ATH 5539

69,50/52112 1

D1710311

ATH 5539

69,50/52112 1

HELICOPTERS before HELICOPTERS

HELICOPTERS before HELICOPTERS

E. K. Liberatore

KRIEGER PUBLISHING COMPANY
MALABAR, FLORIDA
1998

Original Edition 1998

Printed and Published by
KRIEGER PUBLISHING COMPANY
KRIEGER DRIVE
MALABAR, FLORIDA 32950

Copyright © 1998 by Krieger Publishing Company

All rights reserved. No part of this book may be reproduced in any form or by any means, electronic or mechanical, including information storage and retrieval systems without permission in writing from the publisher.
No liability is assumed with respect to the use of the information contained herein.
Printed in the United States of America.

FROM A DECLARATION OF PRINCIPLES JOINTLY ADOPTED BY
A COMMITTEE OF THE AMERICAN BAR ASSOCIATION AND A
COMMITTEE OF PUBLISHERS:
This publication is designed to provide accurate and authoritative information in regard to the subject matter covered. It is sold with the understanding that the publisher is not engaged in rendering legal, accounting, or other professional service. If legal advice or other expert assistance is required, the services of a
competent professional person should be sought.

Library of Congress Cataloging-in-Publication Data

Liberatore, E. K.
   Helicopters before helicopters / E.K. Liberatore.
      p.   cm.
   Includes bibliographical references (p.) and index.
   ISBN 1-57524-053-X (alk. paper)
    1. Helicopters—United States—History. I. Title.
TL716.L484   1998
629.133′352—DC21
                                                                 97-40003
                                                                    CIP

10 9 8 7 6 5 4 3 2

TO
FLORENCE WINSLOW DE LA RUE
ne plus ultra

CONTENTS

viii   **Contents**

PREFACE

The practical helicopter has been in service for about 60 years; fixed-wing aircraft reached this age in 1963. In each case there is today a strong interest in the history of each type of aircraft. Airplane museums are old but what is new is the nostalgia by individuals for the old aircraft. This is expressed in the building of old airplanes found in various states of deterioration, the formation of clubs dedicated to one or all models, in displays and exhibitions, and in the publication of periodicals on the subject. When the favored old airplanes no longer existed they were recreated, usually with masked, modern powerplants. The helicopter has matured enough that it is now following this same sentimental route toward preservation of its past. Emerging in the United States and elsewhere are nonprofit organizations and museums dedicated to rotorcraft as related to hardware, documentation, and education. The industry itself is well into its second generation of practitioners and there is the desire to preserve its past before the machines and their history are lost for good. With this trend in mind this book has been prepared to cover vertical-rising aircraft as envisioned in America from the earliest concepts to the period when the helicopter became a practical machine in the late 1930s. To a great extent the core information comes from an early state of the art study conducted by the author for the U.S. Air Force. (Appendix E)

The present historical account focuses on the American activities enhanced and updated with interpretations using current knowledge of the art. The Epilogue takes the story up to date and into the future. The work is semi-technical, only a few basic equations are used. For those less familiar with the technology an encyclopedic glossary is appended to enhance the concepts used in the narratives (Appendix H). There is an appendix discussing the use here for both the British and SI (metric) systems of units (Appendix G), and finally an extensive, combined listing of references, bibliography, and notes.

ACKNOWLEDGMENTS

The author extends his appreciation and thanks to the following for their review, constructive criticism, and endorsement of this book.

John W. Kitchens, Ph.D.
Aviation Branch Historian
Department of the Army
Headquarters United States Army Aviation Center and Fort Rucker
Fort Rucker, Alabama

Russell E. Lee
Curator, Aeronautics Department
National Air and Space Museum
Smithsonian Institution
Washington, D.C.

Robert C. Michelson
Principal Research Engineer
Georgia Tech Research Institute
Georgia Institute of Technology
Atlanta, Georgia

Leonard E. Opdycke
Publisher
World War I Aeroplanes, Inc.
(Aero and Skyways Magazines)
Poughkeepsie, New York

Raymond W. Prouty
Consultant, helicopter performance, stability, and control
Westlake Village, California
(Former historian of American Helicopter Society.)

For his efforts in obtaining useful information and illustrations recognition and appreciation are extended to William Foshag, Aviation Historian of Carlisle, Pennsylvania.

Chapter 1
INTRODUCTION

1.1 OVERVIEW

This book presents an account of early American helicopter concepts and developments as revealed mainly in the words and literature of the time. As much as feasible an interpretive approach is taken providing both explanation and factual information. This means appreciation and understanding are intimate parts of the account. The work also seeks to define some underlying philosophy in the efforts of these pioneers.

Specifically the history covers the period from the earliest years to the emergence of the successful helicopter in the late 1930s, a total timespan of about 120 years. The oldest American ideas on record date to the early 19th century.

Over 100 investigators are accounted for with about 50 foreign entrepreneurs included to set off the American work. There were certainly more, as can be noted by a count of the patents issued during the interval. Except for special interest patents (mostly related to hardware) the information is from general, published material. A major source was the author's handbook series cited in the Preface, and since donated to the American Helicopter Society.

The history here is a negative one for it is a story of unsuccessful efforts in producing a practical helicopter. Even so, these investigators are worthy of a story because they reveal a lesson in faith and commitment to a principle which is a valid lesson in itself, as important to progress as the technology.

In his *Progress in Flying Machines* (1894) when flight by mechanical means looked gloomy, Octave Chanute wrote:

> "Failures it is said are more instructive than successes, and thus far in flying machines there have been nothing but failures." [1.1]

In hindsight even this wisdom when applied to helicopters did not work well. In today's environment the notion makes sense but in those days there were barrier problems relative to both the state of the art and state of knowledge.

The only wisdom gained was that nothing tried works. It would be erroneous to presume some small bit of helicopter theory, insight, or technology advanced the art. Little of this is evident in the work of individuals described here. Even so, theory was evolving, mainly by way of the autogiro, and one does see in some prototypes awareness of the need for low disk loadings and large diameter rotors. It is curious that the ultimate technological success of the helicopter depended on external agents: the autogiro, the internal combustion engine, and the airplane.

A major observation of the first century interval is the fact the individual efforts were random, lacking the cohesiveness and interaction one usually sees today in successful, evolving innovations. The process of that interval fits the term *empirical groping*. Today theory and practice support each other and progress is made, one leading the other.

There seemed to be an unstated consensus that the ability to hover (and fly forward) was all there was to the question. Until the problem was confronted, there was little realization such accomplishments were merely the admission price to the real questions of vibration, material fatigue, hovering stability, and control. But to their credit first things came first.

The work of these early investigators or experimenters appeared to be mainly isolated attempts to reduce to practice an ancient idea—the idea of a flying machine that could hover, fly forward, and land safely without power. These three concepts were implied objectives. Controllability only became a problem with models or prototypes. The critical notion of control response-

time was not appreciated in the conceptual or design stage, at least not in the 19th century, when navigating in the air was a simple variation of navigating in the water. Ballooning probably reinforced this response idea of a leisurely activity. In that century, stability if considered at all was best solved by some pendulous weight, (an idea the Wright brothers immediately rejected) or through differential control of multiple rotors.

In the early 20th century when prototypes appeared, reliance was on controllability to overcome whatever instability existed in the machine. Since there was plenty of the latter the pilot was kept very busy operating a questionable, somewhat ineffective control system until he tired or met with an accident. In effect each experimenter was attempting to fly for the first time, without foreknowledge.

The Wrights' accomplishment strongly demarcated ideas and models of the 19th century from man-carrying prototype helicopters of the 20th century. Accordingly, this account is divided mainly into two significant, chronological periods.

In the 19th century (the first period) there were influential skeptics who insisted the (aerostatic) balloon was the only thing that would work for aerial navigation. Among flying machines the helicopter approach was not taken seriously. The main interest was in *aeroplanes*, a word that appeared in 1866.

In the early 20th century (the second period) the skepticism remained, however the mere fact of knowing mechanical flight was possible encouraged helicopter advocates to test their own ideas with prototypes. These investigators sorted themselves out into two types, and each exhibited a characteristic approach.

The two types of investigations (or proficiencies) are termed here *inventive* and *scientific*. The inventive type is taken to be pragmatic and intuitive, with no formal training in science or engineering. The scientific type includes the engineer. In the first period (the 19th century) the inventive type was dominant. Since mechanical flight had not been attained, this period also had a speculative component. The distinction appears mostly in the second period. In the latter time there were also inventors whose reputation was derived from creation of useful things. The narratives reveal this distinction.

The first period was identified more by serious efforts dealing with the state of art and knowledge. Popular notions of helicopter flight were subsumed in the quest means. Advocates of mechanical flight not only had technical and financial problems, but they were subject to sharp criticism and ridicule.

In the early 1900s the inventor approach to vertical flight was at times based on some novel principle well beyond the actuator disk concept of rotor aerodynamics. The alternate, engineering approach relied on systematic model testing and trial and error flights with man-carrying machines.

To some extent the narrative spills over in both place and time. This is done to present a more useful perspective of the American technology in a wider context—one governed not by a guiding hand, but by simple, isolated, individual visions of hovering and vertical flight. This spillover means some European (and other) milestones are included along with a few successful flights and entrepreneurs at the end and beyond the second period. Formally the second period end date is 1936 when the Focke-Wulf FW-61 was flown.

In the present context *helicopter* refers to any flying machine with hover capability using airscrews or rotors. In some cases wings were added, for the object was to take to the air in any configuration with this capability, as often an act of desperation as calculation.

In general, the account for each of the two periods consists of its own introduction, followed by narratives and illustrations of individual entrepreneurial activity. The narratives are in chronological order. Because some investigators pursued the idea over a few years, the year selected is taken to be representative of the work under consideration, and in a few cases, one's work may be under more than one entry date.

The narratives themselves have an order that with the best information take the following form: background, technology, performance or

outcome, and assessment. The last item refers to an evaluation of the work in the light of present helicopter knowledge. Since these narratives are accounts of hapless ventures a common outcome can be expressed as "nothing came of it" or "ran out of money". The latter is code for the backer's loss of faith in the viability of the project. Often the investigator himself abandoned the project due to its intractability.

In the spirit of the new century numerical data is given in both the Systeme International (SI) units, i.e., the metric system, and in parentheses, the common British system (foot-pounds-seconds). Unless otherwise noted the patents cited are U.S. patents.

As noted above the two periods have individual introductions. These offer a synoptic view of the activity of the period. Part of this view is a discussion of some technical, theoretical concepts unique to helicopters. Appendix H explains some of the less familiar terminology used here. The introductory views are an attempt at generalizations that should be seen as trends. As such, the generalizations are not without exceptions.

1.2 THE TOY

As a foreword to the narratives it is of interest to trace the idea of the rotor and helicopter through the toy (Figures 1.1–1.24). There were 19th century advocates who used the toy to contend feasibility of a man-carrying machine. This toy, the kite, the wind sock, and the pinwheel are all very old aerodynamic devices.

The earliest known rotor concept is the toy windmill of that vague person *Heron mechanicus*, or as often identified with jet propulsion rotors "Heron of Alexandria". [1.2] In the ancient world the Egyptian city was the great science center and world literature was collected here. As the seat of learning, scholars from the Western world gathered to take advantage of the "Museum" (a kind of university), Library, and the resident philosophers. [1.3] Heron flourished around 62 A.D., and some of his writings survive. These reveal a fascination with gadgets using water, steam, hot air, and compressed air. Seventy-five are identified in his *Pneumatica*. Among other things Heron describes a coin slot machine (to dispense holy water), a hot air engine, and a steam jet-propelled device (described later). Of interest now is his idea of a windmill (wind turbine) for powering a toy organ using an air pump (Figure 1.1). The wind turbine consisted of a disk with blades or vanes, likened to oar blades. While not a thruster it is an early version of a rotor, one that was conceived almost a millenium before windmills appeared in full size. Yet in his time no one picked up the idea of using the wind for mechanical power.

There is little information on Heron as an innovator or as a compiler. Historians differ over his inventive ability. In one view Heron was heavily indebted to earlier work and was an "unintelligent compiler". In another he was only a compiler, but "not unintelligent." [1.4] Despite the different judgments he did have the awareness to collect the known technical knowledge of his time and he did so comprehensively, in effect compiling a "textbook of engineering" [1.5] which was most likely the first of its kind. If anyone had the potential to conceive a windmill it would have been Heron. Regardless of the concept provenance, the nature of the blades for the wheel remain of interest.

Since all illustrations of Heron's work were drawn after this time, one can speculate on the design of the rotor and blades as he or his referent envisioned them. Little is known of the details except Heron called the device *anemurion*, suggesting "something that rotates in the wind on a pivot". [1.6] Blade design here refers to configuration (sail type or vane type) and provision for pitch angle change (Figure 1.1 and inset). Usher [1.7] presents a reasonable argument that the blades were not the sail (i.e., fabric) type. As noted above the idea of a boat oar seemed to be associated with this windwheel. Latter day illustrations [1.8] always show the blades as fixed to the hub (Figure 1.1. inset). However it was not beyond Heron's imagination to recognize the importance of the number of blades and their angle to the wind. There is no point to the concept without at least considering these features. Thus one would expect Heron to prefer replaceable blades to find the best combination of blade number and pitch angle. Hence a hub with many holes in it with blades shaped like oars (part of the blade and stem) would be the best design for his wind wheel. This argument does not carry Heron's thinking ability beyond the wheel function into its usefulness, except as a toy.

The first (power type) windmills apparently were used in Persia in the 7th century A.D. The first windmill description was by al-Masudi in *muruj-adh-dhahab (Meadows of Gold)*, a 10th century work. [1.9] The arrangement consisted of canvas sails (a logical extension of ship sails) driving a vertical shaft. Turning in a horizontal

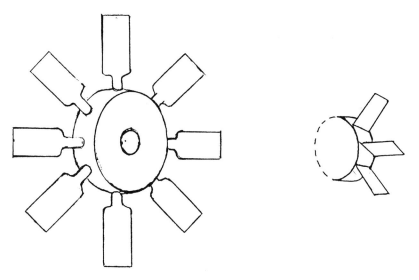

Figure 1.1   Graphical representation of Heron's windmill for a toy organ (ca. 62 A.D.). There are no contemporary illustrations of his ideas.

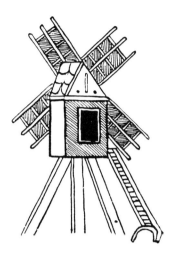

Figure 1.2 Earliest illustration (1390) of a horizontal axle windmill. The "windmill psalter" of the British Museum.

plane allowed the mill to receive the wind from any direction. Such a concept makes the mill the precursor to the modern anemometer rotor.

Al-Masudi was a leading figure in Islamic science, a type often recounted in world history as having been known for encyclopedic knowledge and not for administrative or military accomplishments. The type includes Ko-Hung (China) and da Vinci (Italy), both discussed later. The sail approach had its appeal in the United States in the 19th century in both invention and fiction. Figure 1.2 shows the earliest known illustration of the familiar horizontal shaft windmill (1390).

As a toy, the windmill (i.e., pinwheel) is dated in Europe to the 14th century. It was a popular plaything in Medieval times when children discovered their own toys. Illustrations commonly appear in engravings, tapestries, and manuscripts including psalters (Figures 1.3–1.11). The wheel with two or four blades was pinned to a long stick so it could be used as a jousting lance, for fencing or simply to run with. The idea of controlling mechanical motion in those times must have been half their novelty. It is possible the pinwheel was mainly an improvised toy. Contemporary prints of toy stalls at fairs reveal such items as stick horses, drums, balls, crossbows and arrows, but no pinwheels. [1.10]

Pinwheel popularity is further evidenced by its use in group play (Figure 1.3), probably by students connected to an adult guild associated with the church. The two lollypop-shaped objects in each cap likely had significance to the play. Two insets of Figure 1.3 show knights wearing similar headpieces. Their prominence suggest in heated combat they clearly identified themselves from their foe. The complete illustration shows the schoolmaster with the same objects in his hat, apparently supervising the play with some education in mind. The shape of his hat could be the identifier of a schoolmaster (see inset also) or other learned individual.

A guess at the group game would be playing crusaders. It may involve mock jousting or tournaments. For the former, the opponents would run toward each other with the intent of disabling the opponent's spinning pinwheel. For tournaments the battle in a fenced area would involve groups with the same objective. The cap objects may be marked to represent one team, and possibly to be knocked off. This play would be best on a windy day.

Despite the mock combat and in view of both the privilege of an education and common dress, the children were likely destined for some aspect of church service. The illustration (Figure 1.3) is from a 15th century, French religious work. That this toy and other toys were pictured in Medieval religious texts (Figure 1.4), may be due to the students starting Latin at age 7, and the illustrations put them in a good mood for the effort.

The remaining figures (1.5–1.11) show other pinwheel toys explained with the captions.

There were Asian pinwheels as well. The farm-type windmill is not associated with Asian countries. So the semantic focus is on the toy, which was popular in the late 19th century. [1.11] In Korea the pinwheel was called *to-reu-rak-i* ("revolving wheel"). Made by children, it had two vanes of paper. The configuration was always the same but the colors varied. Often the two vanes separately featured pictures of a man and a woman. The Japanese version was *kazaguruma* ("wind wheel", from *kaze*-"wind" and *kuruma*-"vehicle" or "wheel"). This toy featured several paper vanes radially attached to a bamboo hub. The vanes were colored alternately red and white, but other colors also were used. A special kind had the poetic name *hanaguruma*

Figure 1.3   Children playing with pinwheel lances, revealing the popularity of the toy in group play. From late 15th century "Book of Hours".

("flower wheel"). In Chinese the toy is *feng che* ("wind wheel", "pinwheel", "windmill").

The earliest record of the helicopter idea appeared in China in the works of Ko-Hung (A.D. 283–383). [1.12] He was a Taoist reformer and alchemist from South China, and as mentioned before he was a man with universal knowledge. His idea was to integrate Taoism with Confucianism, which were rival philosophies. Among his thoughts was the notion that morality and beauty are independent of each other. Ko-Hung's famous work is *Pao-P'u-Tzu* (ca. 317), a question and answer document that covered Taoist beliefs and the sciences in doctrine form. The answerer was Ko-Hung who took the pseudonym *Pao-P'u-Tzu*, a phrase borrowed from the Taoist classic, *Lao-Tzu*.

His claim to rotary wing history is from the cited document through the work of Joseph Needham of Cambridge University. He initiated and pursued the definitive historical study of Chinese technology published in *Science and Civilization in China*, a project he started in 1937 and one that has outlived him. [1.13] Needham develops two thoughts related to rotary wing flight, but Ko-Hung had a third less obvious point that is modern. Considering the first, Ko-Hung answering as *Po-P'u-Tzu* to the question of traveling to great heights and through the heavens, he describes flying cars of wood with rotating blades and leather straps to actuate the blades. The reference here is to a man-carrying vehicle energized like the toy helicopters described below. From Ko-Hung's description Needham advances a second point. That the concept describes what

Figure 1.4 Illustrations of children's games often accompanied Medieval religious texts.

Figure 1.5 French print showing one of the "Seven Ages of Man" (1482).

Figure 1.6 Later version of a lancer with a walker. Note tricycle, directionally stable "advanced design", compared with Figure 1.5.

Figure 1.7 Pieter Brueghel's "Childrens Games" includes the detail of a pair jousting with pinwheel lances (1560).

Figure 1.8 A fully outfitted cavalier with sword, lance, and tethered "falcon" (ca. 1600).

Figure 1.9 Detail of print "Kinderspiel" (Children's Games) showing a boy running with a pinwheel (1665).

Figure 1.10 Another "Ages of Man" series detail by French engraver Abraham Bosse (1636).

came to be the 18th century European pull-string toy by then known as "Chinese top." Ko-Hung's third and modern point is in his pseudonym. The expression can be translated literally in three words: embrace- simplicity- in the self.

A transition toy between the pinwheel and a flying rotor is shown in Figures 1.12, and 1.22–1.24. The toy is not a helicopter though the illustrations suggest it. In this case the rotor is turned but it does not fly off the hub. [1.18] The elongated shaft (stem) in the figures suggest this. Most likely its length was to avoid just that. A common feature is the pull-string to actuate the rotor. After the first pull and spin, the inertia in the rotor rewinds the string on its shaft ready for the second pull. The repeated pulls suggest the action of a yo-yo, whereby the child is entertained by a continuous humming sound. Lacking a generic name the toy is referred here as a "hummer", since the purpose of the toy is to produce this sound.

In the earliest of this pull-string toy, considerable friction was present during operation. The yo-yo action along with this friction made it difficult for younger children to pull. Later, internal modifications (in the 1500s) alleviated the problem. Some were made using the shell of a large nut for the hub (Figure 1.24). In 1968 Étienne Bouton [1.18] the source of the latter figure

Figure 1.11 French engraving "Le Petit Soldat" with an elaborate pinwheel lance (1738).

Figure 1.12   Early representation of a "hummer" toy (14th century Flanders) misindentified as a "helicopter". The artist may not have understood how to grip the toy. See Figures 1.22 and 1.23.

called this toy *moulinet noix* (pinwheel-nut). It was a popular plaything in the ancient French province of Maine, particularly around Le Mans.

Figure 1.12 is a hummer as depicted in a 13th century Flemish painting. The hub appears to resemble a nut. Judging from the child's grip, the artist may not have understood how it worked (Figures 1.22 and 1.23). Figure 1.22 is a detail from a "Virgin and Child" painting (ca. 1460) from Le Mans, France. [1.18] Figure 1.23 is a detail from a 16th century English print, suggesting the hummer was a common toy in England as well.

The Bouton sketches of Figure 1.24 lead off with the 1460 toy in the hands of the Christ Child (Figure 1.22). Bouton remarked "Incontestibly this painting from Mans is the most ancient representation known of this plaything". However Figure 1.12 is older. The 1475 sketch (Figure 1.24) is derived from a Book of Hours [1.19] by artist Jean Colombe, produced for a chevalier of the Order of St. Michel. The 1525 toy with a nut hub is sketched from a painting for a French abbey, and now in the Musée de Douai.

The next illustration (1532) is a four-blade hummer from a wood engraving assigned the month of January in a Book of Hours. The original

work was published in Le Mans, showing the pleasures of childhood (the same principle behind Figures 1.1 and 1.4). The trirotor of 1560 is from the same Brueghel painting of Figure 1.7. The three rotors would suggest the toy is not a helicopter.

The following sketch (1530s) is not further identified by Bouton. As for the 1532 design, the stem does not penetrate the shell bottom. This feature not only suggests a design refinement but the idea is closer to the helicopter variant. The next step would be to put pitch in the blades. Apparently this did not happen until a few centuries later. The last illustration shows a 17th century, double-hub concept from Italy. This type was within the grip of an older child.

More recent hummers are revealed in the inset. The one at the left with an inverted arrangement, is from Grand Luce (a town near Le Mans). It is called *girouette* (weather vane). The four feathers are stuck in a small potato. Obviously there had to be some scheme to prevent the potato-hub from slipping on its shaft, possibly something mechanical as spurs on the stem, split stem, or pins through the potato. The middle sketch is derived from Bosse (the engraver of Figure 1.10). It shows the rotor as a wooden disk with the hub an elongated cylinder. This is another example of how the hummer design was approaching the helicopter version. Both 19th century toys are from the present department of Sarthe (which includes Le Mans). The last sketch is a 20th century hummer from Haiti, in which three nuts make up the rotor. The three inset sketches also suggest the rotor was not intended for flight.

After this lengthy "evolution" the true helicopter toy emerged in the 19th century as a popular plaything in different parts of the world, including Europe and America (Figures 1.13–1.18). The early toy consisted of various materials as feathers, bamboo, and metal, with different ways to energize the rotor and launch it. Figure 1.13 is a 19th century Asian version of the stem or palm-launch toy. The blades were bamboo with carved pitch. It was launched by rolling the stem between the palms of the hands. Another type (Figure 1.14) is all metal, appearing in the 1920s. The thin, sheet-metal rotor rests on a slider tube which is on a spiral ribbon. The rotor

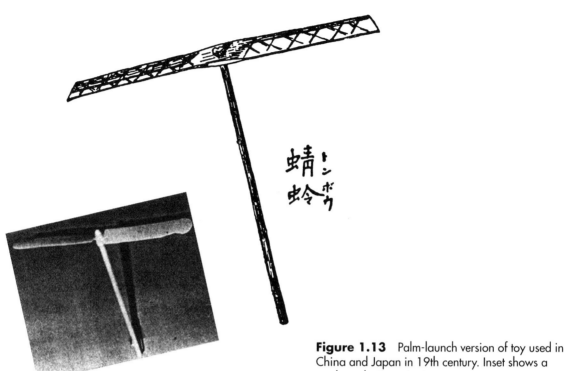

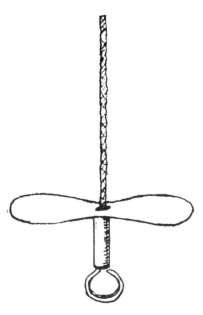

蜻　ト
　　ン
蛉　ボ
　　ウ

Figure 1.13 Palm-launch version of toy used in China and Japan in 19th century. Inset shows a modern plastic variant.

is spun and launched by moving the slider up the ribbon. The detail of Figure 3.98 showing a boy (1930) launching a rotor is a variant of the slider version. Here the slider is a holder and the screw is launched by pulling down on the ribbon, just opposite the motion for Figure 1.14.

The pull-string version of Figure 1.15 (suggested in Ko-Hung's writings) had a rotor a few inches in diameter. It is the one 19th century American proponents used to demonstrate feasibility of vertical flight. There were others who used the toy to gain insights into a man-carrying

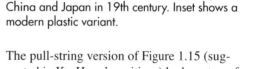

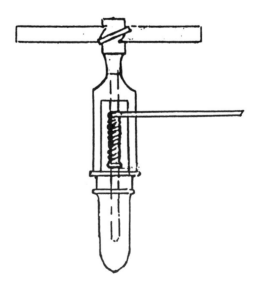

Figure 1.14 All metal American toy using a spiral shaft and tube launcher of early 20th century.

Figure 1.15 Cayley-type demonstrator, known in mid 19th century Britain as "Chinese top".

helicopter. The above figure is the British demonstrator used by Cayley (1843) in advancing his idea of a helicopter.

George Cayley (1773–1857) is considered by many as "the father of aerial navigation" because of his ideas and experiments advanced in the first half of the 19th century. [1.14] His first helicopter model was inspired by the French scientific demonstrator toy of Launoy and Bienvenue (1784). This coaxial rotor toy was the first helicopter concept presented to the French Academy of Sciences (at a time when the word *hélicoptère* was yet to appear).

As suggested above, significant American interest in the helicopter began at the start of the Civil War, however the war postponed serious work and active interest was resumed at its end. In the 19th century the toy had various names. In 1846 it was called *stropheor*, a version with cardboard blades, and later (1860s) *spiralifer* (Figure 1.16), a toy with metal blades. The latter featured a rotor with two blades actuated by a pull-string. As mentioned before with Needham, the British version took the name *Chinese top*.

The Asian toy (Figure 1.13) was called in Japan *tombo* ("dragonfly") and in China *qing ting* (dragonfly) or *zhu qing ting* ("bamboo dragonfly"). [1.15] At times (late 19th century) the rotor alone was called *helicopter*, once the word entered the language. Another name for both the toy, and occasionally the full scale machine was *whirligig*. Since helicopters are now common, *whirligig* belongs to the past; *choppers* has replaced it in the media, while the military use *helo*. (See also *helicopter toy* in the Glossary.)

In 1878 the young Wright brothers received a parental gift of a toy helicopter that was apparently their introduction to flying machines (and later rejecting it as the way to human flight). Figure 1.17 is of particular interest because as a toy it has some features of modern helicopters. The illustration is from U.S. Patent 447,284 filed in 1890 by Eliseo Del Valle of Brooklyn, New York. The helicopter is in the form of a clown with articulated arms and legs, and conical cap. For amusement there is logic in using a clown since the legs extend horizontally in flight. At the shoulders the arms have offset flapping hinges (shown in the cutaway part of the figure)

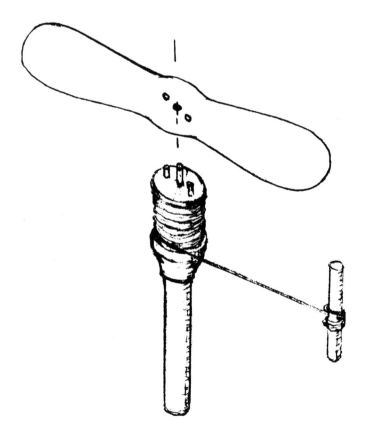

Figure 1.16 Popular American "spiralifer" toy used to demonstrate feasibility of full scale helicopters (1860s).

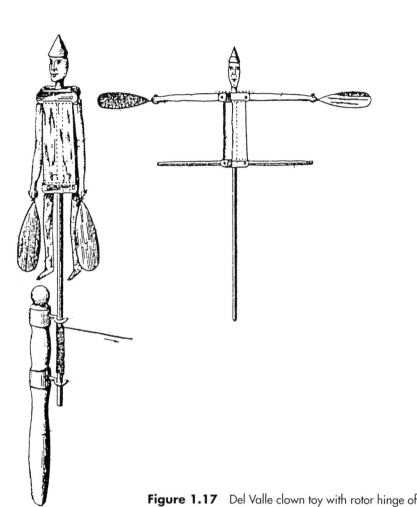

Figure 1.17 Del Valle clown toy with rotor hinge offset (1890).

but vertical flap motion is limited by stops or extensions above the shoulders. Outboard at the wrists, are set screws to adjust blade pitch. The clown holds in each hand a fan or vane serving as rotor blades. The body is attached to a stem or spindle on which the pull-string is wound. The holder (handle) is unusual as the stem rests against hooks (not eyes). The idea is to be able to wind the string on the stem without need of the handle.

Of interest is the inventor's focus on model stability, which he could easily arrive at with trial and error models. The hinge offset of both arms and legs provided a mechanical restoring moment. It is curious the serious investigators of the late 19th and early 20th centuries either were unaware of this patent or saw it as something workable only on a toy. As this account shows with few exceptions they were all convinced rigid propellers or rotors were the answer.

Around 1894 in France Dandrieux created ten different types. Some were produced in France and Japan and sold in the United States. The toy screws of the time were made of cardboard or metal. Some carried a rim to increase energy storage. Heights of 61 meters (200 feet) were attained. An airplane model parts catalog published in Paris in 1911 offered for sale a Dandrieux *papillon hélicoptère* ("butterfly") with a price of 75 centimes (Figure 1.18). [1.16]

At the end of World War II the toy appeared in plastic, launched by a pull-string. The first post-war version was the idea of Bruno Nagler the helicopter pioneer. From Vienna he emigrated to America and produced the toy here. The money he earned Nagler put into his full scale helicopter ventures, yet cheaper versions put him out of this business. Today, spring and battery powered toy helicopters are being sold. Also there are radio-controlled models, "toys"

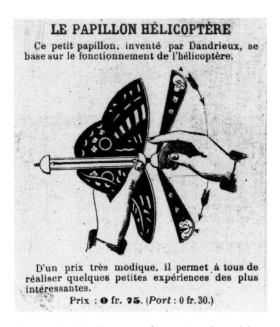

LE PAPILLON HÉLICOPTÈRE

Ce petit papillon, inventé par Dandrieux, se base sur le fonctionnement de l'hélicoptère.

D'un prix très modique, il permet à tous de réaliser quelques petites expériences des plus intéressantes.

Prix : **0 fr. 75.** (*Port* : 0 fr. 30.)

Figure 1.18 Illustration from a French model airplane catalog offering for sale a Dandrieux "papillon hélicoptère" (1911).

the 19th century enthusiasts never could have imagined.

While not toys but models, it is of interest to examine these and the helicopter idea of Leonardo da Vinci (1452–1519). [1.17] The dates reveal he was born a year after Columbus and outlived him twelve years. Figure 1.19 is an IBM model while Figure 1.20 shows one made by Guatelli, a da Vinci modelmaker of recent years. Figure 1.21 is the original da Vinci sketch and beside it are some of his notes on this design. The writing is backward ("mirror writing"), a feature of all his writing. The sketch is the earliest known illustration of a man-carrying helicopter. Da Vinci envisioned a helicoidal screw with an iron rim, covered with starched linen. To support it he added wires connecting the helix periphery to the platform below. Four radial arms are visible, firmly attached to the vertical shaft at a point midway in the pyramid mount. Presumably four operators were required. (See [1.17] for translation.)

Figure 1.19 Leonardo da Vinci model, part of the IBM traveling exhibition.

Figure 1.20 Another model of the da Vinci helicopter also with a platform bearing, by Guatelli.

For the system to work there had to be an unusual drive concept. This point creates a problem in interpreting his drawing. The two models (Figures 1.19 and 1.20) reveal equal interpretations. The four men, facing the direction of rotor rotation are standing on an upper platform. The lower platform (presumably supporting an intermediate thrust bearing) turns with the driveshaft fixed to it and the rotor the men are actuating. With the modelmakers' concept the rotating parts are the helix, shaft, and lower platform (and the wires). The stationary parts are the upper platform they are standing on and the pyra-

mid pylon. The anomaly here is the four men must run around the platform to turn the rotor (neglecting pylon obstruction) or, hand the radial arms to each other. The radial arm length (Figure 1.21) obviates the latter approach. By running around the platform the foot reaction in kicking back would cause an "impedence" (unless they all kicked back in unison), nullifying some of the forward driving motion. In this the men must run in synchronization, as with the alternate interpretation below.

The alternate interpretation (the author's) postulates the system operates as a carousel. More likely the operators using the radial arms held on to (actually leaned on to) an outer housing containing thrust bearings and within the bearings, the rotor driveshaft. The inner shaft connected the helix to the platform (floor). In this case only one platform is required. The rotor is driven by the men "walking" or pumping the platform in unison, in effect using foot friction, kicking the floor opposite the direction they are facing. To pedal in unison, each foot of the four has to leave the floor at the same time. This action required a caller as with galley slaves. With this approach the men face a direction opposite of the helix rotation, contrary to the two models shown.

It is possible to estimate the hovering parameters for his design. The number 8 at the end of the writing indicates da Vinci had in mind rotors with a radius of 8 *braccia* ("arms" length). A braccia is an old Florentine measurement, vari-

Figure 1.21 Da Vinci's sketch and a portion of his brief notes for the helicopter design (1493).

Figure 1.22 A "Madonna and Child" French painting detail (ca. 1460). Mussée de Tessé, Le Mans. The toy is not a helicopter.

able but taken to be equal to about 0.6 meters (2 feet). His rotor diameter would be 9.6 meters (31.5 feet). At best the foursome could produce briefly 1.5 kilowatts (2 horsepower), lifting about 243.2 kg/kW (400 lb/hp). Today's values are between 1.82 to 9.7 kg/kW (3 to 16 lb/hp). Based on the estimated weight, the disk loading would be 2.44 kg/m^2 (0.5 lb/f^2), yielding a figure of merit (hovering efficiency) of 7.44, far beyond what nature is willing to give up.

Mechanical bearings are introduced in the above concepts. Other sketches reveal da Vinci was knowledgeable on the subject of roller bearings, bevel gears, and universal joints. Although foot power was common in his time (as for working bellows), da Vinci's pedal idea for rotation was unusual. The bicycle did not appear until the 19th century. Its pedal-crank mechanism is now used to drive the experimental, human-powered helicopters.

A criticism of the da Vinci sketch is he did not account for external torque reaction in using a single rotor. As mentioned above the men lean on the arms (the reaction) and kick the platform in the opposite direction they are facing (the action). The kicking turns the rotor. Figures 1.19 and 1.20 on the contrary presume the crew, by walking around the upper platform, kick it backward (the reaction) as they push the arms around to turn the rotor (the action). Therefore a tail rotor is required, attached to the platform to keep the floor from turning in a direction opposite the helix rotation. (Without this rotor the crew would more likely be turning the floor rather than the rotor.) Note that for either system to work, there must be some design provision for relative motion between the floor and the rest of the helicopter. For the carousel approach the tail rotor is attached to one of the radial arms.

It is known the helicopter was a quick sketch early in his career with only a few written notes to describe it. Evidently he dropped his design too soon. Among other things he did not account for

Figure 1.23 Detail of an English print showing children's games (16th century). The rotor toy is not a helicopter.

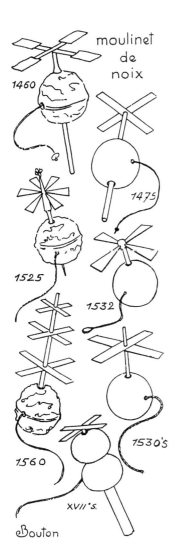

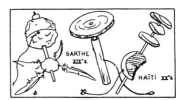

Figure 1.24 A study of the hummer toy *moulinet de noix* (pinwheel-nut) by Bouton in 1968.

takeoff where in either case the lowest platform rotates. The weight and ground friction would prohibit a takeoff, requiring much more power than the crew could produce. With some buoyancy device below the platform, a water takeoff would be consistent with his design. Use of a water helix below the platform could give the crew a vertical, hydrodynamic boost at takeoff.

As discussed previously, Needham credits the Chinese for introduction of the helicopter toy to Europe in the 14th century. There is a loose end to this view, and it relates to the pull-string version. The leather strap (or string) he mentions was not part of the 19th century Asian toy (Figure 1.13) yet Europeans who were using the string method in the 14th century supposedly copied this from the Chinese. Some of the actual tops of the Chinese used strings to spin them, so

to support Needham's argument they knew about this but did not apply it to the helicopter toy. Another source suggests the toy was introduced through Italy by Tartar domestic servants (slaves) brought into that country in medieval times, an activity that peaked in mid 15th century. It has also been suggested da Vinci was influenced by the Chinese, but this view seems improbable. The helicoidal screw (Figure 1.21) would indicate influence by Archimedes, if anyone. Europeans witnessed their own seeds dropping in "autorotation" (maple, sycamore). There were other names for the toy beside the 19th century British term "Chinese top." Other contemporary names were *spiralifer* and *stropheor* (and *hélicoptère*). These suggest the British name was not universally used, thereby not recognizing Asian attribution. Overall there is a good case for the helicopter toy being indigenous to Europe.

Chapter 2

FIRST PERIOD: NINETEENTH CENTURY

2.1 INTRODUCTION

Flying machines existed in colonial America in 1766. In that year the first effort at high speed travel was established using a route from Paulus Hook Ferry (now Jersey City) across the state to Philadelphia. The trip was made in two days with a frequency of twice a week. The speed was so impressive that the wagon-like vehicles were called "flying machines". [2.1] By 1771 the trip took a day and a half in the summer. From New York passengers were first ferried across the Hudson. [2.2] The usual way for the journey was on foot or horseback. With a good wind a coastal sloop took three days. Considering the alternates, two days was as good as flying, this despite the pitching, rolling, and aches and pains that accompanied the wagon ride.

In 1825 Congress was considering admission of Oregon. A New Jersey member declared the prospect of a state on the Pacific an absurdity. By his calculation a round trip would take 350 days. "This would leave the member a fortnight to rest at Washington before commencing the journey home". [2.3] Discovery of gold in California in 1849 increased the desire to get there from the East as fast as possible (the "gold rush"). Ever since, speed and time have occupied the mind at an accelerating rate so it was natural to address serious travel through the air by any means.

In America and Europe there were enthusiasts who focused on balloons to the extent a cult of "balloonism" emerged along with its caricature, visible today in old prints. Advocates of flight eventually split into those sold on aerostatics (balloons) and others convinced aerodynamics held the answer in the form of "planes", screws, or combinations. A popular novel (described later) dramatized this split. Balloonists saw progress in the form of airships outfitted with propellers. This view may be termed "conservative" because it started with something that worked. The heated activity regarding flight with machines effectively began in mid century about 70 years after the first balloon flight. The void suggesting a kind of human consciousness lag, evident also in other parts of this account of technology. The split was more than a simple choice between equals for there were critics who seriously doubted the "radical", aerodynamic approach if only because it was not based on aerostatics.

Aeronautical investigation had its centers both in Europe and America. The word *hélicoptère* appeared. It was coined by D'Amécourt in a monograph on the subject published in Paris in 1863. [2.4] France had its helicopter enthusiasts; some of these were literary figures. In America the locales of serious aeronautical activity were Boston and Philadelphia, both 19th century and earlier centers for the arts and sciences.

Enthusiasm aside, the problems with mechanical flight were enormous. Without a theoretical or empirical base it was not possible to distinguish between an unsound idea and a concept worth following up. This notion supports comments made previously, that 19th century investigators in America involved both "inventive" and "scientific" types. In fact activity fell mainly to the inventive type who could be the promoter as well. Until very late in the 19th century there was little scientific interest in vertical flight in America. There is an underlying factor that apparently contributed to this lack of interest. In that century innovators in a still developing country were pragmatists seeking solutions to immediate problems. On a day in May in 1853 a show opened at the Crystal Palace in New York. The show was an industrial exhibition of "useful arts" (excluding the "arts of ornamentation", or fine arts). The editor of an annual had the following to say:

> "One of the most interesting features of the exhibition was the number and variety of the machines and implements intended for perfecting

or economizing on the various processes of agriculture. . . . In no other department was the exhibition more national and American as this." [2.5]

One can easily intuit the inverse relationship between agriculture and science in the general population, relative to advances in technology. With emphasis on agriculture along with nation building itself, it is easy to understand the low interest in such advanced ideas as mechanical flight. Perusal of the 19th century literature supports this low interest. Europeans long since past the nation building stage could spend more time in scientific investigations.

Helicopter activities of this century in both America and Europe can be separated into four distinct categories:

1. Conceptual designs only of rotorcraft.
2. Tests using rigs.
3. Tests with flying models.
4. Full scale machines.

Except for one American case, man-carrying prototypes were not built. The conceptual design process accounted for the following:

1. General configuration.
   Coaxial or multiple rotors favored for torque compensation. In some cases spiral or helical screws were proposed. Apparently inventors believed such a system would entrain more air or compact it as stage compressor, producing more thrust. It is also possible they accepted the Archimedes screw as definitive.
2. Powerplant (discussed later).
3. Power-off safe descent. Usually proposing parachutes, fixed planes, or wing-parachutes.
4. Theoretical or speculative evaluation of the ratio of rotor thrust available to a given power input. This ratio is the power (also thrust) loading. There was no awareness of the importance or knowledge of the disk loading parameter (also discussed later).
5. Concern for powerplant weight. Some concern for complete machine weight.
6. Little concern for materials. Before commercial aluminum production the lightest, workable sheet metal was copper. Framing usually was iron. There was only one significant exception to this approach (discussed later).

The numerical order above is a reflection of the investigator's priority in confronting the many problems with the helicopter.

The concept for control of the machine consisted of variable speed airscrews. As mentioned before, the importance of control response-time was not factored into the designs. A control design-feature was the use of an elongated rudder (Figure 2.24). There seemed to be a lack of knowledge that this shape would require large control forces to actuate. Or, they never believed they would fly much faster than boat speed and such a rudder would be manageable.

The rig tests involved measurement of rotor thrust and power, yielding thrust loading. The test objective was to obtain the most thrust for the least power. Establishing the value of this loading received most attention. Absent was the knowledge of ground effect which produces optimistic results relative to thrust available or power required. Since rotors usually were not full scale in that century the error was likely to be insignificant. The loading so measured was then assumed to apply to a full scale machine.

In the late 19th century a value of 27.4 kg/kW (45 lb/hp) was considered typical. For a figure of merit of 0.6 (somewhat optimistic for the times) the value implies a disk loading of 3.5 kg/m^2 (0.71 lb/ft^2). The implications of the high thrust (or power) loading is discussed below with reference to scaling test data.

The flying model tests of the late period were European. Except for toys these models did not appear to be of interest to American investigators, probably because the level of sophistication and the discipline were beyond the inventor type, the source of most American efforts.

As noted with the above, the concentration on rotor or screw static thrust loading in the tests and commentary, reveal unawareness of disk loading as it affects the power required to hover. Despite the value of this concept they could extrapolate from models to full scale helicopters without using it. The following is one possible approach. Given the model screw geometry (radius, total blade area), power loading and rotor speed, the parameters of (modern) thrust coefficient can be used for scaling in the following way.

One can assume as a given the thrust is proportional to rotor speed squared and to blade area. The blade was seen as a plane (surface) traveling in a circle, and the assumption was known from experiments with surfaces (for airplane, not helicopter application). If the rotor speed is constant (its value in static thrust optimization), the scaling relation becomes:

$$(SR^2)_f = (T_f/T_m)(SR^2)_m$$

f = full scale
R = radius
T = thrust
S = total blade area
m = model

All the terms to the right side of the equation are known. T_f is the desired weight with extra thrust for climb, as it was then estimated by the individual. Using the same rotor speed, the investigator apportioned blade area and radius as he saw fit probably by geometric scaling of the model rotor and by assuming practical (possibly structural) dimensions for the radius and blade area. In this manner the investigator worked with the parameter thrust coefficient/solidity without actually either knowing about it or recognizing its value in maximizing static thrust efficiency (i.e., figure of merit). The constant rotor speed assumption (for the design point) follows the then idea of varying rotor thrust by varying rotor speed, steamboat style. If rotor speed is included in the scaling, the above equation takes an additional factor:

$$(N_m/N_f)^2$$

where N is the rotor speed

2.2 POWERPLANT PROBLEMS

Because the powerplant was the principal and first barrier to mechanical flight the problem is described at length below. The account covers the investigator's choice and design for an engine, at a time when the internal combustion engine was yet to appear. The powerplant concepts advanced were an unconstrained mix of ideas, and more than steam plants were proposed. However, the steam engine was foremost in the minds of these visionaries.

The first steam engine in America (from Britain) appeared in 1753, for a copper mine pump in

New Jersey. In this country two of the earliest individuals associated with steam power were Thomas Jefferson and Robert Fulton. Among Jefferson's other claims to fame was his support of the idea that America remain a nation of family operated farms. This notion was a moral rather than economic view. He also was known for his fascination with mechanical devices. Jefferson's two interests came together with his knowledge of the giant steam engines operating in England. He envisioned these powerplants reduced to small size, suitable for use by individual families. The engine would not only serve to relieve many of the daily manual chores, but could be used to pump water to a roof tank. The tank would hold drinking water, and this would be available to extinguish fires. [2.6] So Jefferson may also be known as the father of the family owned, steam powered APUs (auxiliary power units).

In 1807 Robert Fulton demonstrated the first practical steamboat. The difference Fulton made is not obvious, but the difference today remains at the heart of any new system development, including the helicopter. Fulton saw the steamboat as a *system* and conducted tradeoff studies of the problem in its many aspects. Therefore Fulton can be seen as the father of the "systems approach" and its central feature, the tradeoff study. Essentially this approach aims to deal with a problem in its totality and not as a set of successive problems, each solved before the next one is considered, and often with much trial and error. In the history of a technology the latter is called "evolution". (The steam engine itself is a good example of the evolutionary path to practicality.) But today the evolutionary approach is too slow, costly, and simplistic in dealing with the grand technological undertakings of modern society. (See also discussion with Figure H.9.)

Oliver Evans (1755–1819) also pioneered mobile steam plants, but of interest here is his reflection on the absence of public information on past technical efforts. Others felt the same way at the end of the 18th century. One proposal was for a Mechanical Bureau to collect and publish all inventions, combined with reliable treatises on sound mechanical principles. Benjamin Franklin in 1755 remarked that America was in great want of good engineers and looked to France to supply them. The next century saw the

emergence of facilities meeting these needs. The first engineering school in America, Rensselaer Polytechnic Institute, was founded in 1824, the same year Franklin Institute was formed in Philadelphia. In mid-century the publication *Scientific American* appeared. Today such organizations as the American Helicopter Society (AHS), and American Institute of Aeronautics and Astronautics (AIAA) focus on aspects of manned flight. (See also Appendix F.)

Steam and "steam mania" were the motivational forces of the age. Enthusiasm had its own twist, with noise revealing a different value. Unlike today the very noise of the early steam engines gave psychological satisfaction to the beholder. James Watt (1736–1819) wrote:

> ". . . the noise seems to convey great ideas of its power to the ignorant, who seem to be no more taken with modest merit in an engine than in a man."[2.7]

It was logical that the mobile steam engine would be considered for flying machines, including helicopters. (Before this there was no chance at all, except by using muscle power, or real horses.) as the story unfolded, steam power application proved to be a futile effort. But to many advocates, it was the only game. Beyond availability concerning weight and output, the problem was compounded because the required values of engine weight and power for the helicopter were uncertain. Essentially, there was no starting point for a rational preliminary design. The objective therefore was less general and experimenters sought the greatest output for the least weight of powerplant, thereby creating a starting point. The parameter kW/kg (hp/lb) became the point of departure for a full scale design.

Presented below is a description of the state of the art for steam engines applied to flying machines. The descriptions refer to the Stringfellow and Thomson units. Stringfellow's designs were purposely very light weight for model airplane flight experiments. The Thomson unit was not designed for flight but it represented the kind of engine some entrepreneurs had in mind for man-carrying flying machines. The two descriptions are followed by a tabular summary of various powerplant ideas considered for flight. [2.8]

Figure 2.1 Stringfellow non-condensing steam plant for his airplane model (1868).

Figures 2.1, 2.2., and 2.3 are illustrations of a serious effort in the last half of the 19th century to create a steam engine for flying machines. These are the work of Englishman John Stringfellow with some help from William Samuel Henson. Henson designed and patented (1842–1843) the first ever flying machine with an arrangement resembling the modern airplane. Stringfellow collaborated with Henson until 1848. Failure to find money and to achieve sustained flight with a 6.1 meter (20 foot) span model led Henson to abandon the work. In 1849 he emigrated to America, settling in Newark, New Jersey. Stringfellow continued the effort with a second model, this time with a 2 meter (6.5 foot) wingspan, using the same engine design. Flight tests were equally unsatisfactory.

Figure 2.1 shows the steam engine exhibited by Stringfellow at the 1868, first ever, aeronautical exhibition. It was mounted at the Crystal Palace in London, sponsored by the Aeronautical Society of Great Britain. The unit weighed 7.4 kilograms (16.3 pounds) including fuel and water. It produced an estimated 0.75 kilowatts (1.0 horsepower) however the plant lacked a water condensing system. The figure shows the steam feed line from the boiler to the vertically mounted piston. Figures 2.2 and 2.3, an earlier version, offer clearer views of the principle. Figure 2.2 depicts a horizontal engine with the crank operating a slide valve. Figure 2.3 is a view of the boiler unit with the burners at the bottom. Without fluids the engine-boiler combination alone weighed 5.9 kg (13 lb). To generate the steam, water flowed through a horizontal pipe just above the flame (Figure 2.3) that converted it to

Figure 2.2 Stringfellow steam engine.

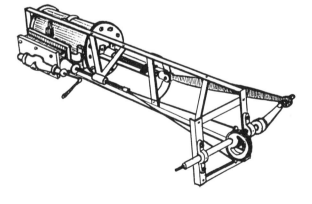

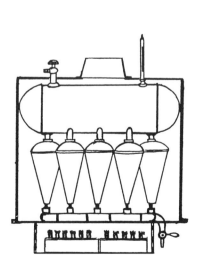

Figure 2.3 Stringfellow boiler (early prototype).

steam at 6.9 bars (100 psi). The vapor rose and expanded in the cones to settle in a header (tank) at the top of the unit. Also at the top, left to right, are a tank valve, for the pipe to the engine, the base of a flue, and a pressure (sight) gage on the header.

Stringfellow used *spirits* for the fuel. Spirits in general referred to the distillate (the spirit) as alcohol extracted from wood (methyl alcohol). With a light weight application as a flying model, this fuel was more practical than the heavy duty type (wood, coal, charcoal). Another fuel for such an application was the distillate *ether*, a highly flammable liquid. This fuel was used in the helicopter concept of French resident Joseph Melikoff in 1879. Ignition was by electric spark.

With development, the Stringfellow engine could have been a practical full scale aircraft powerplant providing that alcohol was available in commercial quantities, as gasoline is today, but today it would have been an expensive fuel.

Figures 2.4 and 2.5 reveal a more business-like, non-condensing steam plant with a vertical boiler and engine. For later locomotives of that era, both would be horizontal with a right angle turn to the smokestack. The engine shown was built for the son of Elihu Thomson, a founder of General Electric Company, to operate on a narrow gage railway. This steam plant is of interest because it reveals the typical components, functions, and construction applicable to a full scale flying machine of the period. On a large scale the unit easily could be the one envisioned for the design of Figure 2.17. The latter shows four engines connected to one vertical boiler.

In Figure 2.5 the feedwater inlet connection is to the right of the boiler. The water flows through pipes inside the boiler while being converted to steam in its passage. The fuel is likely coal or charcoal, located in the fire box at the bottom of the boiler. The steam produced flows through piping to the engine cylinder by way of a slider valve mounted on it. The valve is inside the rectangular part of the cylinder (Figure 2.5) permitting alternating steam flow to the piston faces. The spent steam in this design is returned to the firebox through a high looping tube presumably to reduce the amount of makeup water. The pur-

Figure 2.4 Thomson steam engine, full view. Museum of Science, Boston.

posely high loop would preserve the fluid head for flow in one direction, into the boiler water supply. Observe that the engine is vertically mounted with parts cut away for museum exhibition (Figure 2.5). The piston rod drives an eccentric pin by means of an elongated connecting rod. This pin is attached to a disk that drives a horizontal shaft. At the opposite end of the shaft is a flywheel. Not visible are the mechanisms that drive the slide valve and the propelling car wheels.

The steam plant in general is very primitive, with few auxiliaries. One of fundamental importance is a water flow regulator, not only to maintain a steady flow of steam, but to avoid the boiler operating low on water. The latter problem was the cause of the notorious steam engine explosions of the 19th century. The engine explosion of the

Figure 2.5 Thomson steam engine details.

Davidson, 1909 helicopter was most likely due to this deficiency. (See Davidson narrative with Figure 3.20, and also cartoon, Figure 2.42.) For this control, Figure 2.5 shows on the boiler, a lever-actuated water valve with a weight hanging off the free end. Inside and connected to this is a ball float (similar to one found in a household water tank). The vertical tube on the discharge end of the boiler is the protective cover for a glass sight gage with its own shutoff valve.

What this steam plant evokes is the scarcity of automatic controls in those times. The common ones were the ball float valve for water and the flyball governor for rotating machinery. A third, the electromagnetic relay appeared late in the 19th century. The Thomson steam plant appeared to lack a normally operated throttle. The engine probably was given a starting boost by manually spinning the flywheel. Today, automatic controls and automation, as well as the computer driven analytical methods are extensive and pervasive elements of modern, progressive technology one with a strong social impact as well.

Table 2.1 is a nominal count of powerplants considered or used for flying machines, designs, test rigs, and flying models. The survey covers both the United States and Europe. Concepts numbered around 20. The table itself accounts for 119 separate efforts directed at mechanical flight, including the work of Australian Lawrence Hargreave. No person in the 19th century surpassed him in the quest for a viable steam or other engine for model or full scale aircraft. He worked on at least 26 variants, designing and constructing five engines. Figures 2.6, 2.7, 2.8, and 2.9 are representative of his work. [2.9] Figure 2.6 is most likely the first ever design for a rotary engine, the type popular in the first world war. Figure 2.7 shows the design of a steam turbine driven propeller, with the turbine at its hub. In the 1960s a similar concept was tried in the United States using a gas turbine driving the tip buckets of a multi blade lifting fan. Practically, turbine wheel peripheral speed must be very high. To maintain an appropriate rotational speed, the turbine diameter is much higher than that shown in the figure. For this reason the

Table 2.1
Powerplant Concepts Count, Nineteenth Century
(American and Other)

No.	Type	Full Scale Concept	Test Rig	Flyable Model	Total
1.	Steam, complete	4	0	0	4
2.	Steam, less condenser, boiler	5	0	5	10
3.	Steam, boiler only	0	1	2	3
4.	Steam, jet	2	0	1	3
5.	Steam, unspecified	16	3	1	20
6.	Electric motor	0	4	0	4
7.	Gunpowder	3	0	0	3
8.	Guncotton	1	0	0	1
9.	Compressed air	0	1	2	3
10.	Carbonic acid gas	2	1	1	4
11.	Pulsating cells	1	0	0	1
12.	Muscle	0	8	0	8
13.	Other types	4	2	1	7
14.	Undefined	10	4	1	15
15.	Hot air	2	0	0	2
16.	Internal combustion concept	4	0	1	5
17.	Hargreave projects	—	—	—	26
Total					119

drive should be at the blade tips, rather than at the hub as shown. With a hub turbine designed to rotate at a high peripheral speed, there could be a reduction gear stage driving the propeller. With the reduction gearing, the concept would approach that of a modern turboprop engine.

The idea of a steam jet driving a turbine wheel dates at least to 1627. In that year the Italian engineer Giovanni Branca demonstrated publicly in Milan its first application for crushing ore (Figure 2.10). Branca appealed for support to the government, at the time under control of the Spanish Viceroy, but was turned down. If followed up the concept easily could have been a successful alternate to the piston version of the steam engine. [2.10] In hindsight the idea was promising, and its demise is an example of the

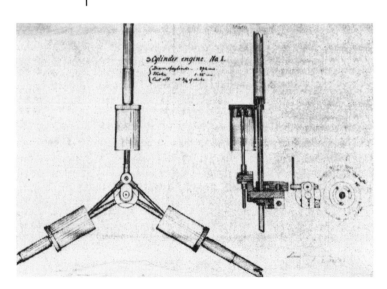

Figure 2.6 Hargreave aircraft rotary engine, the first of its type (1899). Exhibit of Sydney (Australia) Museum of Arts and Sciences.

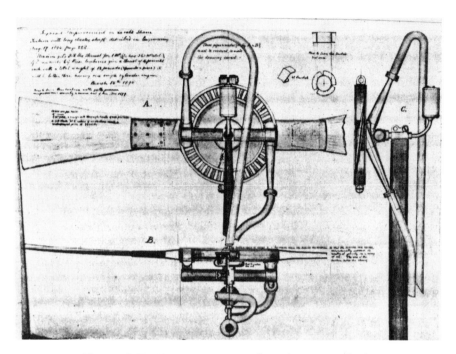

Figure 2.7 Hargreave steam-turbine driven propeller (1895).

Figure 2.8 Hargreave engine No. 23, two-cylinder rotary engine (1898).

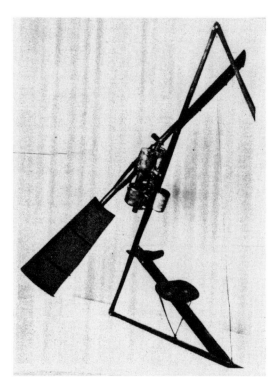

Figure 2.9 Hargreave No. 24 four cylinder gasoline engine (1900).

many good ideas that were not supported. The working version would be very inefficient, but in those days *efficiency* had less meaning when the real interest was in getting any machine to work at all. Improvements naturally would follow.

Figure 2.8 shows Hargreave steam engine number 23 (1898). This was a two cylinder rotary engine producing 3.7–4.5 kW (5–6 hp). Variant 24 (Figure 2.9) was a four cylinder gasoline engine, turning a propeller at 8.3 rps (500 rpm) (1900). The engine is pictured on a rig with seat for the operator.

Very likely the best engine of aircraft quality was the five cylinder radial of Charles Manly, Figure 2.11. [2.11] It was built for the Langley *Aerodrome*, a machine that crashed on its first flight (1903). The engine produced 38.8 kW (52 hp) and weighed 94 kg (207 lb) or 2.4 kg/kW (4 lb/hp), complete with radiators, batteries, and 9.1 kg (20 lb) of cooling water. The unit weight practically halved the maximum value specified by the government: 5.1 kg/kW (8.3 lb/hp). Manly's engine ran 10 hours in bench tests. Aeronautical history would have had a different

twist if the *Aerodrome* was as reliable as the Manly engine.

The task of contending with a man-carrying flying machine was the most demanding of the lot (Table 2.1) because all the components of a complete airborne system required accounting in the total weight. In this case the engine unit weight had to be included in the total weight and in the total power loading. By subtracting the powerplant weight per unit power from the measured thrust loading in kilograms per kilowatt (pounds per horsepower), one could determine the available (or allowable) weight per unit power for the rest of the helicopter. This subtraction could just as easily be negative (or more likely so). A reverse calculation would reveal the maximum allowable engine weight per unit power. Such was the analytical reasoning of the time.

The flyable models were less demanding because some of the powerplant components (and manning) could be eliminated from the total weight lifted. For example, with a steam engine, the condenser and steam generator (boiler and fuel) could be omitted by use of an airborne tank of water that was heated to steam before launching. In this case, emphasis was placed on flight characteristics rather than on weight or endurance.

Least demands on a flyable powerplant were attained in use of a tethered model, or on a ground based test rig. In the latter case, focus was on establishing a practical value of thrust loading, thereby approaching the problem one parameter at a time.

Referring to Table 2.1, steam power was most favored in the investigations (lines 1–5). As suggested above, the essential components of a complete (closed) steam plant consist of the engine itself, boiler, and combustor (the latter two being the steam generator), recirculating pump, and water condensing system. With a closed system the major consumable was the fuel. The latter could be wood, coal and later, petroleum.

In the late 1890s the best weight for a closed system was around 4.9 kg/kW (8 lb/hp). This low weight was obtained on a prototype airplane

Figure 2.10 Italian Branca's steam turbine concept (1627).

using a complicated condensing system with a surface area of 9.3 m² (100 ft²), a feat of design desperation not feasible for a helicopter. To this day, the steam to water condensing problem with its large surface area requirement (permitting water recirculation) inhibits use of steam as the prime mover in aircraft. (Steam locomotives pick up water along the way.) The late 19th century state of the art for stationary units revealed powerplant unit weights of 36.5–103.4 kg/kW (60–170 lb/hp) and more. [2.12] One 1864 kW

(2500 hp) stationary plant (1876) weighed 334 kg/kW (550 lb/hp).

The most favored alternate relative to a complete system was the steam plant with a generator (boiler) but without a condenser (Table 2.1, line 2). This approach was incorporated in most of the flying models, including the Stringfellow engines (Figures 2.1 to 2.3). In the late 19th century typical water (or steam) consumption for an uncondensing system was (optimistically) 4235

Figure 2.11 Manly water-cooled radial engine (1903).

micrograms/Joule (25 lb/hr/hp), hence model flight duration was brief. [2.13] Some full scale studies simply ignored the condenser problem. To reduce model weight even more, the generator was replaced with a reservoir of water as remarked above. It was heated to steam by an external source, and the model was launched with this fixed supply. The first successful model helicopter was flown with this system in 1877. This project, described later, was the work of the Italian, Forlanini.

An alternate to the engine (line 4) used steam vapor to produce a jet reaction, driving a screw. In one case the energy was produced by the combustion of gunpowder (nitre, charcoal, gypsum). The steam jet idea dates to a description by Heron. Figure 2.12 is a current interpretation of his *revolving ball* concept. The features called out in the figure are those identified by Heron. [1.2] His *aeolipile* (apparently not the correct name for the device) was a spherical steam chamber that rotated on two supports, driven by steam escaping from two hollow arms attached to the sphere. The rocket rotor helicopter of today is steam driven by the conversion of almost pure hydrogen peroxide by means of a catalyst (as potassium permanganate) located in the

blade tip, nozzle chamber. This chemical is a highly corrosive and hazardous propellant that will detonate if contaminated (as with an accidental impurity). Domestic hydrogen peroxide is diluted with water, the solution containing 3–6% pure hydrogen peroxide. The rocket rotor discharge products are steam and oxygen, the former about 60% by weight. [2.14] Less known is Heron also conceived a hot air driven rotor (Figure 2.13) to carry "dancing dolls". Presumably he had convection heat in mind.

Referring to line 5 of Table 2.1, there were also many inventors who proposed flying machines but left undefined the steam engine. Others gave up on steam and looked to alternate systems (lines 6–13). These included a hot air engine and those described below.

Line 14 shows some ignored engine identification altogether, the inference being someone eventually would produce a powerplant suitable for flying machines, an obviously correct inference. Ignoring the engine allowed the inventor to investigate other aspects of mechanical flight.

The electric motor (line 6) was used for ground testing rotors. Few applied it to flying machines. Motors powered the science fiction helicopter of Jules Verne (1886) described later in the narratives but the inventor of the machine kept the details of electric propulsion to himself.

Gunpowder and guncotton engines (lines 7 and 8) were considered by a few. Both relied on using the explosive force in some kind of powerplant. The idea of a gunpowder fueled engine has a longer history than one might expect. The principle even could be taken as the precursor of the liquid fueled internal combustion engine. Leonardo da Vinci and Dutch physicist Christi-

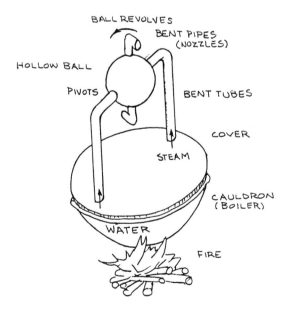

Figure 2.12 Heron's "aeolipile" stem turbine (A.D. 62). Illustration is based on his description of the unit. The items called out are those Heron identified.

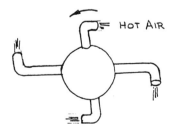

Figure 2.13 Heron's hot air concept.

aan Huygens (1629–1695) had ideas for gunpowder engines. The latter produced an experimental piston engine in 1673. [2.15] In the late 19th century peak pressures in firing a cannonball were around 5516 bars (80,000 psi), indicating what the engine designer was up against. [2.16] In one engine design (1871) the gunpowder explosion produced a jet of gas that impinged on turbine buckets (blades) driving an airscrew. As an afterthought on the use of gunpowder, an anonymous writer in *Scientific American* offered the following, published in 1871:

> "The world seems to have concluded that the cycle of invention is complete that the telegraph has taken the last and topmost place, and that men must be satisfied with the great time and labor saved which they now possess." [2.17]

The writer may have had in mind the laying of the Atlantic cable in 1866, which in its time led to connection of all the national telegraphic systems. By 1862 the world's telegraphic system extended over a distance of 241,000 kilometers (150,000 miles). Apparently this era experienced the first "end of technology".

Application of guncotton (explosive nitrocellulose) invented in 1865 took advantage of the latest propellant. With one particular engine the idea was to put a small charge between two pistons and detonate it. Though few advocated the explosion engine, compressed air engine (line 9) like the electric motor found its use in test rigs or models, mainly serving to bypass the powerplant problem to concentrate on rotor performance. The air source was a ground based power supply. Analogous to one steam system, compressed air could be stored in an airborne tank, permitting a brief free flight. A different approach to the steam engine principle without its auxiliaries, was to use carbon dioxide as the motive fluid (line 10). The gas was produced using pressurized carbonic acid, a compound of carbon dioxide and water. One problem with this concept was caused by the low fluid temperature. The cold not only resulted in freezing valves, but it produced dry ice snow, clogging pipes. Nonetheless a carbonic acid engine was found in a European airplane as late as 1906 (the Serpollet engine in the Vuia airplane). [2.19]

Line 11 lists the strangest concept aimed to create an ultra-light powerplant. The idea was to rely on pulsating cells to produce a reciprocating motion. The powerplant consisted of a wood cylinder containing rubber cells in tandem. Introduced periodically within each cell was a mix of hydrogen and air. Ignition by electric sparks produced explosions which by proper timing caused the cells to expand and collapse. This axially-cyclic action drove an accordion-like member at one end of the cylinder. The member produced the reciprocating motion necessary to turn a crankshaft, ultimately driving the airscrew.

Line 12 shows some experimenters used themselves as a human powerplant. The intent was not always to attempt flight, but to evaluate rotor performance with a test rig in which the investigator estimated his own power input. This way one avoided altogether the powerplant cost in testing.

There were some investigators who postulated other powerplants (line 13). Included here were turbines and powerful springs. The turbine could be a blower for jet lift, but this did not account for the turbine powerplant. In another case the impeller relied on jet impingement produced by an explosion. A third (cited earlier) used ether vapor combustion as the motive fluid. The inventor Hiram Maxim in 1872 proposed a powerplant using the Brayton cycle. Today the unit would be called a turboshaft engine.

The final powerplants of interest (lines 15 and 16) relate to internal combustion engines, the type that made mechanical flight possible—an accomplishment of the first years of the 20th century. The aeronautical pioneer George Cayley not only invented a helicopter, but addressed himself to a light weight powerplant for flying machines. His concept prefigured the internal combustion engine. In 1809 he wrote:

> "It is only necessary to develop a suitable engine . . . but as lightness is of so much value there is the probability of using the expansion of air by sudden combustion of inflammable powders of fluids." [2.20]

Cayley designed a hot air engine (Figure 2.14) and conducted some tests. Structural failure and worker injury caused him to drop the project.

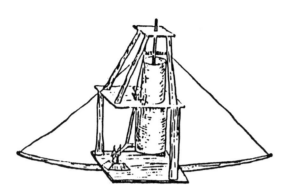

Figure 2.14 Cayley two-cylinder "internal explosion" engine test unit (1807).

Another visionary was Frenchman Joseph Niépce, the photography pioneer. About 1807 he tested an engine (called *pyrelophore*) fueled by lycopodium powder, a flammable kind of moss spore he well knew, used in photoflash powders, fireworks, and stage lighting. In this case the intermittent explosion engine was used for direct propulsion of a boat on the Sâone. [2.21]

The first practical internal combustion engine was produced in France in 1860, by J. J. Étienne Lenoir. His water-cooled engine ran on coal (illuminating) gas, introduced into a cylinder at atmospheric pressure, and exploded by an electric spark. There was no compression stroke in his two-stroke cycle engine. Without a significant pressure ratio, the thermal efficiency ran about 4 percent. (From thermodynamic theory, the thermal efficiency of an internal combustion engine increases exclusively with increase in compression ratio.) Several hundred were built. In 1872 one was installed in the first airborne application of this type engine, specifically in an airship. [2.22]

Despite the promise of the internal combustion engine, the following appeared in *Scientific American* in 1864:

> "Flying is impossible by 'pneumatics' using fixed wing and propeller because a 50 hp engine and etc., will never weigh 150 pounds."
> (37.3 kW, 68.1 kg). [2.23]

Today aircraft piston engines weigh around 0.85 kg/kW (1.4 lb/hp) while helicopter turboshaft engines weigh 0.15 to 0.24 kg/kW (0.25 to 0.40 lb/hp), much less than the 1.8 kg/hp (3.0 lb/hp) cited above.

It was not until 1876 that the true four-stroke cycle engine was reduced to practice by the German N. A. Otto. [2.24] The compression stroke was an important addition, which as implied above is the key to a relatively low fuel consumption. The idea of precompression was advanced by Carnot (1824), and such an engine was suggested by Beau de Rochas (1862). [2.25] To the Otto engine, Daimler added a carburetor producing a light weight, 20.1 kg/kW (33 lb/hp) roadable, i.e., mobile version. Benz introduced the spark coil and plug. Evolution was complete in 1902 when the high-tension magneto was developed. The last eliminated batteries to sustain operation. [2.26] By the end of the century over 20,000 Otto engines were produced.

The turn of the century saw introduction of the radial engine for aircraft, both water and air cooled. Initially the latter was a rotary engine, favored for early helicopter prototypes because of its self-cooling feature in hovering and relatively light weight.

The powerplant mystery of the 19th century is why the idea of the internal combustion engine was not immediately seized upon as the answer to the long quest for a powerplant suitable for flying machines.

2.3 CHRONOLOGY

What follows are the narratives of individual visionaries, inventors, and experimenters for the first period. Where indicated the ideas are in their own expressive language. As noted before, the date is considered the most representative period of their work.

1828 Pennington

The earliest American known to give scientific thought to a lifting rotor appears to be John H. Pennington of Baltimore. He appreciated the aerodynamic force of an inclined plane moving through the air and that the common windmill driven in reverse could be used for lift or as a propeller. In a letter to John Wise a famous balloonist [2.27] he cites an article in the U.S. Gazette signed E. L. B. E:

"I hold that a current of air acting against a system of confined inclined planes causes them to revolve with great power, increasing in proportion to their surface and strength of the current. So if the power were reversed, the planes set free and the force applied directly to them, they would propel themselves forward with a corresponding force and velocity . . . for contrary to common conception three-fourths of a ship's sailing is performed by sails acting as inclined planes against the current of wind, instead of direct line impulse." [2.28]

Pennington postulated an engine of steel, fueled by turpentine or alcohol. The weight of a 1.9–2.2 kW (2.5–3.0 hp) engine including fuel and "dilating fluid" (the expansion fluid) was estimated to be 227 kg (500 lb). In a design using a balloon, Pennington proposed the addition of "fan wheels" for lift and propulsion. He remarks further that while the idea was original with him, others could have just as easily come up with the same concept. Even so, he showed early aerodynamic recognition that suction acting on a lifting surface is much greater than the dynamic pressure impacting the lower surface. (See also Bernoulli theorem in the Glossary.)

1834 Mason

As reported in local papers at the time, A. A. Mason of Cincinnati, Ohio announced a demonstration on the Fourth of July of a flying machine that was essentially a helicopter. [2.29] Powered by a 1.5 kW (2.0 hp) steam engine, the craft consisted of four spiral-shaped lifting screws mounted on a 3.1 m (10 ft) long hull. The latter was made of frames covered with silk. For propulsion two additional screws were fixed to the stern. The machine included a cover of silk, apparently meant to serve as a parachute as well as to provide lift and propulsive components. The fate of the project is unknown, and as a man-carrying machine it was obviously underpowered and using Pennington's estimate, it was also overweight. However, the Mason helicopter appears to be the only example of a "complete", man-carrying machine of American origin in the 19th century.

1842 Taylor

The concept for a kind of convertiplane was advanced by American Robert Taylor in 1842

(Figure 2.15). The coaxial system consisted of a large and small diameter rotor. In forward flight, the surface of the lower rotor was to cover the open (inboard) area of the upper rotor, by an axial movement upward. In this manner the two lifting screws were converted to a solid circular surface for "progression". The rotors appear to be contrarotating, a feature that would complicate conversion [2.20]

Taylor contacted George Cayley relative to the idea. It showed up in Cayley's convertiplane design of 1843 (Figure 2.16). [2.31] Apparently he did not give much credit to Taylor for the idea. Even so, Figure 2.16 shows Cayley avoided the nesting problem by providing single, separate rotors, each with the ability to depitch its blades, forming circular wings. The craft could fly just as well as a compound helicopter. By forming a wing instead, Cayley deliberately or inadvertently avoided the problem (aerodynamic dissymmetry) with rotors in forward flight.

Cayley called his design *Aerial Carriage*, a potent concept in the 19th century. To people of the time, *carriage* was a wheeled vehicle ("a carriage and pair"), or with reference to steam locomotion, *railway carriage*. One presumes Cayley applied the concept to a flying machine to stimulate public imagination with the vision of a wheeled commonplace moving through the air carrying many people. Despite the appearance of the design in Figure 2.16, Cayley was no helicopter enthusiast, for most of his work involved fixed wings.

1848 Anonymous

In 1848 there appeared an account of a proposed helicopter by an unidentified letter writer to the *Jacksonian*, of Pontiac, Michigan. The idea reappeared in *Scientific American* with editorial comments. [2.32] The inventor describes his machine:

"Let us suppose a machine to be constructed resembling a long railroad car with arms projecting at certain distances from roof to floor . . . At the extremities of these arms, the axles of screw wheels or wings are inserted which will work parallel to the earth instead of perpendicular as in a vessel. At the stern of the car are two or four wheels to serve as propellers. The side wheels being merely to elevate and suspend the

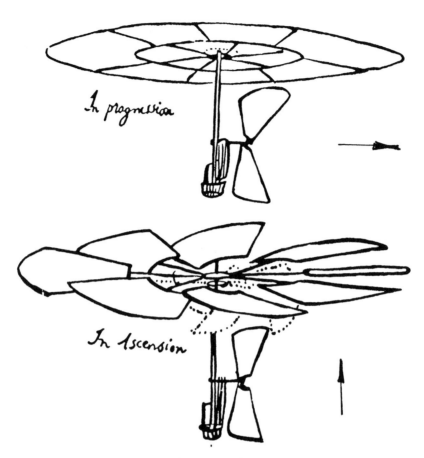

In progression

In Ascension

Figure 2.15 Taylor convertiplane concept (1842).

car. In the interior of the car at the center, is a steam engine with fuel and water, while the extremities are reserved for passengers and baggage. The wings are moved by independent bands connected with the internal machinery, so that whole or portions of them may be used at once for convenience in ascending or descending. Unlike the railroad car, the frame should be constructed of wrought iron and the roof and sides be covered with sheet iron or copper, suitably supported by light frames where necessary. The wheel wings should be constructed in the same manner . . . strength combined with lightness being always kept in view."

Figure 2.17 shows the general arrangement as conceived by the author. The inventor proceeds with an explanation justifying use of a marine steam engine as a feasible powerplant for aerial navigation. He then continues:

> "The machine . . . will have four to twelve wings according to length. The forward end should be built sharp to offer less resistance to the wind.

Having more wheels than necessary for elevation, no danger can occur from any accident that might occur to one or two of them. The machine can be guided by some kind of rudder attached to each side of the stern. The car forty feet long with five wheels on each side eight feet in diameter and three smaller propellers at the stern would certainly appear a novel object roaring along through the air. If a certain breadth of wheel be not sufficient, try broader ones . . . if the velocity be too slow, increase it."

Regarding wing wheels, the reviewing editor had the following to say:

> "We would greatly have preferred the paddle wheel to the screw, in the atmosphere, as we certainly do for navigating the Atlantic or the Hudson."

To function in air, the paddle wheel concept had to be some form of cyclogiro rotor with its movable blades. (See cyclogiro in Glossary.) The inventor assumed some of the rotors could fail

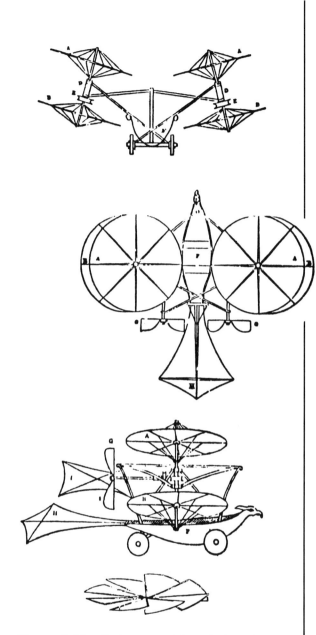

Figure 2.16 Cayley convertiplane design using Taylor rotor concept modified.

without a catastrophe, but if blades separate they could destroy other rotors creating lift dissymmetry. Overall, this design was the most complete to date conceptualizing a helicopter in America, and one that did not rely on the coaxial rotor configuration.

1849 Smith

In 1849 a Princeton University student J. Henry Smith designed an electric powered, captive helicopter that included a parachute (Figure 2.18). The craft was intended for military observation. [2.33] The coaxial, contrarotating system was coplanar, with one set of blades mounted on a rim outside the inner rotor, suggesting the Taylor (1842) concept. The rotor overall diameter was about 7 meters (23 feet). A ground based steam engine drove a generator producing the current for the motor on board. Smith's idea showed progressive thought. The first electric motors were introduced in the 1830s, and practical ones in the latter part of the 19th century. A similar captive concept was tested in Austria during the First World War by Petroczy and von Karman. [2.34]

1857–1861 Edwards

In a letter to *Scientific American* [2.35] titled "Suggestions about flying—the thing accomplished", Charles Edwards reported on his work with the commentary:

> "Since the creation of the earth, men have longed to take themselves to wings and soar away like birds of the air. The thirst for amusement, for knowledge, for novelty, for fame, for wealth, in fact for almost every object that man holds dear has conspired to incite inventors to exertion in this particular field. Especially as the almost boundless wealth which would be the reward of the successful inventor served as a powerful incentive to that proverbially poor class. Yet, although inventive genius has accomplished results little short of miraculous in other directions, we have been, up to the present time, particularly as far from attainment of that desire as in the days of Adam. To be sure, we have the balloon, but that is a mere plaything, and, as is evident to all who have considered the subject, can never be anything more. The requisites of a serviceable 'airship' are, the ability to move in any direction regardless of the winds or currents of air, and, if need, to maintain a stationary position in the atmosphere at any place and for any required length of time."

Edwards listed the three major problem areas requiring solution: the body, which is the least problematic;

> ". . . the construction of the propeller or contrivance by whose action upon the atmosphere is given to the vessel; and the third the motive

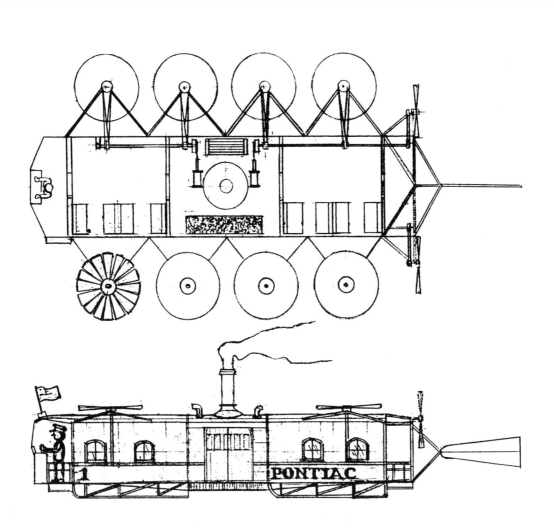

Figure 2.17 Author's interpretation of the "48 Pontiac" (1848).

power. This in absence of any specially adapted to the purpose, might be supplied by some of those already known but at ruinous disadvantage, were it practicable."

He cited the work in France of "M. DePouton" (DePonton D'Amécourt) the inventor who:

> ". . . made a great sensation and yet all that has been done, admitting fully the claims of the inventor, is the elaboration or calculation of a method of propelling an airship."

D'Amécourt was a champion of helicopter flight in mid-19th century France. Along with de la Landelle his work is described later in conjunction with Nadar (1861–1865). Edwards then cited the criticism of de la Landelle regarding theory without practice:

> "This (theory) amounts to saying that the problem already solved by mechanical skills awaits only the aid of some sufficient physico-chemical force in order to attain a perfect development, and Heaven be praised, the resources of modern science are of miraculous fecundity."

Edwards followed with his own work, maintaining he had solved the first two problems (hull, propeller) without describing how, and that he had a solution to the motive power. Details of the powerplant were not revealed. However he described earlier tests with a model powered by a steel spring that ran about 135 sec (2¼ minutes). The model weighed 35 kg (77 lb), and a 28.1 kg (62 lb) weight was added. It was tethered to a post with a 9.2 m (30 ft) line. He conducted 36 trials and calculated the model flew around the post at 145 km/hr (90 mph). Based

Figure 2.18   Smith tethered observation helicopter concept (1849).

on these tests and scaling up the model propeller, he believed a speed of 5 miles a minute was attainable (483 km/hr).

> "I have not only invented a flying machine, but made a working model, which operated in a manner eminently satisfactory-being, I think, the first on record."

Edwards concluded his letter with a solicitation of capital to continue tests of the propeller and motive power on a large scale.

1861 Mitchel

In late 1861 at the start of the Civil War there was a Union proposal to build a helicopter for reconnaissance. The proposal was put to General Ormsby M. Mitchel [2.36] who reviewed the idea with his chief engineering officer. At this time a report noted the officer demonstrated a metal toy of a type described before (Figure 1.16). A model

> ". . . that, wound up with a string like a humming top . . . would fly into the air one hundred

feet or more, vertically, according to the force exerted upon it, and would carry a bullet or two if the force were hard enough. A device like this supplied with propelling screws could carry an observer out and back."

The project was dropped temporarily due to the death of General Mitchel by yellow fever. It was later revived by General Benjamin Franklin Butler. (See 1865 Butler entry.)

Although Mitchel, a former teacher of mathematics and astronomy, was a helicopter proponent, he is remembered for his approval of a daring Union attempt to disrupt the Confederate rail line between Atlanta and Chattanooga, and for the raiders to meet with Mitchel advancing toward the latter town. [2.37]

The raiders seized the locomotive *General* north of Atlanta at Big Shanty (now Kennnesaw), but were frustrated in their plans by another Confederate locomotive in pursuit. The chase continued for about 145 km (90 miles) before the raiders dispersed or were captured. The locomotive lost its steam, being unable to stop for fuel. The chase was the subject of a well-known silent movie *The General*, featuring Buster Keaton as the Confederate pursuer, and hero. The locomotive was built by the Rogers Works of Paterson, New Jersey [2.38] (America's first industrial city). The first Medals of Honor granted by Congress went to the raiders. [2.39] In 1994 the U.S. Postal Service issued a 29 cent commemorative stamp depicting the locomotive.

1861–1865 Nadar and D'Amécourt

The French activity of Nadar and his associates is of interest because it reveals the most advanced efforts at helicopter flight in mid century. Nadar (Gaspard Félix Tournachon) was a famous aerial photographer and aeronaut. By recording the bird's eye view, his photographs revealed a picture of communities never seen before in this perspective or in such totality. [2.40] He was the promoter in a group of helicopter enthusiasts led by D'Amécourt. Nadar wrote:

"It is the screw which is to carry us through the air, it is the screw which penetrates the air as a

gimlet does wood . . . you can rise, descend, or remain motionless according to the number of revolutions which you cause your screw to make. . ." [2.41]

Nadar's proposals are shown in Figure 2.19. The steam powerplant, to be built by the Bariquand Company, consisted of two cylinders driving coaxial rotors by means of rods, cranks, and bevel gears. (This company later built engines for the Wrights.) As Nadar states above, rotor control is through speed change. His design is a pure helicopter, showing no propeller (thruster). D'Amécourt's patent (British 1929 of 1861) includes both a propeller and a rudder, along with a powerplant and drive system similar to Figure 2.20. Nadar held: ". . . . that which aerostation refuses we must demand of dynamics and statics." A monograph by Jeune Duchesne in 1864 reveals the skepticism toward helicopter flight in particular. Published in Paris by E. Dentu, the title discloses the critics position. "Exposé de divers systèmes de Navigation Aérienne et Réfutation de L'hélicoptère Nadar."

D'Amécourt who began helicopter work in 1853, produced models of his helicopter ideas. A steam powered aluminum version was built by mechanic L. Joseph of Arras (Figure 2.20). The powerplant technology was the best of the time. The coaxial rotor helicopter weighed 2.3–2.7 kg (5–6 lb). For flight the two cylinder engine carried no steam generator nor condenser, the only energy available was the steam stored in coils. In tests, the model failed to lift its own weight. The model is now in the Musée de L'Air (Meudon). D'Amécourt was part of a famous trio that included Nadar and de la Landelle. French physicist Jacques Babinet named them *triumvirate hélicoptèroidal*. In their enthusiasm they undertook balloon ascensions with *L'Géant* to raise money to build a full scale helicopter. Subscribers included Offenbach, Dumas, Hugo, George Sand, and Jules Verne. Even so, the venture proved unprofitable. [2.42] The helicopter activity inspired Verne to write a novel on the subject. (See 1886 Verne.)

1862 Powers

During the Civil War the South also had a helicopter project. It was the work of William C.

Figure 2.19 Nadar and D'Amécourt concepts (1861–1865).

Powers of Mobile, Alabama [2.43] however he did not go beyond construction of a static model. Powers believed a full size machine ". . . could carry a weighty explosive, and move swiftly at the will of the pilot". His steam powered design (Figure 2.21) used two helicoidal screws in tandem for lift and two for propulsion. The model featured a rudder for directional control, while a rolling weight served to maintain trim by shifting the CG of the craft. The model, discovered in an attic in 1940, was donated to the Smithsonian.

1865 Barbour

In 1865 *Scientific American* carried an editorial reviewing the work of Barbour who was affiliated with the Polytechnic Association. [2.44] The editorial is a good summary of the then state of knowledge. It discusses a novel powerplant (carbonic acid engine) and the possibilities of mechanical flight.

Barbour claimed he obtained 1.5 horsepower (1.12 kW) from an engine weighing 450 pounds (204 kg) as a functioning unit. It ran continuously for an hour and twenty minutes with a maximum reservoir (tank) pressure of 1100 psi (75.9 bars). The editorial postulated an improved engine of aluminum, and substantial increase in pressure ratio to obtain a greater output. (Note aluminum was not commercially produced until 1886.) A half-hour operation using carbonic acid was considered an acceptable duration. This time interval was taken to be satisfactory for a trip of 30 miles (48.3 km) at 60 mph (96.5 km/h). It was believed feasible to build a 2 horsepower (1.5 kW) engine weighing 150 pounds (68.1 kg). The editorialist then analyzed the powerplant in a one man rotorcraft. The weight of the machine and its burden was estimated to be 330 lb (150 kg), including a 180 pound (81.7 kg) man. Using test data from a flat plate, he derived the following rotorcraft: The powerplant is an aluminum engine using carbonic acid, delivering 2 hp (1.5 kW). The lifting

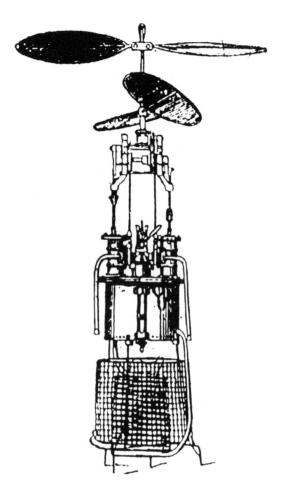

Figure 2.20 D'Amécourt steam powered model (mid 19th century). Meudon (France) museum.

system consists of two, two-blade rotors (presumably counterrotating) of a 4 foot radius (1.2m) and 10.5 inch (26.7 cm) chord, turning 360 rpm. These values would then yield a vertical climb of 100 fpm (30.5 m/min).

Using current parameters, the power loading is 100.3 kg/kW (165 lb/hp), and the disk loading 16.1 kg/m² (3.3. lb/ft²). The resulting figure of merit is 7.9, far in excess of the maximum theoretical of 1.0. It is obvious the power required is grossly underestimated.

The editorialist concluded his study with the following remarks:

> "The only plan for navigating the air that has any hopes of success is that of flying-beating the air with wings driven by mechanical force; and certainly no machine (engine) heretofore proposed comes so near possessing the requisite power in proportion to its weight as a carbonic acid engine constructed of aluminum."

In the context of the editor's analysis, "beating the air" apparently refers to a rotor (not flapping wings). As discussed previously the carbonic acid engine is seen as a precursor of the internal combustion engine, because the former was a production unit. Aside from optimistic performance estimating, a common deficiency, the editor was on the right track. However beyond aerodynamics,

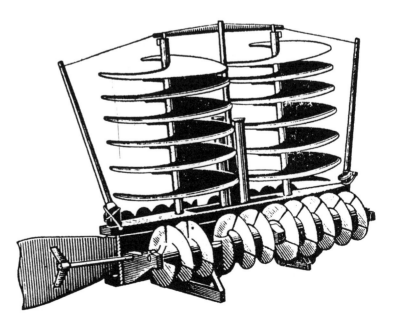

Figure 2.21 Powers static model of a compound helicopter (1862). Smithsonian Institution.

the problems of stability and mechanical reliability remained to be resolved far in the future, beyond even the second period described here.

1865 Butler/Serrell

The helicopter project supported by General Mitchel in 1861 was reactivated in 1865 by General Benjamin Franklin Butler. [2.45] A 10.2 cm (4 in) tin toy was demonstrated, and the show intrigued Butler enough to order Lemuel W. Serrell to provide a full report on the subject. [2.46] The intent was to scale up the model, adding wings ("gliding planes") producing a vehicle 15.9 m (52 ft) long, weighing 5450 kg (12,000 lb). The design reviewed used four fans for lift, two above and two below the powerplant. The latter being a high-pressure steam engine. There were two additional fans for propulsion, one at each end of the craft. Balance was by movable weights, one on either side of the hull (fuselage). A retractable weight was suspended from the car center, presumably for its "pendulum effect". The design of the machine apparently was based on the ideas of Mortimer Nelson (1865) described later.

Butler gave Serrell the go-ahead to build the machine. However no money was alloted to the project, and there were no tools at the "engineer's park." The enterprise was picked up and funded by civilians named Sully and F. P. Clarke, and the Butler project was superseded in 1865 by the Hoboken project that follows.

General Butler was a colorful, flambuoyant individual, harsh and notorious while serving as military governor of New Orleans (1862) [2.47] He was harsh enough for Jefferson Davis to issue an order to hang him if caught. [2.48] The general earned the epithet *Spoons Butler* for his inclination to profit personally from looted household silverware. He antagonized the women of the city by surmising of them collectively certain proclivities. In the PBS-TV series on the Civil War, Butler was declared the most inept Union general of the war. He obviously had the personality to be interested in far-out ideas such as helicopters. The following account supports this.

In 1864–65 Butler was involved in the siege of Petersburg (and Richmond). At the time his

ideas on warfare technology were met with disfavor, revealed in a letter (1864) critical of the general:

> "Butler never is happy unless he has half a dozen contrivances on hand. An idea that Benjamin considered highly practicable was a fire engine, wherewith he proposed to squirt water on earthworks and wash them all down. Then with Greek fire, he proposed to hold a redoubt with only five men and a small garden engine. 'Certainly' said General Meade. 'Only your engine fires thirty feet and the rifle 3000 yards, and I am afraid your five men will be killed before they had a chance to burn up their adversaries!' Butler also was going to get a gun that would shoot seven miles and, taking direction by compass, burn the city of Richmond with shells of Greek fire. If that didn't do, he had an auger to bore a tunnel five feet in diameter, and he was going to bore to Richmond and suddenly pop up in somebody's basement while the family were at breakfast! So, you see, he is ingenious." [3.49]

(A garden engine was a portable, steam driven force-pump for watering gardens.)

1865 Hoboken Project

In 1865 there was a helicopter project in Hoboken, New Jersey that grew out of the earlier Mitchel and Butler initiatives. An account in *Scientific American* reported the following:

> "A flying machine of novel form is now in the process of construction at Hoboken for the United States Government. It was commenced during the war and it was intended for use in aerial reconnaissance of enemy's positions. The war is over, but the machine is going on until success or failure is an established fact. The idea of the invention is an old one, but this is the first time that an attempt has been made to put it in practice. The government was induced to embark on the enterprise on the strength of certain experiments by the late distinguished general (and professor) Mitchel. He has long been interested in the subject of aerial navigation, and believed that the principle of screw propulsion could be made to work in air as well as water. The first and only way to demonstrate the lifting power of a screw in moving horizontally at different rates of speed. The experimental fan was placed upon a pole

as an axis, up and down which it would move freely. The fan was then made to revolve at various rates of speed at the pleasure of the operator. At one rate it would merely lift itself; at another it would rise twice its own rate; and another three times and so on until the fact was ascertained that a fan thirty feet in diameter revolving at a certain rate of speed would raise six times, and have considerable power to spare. It is only a child's toy upon a large scale. We see every day in the streets toy vendors who give a quick twirl with a string to a little fan upon a stick and let it. . . fly . . . in the air to heights of thirty feet and descend slowly still revolving as it comes down. The government toy-as some persons will probably call it-is a cigar-shaped canoe built of copper with iron ribs. An engine is placed in the center with sufficient power to work a screw with thirty foot blades. There are four fans connected with the engine-one below and one above the canoe and one at each end. The upper and lower fans are worked together to produce an ascent; and the terminal fans are made to revolve together or separately in the same direction or opposite direction." [2.50]

As mentioned before the projected weight of the helicopter "fully equipped and manned" was 5450 kg (12,000 lb). A critique in the *Journal of Commerce* offered the following:

> "If a vessel can be propelled through the air at a given miles per hour, it may be made to stem the wind of an equal number of miles per hour. If the power of the headwind exceeds or is less than the propelling power, the machine actually falls back or progresses in exact proportion to the difference between the powers. This truth should be borne in mind in considering schemes for air-sailing. An accomplished government officer is superintending the work, and hopes to have it done in a month, when the pretensions of the new flying machine will be tested." [2.50]

The writer was concerned with the difference between air speed and ground speed. Apparently he did not expect much magnitude to the ground speed, probably because he related mechanical flight speeds to the familiar balloon values.

A rotor test stand was built and operated. The steam powerplant was based on recent fire engine technology using copper and steel, and many parts were hollow for lightness. The 29.8 kW (40

hp) steam plant weighed about 227 kg (500 lb). This drove a 3.7 m (12 ft) rotor made of iron.

It was claimed the rotor lifted 1100 lb (4.9 kN) at 300 rpm. Using full power and a height-diameter ratio of 0.25 would give a figure of merit of 1.23 out of ground effect. Derived using a disk loading of 31.7 kg/m^2 (6.5 lb/ft^2), and power loading of 11.1 kg/kW (18.3 lb/hp), both estimated OGE values. Using the test data directly (assumed IGE) results in a figure of merit of 2.3. In either case the test results are suspect.

A project critic, S. D. Engle of Hazelton, Pennsylvania in a letter (oblivious of the complete configuration) wrote:

> "In looking over the . . . design . . . of the machine being constructed at Hoboken, the thing looks very squally to me. How can they give a rotary motion to the lifting fan without causing the car to rotate in the opposite direction without having a fan to act against it? It looks to me as though the motion would be more like a boomerang than anything I know of." [2.51]

Apparently Engle presumed a coaxial rotor arrangement, it is unlikely he had a tail rotor in mind.

1865 Nelson

In mid-19th century Mortimer Nelson was a prominent figure investigating mechanical flight, and helicopters in particular. His ideas are of special interest because they represent serious thought on the state of the art, particularly regarding configuration, materials, and powerplants. [2.52] In May 1861 he was granted a patent (32,378), the first (in the United States) for a flying machine (Figure 2.22). His helicopter (Figures 2.23 and 2.24) he called *Aerial Car* or *Flying Machine*. As a generic name *helicopter* was not in use in the United States until the early 20th century.

The device was not a pure helicopter but a car to be attached to a balloon, a temptation others also submitted to. The rotor was tiltable for lift and propulsion and the car included an inclined wing for added lift. The patent specified extensive use of aluminum.

Late in the 19th century Nelson claimed his idea was appropriated by the government. Shortly after the patent, Nelson wrote, a government officer called on him to examine his design, which was disclosed. There was no response until he heard of the government constructing a *flying machine* in Hoboken (now 1865). He called on the superintendent who turned out to be the engineer who examined his design in 1861 (presumably Serrell). The engineer noted tests were made that proved satisfactory, and construction had begun on the car.

Nelson commented on the rotor test results (the Hoboken project described above) and noticed the *Aerial Car* resembled his idea. He concluded

Lower Manhattan, ". . . one door west of Broadway. . .". In describing his invention Nelson revealed equal ability in vision and locution:

> "The important subject of Aerial Navigation, on which some of the greatest minds have in vain lavished a profundity of thoughts, is that which I propose to treat in a description of my Aerial Car, or Flying Machine: and when the facts (of my invention) are compared with the laws that govern mechanics, it will be seen that the subject above referred to has, after mature consideration, been scientifically solved. . ."
>
> "Hitherto the many contrivances made with this view have failed to achieve the ends intended, and no one has yet shown the exact device by which so great an object may be at-

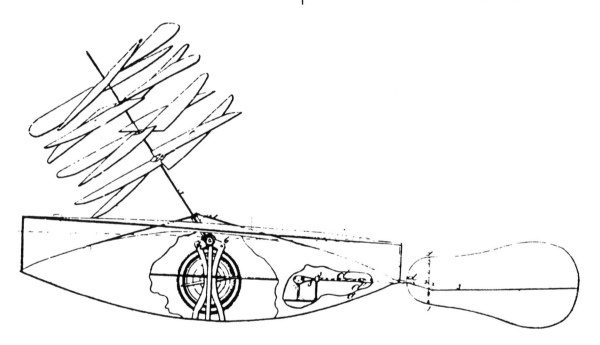

Figure 2.22 Nelson Aerial Car and balloon attachment (1861).

his complaint by repeating the project test results, and remarked.

> "I have learned that since the termination of the war, the work has been taken out of the hands of the government, and made an individual enterprise."

He did not follow up on his complaint, and after the war Nelson released a prospectus. The plan was to organize a company with a capital of $10 million and a working capital of $1 million. He set up an office at 444 Broome Street in

tained. But the feathered tribe have long illustrated and proved to the minds of reflecting individuals, that air, as well as water can be made subservient to the will of man, and navigated with equal facility."

> "The present century, remarkable for the discovery and application of steam power on land and sea, is probably destined to witness a still further development of science, in which the chief difficulty of ages will have been overcome, when the true design for a Flying Machine shall have been practically tested and launched into the blue expanse of air. The distant portions of the earth, from the rapidity

with which we shall be enabled to communicate with them, will seem as our adjoining States do now and, uninfluenced by its mighty forces, we will find the ocean presenting no obstacle to our rapid progress above its depths."

Nelson's *Aerial Car* (Figure 2.23) was a helicopter with lifting rotors and thrusting propellers. (He had variants depending on the screw arrangement.) The spindle-shaped fuselage included a skid landing gear. The *awning* (wing) could be inclined for additional lift. In comparing his design to the natural strength and weight of birds, Nelson concluded his system would put out 10 times more power per pound than a bird. He appreciated the need for light weight materials preferably steel tubing, or processed wood, the latter a new discovery making it "as a durable as whalebone". The wood was used in making umbrella ribs. He reasoned the framework could be made of this material and covered with light cloth or canvas, impervious to air or water. Recall that others used copper sheeting for the skin. Nelson recognized the fabric had to support air

pressure without leaking. The framework itself consisted of bowed longerons of processed wood, giving the car its external shape. His construction materials prefigured those of the earliest airplanes fifty years later, consisting of bamboo or other wood longerons, and cotton fabric for covering. The car was 10.1 m (33 ft) long and 1.8 m (6 ft) square, divided into compartments. The central one held the steam powerplant, while the outer compartments were for engine auxiliaries, coal-oil, mail, and freight.

In one configuration the lifting rotors were located at the center of the car, with one rotor above it and the other below, operating in contrarotation (Figure 2.24). The wire-braced rotor blades consisted of steel tubing covered with the same fabric as the car. The steam powerplant could be used "directly", or with carbonic acid gas as the motive fluid, driving the piston. The steam plant was similar to the unit used in the Hoboken tests: 29.8 kW, 227 kg (40 hp, 500 lb). Considering fuel and also a steam condensing system, Nelson says the following:

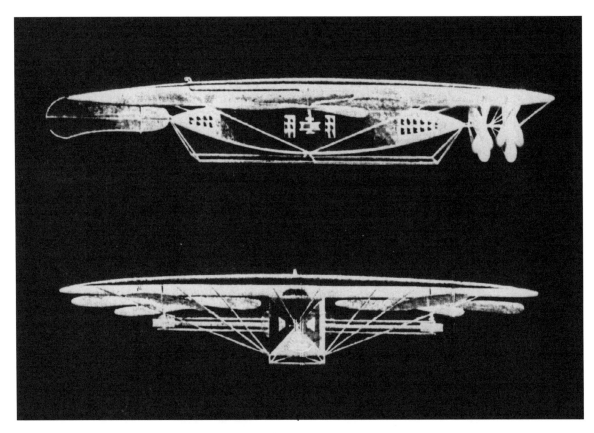

Figure 2.23 Nelson Aerial Car No. 2 (1865).

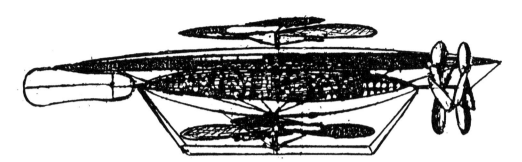

Figure 2.24 Nelson Aerial Car variant with "over and under" rotor system (1865).

"The material to be used as fuel is coal-oil, which is well adapted for the purpose, and might be carried in sufficient quantities for long journeys. It has been shown petroleum is many times more powerful than the best coal as steam fuel, that it can be burned in perfect safety, and without the slightest danger; but I do not think it would be so cheap and practicable as the combination of naphtha and air which is now coming into general use for domestic purposes. The condensation of steam is produced by a strong current of air which is forced through the condenser by the current from the forward propellers."

As noted above, Nelson's other choice of powerplant for this design was the carbonic acid engine. He favored the Barbour concept described previously (1865). Nelson based his reasoning on the information that at 1000 psi (69 bars), 1 cubic foot ($0.028 m^3$) of gas if released on a steam engine piston would deliver 4 hp (3 kW) for 1 hour (3600 s). The weight of the compressed gas being 22.7 kg (50 lb). Barbour claimed his engine would result in a size about ¼ that of a steam engine with the same power.

In his prospectus Nelson then develops his design using the Hoboken test data. He assumes 32 hp (23.8 kW) is sufficient to lift the machine with the following weights:

Compressed gas, 4 cubic feet ($0.113 m^3$) (32 hp for 1 hour) (23.8 kW for 3600 s)	200 lb (90.8 kg)
Steel cylinder for the gas	160 lb (72.6 kg)
Engine	100 lb (45.4 kg)
Car	300 lb (136.2 kg)
Engineer	150 lb (68.1 kg)
Total weight	910 lb (413.1 kg)

Nelson compares this weight with the Hoboken tests: 12 ft fan, 300 rpm, lifting 1100 lb with 40 hp (3.66 m, 50 rps, 4.9 kN, 29.8 kW), showing a positive margin. However, based on the previous figure of merit discussion he was using optimistic test data. Assuming his total weight is attainable, today the helicopter "fan" would require 37 feet in diameter just to hover on 32 horsepower.

Regarding weight reduction of the steel, gas cylinder he cites use of *papier mâché*:

> ". . . a material of which cannon have been made, and the great strength of which has been established by experiments in France and Germany."

He refers to a report in which its author describes bitumenized paper pipes of 5 inch (12.7 cm) diameter, ½ inch (12.7 mm) thick tested alone and jointed, withstood 500 psi (34.5 bars) satisfactorily.

Considering the above two studies of lightweight materials, he is clearly a pioneer in investigating composite structures for helicopters. As an alternate working fluid Nelson suggested a mix of hydrogen gas and air. Hydrogen was commonly used in balloons. He also patented a liquid fuel *carbo-sulph-ethal*, the third part presumably *ethyl* (or *ethule*) which dates to 1840. The inventor reviewed the experiments of Lenoir, observing he exploded in a cylinder a mix of hydrogen and air, using an electric spark. He theorized this system to eliminate the boiler, fuel and water, and would be a big step forward in aerial navigation. He recalled a company was formed in New York City to build the engines, and one was exhibited at the foot of Tenth Street and East River.

Nelson ends his prospectus with the following:

> "In conclusion I would like to call attention to the comparatively recent discovery of a metal called *aluminum*, as I believe it to be of great importance in construction of nearly every part of the engine and car, although its great costliness at present will probably prove an obstacle to its general use. Monsieur Deville, an eminent French chemist, has been chiefly instrumental in bringing it to its present perfection. This metal is capable of being rolled out to any required thickness, and when alloyed with copper, combines nearly the tenacity of iron; with the lightness of *lignum vitae*. Its price per pound averages twenty dollars. Thus its adaptability for the construction of aerial cars and engines, so soon as they shall come into use, will be seen; and although the chief obstacle to the employment of this valuable metal is the expense at present attends its manufacture, we have reason to hope that even this consideration would be accounted as of no comparative moment when weighed in the balance with a great and important enterprise, in which nations of the earth have a common interest."

1865 Partenscky

In 1865 Charles Partenscky of Oakland, California wrote to *Scientific American* [2.53] on the "power . . . to be expended in beating the air in order to raise a given weight . . ." Addressing this problem, Partenscky postulated a six-blade "spiral fan" having the same area as a circle of the same diameter. The fan had a 2.3 m (7.5 ft) diameter, with a 45 degree pitch angle, turning 500 rpm. The writer concluded it took 562.3 lb (2.5 kN) of thrust to fly at 60 mph (96.5 km/hr),

although he did not actually specify the power required. It is not clear how he distinguished between lift and propulsion power, but the total power required for the parameters (assuming thrust only) would be at least 90 hp (67.1 kW) with an ideal propeller, and 120 hp (90 kW) for a practical, 75% efficient propeller.

1870 Oakes

Citing *Aerial Age* [2.54], the "first" U.S. patent (106,862) for a helicopter-aerostat was given to "Edwin Oaks" (properly Edward Oakes) of Richmond, Indiana for an *aerial car*. (Nelson's patent was in the helicopter-airplane category.) Regarding the state of the art, *Aerial Age* had the following to say:

> "Up to January 1, 1920 a total of 291 patents were issued in these divisions: helicopters, balloon helicopters, and helicopter-airplanes. Most patents were puny, grotesque and, or complicated. Very few of these contributed to the evolution of helicopter flight. . . . It was not till about 1870 that the U.S. patent office allowed patents for airplanes or helicopters because they were considered impractical, along with perpetual motion machines, which today are still unpatentable."

1871 Croce-Spinelli

The propeller (or rotor) collective pitch control of Italian Joseph Croce-Spinelli is of interest because it is a credible 19th century approach to the problem (Figure 2.25). [2.55] Blade pitch is changed by a hydraulic piston acting against a

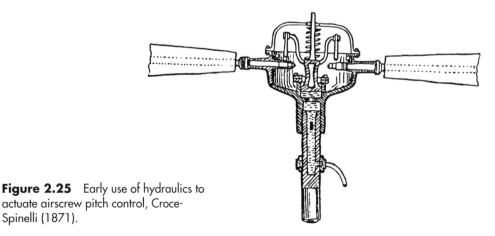

Figure 2.25 Early use of hydraulics to actuate airscrew pitch control, Croce-Spinelli (1871).

spring. Pitch is increased by hydraulic pressure. It is reduced by relieving the pressure, allowing the extending spring to depitch the blades. The hydraulic idea is modern but use of a spring is not good practice. The blades could be subject to flutter if not locked in to their selected pitch position, or could lose the setting. A modern hydromatic propeller uses a piston and cam system for pitch change, with oil pressure acting on either face of the piston. Modern helicopter blade pitch control is usually mechanical, frequently with hydraulic boost. Advanced concepts include "fly-by-wire" systems, with no mechanical connection in the primary controls. In this case a synthetic "feel" is added to the pilot's controls.

1872 Maxim

Hiram S. Maxim (1840–1916) inventor of various devices as a machine gun and mousetrap,

became interested in aerial navigation in 1859. He sketched a helicopter design with two lateral, counterrotating rotors separated by a car (Figure 2.26). In 1891 Maxim described his systematic tests with rotors. The screws were configured like those of French tests by Charles Renard. But the results were just the opposite. Renard concluded that there was a specific, optimum screw design, with other designs either side of it showing drastically reduced efficiency (thrust per unit power). The optimum was a two-blade, 23 foot (7 m) diameter screw (solidity 0.10).

Maxim tested 50 different screw configurations and the best one selected by Renard (intended for the war balloon *La France*) gave the worst results. [2.56] The anomaly probably was due to lack of a theoretical base at the time, which would show the direction for rotor design optimization. Renard himself in 1903 introduced the parameter that empirically (but not theoretically)

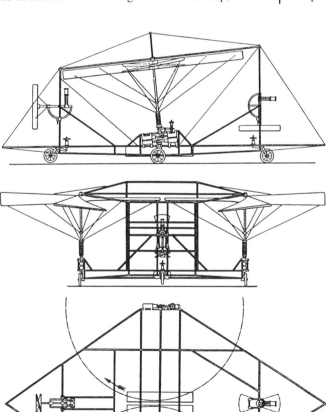

Figure 2.26 Maxim lateral rotor helicopter design (1897).

permits optimization of modern rotors in hovering. The parameter he named *qualité sustentatrice*, known in the United States as figure of merit (the term used in this book). [2.57]

Maxim appreciated the use of an "explosion engine" because of its low weight. In a design of 1872 he studied the two-rotor system powered by the then new Brayton cycle engine (i.e., a turboshaft engine concept). He decided the art was insufficiently developed and dropped the project.

Maxim gave up on the helicopter for the airplane, a machine he tested in 1893. Static thrust measurements of the propellers 5.4 meters (17 ft 10 in) in diameter yielded a figure of merit of 0.35. This value is less than half today's typical value for rotors, and about 56% of that for static thrust of a modern propeller. For his airplane he produced a complete steam powerplant, weighing 4.9 kg/kW (8 lb/hp). Remarkable for its day, but with a condensing system strewn around the airplane. The overall impression of his approach to airplane design is he sought to determine just what could be done practically with current knowledge and technology rigorously applied to the problem of mechanical flight. Despite this the machine never made it beyond a ground run. Fortunately, from its appearance a hard landing would have caused the machine to collapse on itself. If there is a message in this tour de force, it is that structural integrity also counts in problem solving.

1873 Wise

John Wise was the leading American balloonist in the latter part of the 19th century. His activity in the Philadelphia area probably contributed to the locale selected by Jules Verne for his science fiction novel about helicopters (1886). Wise's work is of interest because of a book he published in 1873. [2.58] It covers the history of balloons, their construction and inflation, as well as the state of the art of mechanical flight. The latter accounts for helicopters and the critical problem of a suitable powerplant. (Figure 2.19 is from the book.) His observation of attitudes regarding aerial navigation is expressed in a summary remark:

> "The almost universal opinion, and to a great extent among really scientific men, that aerial navigation cannot be turned to a useful ac-

count, is almost as prevalent as the opinion that aerial voyages are extremely dangerous, and is just as wrongly founded." [2.59]

1874 New York Novelty Works

There was a brief cryptic note in *Scientific American* referring to the flying machine project of an unknown and most likely forlorn constructor. [2.60] The item reported on a coaxial rotor helicopter built in New York in a "novelty works" shop. (In the late 19th century "novelties" referred to small, manufactured articles for household or personal embellishment.) The helicopter, powered by a 2 horsepower (1.5 kW) vertical boiler (probably like Figure 2.4), was apparently abandoned. One could write a novel around this singular account of a forsaken helicopter dream of flight.

1876 Lewis

Leslie's Weekly [2.61] reported on a helicopter project of W. J. Lewis of New York City. The concept (Figure 2.27) featured tandem coaxial screws of fabric, inflated by rotation. Apparently the inventor sought to take advantage of the "thrust" produced by ship's sails. (See 1828 Pennington.) The Lewis propeller system needed to "furl" for takeoff. The angular structure alone suggests the thrusting screws operated in flight but not at takeoff. The sails also may have served as parachutes. The sail material is identified as *frock*. This fabric is a wool jersey used by sailors, the word dating to 1811. Probably the material was lighter than available sail canvas, and more pliant. Lewis claimed he flew a model of his "winged cabin", and that a full sized machine could make a round trip to Philadelphia at 100 miles per hour (161 km/h).

It is of interest to study the design of such a rotor system and the aerodynamic principles behind it. The logic of the choice over the ordinary rotor as Figure 3.1 is not clear. It may have seemed more practical because of its relation to the proven ship sail. The relatively small size of the rotors would suggest an objective of producing a more compact and lightweight method of entraining air. Referring to Figure 2.27, each sail (i.e, "blade") consists

Figure 2.27   Lewis helicopter concept showing fabric blades inflated by rotations (1876).

of fabric attached to a driving spar at its outermost point. The inner end of the sail is connected to a yard at two points, located at the axis of rotation, and a batten (shown) . . . necessary to assure proper inflation on starting the rotor. The batten could be whalebone. In hovering the air is scooped by the outer part of the sail and flows inboard and downward, parallel to the driveshaft thereby producing thrust. The inboard flow is mainly axial because there is little rotor peripheral velocity in this area. In forward flight the lift-drag ratio of such a system must be very low, probably 0.25 to 1. This compares with 6 to 7 for a modern rotor.

1876 Rotor Tests

Scientific American on the prospects of aeronautics reported experiments with vertical screws. [2.62] The tests show 2.24 kW (3 hp) will support 45.4 kg (100 lb). The editorial stated further that a 1 hp (0.75 kW) engine had been built weighing under 15 lb/hp (6.8 kg/kW), however the powerplant was not described.

1876 Ward

In 1876 John B. Ward of San Francisco obtained a patent that had some advanced ideas.

His invention was to use separate blowers for both lift and propulsion. Ward also envisioned use of aluminum. [2.63] The concept anticipated modern jet lift and jet propulsion aircraft.

Chanute discusses the invention along with a similar idea of Walker's in 1892, offering the final comment: ". . . it seems a question whether air blasts can be advantageously used in aerial navigation." [2.64] In one sense he was correct for without adding energy (burning fuel) to heat the air the system would be unacceptably inefficient. However to win an argument one could very likely design a machine to work using "cold air" alone.

1877 Pickering

W. H. Pickering, a professor at Harvard, was one of the few 19th century investigators who assumed a scientific approach to his work. [2.65] The experiments were systematic tests with lifting screws, to determine the thrust capability of rotors 6.4 meters (21 feet) in diameter. Testing extended to 1903, and it included a lateral rotor rig powered by two electric motors. The unit was capable of lifting itself a few feet, restrained by its tether.

1877 Forlanini

The first successful flight of an engine-driven, reduced scale helicopter (Figure 2.28) is credited to Enrico Forlanini, in Italy. [2.66] His model featured coaxial rotors with the lower rotor of 3.0 m (9.2 ft) diameter, larger than the upper one, 1.7 m (5.6 ft). Blade pitch was equal to the diameter (about 17.6 degrees). The lower blades were located outboard on a triangular truss so the wake of the upper rotor passed inboard of the lower blades.

The system operated on the corotor principle. The upper rotor was shaft-driven while the lower one fixed to the cylinder mount, turned in opposition. In so doing, the latter reacted the shaft torque. In hovering there is no stationary part to the system, thereby saving weight. To reduce weight further, the two cylinder engine was driven by pressurized steam contained in a spherical chamber suspended below the rotor (Figures 2.28 and 2.29).

With an engine nominal power output of 0.15 kW (⅕ hp), the 3.5 kg (7.7 lb) model flew to a height of about 12.2 m (40 ft), remaining in the air 20 seconds. Initial pressure was 12 atmospheres, falling to 6 at the end of the flight. The first successful flight took place in Alexandria, Egypt 29 June 1877.

Lacking a steam generator, the powerplant weight was 16.1 kg/kW (26.4 lb/hp), while the power loading came to about 23.4 kg/kW (38.5 lb/hp).

Forlanini designed a generator to weigh 8.0 kg/kW (13.2 lb/hp). Thus the optimum (complete) steam powerplant by his estimates would weight at best 24.3 kg/kW (40 lb/hp). This compares with the 9.1 kg/kW (15 lb/hp) presumed the upper value for flight by Chanute (1894), and the 4.9 kg/kW (8 lb/hp) attained by Maxim through an extensive and complicated system. From these figures it is evident there was no convergence on a practical steam plant for a helicopter.

Forlanini's machine was formally shown at La Scala in Milan. While there is no obvious connection between helicopters and opera, there can be an explanation. In 1892 the East Prussian, Hermann Ganschwindt demonstrated his helicopter model as Part II of a piano concert in Allenstein [2.67] (now Olsztyn, the Polish city southeast of Gdansk). In those days there were few choices in captive, affluent audiences.

1879 Bagdley

The aerostat-helicopter of Figure 2.30 [2.68] was the invention of Henry Bagdley of Virginia. (Patent 214,546). The illustration has often appeared in advertising for its quaintness. A steam powerplant drives two propulsion screws and a lifting rotor. The rear propeller is a "steering wheel" capable of swiveling. The rotor blades are panels with cables at the tips for restraint. The panel outer edge was turned down 15.2 cm (6 in) "to prevent the air from slipping off." For thrust change the rotor operates at variable speed.

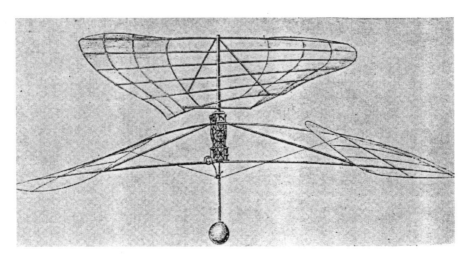

Figure 2.28   Forlanini helicopter model, first one to make a successful flight (1877).

Figure 2.29   Forlanini steam engine (1877).

1879 Quimby

Chanute [2.69] describes a patent by Quimby (presumably Watson Quimby of Wilmington, Delaware) for a rotorcraft concept using sails, as the case for the 1876 Lewis concept. In Quimby's design two sets of "screw-like sails" each with two blades of fabric were mounted on a light framework. On set was for lift and the other "inclined" for propulsion. Drive was by "rope gearing", but the powerplant was not specified.

1880 Edison

In the late 19th century Thomas Edison developed an interest in flying machines of both the helicopter and airplane configurations. [2.70] He was encouraged by a grant from the *New York Tribune* which established an aeronautical trophy. Figure 2.31 shows sketches by Edison of an idea using electrical power. His initial work involved a guncotton engine, but an explosion resulting in injuries turned him from this concept. He then conducted rotor experiments powered by an electric motor with a nominal rating of 7.5 kilowatts (10 horsepower). The scale-mounted motor drove a rotor consisting of two panels mounted on radial arms. Screws of different sizes were evaluated with the best thrust in the 17.8–22.3 N (4–5 lb) range. The poor results suggest inaccurate measurements, but they did not affect Edison's projection of an optimum single-seat helicopter. He predicted the need for a large diameter, low solidity rotor. The powerplant required 50 horsepower (37.3 kilowatts), and could not weigh more than 3 or 4 lb/hp (1.8–2.4 kg/kW). This prediction showed Edison had a realistic, practical understanding of helicopter rotor design and performance.

Figure 2.32 shows a helicopter concept disclosed in Edison's patent 970,616 of 1910. The rotor consists of boxkite blades that could be retracted up to the hub. The system reeled out under centrifugal force, along with cables that resisted the lift and centrifugal forces on the boxkite. It is difficult to see the merit of such a design today, but the intent could be to obtain a large sweep and high tip speeds without an ungainly rigid structure, and obviously retraction created a compact design.

Figure 2.30   Bagdley aerostat-helicopter. Illustration from his patent (1879).

Figure 2.31   Thomas Edison helicopter sketches (1880).

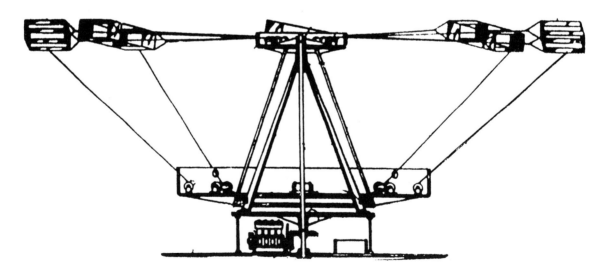

Figure 2.32   Edison retractable, boxkite rotor helicopter patent (1910).

1885 Ayers

Doctor W. O. Ayers of New Haven, Connecticut conceived a multi-screw helicopter driven by both compressed air and human power (Figure 2.33). [2.71] The structure consisted of a rectangular, tubular frame holding six screws for lift and one for propulsion. The tubular frame dimensions were given as 4 feet (1.2 m) length, 3 feet (0.92 m) width, with a vertical height of 4 feet (1.2 m). The operator was in the center of the frame, seated on a wire-suspended saddle. Two compressed air tank engines (air motors) drove four of the lifting screws. The operator's pedaling drove two others. With his right hand he powered the aft (propelling) screw, while his left hand selectively controlled the engines. (Air control valves are shown by the aeronaut's left hand.) Each of the air tanks was charged to a pressure of 207 bars (3000 psi). According to the description the air operated a "paddle wheel brought into rotation by the flow of air". One air motor on each tank turned a vertical driveshaft, mounted at the forward and aft ends of the frame.

The editorial appraisal of the design included the following:

> "It is possible the propellers may require to be longer, but providing the principal is main-

tained, we consider that a machine such as this can do successfully what is expected of it."

Presumably the inventor expected it to fly. There is no accounting for stabilization (possibly by body shift), and the control concept using crank actuation ignores the need for rapid response. The manually driven propeller suggests its speed was about 450 rpm; using a maximum human crank speed of 100 rpm and a step-up of 4.5 to 1. Its maximum diameter would be 0.92m (3 ft) at most. For M = 0.4 static propulsive thrust becomes 22.3 N (5 lb), decreasing with forward speed. Inadequate by any standard.

The Ayers illustration elicits the general notion of human factors in mechanical flight, factors concerning the operator's position and human power available. The upright seating (as today) became the accepted mode in the early 1900s even though the Wright Flyer I was flown with a prone pilot. In some cases the operator was seated on a saddle (as Figures 2.33 and 3.36). While this seems strange today, recall that then men were accustomed to saddles on horses and bicycles. (Autos were yet to appear.) Aside from other problems, the wire-suspended saddle would develop a swinging natural frequency in flight. Depending on the size of the machine, this oscillation would induce motion in the ma-

Figure 2.33 Ayers multi-rotor muscle-powered helicopter concept (1885).

chine itself. In other cases standing was preferred (Figures 1.19, 2.18 and 2.19) probably derived from steam locomotive practice. Undefined is how an operator would mount such a machine or escape from it.

Considering human power there seems to be little mutual understanding of the amount available in relation to what is required, partly due to quantitative ignorance in both cases. Therefore one worked completely by intuition. As implied in the da Vinci discussion (Figure 1.21), Ayers' effort would be expectional in producing continuously half a horsepower (0.37 kW) with bursts at the ¾ horsepower (0.56 kW) level.

1886 Verne

As mentioned before Jules Verne was one of the French enthusiasts supporting the helicopter. Among his many books of science fiction is one known in the English edition (1887) as *Clipper of the Clouds*. The first illustrated edition appeared in France in 1886 titled *Robur le Conquérant*. [2.72] The story was a deliberate poke at the balloon advocates, and Verne expected a reaction from them.

The story is about an engineer Robur who built a giant *aéronef* (helicopter) on a secret island in the Pacific. Figures 2.34 and 2.35 are the work of L. Benett, engravings typical of Verne's 19th century book illustrations. The story was based on the ideas of de la Landelle. Verne carefully reviewed his concept with an engineer, presumed to be one Badoureau, to assure the design was plausible. Called *Albatross*, it consisted of a seaworthy hull on which were mounted 37 masts; each mast held two rotors. Pusher and tractor propellers were located at each end of the hull. The *Albatross* was powered by lightweight electric motors energized by *piles* (batteries). Robur claimed the *aéronef* could go around the world in less than eight days.

The story concerns a real conflict of the times mentioned in the Introduction, and suggested above. The contention was between advocates of the balloon as the way to fly and the few like Robur who believed man could conquer the air by mechanical means, and by helicopter in particular. The novel begins in Fairmount Park in Philadelphia. A fitting locale and prescient, for

Figure 2.34 On the open deck of the *Albatross*. Robur, unmindful of liability insurance, contemplating the structural integrity of the slender driveshafts. (Verne, 1886).

60 years later the city became the cradle of rotary wing flight in America. In Verne's time it was the center of balloon activity undertaken by John Wise, as mentioned before. In the novel the balloon advocates were members of a group called the Weldon Institute. This was in imitation of the Franklin Institute, which coincidentally became an early forum for rotary wing flight. Members of the Weldon Institute were skeptical of mechanical flight. In a sudden appearance at a conference there, Robur was repudiated for his committment to flying machines, and for his declaration that he had solved the problem.

To demonstrate his creation to skeptics, Robur's crew abducted three of the Weldon members, taking them on board the *Albatross*, which had landed in the park. They took to the air with Robur, for a trip around the world. Much of the novel deals with their aerial adventures in different lands, introducing the reader to a less known world than today. This included an unintended flight over the South Pole.

Figure 2.35 Contemporary engraving of the *Albatross* in Jules Verne novel (1886).

Along the journey the three hostages managed to escape but after severely damaging the *Albatross*, and they made their way back to Philadelphia. Despite the misfortune Robur was able to rebuild the *aéronef* on a secret island. He returned to that city just in time to witness the flight of an improved balloon (with pusher and tractor propellers). The balloon crew, the former hostages, sensing a threat from Robur, ascended higher in the atmosphere to avoid an imagined attack. In doing so, the bag burst. As the wreckage fell, the *Albatross* undertook an in-flight rescue of the balloon crew, returning them to land safely.

Despite Robur's demonstration of the feasibility of mechanical flight, the Weldon members remained unimpressed. Robur departed with the *Albatross,* convinced the times were not favorable for such an advanced idea to find acceptance among the more conservative advocates of aerial navigation.

Verne however did not abandon Robur and the *Albatross.* They both reappear later in a dark novel *Maître du Monde.* [2.73] Robur is more aggressive in this story. Surveillance was revealed in the nighttime appearance of the *Alba-*

tross over the city of Paris exposing its citizens to a giant spotlight emanating from the airship. The English version as *Masters of the World* was published in 1904. It revealed Verne's change in attitude over the limitless benefits of science. Robur was recast from a well meaning engineer into a "mad scientist". With this change the author was expressing a disillusionment shared by many at the turn of the century.

Verne chose Robur's name with thought. The word is the name of a hard wood oak, suggesting strength. In his time Roburite, a flameless, highly explosive mix of chlorinated benzine and ammonium nitrate, was a catchy word.

Long distance travel through the air was in the air. A New York paper reported on a proposal to fly to California in a steam powered airship (a propelled aerostat), cruising at 200 mph (322 km/h). One critic wrote the idea "seemed too much for sober-minded people". [2.74] Rufus Porter, editor of *Scientific American,* was an advocate (1849) of the steam powered airship for a New York-San Francisco run. He expected the trip to take 3 days with passengers equipped with parachutes. Normal transit took 5 months by ship or overland by mule train. The latter averaged about 32.2 km (20 miles) a day. [2.75] In 1853 a clipper ship made the trip in 83 days. [2.76] In mid 19th century California meant the "gold rush". From the East the only ones taking the rush seriously were advocates of a trip through the air, and by propelled airship in particular. Another champion of this configuration was Frederick Mariott, who was ready to start a transcontinental service in 1869. Failure with an unmanned prototype led him to drop the aerostat approach for a machine propelled by a helical screw. In 1881 his invention was rejected by the Patent Office as impractical. [2.77]

In 1948 C. W. Tinson in Britain took the Verne description of the *Albatross*, and produced a preliminary design, published along with an illustration. [2.78] Verne's novel with the helicopter is of technical interest only, for the story contains a thread of racism, today offensive to enlightened sensibilities. This novel is unlikely to appear in print in any new editions. The book read is dated 1962. Bookstores always carry a few of Verne's novels, but apparently never the one on helicopters.

1890 Holland

The inventor John P. Holland is usually associated with submarines. His original submarine proposal in 1875 was rejected by the U.S. Navy. With financing from the Fenian Society (he was a native of Ireland) Holland launched a prototype on the Hudson in 1881. The then novel idea was to use multiple powerplants, one for surface operation (internal combustion) and the other (electric) for underwater propulsion. The organization he formed later became Electric Boat Company, later a division of General Dynamics Corporation. [2.79] In an 1890 letter Holland maintained helicopter flight was possible within the state of the art by combining known principles. [2.80] He proposed a steam powered machine weighing 7000 pounds (3180 kilograms) to carry two men and supplies. Projected endurance was in the range 8 to 24 hours. Considering the size of his design, this is one of the largest proposed in the century. Apparently Holland was not intimidated by weight or large numbers, in view of his work with submarines. Regarding powerplants, he chose as some others did, (including Maxim) to accept the state of the art, (his philosophy) rather than innovate. However he did not pursue this proposal.

1891 Means

James B. Means, an MIT graduate and successful boot manufacturer, was a prominent figure in aeronautical circles around the turn of the century. He was a leader in popularizing the activity through the Boston Aeronautical Society, which he helped form. [2.81] Using the society, Means published compilations in three serials starting in 1895, providing a unifying influence on the various investigations underway.

In 1891 Means proposed a helicopter with a single lifting rotor and tractor propeller. (Rotor torque was not accounted for.) Later the arrangement was changed to a single tiltable rotor with control surfaces in the rotor wake. In a pamphlet Means declared: "If you want to bore through the air, the best way is to set up your borer and bore." [2.82] Octave Chanute in contemplating the "chaotic state of theory applied to the screw", found Means' experimental view as good as any theory. Even so, the thrust of the society was toward the airplane. Around 1893 Means himself abandoned the helicopter ideas, supporting the advocates of fixed-wing flying machines.

1892 Veyrin

A significant but misinterpreted experiment was conducted in France by Émil Veyrin. In the course of testing some single rotor helicopter models, he flew one with the rotor below the fuselage (CG above the rotor). Of this Veyrin wrote . . . "this machine flew perfectly, which seems contrary to the law of gravity. . . ." [2.83] He had witnessed an inherently stable system. But without understanding the dynamics of a rotor, Veyrin (as all others in the period) presumed stability was simply equivalent to balloon static stability with the rotor replacing the gas bag. His interpretation of the result as an anomaly was due to an erroneous premise. Very likely for his model to be stable he also unknowingly used

blades that were flexible in the flapping plane. (See also stability in Chapter 3, Introduction, and in Appendix H.)

1893 Science Fiction

In the late 19th century a natural habitat for flying machines in general and helicopters in particular was found in what later was called *science fiction* (sf). For purposes of this book the category began with Jules Verne, previously accounted for (Figure 2.35). Verne had his imitators as shown in Figures 2.36 (1892) and 2.37 (ca. 1899 and later). The source of Figure 2.36 is not identified but letters on the pennant suggest *Frank Reade Library*, the case for Figure 2.37. The latter is from the series of "dime novels", popular around the turn of the century. The long running story that extended to 179 titles was about Frank Reade Jr., "boy inventor" and his *Queen Clipper of the Clouds* (1893).

Figure 2.36   A science fiction helicopter with inflatable rotor and sails. Pennant with FR suggests the Frank Reade Library "dime novel" (1892).

Figure 2.37 Helicopter illustration from Frank Reade Library science fiction novel.

The books were published with the author listed as "Noname". They were predominately the work of Luis Senarens who wrote under at least 27 pseudonyms. A significant amount of the writing would be unacceptable today for a general readership, even though of professional interest. Everett F. Bleiler an sf editor, bibliographer, and reprinter of the complete *Franke Reade Library* series (1979–1986) observed the following:

> ". . . en masse they suffered visibly from this hugely prolific author's carelessness, cheap jingoism, racist stereotyping and lackadaisical plotting." [2.84]

From the design viewpoint all three figures cited above show a lack of understanding of the proper alighting gear for a helicopter, particularly a giant one. Nelson (ca. 1865) who had a good grasp of contemporary state of the art was prescient with his skid gear. Verne's rotor design does not reflect modern practice. Later, some into prototypes chose a similar slender, elongated shaft to drive the rotor, guaranteed to whirl, bow, and vibrate. The rotor design itself was unlike anything finally used. Figures 2.36 and 2.37 feature sail rotors, contrary to the serious designs of the time, (also not practical), probably just to be different.

As science fiction the Verne *Clipper* novel was not typical in content. Unlike most sf this story takes place in his time and the vehicle itself is the story. Usually in sf stories the vehicle is used mainly to transport the characters to a new or alternate reality in which they interact, and in a future time. Fantasy also part of science fiction seems to be basically a product of the intuitive brain while science stories are cognitive. Aficionados tend to take sides, some preferring the cognitive, meaning the story is plausible as a future reality. In hindsight many of the 19th and early 20th century patents on vertical flight, far beyond those cited in this book (several thousand being examined and classified) unintentionally could reside in the world of cognitive science fiction. Beyond this, science fiction of one era can be science fact of another. Consider helicopters, for example.

Futurology is an allied discipline, mostly based on extrapolation of the present despite the fact the actual future often comes to pass after a dramatic discontinuity (part of science fiction as well). It is interesting that Mortimer Nelson had many ideas suggesting modern technology, yet he was not concerned with futurology. We look back on such individuals as "visionaries". In the domain of mechanical flight a futurist of 1910 projecting a machine of the 1930s would take the Wright biplane and see it (i.e., extrapolate it) as a giant with many more wings and wires, carrying many more passengers (Figure 2.38). Yet in the early 1930s what did appear was the Douglas DC-3, the first modern airliner both in con-

Figure 2.38 Airplane of the future from the vantage point of early 1900.

struction and configuration. Aside from the design, no futurist of 1910 would have the courage to predict this 1930 flying machine would be produced in numbers beyond 10,000.

Figure 2.39 is a whimsical concept from a set of collector's cards published in France, poking fun at flying enthusiasts. [2.85] As suggested before with balloonism, excess in a popular culture seems to elicit a satirical response. Apparently the artist had in mind the extreme variety of con-

figurations builders were flying or attempting to fly in the early 1900s, taking a little from each one for his design. It is not a futuristic concept but a parody of contemporary enthusiasm for the new found sport of mechanical flight.

The machine included boxkite wings, flapping wings, a lifting screw and tractor propeller, but no alighting gear nor horizontal tail surface. (The airscrew could replace the last.) The forward operator is standing while the aft one is

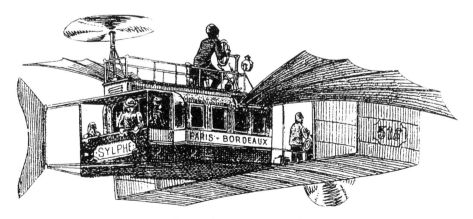

Figure 2.39 Whimsical aircraft with a little bit of everything (1910–1912).

seated. The rear crew member above the front one anticipated today's two-man attack helicopters. The guard rail around the aft operator allowed him to take a stretch, unmindful of the airscrew nearby, bumpy air, and the heavy liability insurance carried by the machine's owner. This operator has both a control wheel and two control levers, combining two different actuating systems in one aircraft. The combination suggests the period of the illustration to be 1910–1912 when the Wright-designed lever system was being replaced by a wheel.

The role of the forward crew member is not clear. He appears to be handling controls. The artist may have added him to increase the redundancy of the whimsical design. He could be the captain, possibly in control of the engine, as on a steamship where engine and helm had separate manning. Up front, he could be the navigator, literally pointing the way.

The French artist named his creation *Sylphe* (Sylph), referring to the genie that inhabits the air, in the mythology of Celtic (Gallic) and Germanic people. Since each machine has a particular name, one would expect Sylphe to have serial number 1 and not 516, the number on the wing curtain. The latter number would suggest there were many of them flying. It could be a registration number supplied by the government, unaware of the need to mark the lower wing.

The importance today of Figure 2.38 and as suggested by Figure 2.39 is that one cannot always predict the future by mere extrapolation. As graphic metaphors and discounting political intent, the two figures reveal the care that must be taken in predicting or envisioning the future (including the author's in the Epilogue). The future is always full of "surprises", that is, discontinuities.

1894 Chanute

In the late 19th and early 20th centuries Octave Chanute was the leading aeronautical figure in America. His ideas and work were both scientific and influential. Chanute's influence entended to the brothers Wright and European engineers. In 1894 he published *Progress in Flying Machines*, in its day a masterpiece on the state of the art. [2.86] One chapter describes heli-

copter activities in the United States and in Europe. Overall, Chanute was an airplane advocate who was skeptical of the helicopter. On the subject of *aeroplanes* he offered a remark that seems quaint today:

> "The idea of obtaining sustaining power from the air with a fixed, instead of a vibrating or a rotating surface is not obvious." [2.87]

This means the obvious support from motion of flapping or rotating wings was easier to comprehend than the "static" appearance of a plane surface. However even today some people wonder what keeps an airplane in the air. (See Bernoulli theorem in the Glossary.)

Chanute saw the screw as a propeller only. He observed:

> ". . . such aerial devices (aerial screws) do not seem to have received much attention from inventors and there have been few patented proposals (to 1894) therefore in the United States."

Even though he believed the aerial screw slightly more tractable than the marine equivalent, the following applied to both:

> "There is no mathematical theory of them (the screws) which has found general acceptance, or which connects their action with that of plane surfaces, so as to agree with observed facts."

Around the time of Chanute's summary, it happened there was emerging the airscrew theory as we know it today. What made the problem tractable for both propellers and rotors was the combining of the momentum theory (Rankine, Froude, 1878), the blade element theory (Drzewiecki and others, 1892–1920), and the vortex theory (1920s). The last making possible the calculation of the induced velocity at the rotor disk.

In the early years of the 20th century there was disagreement on the theoretical approach, one group led by Bréguet and the other by Drzwiecki. It started in March 1909 when the latter in an *L'Aérophile* article stated the helicopter people were taking a "false route". Sides were drawn and throughout the year there were exchanges of letters in the magazine regarding the correct helicopter rotor theory. [2.88]

A principal argument by Drzwiecki was Bréguet based his thrust and power on the swept area of the rotor, when it should be on the blade area. Considering current elementary hovering theory, they were both right. Momentum and blade element theories are combined to calculate hovering (or static) performance.

Despite this airscrew theory development that took place decades either side of 1900, the theory does not appear to be factored into helicopter projects of the time. Only Hewitt (1917) seemed to grasp its practical significance in helicopter work. Otherwise the knowledge was empirical. The first significant application of theory came with autogiro development after the First World War.

1895 De Los Olivos

In 1895, Estanislao Caballero De Los Olivos a Mexican living in New York City patented a tandem rotor helicopter that included an elliptical wing (Figure 2.40). [2.89] The latter had an opening for the rotors. The wing incidence an-

gle could be changed using ropes, as shown in the figure. There also was a rotor-rim belt, apparently causing the rotors to turn in the same direction. With two vertical drive shafts showing, the inventor may have used two engines for multi-engine reliability. But he did not specify the powerplants. In his design the alighting gear featured springs for energy absorption.

1900 De Leftwich-Dodge

The steam powered helicopter-airplane of William De Leftwich-Dodge (Figure 2.41) is dated around 1900. The illustration is included here as the last of this era because it has the primitive, late 19th century look. The "stacked" appearance of the invention is symbolic of the complete century when no one quite knew what a flying machine should look like, or what it took to propel it.

Figure 2.42 looks like a related design. Actually

Figure 2.40 De Los Olivos concept (1895).

Figure 2.41   De Leftwich-Dodge airplane-helicopter model (1900). Smithsonian Institution.

Figure 2.42   Two turn of the century, top-hatted entrepreneurs conferring on their latest problem. (Sketch ca. 1950.)

it is a latter day (ca. 1950) cartoon that captures the aplomb with which turn of the century entrepreneurs accepted misfortune. Apparently a boiler explosion where the head blew off, with a backfire through the firebox.

2.4 THE CRITICS

In summarizing the most common attitude of this century regarding mechanical flight and helicopters in particular, it is fitting to present the views of some of its strongest, contemporary critics. This in the United States and France, where most the helicopter excitement took place.

In response to the 1848 ideas of "Anonymous", an editorial in *Scientific American* offered the following:

> We have not a mite to contribute to this cause . . . the mechanical appliances for counteraction explained is altogether different from our notion. Every artificial object that can float in the atmosphere must be lighter than its bulk of atmosphere, let the appliances be as curious as they may . . ." [2.32]

The editorialist concludes with the admonition: "We hope he won't forget the law that was discovered by the great Newton in a falling of an apple."

In 1869 there was an editorial change of heart. The *Scientific American* asked and answered the question: "Is the flying machine a mechanical possibility?" [2.90] The editor then asserted this form of flight is not possible until a light weight and stronger material is found. Presumably he had it in mind for the powerplant as well as the rest of the machine.

In France the 1864 criticism of Duchesne was cited in the Nadar account. In 1876 the reaction was still strong. One Charles du Hauvel called the screw an *engin détestable*. As an advocate of the artificial bird he openly declared himself an "enemy of all rotating organs". In response de la Landelle wrote: "The draconian sentence is certainly excessive in view of the services of the wheel, a rotating organ par excellence." [2.91]

Chapter 3

SECOND PERIOD: EARLY TWENTIETH CENTURY

3.1 INTRODUCTION

The second period accounts for the interval 1900 to around 1936. There is also brief coverage to 1941 and later, to introduce some formative activities that became the antecedents of today's continuing helicopter endeavors. As remarked before, the significant difference from the first period is a shift from the speculative, with some testing, to large scale "hovering" test stands and flight attempts with man-carrying prototypes.

In the first period, early road travel amounted to 20–40 miles (32.2–64.4 kilometers) a day. In 1914 on the eve of World War I, travel urgency switched to airplanes. In that year a magazine announced one F.C. Hild ". . . will attempt a non-stop flight from New York to Washington,

D.C." In trials at Paterson, New Jersey his monoplane hit 65 mph (105 km/h). [3.1] Balloons were not forgotten. In the same year the *Philadelphia III* took to the air to drop bundles of suffragist leaflets. "Pennsylvania and New Jersey farmers were surprised to see suffrage leaflets descending on them from the clouds". An event declared by the editor ". . . the most advanced form of publicity that has been devised". [3.2]

The following discussion is separated into discrete time intervals for the period. In addition this introduction covers rotor aspects of theory and design from the historical perspective, and the typical sequence of development problems encountered by experimenters. As in the previous century, there were two approaches to investigation: the *inventive* (or intuitive) and the *sci-*

entific (or engineering) styles. The projects described in the narratives reflect these approaches. The discussion below applies only to the *scientific* approach.

Each of the discrete time intervals (or spans) was identified by characteristic technical and design features. The first timespan is the period from 1900 to the onset of World War I. The second accounts for the war, and the third includes the period from war's end to the late 1930s (and beyond).

The period to the First World War was marked by the successful flights of the Wright brothers, and the promotion of their flying machine. Proof that mechanical flight in general was feasible meant there was a system of knowledge and technology available for practical flight, features absent from the 19th century projects. The timespan was occupied in developing the airplane for its own sake exemplified by the above flight attempt. Its utility was yet to be exploited. Fixed wings had a monopoly in the air as the proven way to fly in a machine. Utility came about because of the war. World War I not only put the airplane to use but it accelerated technology to the extent helicopter prototypes of the first timespan appear fragile and crude relative to the postwar efforts. The war itself preempted helicopter activity.

If from the helicopter's viewpoint the first timespan was the era of the airplane, the third was the era of the autogiro. It is generally accepted the autogiro had the elements of a practical helicopter, and a lengthy patent infringement case legalized the point. Yet it is an anomaly that the majority of the experimenters ignored one or all of the elements critical to the helicopter (low disk loading, flapping hinge, blade pitch control) until the late 1930s.

The postwar (World War I) years were an active time for helicopter projects. This activity was consistent with the general euphoria among the numerous companies building airplanes for private use. These included everyman's "flying flivver" and "baby airplane". Some entrepreneurs envisioned the helicopter as meeting this goal.

In 1919, Michelin in France, patron of aviation, announced a prize of $100,000 for a helicopter to demonstrate the following performance: [3.3]

Rise vertically from the ground.
Demonstrate the greatest speed up to 200 km/h (124 mph).
Land vertically within a radius of 5 meters (16.4 ft).

Active with machines in France in the early 1920s were Pescara, Damblanc and La Coin, and Oehmichen.

In May 1923 a helicopter competition was to be held in Britain sponsored by the Air Ministry, with a prize of 50,000 pounds ($250,000). The entrants were to meet these conditions: [3.4]

Attain an altitude of 650 meters (2130 feet), climbing straight up and down.
Hover 30 minutes with a 35 km/h (22 mph) wind.
Perform a circular flight of 32.2 km (20 miles) at 95.5 km/h (60 mph).
Land safely, power-off in a small area from 91.5 meters (300 feet).
Ascend and descend in calm air, and in a wind not to exceed 40 km/h (25 mph).
Each machine to carry a pilot, 1 hour fuel and a military load of 68 kg (150 lb).

At the time the best a helicopter could do was reach a height of about 15.3 meters (50 feet), and remain in the air 9 minutes. (With a low confidence level such feats could be repeated consistently and reliability.)

The competition closed in April 1925. There was no formal contest in 1924 and the offer was carried over to 1925–1926. Again no competition ensued. There were 18 applications for the 1924 event, eight were from America. Thirty-five entered the following one, and thirteen were American. Of the latter only four were carry-overs from the 1924 tender. The American entrants are described in the narratives. (A complete list of the entrants is given in Appendix B and C.)

That the competition did not materialize created suspicion that it was cancelled because the British entry was not ready. However it is doubtful any of the machines proposed could have met the requirements. In any case the contest was quickly forgotten and little has been published on the details of it. Most likely the Focke

FW-61 that appeared later could meet all the requirements, but it is doubtful the VS-300A could (at least judging from public information).

Apparently the British entry was the Brennan three-blade, propeller-driven rotor helicopter. The machine first flown outdoors in 1924, was supported by the Air Ministry to 1929. Hovering tests revealed severe oscillations of the lightweight car, which was suspended below a heavy rotor system. Tests continued until October 1925 when an accident destroying rotor propellers and their gearboxes, resulted in eventual cancellation of the program. [3.5] The decision to drop helicopter development was reinforced by the promise of the Cierva autogiro.

Even so, helicopters were taken seriously elsewhere. Staring in April 1924 The *Fédération Aéronautique International* (FAI) officially recognized helicopter records. The first holder was Frenchman Étienne Oehmichen who, in the same year flew a straight line for 525 meters (1,720 ft). [3.6] He later made the first closed circuit flight (1 kilometer, 1.6 miles) in a helicopter. The machine designated No. 2 was a quadrotor powered by a 120 hp (89.5 kW) Le Rhône rotary. Vittorio Isacco the helicopter pioneer of Italian origin was involved in nine helicopter projects, including some of his own design. He summarized the period well with the following statement published in 1936:

> "Taking the year 1906 when the first helicopter of Cornu left the ground, as the starting point of modern helicopters, 30 years have already elapsed which 50 different types have been built and tested, and yet the problem of vertical flight is not completely solved."

Addressing his own work Isacco continued:

> "We believe that the single airscrew type, the Brennan helicopter is the one which has succeeded in giving the best performance with vertical flights inside a shed, lifting up to four passengers to a good height. The author's (i.e., Isacco's) *hélicogyres* No. 1 and No. 2 have also lifted several times inside a shed, but none of them has been able to perform successful flights in the open air." [3.7]

Unknown to Isacco, the first successful flight of the Focke helicopter was made the same year.

It is of interest in the narratives that follow, to review the theory and design of the rotor system, the element that makes the helicopter what it is. Rotor, i.e., airscrew, theory development was described previously. The following discusses figure of merit, rotor design, blade articulation and finally, stability and controllability. (See also blade and rotor design in the Glossary.)

Figure of merit (Appendix H), a measure of rotor hovering efficiency is based on momentum theory alone. This theory deals only with the flow of air and is not concerned with the object producing it. The ideal value, $M = 1.0$ (accordingly) assumes zero viscous (i.e., air friction) effects on the body that is producing the flow, in a uniform wake. This idealized airflow is produced (conceptually) by what Herman Glauert called the *actuator disk*. [3.8] Expressed as a special interpretation of efficiency, figure of merit is the ratio of the ideal (momentum) power to the actual power driving the rotor. Sometimes the engine shaft power is used instead of rotor power. However this is arbitrary because it includes power supplied to other items between the engine and rotor shafts, i.e., losses due to installation, gearing, driving accessories, and a tail rotor, if applicable. In this book the distinction is usually not important because only gross effects on this efficiency are of interest. However in some cases rotor power required is explicit (as for a whirl tests). In others only engine rated power is known, and there is little between the engine and rotor shaft but a reduction gearbox.

In the early 1900s there were several different parameters proposed for determining the hovering efficiency (or performance) of a rotor. As noted before the equation used today was introduced by Renard in 1903. Later it was popularized by Glauert and used in the coefficient form by NASA (NACA). The term *figure of merit* and its engineering units were introduced by Richard H. Prewitt in the 1940s when he was chief engineer at Kellett Aircraft:

$M = (PL/38)(DL/\text{density ratio})^{0.5}$
$PL = \text{Power loading (lb/hp)}$
$DL = \text{Disk loading (lb/ft}^2)$
density ratio (rho/rho_o) of air
(See Appendix G for metric units.)

It has been argued the comparative values of M are misleading unless calculated at the same disk loading. From the above equation this means two rotors are compared on the basis of power loading only. This is the very parameter of concern to the 19th century experimenters, as discussed previously. Even so, figure of merit has value for a particular rotor in the preliminary design stage. It is used in conjunction with rotor mean lift coefficient (= $6.0 C_T/sigma$). C_T = thrust coefficient. The latter is a parameter useful in establishing rotor solidity $sigma$, the ratio of blade area to disk area, and hence blade area, for a maximum value of figure of merit. A common characteristic, and empirical curve for a rotor is a plot of M versus mean lift coefficient. Empirical tests show an important feature of the curve is rotors exhibit their maximum figure of merit around a $C_T/sigma$ of 0.10 (or a mean lift coefficient of 0.6). This information permits one to establish the best blade area for hovering performance. How the total blade area is divided into a number of blades is arbitrary. This point is discussed later.

In retrospect it is curious the early experimenters made no big point of disk loading anymore than they did in the previous century, not only for power reduction, but for understanding autorotation. The design of rotors took three general, successive forms. Until late in the period, all helicopters built used blades rigidly attached to the hub, acting as lifting propellers. Apparently what was good for propulsion was considered good for lift.

Before the First World War the screws were simply offset, crossed tubes covered with fabric, or fabric covered tubes of special planform (Figure 3.1). After the war, when conventional wood propellers attained their typical construction, the type was adapted for helicopter use. In some cases the propellers were specially carved with the idea of optimizing static thrust and autorotative properties, by means of special twist, planform or articulation. Figure 3.2 shows a design of Oscar Asboth who by 1939 built and flew four helicopters in Europe. [3.9] The figure (Patent 2,162,794) discloses a split, pivotable blade. In hovering the inboard part is set in low pitch, while the outboard part is at a positive, hovering angle. For autorotation both parts are set at a low angle. Asboth's work is of interest

because no one tried harder to make a propeller work on a helicopter. Others who perceived rotors as light, elongated rotating wings were closer to the answer. In one case (Pescara) the inventor used biplane blades on his prototype. [3.10]

In the early 1920s true helicopter rotor development took place in its surrogate, the autogiro. Cierva demonstrated the value of a flapping hinge. Though Cierva discovered the hinge empirically, the idea was not new. There is a 1913 patent (Figure 3.34) cited in the narratives showing this hinge. The idea was even advanced earlier (1904) by Renard. [3.11] Recall Figure 1.17 (clown toy), and the idea of Rochon (1911), described later.

Anyone studying rotary wing patents before and after autogiro technology will be impressed by the quality, purpose, and detail as well as the professionalism of the autogiro and later, helicopter patents.

The first successful helicopter (Focke's) was imputed by one critic (described later) to be using an "autogiro rotor", and therefore the machine itself was an autogiro that could climb vertically, but not "straight up". Another critic early in World War II attempted to discredit Focke's accomplishment insisting it was just another autogiro because of the obvious "propeller" at the nose of the engine (Figure 3.116). The device was not a thruster but a simple fan to cool the engine while hovering.

The very flapping hinge introduced in the autogiro, created a lead-lag force (due to momentum conservation in the flapping motion) that was alleviated by addition of a lag hinge. In forward flight the blade is maintained in its instantaneous, autorotating position by a balance among lift, drag, centrifugal, and inertial forces. The rotor is free wheeling, by virtue of the rotor disk tilt away from the direction of flight. In contrast, a helicopter rotor is shaft-driven, and the rotor disk is inclined in the direction of flight.

When turning on the ground, presence of a lag hinges without dampers (regardless of the lift on the blades) can cause an unsymmetrical, cyclic pattern (i.e., unbalance) to the rotor as a system. This dissymmetry creates a cyclic force in the

Figure 3.1 Typical paddle rotor and propeller construction of the late 19th century, and for helicopters with low disk loadings, into the 1920s.

plane of rotation that turns with the rotor, shaking the helicopter in pitch and roll on its landing gear. On the ground the helicopter will have a natural frequency in roll, measured in cycles per minute (cpm). A helicopter will also have a natural frequency in pitch. Since this is usually much higher, the phenomenon to be described will appear first in the roll mode. (The difference means the helicopter rests on "anisotropic supports".)

When the cyclic or exciting-force frequency from the unbalanced rotor pattern (in rpm) equals the roll natural frequency (in cpm), a mechanical instability (blades flailing about their lag hinges) occurs that reinforces itself with each cycle until something fails. Failure is usually in the rotor system and the helicopter rolls over, aggravating the catastrophe. The phenomenon is popularly called "ground resonance". The above description applies if there are no design

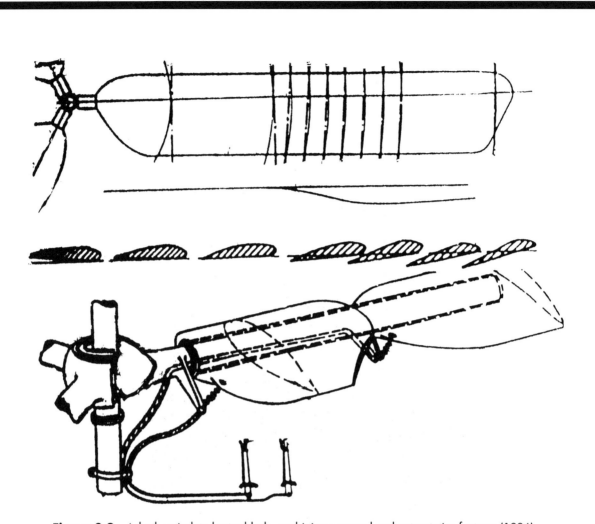

Figure 3.2   Asboth articulated rotor blade combining powered and autorotative features (1936).

provisions nor pilot procedures to avoid the problem. (See also ground resonance in Appendix H.)

The solution to this problem, which appeared first with autogiros, was to add dampers at the lag hinges and in the landing gear. (The lag dampers also act as snubbers in forward flight.) The theory for solving the problem was the work of R. P. Coleman and A. M. Feingold. [3.12] An important finding was the requirement that landing gear damping is as essential as blade damping. This revealed itself in the theory as a "damping product", meaning the total damping required could be apportioned between the rotor and landing gear, desirably in equal orders of magnitude.

Rotor and helicopter control are unique features of the design because of its versatility. Modern cyclic and collective pitch control of the rotor

evolved by way of the blade pitch angle, for jump takeoff. Practical cyclic pitch control of a helicopter dates to the early 1930s. The essential component is the swashplate, a large-bore ball bearing. It is used to transfer the axial (collective pitch) and tilt (cyclic pitch) motions from the fixed part of the helicopter to the rotating part. The idea of transferring only axial motion is probably as old as control of any rotating machinery. The novel part is the tilt, which requires a gimbal mount, along with a slider (on the rotor shaft) to effect cyclic and collective pitch control.

There are early helicopter patents incorporating the collective and cyclic swashplate system. One is the British patent 14,455 of 1910 to Jakos Wojciechowski of Warsaw, Poland. Apparently the first helicopter to use the swashplate was the Austrian *Revoplane* of 1929. [3.13] In the United States George Exel used it on his

1930–33 machine (Figure 3.51). The idea of a cyclic pitch control mechanism could have more than one design treatment. Apparently Crocco in Italy suggested this type of control, and Ellehammer in the Netherlands in 1914 briefly hovered a helicopter using cyclic pitch control of blades mounted on the rim of a large disk. [3.14]

An alternate cyclic system resorted to a tiltable, control spider above the rotor head. It was first used on gyroplanes (non-Cierva "autogiros") and on some early practical helicopters. The term *gyroplane* in fact refers to rotorcraft featuring cyclic (or feathering) control in contrast to *autogiro*, (Cierva's word) which obtained control by tilting the complete rotor. On some early prototypes with rigid rotors, control design bypassed the rotor, relying (usually ineffectually) on vanes on the slipstream. On others, blade appendages, or blade warping were used for helicopter control.

For most of the 1920s and early thirties, autogiros far outshone the helicopters of the period. When the practical helicopter did appear, the relationship abruptly reversed. What made a world of difference was one could hover and the other could not. Aside from sport, the autogiro today lacks a dramatic feature (as hovering or high speed flight) to find a place for itself in the transportation spectrum. Early practical helicopters had the flaws of the autogiro, as limited CG travel, blade fatigue, vibration, and stick shake, and added a few of its own complexities such as a transmission system and tail rotor. Autogiros were flying 240 km/h (150 mph) when the best a helicopter could do was 107 km/h (100 mph). Even so, all was forgiven because the helicopter could hover. The point is important for the future as well, for nothing hovers as efficiently as a large rotor with a low disk loading. With hover ability, an unstated property of the helicopter becomes its ability to work from the air to the ground while hovering, which is as useful as its vertical flight capability.

The previous discussion of the flapping hinge leads to the concept of helicopter stability, particularly in hovering. In this early period there is little evidence in understanding stability except through control. Frequently the inventor relied on "gyroscopic stability", a notion that did not account for the aftermath of a disturbed rotor.

As noted below, the problem was one of priorities, if anything.

In its usual relationship on a helicopter, the flap-hinged rotor is theoretically unstable. However the inertia of the flapping blade mitigates the problem. What is termed *stable* with this configuration actually means *less unstable* and therefore more controllable. Flap-hinged rotor "speed stability" property in hovering allows it to tilt away from the direction of the gust, or velocity vector. This is a restoring effect, but the helicopter instability manifests itself at the end of the first, lateral swing. Inertia of the pendulous fusclage "overcorrects" the restorative rotor inclination at the end of this swing, tilting the rotor at a greater angle into the velocity vector. As the helicopter heads back to its original position, the fuselage again overcorrects the rotor with an increasing amplitude. For each swing the fuselage attitude increases, resulting in a divergence (instability). This explanation assumes there are no "black boxes" or feedback mechanisms in the system.

The fact the period of oscillation is slow enough (8–12 seconds), combined with effective controls, permit the pilot to maintain control of the helicopter in hovering, and even to anticipate unstable motion. The more skilled the pilot, the less obvious the instability, or one's cyclic stick motion. Conversely to the student, hovering is the most difficult part of learning. Except for autorotation, the other regimes require a skill level comparable to flying a fixed-wing aircraft. The common use of rigid rotors in these early prototypes, devoid of flapping inertia made the instability more abrupt and adverse.

In reviewing the ensuing narratives dealing with prototype tests, an important factor to recall is the lack of stability accounting in the claims of the experimenters. In hovering, if accomplished at all, the claims focus on hover height, never mentioning the attendant stability problem. The machine could be steadied from the ground, the hover height could be just a hop off the ground, or the machine could bounce along the ground in forward flight. The more scientific the program the more credible the claims.

As mentioned at the start of the present introduction, experimenters encountered a sequence of development problems. One need not know the specific technical and operational problems for a particular experimenter for there is an implied sequence of events in what they tried to accomplish, and this submits to a reasonable generalization. The individual experimenters went as far as they could along the same route. If one were to postulate a priority in major design concepts leading to a practical helicopter, they would take the following form.

1. Suitable powerplant.
2. Adequate thrust in hovering.
3. Adequate stability and controllability.
4. Safe descent, power-off.
5. Reliability.
6. Performance (forward flight).
7. Maintainability
8. Cost reduction.
9. Noise abatement.

Early in the 20th century the desirable powerplant was the aircooled rotary engine. It was self-cooling for hovering, of relatively light weight, 1.34–1.52 kg/kW (2.2–2.5 lb/hp), and inexpensive being World War I surplus. Prior to the war, experimenters on a low budget found it easy to construct the airframe but engines were costly, hard to come by, and power categories limited. Borrowing an engine was feasible, but the lender required assurance it would not be damaged. Regardless of the powerplant selected, the helicopter often proved to be underpowered.

Lifting thrust was often marginal in the early 1900s, but after the war, lifting off with a pilot was not so much a problem as remaining in the air under control. The power-off design problem was not taken seriously because flying was usually a few feet off the ground. The other items on the above list were accepted as chance could dictate. Only in recent times were all the items accounted for in the design stage.

There was a progression or sequence of testing responding to the problems as they turned up. As noted above, experimenters were governed more by unanticipated situations than by plan. There were two results for testing, both with the initial object of a free controlled flight. In one case, circumstances kept one's effort always on the ground, while in the other a free (but uncertain) flight was made.

In the first case, ground operation would result in functional or structural failure, requiring repairs. Ultimately a hover was attempted. This led to an instability not compensated for by effective control. The result was a rollover damaging the machine. Repeated trials brought no improvement. Somewhere in this trial and error process the helicopter would be severely damaged or destroyed, terminating the work.

In the second case of testing, the helicopter survived the lift-off and the pilot attempted to hover and fly forward, the latter perforce if there was a wind. In this movement the instability could not be controlled, leading to a hard landing and damage. Since wind only aggravated the problem it was sometimes preferable to test fly in calm air or in a hangar, as remarked before. This approach avoided the worst of the stability problem, but was no solution. Any time in these test hops one could experience a mechanical or structural failure. Finally if the barely controllable machine (the pilot very busy with the controls) remained in the air a few minutes, it became a world's record. The endurance was limited in order to avoid an accident, for the pilot was straining to keep the machine in the air. In truth the world's record for endurance belonged to the pilot, not the helicopter. The intractability of the pure helicopter tempted some to add wings to make the machine flyable. But this did not solve the hovering problem. What is remarkable about this kind of development testing is the insistence on using rigid, propeller-like rotors, and the use continued up through the mid thirties.

The drift of technology toward fixed-wing aircraft is revealed in the listings in Jane's *All the World's Aircraft* from its first edition in 1909. Considering just American aircraft entries, there were about 21 in the helicopter category in the first annual. The second edition listed 24. In the third edition (1912) there were no new aircraft of this configuration. From 1914 on, there was scant information on rotorcraft until the 1920s and 1930s when a few autogiros were described. Only in recent years did helicopters reappear in the annuals.

What follows are the chronologically-ordered narratives for the second period. In the early decades there was a category of flying machine then called *air sucker*. As remarked before, Chanute called the function the *air blast principle*. Today they would be classified as VTOL aircraft, or *jet-lift* aircraft. These indeed suck in air and discharge it downward. As noted earlier, the main difference between then and now is the modern types heat the air before discharging it. This adds energy and hence thrust to hover the machine.

Consistent with the previous narratives, some European activities are included because they are significant to helicopter engineering history. In fact the first two accounts are from Europe. One deals with theory and the other with practice.

3.2 CHRONOLOGY

1906 Crocco

In 1906 Colonel Gaetano Arturo Crocco of the Italian army applied for a patent (Italian patent application 81,078) that described the use of blade pitch change for power-off autorotative descent. He also proposed use of cyclic pitch control. Both came to be accepted ideas common to helicopters. In 1922 Crocco designed a twin-rotor helicopter, and in 1923 NACA translated his theory of inherent stability of helicopters. [3.15]

1907 Cornu

The first man-carrying flight in a helicopter took place in France. In 1906 Paul Cornu conducted

model tests that encouraged him to build a full-sized machine. The helicopter, described in Patent 902,859, was built in Lisieux, a town close to the English Channel. The two, two-blade rotors in tandem had a diameter of 6 m (19.7 ft), and turned 90 rpm. Total power to the rotors was about 10.4 kW (14 hp), transmitted by belts. Vanes in the slipstream were fitted for forward propulsion and directional control. With the pilot the machine weighed 260 kg (573 lb). [3.16]

Cornu's first flight was a short hop, lasting a few seconds. Overall he conducted more than 300 tests, fifteen with a pilot on board. However Cornu was unable to obtain satisfactory stability or control of the machine, and was beset by drive belt problems. While Cornu did leave the ground briefly, he never had control of his machine. He continued work with a helicoplane, remaining in his hometown during World War II. With the invasion of France on D-Day in 1944, Lisieux was bombed. The pioneer lost his life, a victim of the war.

1907 Luyties

Around 1907 in America, Otto Luyties built a coaxial rotor system (Figure 3.3), with the intent of collecting data for "construction of rotary flying machines". The rotors of fabric-covered tubes, were driven by a 14.9 kW (20 hp) air-cooled engine. Helicopter propulsion was to use shaft inclination. The complete device mounted

Figure 3.3   Luyties helicopter test stand with slack tiedown cables (1907).

on a spring system, allowed some vertical motion. The total apparatus weighed 454 kg (1000 lb). The two four-blade rotors had a diameter of 10.7 meters (35 feet), and turned 31 rpm. The pitch of the lower rotor was set one degree higher than the upper one, apparently recognizing the effect of the upper rotor wake on the lower rotor. [3.17]

In tests of 1907 the rotors failed to lift the apparatus weight. Luyties continued testing in 1909, but was only able to develop 3.1 kN (700 lb) of thrust. On several trials he was confronted with high winds that often damaged the rotor system. A lack of funds caused the project to be terminated.

As a result of his tests Luyties proposed a helicopter with the following characteristics, retaining the coaxial arrangement:

Gross weight	318 kg (700 lb)
Maximum thrust	4.9 kN (1100 lb)
Power	29.8 kW (40 hp)
Blade loading	12.0–47.9 N/m² (0.25–1.0 lb/ft²)

Apparently Luyties used his measured maximum thrust in the design of the above helicopter. This permitted him to fix the weight and climb margin. He also doubled the engine power. The test figure of merit is calculated to be 0.79, a highly optimistic value. It is possible ground effect produced the favorable reading, however even correcting for ground effect would produce a favorable, but plausible figure of 0.65. Plausible because of his very low disk loading range. For an estimated M = 0.5 his proposed design would require at least 46.2 kW (62 hp). In general Luyties was working in the right design direction with his low disk loadings and low rotor speed.

~ 1900 Gabbey

Around the turn of the century a Doctor Gabbey was involved with design of a multi-rotor helicopter. With a design weight of 681 kg (1500 lb), the craft featured six rotors, three on each side of the helicopter. The configuration predated one of E. R. Mumford built at the Denny Shipyard in Scotland, in 1914. With the Gabbey system the rotors also served as parachutes. The

powerplant was a 112 kW (150 hp) gasoline engine. It was estimated the machine could lift 1230 kilograms (2700 pounds). This amounts to a power loading of 10.9 kg/kW (18 lb/hp). It is unlikely the design could produce the thrust indicated. The rotor diameter would have to be about 7m (23 ft), giving an overall length to the craft of at least 21.1 meters (69 feet), which is improbable. Neglecting the stability problem, the helicopter could hover 681 kg (1500 lb) with rotors of 2.8–3.1 meter (9–10 foot) diameter. [3.18]

1907 Paul

W. Luther Paul [3.91] was the apotheosis of the inventor-gadgeteer and entrepreneur common in the early years of the 20th century. Another was the builder George Exel (1920–1923) described later. Paul was a resident of Davis, North Carolina, a town about 161 km (100 miles) southwest of the Wrights' test site near Kitty Hawk, and 19.3 km (12 miles) north of Beaufort. By trade he was a machinist and blacksmith, and typical of the inventive mind of that era he became interested in mechanical flight.

Paul was instrumental in obtaining financial backing for a helicopter he had designed, and in 1907 produced a test rig. The configuration he favored was in fact a compound helicopter with two rotors in tandem and a tractor propeller (Figure 3.4). It is not clear how complete the test rig was, but it was powered by four motorcycle engines, which in that period were delivering around 2.24 kW (3 hp). The helicopter was tested in a large barn that had an unusual aerodynamic feature caused by the prevailing winds. With both ends open there was a significant draft through it. This Paul considered a desirable feature for his "wind tunnel" simulated forward flight for the tests. In a 1937 news item [3.20] headed "Paul Invented Queer Airship", the best performance achieved was to lift the nearly 500 pound (227 kg) craft to height of about 4 feet (1.2 meters). The progress of the Wright brothers caused Paul to lose his financial support and the project was abandoned.

In a later account to his granddaughter [3.21] Paul mentioned his efforts toward reducing engine weight and increasing its power. In the

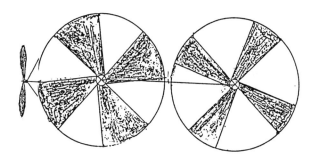

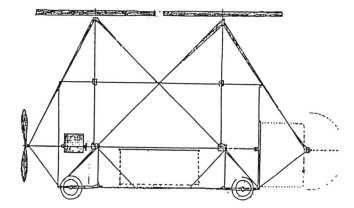

Figure 3.4 Paul compound helicopter concept (1907, 1942).

same account he revealed the machine hovered with sandbags totaling 60 pounds (27.2 kg). Paul regretted not flying it outdoors believing that "with a good breeze and a hefty push it could have flown as high as far as the Wright brothers". Not very likely.

In March 1942 Paul submitted his concept including Figure 3.4, to the National Inventor's Council of the Department of Commerce. The unit was instituted during the Second World War inviting from the public ideas that could be useful to the war effort. [3.22] He called his design *Bumble Bee*. The control surfaces consisted of a conventional rudder and elevator plus side vanes for lateral control, operating in the rotor wake. The vanes were connected to a cradle containing the operator's shoulders. Lateral shoulder motion actuated the vanes. The propeller featured reversible pitch, controllable by the operator. It was directly connected to the engine and set at zero thrust angle for vertical flight. The rotor drive system included a clutch, disengaged for engine starting and idling. The four-blade rotor diameter was given as 8 feet (2.44 meters), and apparently of tube construction as was the Luyties (Figure 3.3). There was no pitch control and thrust was varied by speed

change. Paul also described the design as having steerable front wheels "to make it a good land machine", and with a water-tight bottom it makes "a good water duck." On land or water the rotors were disengaged and the propeller drove the machine as an auto or an airboat.

Overall the 1942 concept looks more like it belonged to 1907. By 1942 the rotors had the slender look they have today. The triangular planform was a primitive approach that presumed the local area should be proportional to the local rotational velocity. Most likely Paul's earlier test rig configuration was limited to the two rotors shown in the figure. It is unlikely this arrangement could hover freely without some steadying from the ground, and there is nothing in the concept that reveals instability was accounted for. If he had solved this problem he would have made a big point of it.

Testing with a barn wind would be unfortunate in complicating the effort in controlling an unstable machine. The winds at Davis on Core Sound fronting the Atlantic were comparable to those the Wrights experienced. While the average at Kitty Hawk was 24.1 km/h (15 mph), they could vary daily from zero to 96.6 km/h (60 mph). The Wright flights were limited to 32.2–48.3 km/h (20–30 mph) winds. As described with others, winds were undesirable in testing in view of the controllability problem. Recall also, rotor speed control is too sluggish to be practical. However modern helicopter performance would be enhanced if the the normally constant speed rotor could have (at least) two speed ranges: low rpm for hovering and low speed flight and high rpm for altitude and high forward speed.

Judging from the date (1907) it appears Paul was first in America to hover a test rig (helicopter). It was unmanned and certainly had to be steadied from the ground. There is no factual information he hovered a rig with two rotors; it too would have been steadied from the ground. The comments here on stability reflect the lack of understanding of both stability and control and their interaction by the early prototype builders. (See Chapter 3, Introduction.)

In other areas Paul was very successful in his ideas, particularly those involving motion picture exhibition. Among other activities he was an early operator of a theater and pioneered a sound system of his own. (He proposed the idea to Thomas Edison, but was turned down, believing the latter was satisfied with just one inventor on his team.) Paul had his own version of social security long before the federal government got the idea. With the birth of each child he started a new business the kid could eventually take over.

1908 Berliner

Emile Berliner was an American inventor born in Germany. His inventions related to telephones and the "talking machine". He created the disk-type record (in contrast to Edison's tubular design) that is in common use today. He designed what may be the first (production) rotary aircraft engine (Gyro rotary, Figure 3.5). It was also known as the Adams-Farwell rotary. Versions were used in his helicopter tests. The other contender for rotary engine primacy was Frenchman Laurent Seguin who tested one in 1908. However the earliest idea of the engine is attributed to Hargreave who designed one around 1889 (Figure 2.6).

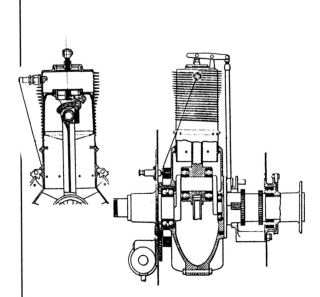

Figure 3.5 Rotary engine cross section views. A popular engine in World War I, and desirable for later helicopter prototypes because of surplus availability, light weight and self cooling properties in hovering.

Berliner's first rig, tested July 1908, (Figure 3.6) consisted of a two-blade rotor with a 5.2 meter (17 foot) diameter, powered by a 26.8 kW (36 hp) Adams-Farwell rotary engine. At an engine speed of 1200 rpm (rotor speed 150 rpm) the best thrust measured was 1.5 kN (340 lb). This yields a reasonable figure of merit (for the time) of 0.37, presumably in ground effect. [3.24] He later conducted forward flight tests with a wheeled rig (Figure 3.7) in which the rotor shaft was inclined 15 degrees, to examine lift and propulsion components of rotor thrust. With these tests, applicable to his *Aeromobile* design, Berliner discovered the power-reducing (induced) effects of forward flight. In 1908 he explained the phenomenon:

> "In order to propel the *Aeromobile* horizontally the propeller will have to be tilted forward, and I have calculated that, while this will reduce the lifting power less than three percent, the resulting thrust would be one quarter of the lifting pressure. It is an accepted theory, which has been proved by practical tests, that a propeller moving forward is more efficient than moored fast in one position. Hence the lifting power of the *Aeromobile* would increase in free flight." [3.25]

Practically, for a constant weight helicopter this meant a reduction in induced power with for-

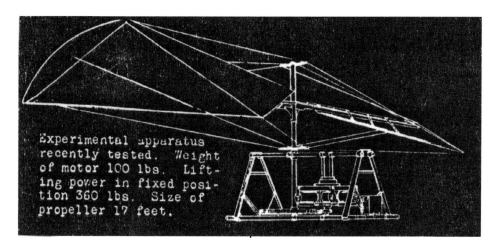

Figure 3.6 Emile Berliner test rig (1908).

ward speed. (See also helicopter power in the Glossary.)

From modern experience the minimum power required is at a flight speed of about 64.4 km/h (40 mph). At the low disk loadings Berliner used, about ⅔ of the hover power would be required. Hence for a 25 percent reduction his tests were conducted around 40.2 km/h (25 mph). Had he increased his test speed he could have realized as much as a 33 percent reduction.

Berliner's wheeled rig tests represent pioneering work in investigating the induced effects of forward flight. The first to evaluate these effects in a wind tunnel was Zhukovskii (Joukowski) who in the early 1900s added a tunnel to the aero laboratory of Moscow University.

In 1908 J. Newton Williams of Connecticut constructed a coaxial rotor helicopter tested at

Berliner's farm in Maryland. The machine used two Adams-Farwell rotaries. Williams left Berliner to undertake independent work, described below. The coaxial system development was continued by Berliner's son Henry. (See 1919 Berliner.)

In 1909 Berliner had under construction the *Aeromobile* (Figures 3.8 and 3.9), an "interlocking" rotor helicopter. The rotors intermeshed in tandem. The estimated empty weight was 227 kg (500 lb), with a maximum thrust of 3.1 kN (700 lb). Power was supplied by a 41 kW (55 hp) Adams-Farwell weighing 79.5 kg (175 lb) yielding 1.95 kg/kW (3.2 lb/hp). The fate of this machine is unknown. However around 1910 he conceived the *gyrocopter,* a single rotor design. To account for rotor torque he added a tail rotor 3.1 m (10 ft) from the main rotor. See Figure 3.10 from Patent 1,472, 148 (1918) also 1,361,222.

Berliner continued this work until 1914 when he suffered a nervous breakdown. His son Henry took over the helicopter activity, an effort that persisted through the 1920s.

1908 Williams

J. Newton Williams of Derby, Connecticut the inventor of a typewriter, experimented with toy-sized, powered helicopters in 1904. He conceived a coaxial rotor helicopter disclosed in Patents 1,023,233 and 1,076,803. [3.26] The

Figure 3.7 Emile Berliner rotor test vehicle (1908).

Figure 3.8   Emile Berliner *Aeromobile* test rig (1908).

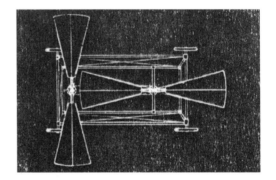

Figure 3.9   Emile Berliner tandem design plan view (1908).

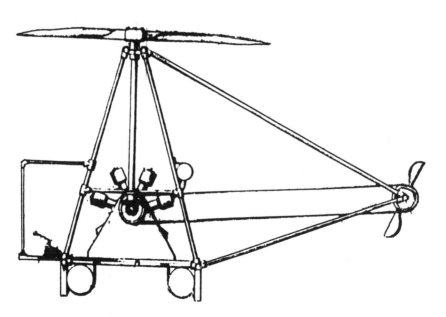

Figure 3.10   Emile Berliner tail rotor design (1918).

helicopter as mentioned above used two Adams-Farwell rotaries, powering rotors of 5.7 m (18.7 ft) diameter at 120 rpm. The machine weights were 209 kg (460 lb) empty and 277 kg (610 lb) with the operator. The design included a parachute for emergency. In Maryland some hover attempts were made with Williams as the pilot. The prototype lifted the 277 kg (610 lb), and a larger variant lifted 354 kg (780 lb). Such accounts do not reveal if the helicopter was steadied from the ground, a credible possibility.

Williams in mid 1908 and prior to Berliner worked in Hammondsport, New York, the home base of Curtiss and other flying machine experimenters. He at one time was employed by Glenn Curtiss. The helicopter was fitted with a Curtiss engine (Figure 3.11) of 30–34 kW (40–45 hp), which was fan cooled (Figure 3.12), being an early version of the system for current reciprocating engines. With the Curtiss engine the best result was a 0.92 meter (3 foot) hover, but the machine was unstable and uncontrollable. Ultimately it experienced a "sprung shaft". Williams' patent and prototypes reveal his interest in using rotor collective pitch control by means of a blade warp-ing system. Apparently body weight shifting proved to be inadequate to control his machine.

Williams was an entrant in the British helicopter competition (1925–26). This coaxial design took a 59.7 kW (80 hp) Le Rhone rotary engine. The project most likely involved a hovering test stand. (See 1924 Anonymous [Williams].)

1908 Chalmers

The work of C. H. Chalmers, an electrical engineer is of interest because his rotor system did not follow the usual airscrew approach, and he was systematic in his tests. [3.28] The idea for the novel rotor system was suggested by his observation that the airplane wing (e.g., Wrights') flying in undisturbed air supported 30.4–36.5 kg/kW (50–60 lb/hp), while a (static) propeller produced only 3.0 to 4.3 (5 to 7). He postulated a two-blade system ("air helix") in which only the outer 16 percent of the radius was a structural, aerodynamic surface. In rotation the two surfaces (panels) swept an annular path. The panels were attached to rigid arms that extended

Figure 3.11 Williams coaxial rotor test stand (1908).

Figure 3.12 Williams and the Curtiss, fan-cooled engine for his helicopter (ca. 1908).

from the hub to about a 40 percent radius. Between the arms and the panels were cables holding one member to the other. The cables allowed the panels to be retracted, to abut the arms. This retraction was automatic, by means of a helical spring.

When rotating the panels were held out at full radius by equilibrium between the aerodynamic and centrifugal forces, defining a kind of coning angle. In retrospect Chalmers was carrying a "strip analysis" into the test stage. He reasoned the system efficiency would approach that of a wing in free air. Further, the "blade" stresses (centrifugal only), and hence system weight could be reduced significantly.

The designer built a fixed test rig driven by a 11.2 kW (15 hp) electric motor. The air helix diameter was 7.6 m (25 feet), with a panel span of 0.61 meters (2 feet). With panels retracted the diameter was 3.4 meters (11 feet). On his first runup he observed the blades "flounced". The flutter was corrected by adjustment of two trailing tabs called "rudders". These were spaced about two chord lengths behind each panel. During tests he noticed the difference in effect in calm air and with a breeze. Chalmers wrote:

"The noise was startling, and some curiosity seekers who refused to heed warnings of possible danger quickly fled when the blades got up to fair speed. The sound would compare favorably with a Pullman sleeper full of fat men badly addicted to snoring."

The best results of his systematic tests (4–6 degree tab angle) occurred at a rotor speed of 168 rpm with a tip speed of 67.1 m/s (220 fps), yielding a thrust of 6.8 kg/kW (11.2 lb/hp). Thus he was able to double the unit value of a contemporary propeller, but it was about 1/5 the value for the wing.

Chalmers planned to continue tests with 0.46 m² (5 ft²) panels vs. 0.93 (1.0) for the test blades, but there is no record of his work. In a 1908 article in *Aeronautics* Chalmers concludes:

"There are two important considerations in this type of air helix. First the centrifugal force must be made quite large as compared with the lift and drift (drag). By doing so the blades remain more nearly horizontal, and also more radial. Second the rudders on the blades must be carefully proportioned as to size, angle and weight. With proper care in these respects a perfectly steady lift is obtained."

Overall Chalmers was ahead of his time in areas he did not appreciate, such as flexible blades, hinge offset, trim tabs, and "self folding" rotors. He was on a track similar to 1911 Rochon described later, but he lacked Rochon's awareness.

1908 Kimball

Wilbur R. Kimball was Vice President of the Aeronautic Society of New York. The organization was founded to promote aviation and to financially support promising experimenters. These included Glenn Curtiss and Kimball. The first machine completed was Kimball's, a helicopter with 20 lifting screws (Patent 1,843,643 and Figure 3.13). [3.29] The idea was to save weight. He believed a large number of small screws would be lighter than one large one of the same total disk area. (See also Figures 3.14, 3.15, and 3.16)

The four-bladed screws, 1.22 meters (4 feet) in diameter turning 1000 rpm, were mounted in a

Figure 3.13   Kimball multi-rotor helicopter (1908).

Figure 3.14   Kimball helicopter, view from front (1908).

Figure 3.15   Kimball helicopter, side view (1908).

rectangular frame above the pilot. The screws were belt driven by a 37.3 kW (50 hp) at 2000 rpm, water-cooled Aero & Marine Company (Boston) engine. The latter which weighed 81.7 kg (180 lb) with coolant and fuel, was located to longitudinally balance the pilot. The frame was inclined at an angle to give a propulsive component to the thrust. Vanes behind the pilot were for yaw control. The pilot's seat shifted for longitudinal control, and lateral control was obtained by blocking some of the airscrew wake. With the pilot the machine weighed 272.4 kg (600 lb). Helicopter control was by two hand-wheels, which probably served as grips in weight shifting. The craft appears to have only two wheels located at the forward end (Figure 3.14). The forward wheel arrangement suggests Kimball expected the machine to start off by

lifting the aft end, pivoting on the forward wheels.

The inventor first experimented with scale models. Full scale tests were to take place at Morris Park in the Bronx. The helicopter, considered underpowered by Kimball, had drive system problems that caused the project to be set aside. Later the machine was destroyed in a fire. One account notes $10,000 was put into the venture. (See also 1909 Rickman).

1908 Lane

A project of Lane Automatous Airship Company of San Francisco [3.32], the design was an airplane-helicopter with a single wing 12.2 × 6.1 meters (40 × 20 feet) in size, in the center of which was a lifting screw powered by a 27kW (36 hp) engine. The machine was an "air sucker" in which air was taken in from above and discharged below from special cups, at 250 times a minute.

It was claimed in September 1908 the craft flew 1½ miles (2.5 kilometers) using hand and foot power only. The claim is not credible. As mentioned in the da Vinci discussion, a single operator using human power would be capable of producing a fraction one horsepower (0.75 kW).

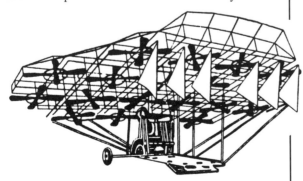

Figure 3.16   Kimball helicopter isometric (1908).

The air sucker design alone would require far more power than a comparable helicopter with a large diameter rotor. If anything the inventor was driving a low-powered ventilating fan. The best he could claim is a flight with a kind of glider with insignificant input from his high frequency scoops.

1909 Metcalf

In 1909 a helicopter (Patent 908,794) was under construction by George A. Metcalf of Malden, Massachusetts. [3.30] The craft had two rotors in tandem with a 2.4 meter (8 foot) spacing (Figure 3.17). The rotors were mounted so they could be tilted in opposite directions for yaw control using two hand-operated levers. The frame around the rotors consisted of structural members and "buffers" for protection.

Characteristics:

Rotor diameter	6.1 m (20 ft)
Maximum length	14.6 m (48 ft)
Maximum width	6.7 m (22 ft)

1909 Wilmington Model

A Wilmington, North Carolina newspaper in 1909 carried a brief item on vertical takeoff aircraft that "requires no skids for it to get right up

in the air". [3.32] Reference to *skids* for comparison in the statement was recognition by the writer that in 1909 airplanes still featured skids not wheels. Wheels appeared on Wright machines in 1910. The transition in Europe occurred in the 1906–1910 period.

The item continues:

"Its startling flight is not at a slant but its flight upward is from the ground. The inventor has not built a machine to carry a man or two, but we would like to see one built according to the model that actually flies."

The builder's name is not mentioned. Most likely the design was a rubber-powered coaxial rotor model.

A Wilmington newspaper account in 1911 describes two local flying machine projects, one a monoplane the other a multiplane. [3.33] A third machine was attributed to Frank Herbst, promoter of an air show in January 1912. However it is not clear he was the model builder.

1909 Bultzingsslowen

A biplane helicopter was reported under construction in New York in 1909. [3.34] The craft featured two 1.8 meter (6 foot) diameter rotors turning 120 rpm. Calculated lift was 2.2 kN (500 lb) per rotor. Two 1.8 meter (6 foot) propellers

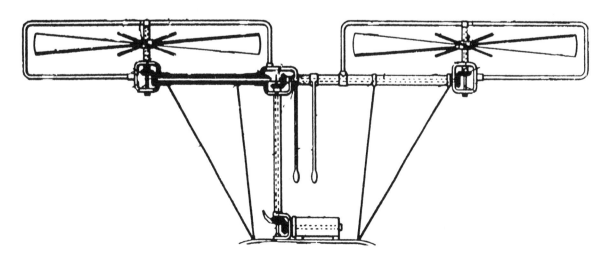

Figure 3.17 Metcalf tandem rotor helicopter concept (1909).

were located aft. The machine weighed 341 kg (750 lb) and was powered by a 27 kW (36 hp) engine.

1909 Thompson

A monoplane air sucker (jet lift) machine was reported under construction by George Thompson of Kingston, Oklahoma. The jet-producing airscrews were inside the body of the machine. [3.35] This arrangement suggests a ducted fan, a system requiring more power than a large diameter rotor, and a lack of concern for hovering stability.

1909 Snell

H. B. Snell of Toledo, Ohio had under construction a flying machine with supporting surfaces that rotate "opposite the direction of flight". [3.36] Apparently the craft was a cyclogiro. (See Glossary.)

1909 Lake

An air sucker machine was under construction at the Lake Submarine Company of Bridgeport, Connecticut. The builder was C. J. Lake, apparently related to Simon Lake, the rival of John P. Holland for submarine business. The jet-lift design featured hollow curved surfaces from which heated, expanded air was discharged. Unlike others with this configuration, Lake's novel feature was use of heat to increase the discharge energy of the air and hence lift.

As mentioned before with jet-lift ideas, stabilization and control present problems more severe than that of simply attaining lift. It is unlikely such systems would be capable of hovering without relying on stabilization devices well beyond the state of the art. The first practical jet-lift machine to hover, the British Rolls-Royce "flying bedstead", made its initial free flight in 1954. [3.37] The first useful VTOL "jump jet" featuring vectored jet lift was the British Harrier, an aircraft that underwent many years of development. It finally entered squadron service in 1969. The machine performed well in the Falklands War in 1982.

1909 Jean

A company was formed in 1909 to exploit a design consisting of rectangular frames having airscrews installed within the structure. The craft powered by a two-cylinder engine was reported under construction in 1909. [3.38]

1909 Davidson

George L. O. Davidson was one of the more active entrepreneurs. His work covered the decade either side of the turn of the 19th century. Davidson's initial venue was Britain, later emigrating to America.

In 1896 he patented a vertical-rising aircraft with a birdlike configuration (Figure 3.18). The wings were fitted with 22 small airscrews that were belt driven. In forward flight these were to

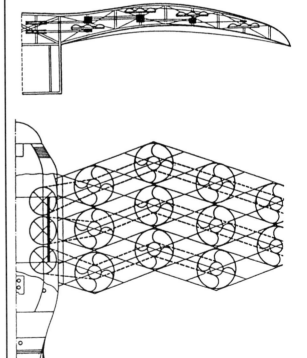

Figure 3.18 Davidson multi-rotor concept (1896).

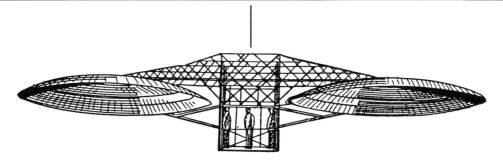

Жироптер Давидсона.

Figure 3.19 Davidson prototype front view (1909).

be stopped and covered. In 1898 Davidson turned to a different configuration featuring two, laterally arranged rotors of very large size. Each of the 9.2 meter (30 foot) rotors was composed of 120 blades. A large model was built and promoted at shows, identifying it as the "flying machine of the future". The design was to transport 20–30 passengers at a speed of 322 km/h (200 mph), apparently the largest helicopter design of the period. Even so, he failed in his efforts to raise money for the full scale machine.

Davidson's work continued in Denver, Colorado, and in 1909 had a lateral rotor prototype under construction. [3.39] Named *gyropter* it was a giant machine for its time, weighing over 908 kilograms (2000 pounds). Each of the rotors was shaft driven by its own steam engine located in the fuselage (Figures 3.19 and 3.20). During development he increased the engine size due to poor rotor performance. A powerplant explosion (most likely steam) terminated the project.

The belt drive, multi-screw idea of 1896 antici-pated approaches by Cornu (1907), Kimball (1908), and Whitehead (1911). As mentioned before this drive system was almost a guarantee of malfunction. Recall in those days of the late Industrial Revolution, belt drives were a common feature of factories with their multitude of individually operated machines, driven off a single shaft. Using belts was standard practice, however helicopters lack the structural rigidity for using such a method. Even today with mechanical drives, airframe flexibility contributes significantly to the relatively short time between gearbox overhauls. Compared for example with a turboprop, propeller-reduction gearbox. Small helicopters use belt drives, but these are compact units. Including safety factors these vee belts are designed to absorb 37.3–44.8 kW (50–60 hp) per belt. (A 94 kW–126 hp- auto engine fan with a similar drive will absorb 2.2–3.0 kW (3–4 hp.) On a statistical basis alone, and considering the large number of flat belts, slippage, the flexible structure, and outright failure, these together would inhibit screws working at the same speed, if at all.

Figure 3.20 Davidson prototype helicopter, steam powered (1909).

1909 Rickman

The Rickman Helicopter (Figure 3.21) was a muscle-powered craft, and an early prototype using this form of power. A single rotor was mounted on a tricycle frame through a long, slender driveshaft, about 5.1 cm (2 in) in diameter. The machine was a two seater with two sets of handlebars. [3.40] The rotor with an estimated diameter of 6.7 meters (22 feet) consisted of a number of (about 32) separate blades independently attached to a peripheral framework, the rotor probably serving as a parachute as well.

It is unlikely the two man effort did much more than turn the rotor. Using a figure of merit of 0.3, and an estimated weight of 182 kilograms (400 pounds) with operators, the maximum thrust they could produce is around 222.5 newtons (50 pounds). The calculated thrust is based on assuming a brief vigorous output per man of 0.56 kW (3/4 hp). Considering the problem of maintaining rotor balance while pedaling, they probably introduced a lateral shake due to shaft whirl or rotor unbalance.

The Rickman project can be viewed in context. He was a member of the Aeronautic Society of New York. [3.41] The organization planned what was to be the first major aviation meet in America in 1910, at Belmont Park racetrack in Elmont, Long Island. Morris Park, along the Bronx River, also had a track suitable for flying. An airshow was held here in 1908. These tracks were relevant because the airplanes of the period featured low wing-loadings and therefore had short takeoff runs.

Entrants to the meet included members Rickman and Kimball (1908), described previously. The Aeronautic Society decided to enter an airplane of its own and funded Glenn Curtiss (another member) to construct and fly it. One other entrant was Stanley Y. Beach mentioned subsequently with Whitehead (1911). The meet itself was an anticlimax, being nothing like the milestone in aviation history expressed by the meet in Rheims, France in August 1909. As mentioned before, the Kimball machine was destroyed, Curtiss performed a nominal flight demonstration, and the event ended more as a static exhibition than an air show.

1909 English

The inventor English of San Francisco in 1909 tested a helicopter (Figure 3.22) that was part of a single wing helicoplane. [3.42] The machine consisted of tandem rotors mounted on a tubular steel frame, with a platform at its center. The pilot sat forward of the centerline, balanced by the engine located aft. The blades had a guitar-pick planform, while a wing was incorporated for safe power-off landing. The wing chord ex-

Figure 3.21   Rickman muscle-powered helicopter, apparently at Belmont Park racetrack in the days when all men wore hats (1909).

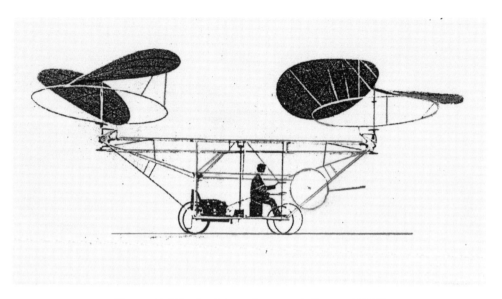

Figure 3.22 English tandem rotor helicopter (1909).

tended the full distance between the rotor shafts. Control was obtained by a surface located below the forward rotor.

Characteristics:

Rotor diameter	4.9 m (16 ft)
Powerplant (vee engine)	44.8 kW 960 hp)
Weight	272.4 kg (600 lb)
Wing area	9.3 m² (100 ft²)

It was claimed the machine could lift 754 kilograms (1660 pounds). The first test hop resulted in a crash caused by the craft breaking away from its tiedowns. Apparently this accident terminated the program.

1910 Purvis-Wilson

William Purvis, an inventor from Goodland, Kansas was inspired by the *whirligig*, on observing a youth playing with the toy. Purvis a machinist for the Rock Island Railroad gained the interest of a friend Charles A. Wilson, and together they designed and constructed a coaxial rotor helicopter (Figures 3.23, 3.24 and Patent 1,028,781). [3.43] A novel feature was the use of control surfaces mounted outboard on either side of the frame. These surfaces could be inclined collectively or differentially. The collective angle was employed to tilt the machine for forward flight. In a banked turn,

the differential control was used in conjunction with a rudder. In vertical flight the vanes were set at zero angle of attack, to reduce air resistance. The machine featured a tricycle landing gear, however, the single wheel is aft, not forward. For ground roll directional stability, the single wheel should have been forward (Figure 1.6).

The helicopter weighed 182 kilograms (400 pounds), and was powered by two 5.2 kW (7 hp) air-cooled engines. Figure 3.23 shows one of the engines, the large ring assembly behind the engine may be the cooling fan. It would take about 0.38 kW (½ hp) to continuously cool each engine at full power. Reports of the initial tests indicate the machine was flight-damaged, or experienced a structural failure. Either way, development was suspended. The inventors had formed Goodland Aviation Company to raise money to continue the project. With no financing forthcoming the project was dropped.

A full scale replica of the machine is on exhibit at the High Plains Museum in Goodland. It is identified as "America's first patented helicopter". Aside from this claim, its "firstness" also can be due to what may be the first helicopter in America that fully accounted for all the design features necessary for flight. It was a *complete* helicopter, one devoid of wings, and not a hoverable test stand.

Figure 3.23 Purvis-Wilson prototype (1910).

Figure 3.24 One of two 5.2 kW (7 hp) engines of Purvis-Wilson (1910).

1910 Hunt

A. E. Hunt of Jetmore, Kansas, a blacksmith by trade, was inspired to build a tandem rotor helicopter (Figure 3.25). The machine, called "Hunt rotary airplane" included wing panels, making it a helicoplane. [3.44] The counterrotating rotors were of special design, driven by a 30 kW (40 hp) engine. The panel blades were contained by an attached shroud, and the assembly rotated as a unit. Tests proved the machine to be underpowered and overweight. The weight problem was due to the use of iron (literally *ironmongery*) instead of lighter materials unavailable to him. Hunt appealed to a local farmer to put to use his thresher steam engine to boost helicopter power. The effort to increase rotor speed did not work, and the inventor abandoned his helicopter. A local newspaper reported Hunt developed a salve for treating boils, a venture more successful than his helicopter project.

Figure 3.25 Hunt tandem rotor prototype (1910).

Regarding the design, a reason for the rotor shroud apparently was to obtain a uniform airload to the blade tip, thereby avoiding tip losses. A similar deep rim (ring) concept was tried in France by Renard in 1873. He used a 4.6 meter (15 foot) diameter rotor. The intent was to keep the air from being driven from its circular path by centrifugal force. In both cases the focus apparently was on hovering, ignoring the unsymmetrical aerodynamic forces and pitching moments introduced in forward flight by such a shroud.

1911 Rochon

Achille Rochon was an experimenter who had some progressive ideas that ran counter to certain assumptions that were both prevailing and wrong. Even so, he was defensive about his views, unaware he was on the right track. His ideas make him unique in this account of early helicopters.

Rochon's concepts were disclosed in Patent 1,145,388 and in a letter published in *Aircraft*.

[3.45] His calculations are of less interest than his concepts, which relate to blade (root end) articulation and blade flexibility. The report was based on model experiments, and at the time of the letter he was appealing to the Aero Club for the loan of an engine for a prototype under construction.

Rochon envisioned a rotor with very thin, flexible metal blades that held their position in rotation by virtue of the centrifugal force and air load acting on them. He further advocated use of both a flapping and lag hinge as part of his overall rotor design. This approach is modern in its treatment. More than he realized, an elastic (flexible) blade as distinct from a rigid, propeller-like rotor blade, provides "centrifugal relief" of the bending stress, resulting in a lighter weight blade. The relief can be ¼ and more of the bending stress in a rigid blade. (See the Glossary for further rigid and hinged blade design treatment.)

As described before, a blade with a flap hinge (or a very elastic one without a hinge) makes hovering instability controllable, a notion neither Rochon nor his contemporaries appreciated. Because of his unusual design, Rochon was compelled to reinforce his point:

> ". . . . Probably some think hinges are not the thing but this is a mistake-they are an indispensable part of the combination and not a defect."

The inventor had two other ideas regarding his rotor: the blades could be coiled into a drum and pulled out by centrifugal force, and by proper chordwise weight distribution the blade would assume a natural twist while rotating. In power-off (safe) descent he believed the blades would untwist by virtue of the upflowing air permitting the helicopter to ". . . . fall from any height without a motor, with more security than a gliding aeroplane".

Rochon's advocacy though modern was not accepted by those who followed him for two probable reasons. Rochon was not well-known enough to be taken seriously, assuming others knew of his work, and more importantly, none including Rochon had the basic helicopter engineering knowledge to appreciate what he discovered. Philosophically, and in view of the many missed cues in this history (and others) one can wonder if there is a way to appreciate what is not appreciated. The simplest answer is to be alert to new ideas, and not dismiss them out of hand.

Unaware of Rochon's work, in the 1948–1951 period, a similar rotor system was under development in the form of a rotorchute at Prewitt Aircraft Company of Wallingford, Pennsylvania. [3.45] The details are in Patent 2,614,636. Twelve to 20 foot (3.7 to 6.1 meter) diameter, two-blade rotors were tested. The blades with a 7 inch (17.8 cm) chord were made of thin sheets of stainless steel. The leading edge was built up to a 0.10 inch (2.54 mm) thickness by adhesively bonding additional steel strips to the sheet. In one configuration, the blades were coiled into a cylindrical drum of 14 inch (35.6 cm) diameter (Figure 3.26). The drum had two slots with a slotted flap hinge attached to each opening. Each blade had a pin attached to its root end, allowing engagement with the flap hinge when fully extended. With this arrangement, both flap and lag hinge articulation were provided (Figure 3.27).

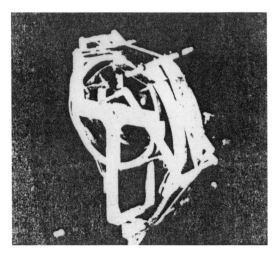

Figure 3.26 Prewitt rotorchute with two blades coiled inside the hub (drum). The tips remain outside to start autorotation (1948–1951). In one test a blade tore as it exited the drum, losing its lift. It trailed vertically as the rotochute fell. The other blade established autorotation and the rotorchute descended as a single-blade rotor.

Design variants of rotorchute were mounted on a weighted spike and launched from an airplane at 80 mph (129 km/h), using a 15 foot (4.6 m) static line (Figure 3.28). The device weighed up to 75 pounds (34.1 kg). In rotor speed tests, the minimum to extend the "stub" blades was 200–250 rpm, while the maximum as tested was 400. The minimum altitude to stabilize autorotation was 225 feet (68.6 m).

As a two-blade rotor without lag dampers (later installed) it was discovered the blades experi-

Figure 3.27 Prewitt rotorchute blades extended showing flap and lag hinges. The vertical pin at the blade root stops its extension (1948–1951).

Figure 3.28 Prewitt 4.9 meter (16 foot) diameter rotorchute weighing 34.1 kilograms (75 pounds) descending in autorotation (ca. 1949).

enced "ground resonance" in the air, probably the first time this phenomenon was recognized. The drum-wrapped blade concept could be of use in a human-powered helicopter because of its low starting torque, where significant pre-flight energy is expended. With the present design, a force of 40 pounds (178 N) of "pull" was required to overcome the initial friction of a blade wrapped in the drum.

1911 Scott

Figure 3.29 shows a prototype so strange it is in a class of its own. The machine was the creation of James F. Scott of Chicago, a stage set builder. In some rotorcraft histories it is presented as a kind of aircraft designed to hover, a "helicopter" or a craft with "wings" that flutter or reciprocate. [3.46]

A close study of the illustration does not support the point it is a helicopter or other VTOL type. Assuming the picture is a complete machine, there is no evidence of driveshafting or other driving mechanisms for the disks. As a would-be helicopter the craft is worth a closer look, based on the illustration alone. What follows is a mix of the obvious, conjecture, and analysis.

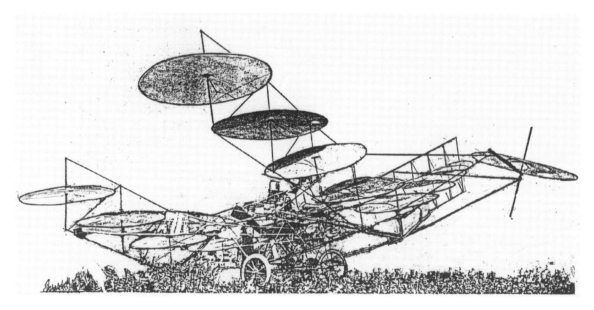

Figure 3.29 Scott multi-disk prototype sometimes cited as a kind of rotorcraft but the structure does not indicate this. The other possibility is the disks are designed to flutter (1910).

The machine (Figure 3.29) consists of an open structure carrying two vee-frames on which disks are mounted. The forward frame supports nine of them, constituting the forward "wing", while the aft frame holds seven disks. Along with a nose disk, apparently a pitch control, the total number is seventeen.

The pilot sits high between the forward frame and the powerplant. The engine bed-rails extend forward on either side of the pilot, serving also as arm rests. It would seem mounting the craft was as involved as the machine itself. A water-cooled engine with the radiator below it drives a pusher propeller. The wide-tip propeller reveals a design still under the Wright brothers' influence. Not obvious, but the undercarriage has a tricycle arrangement.

The disks about 2.44 meters (8 feet) in diameter appear to be fabric and radially ribbed like an umbrella. The features may indicate reciprocating action, but this notion lacks mechanical verification. The disks overlap by about a radius, and this scheme alone would negate disk rotation. They appear to be installed to operate in the free stream-like independent circular wings, which in forward flight would leave a wake of tubular airstreams. It is very likely the disks were designed to flutter (by self-excitation) in the airstream. The inventor may have expected this action to produce more lift than a conventional wing. The long staff per disk suggests Scott sought to avoid disturbed airflow and allow freedom of angle of attack change. Each disk has a cable attached to the underside, all leading to the pilot's feet, implying a possible pedal control of the angle. A pilot's control stick or lever is not evident.

The machine has an estimated empty weight of 307 kg (675 lb), and a gross weight of 409 kilograms (900 pounds). The engine was probably rated 34 kW (45 hp), a typical value for the time. Based on using 16 disks, the lift per disk is 26.1 kg (57 lb.) This makes the disk loading 5.4 kg/m^2 (1.1. lb/ft^2) which the disks could withstand. However the staffs look like they would not take much bending, and might vibrate due to the aerodynamic moments on the disks. If so, the inventor would be realizing more flutter than he predicted. The vee-frames themselves lack any structure to resist the drag forces on the system. In any case the machine is not a helicopter.

1911 Whitehead

Gustave Whitehead (Weisskopf) (1874–1927) is a little-known but controversial figure in aeronautical history, even though he was a persistent investigator of mechanical flight dating to 1895. A native of Germany (Bavaria), he was recognized there during World War II as an aeronautical pioneer, [3.47] and a monument was erected to him in his native town of Leuterhausen.

Including models and man-carrying machines, he claimed to have built 56 flying machines before 1901, and on August 14, 1901 made a successful flight in one of his airplanes, thereby preceding the Wrights'. Among his machines were helicopters. The inventor's work is covered in a 1937 book by Stella Randolph: *Lost Flights of Gustave Whitehead.* [3.48] Some of his activity took place around Bridgeport, Connecticut, and the *Post* of that city examined the veracity of the first flight claim (in 1940). Although there were witnesses to flights, no date could be established. The paper reports the statement of Stanley Y. Beach, son of a former editor of *Scientific American.* Beach, a long-time associate of Whitehead, was an aeronautical promoter as well as a collaborator. (See also 1908 Kimball entry, and 1925 Beach, S.Y.) His view and that of others who investigated the claim was it had no validity. Even so it is controversial to this day. [3.49]

Whitehead's first helicopter was built around 1911 (Figure 3.30), apparently powered with his own engine, fueled by acetylene. It was a multi-rotor type that proved to be underpowered. The 1911 helicopter consisted of an open, tubular framework, carrying an array of lifting screws. The two rows of screws on either side of a central frame may be seen as "hovering wings". The two-blade screws with X-shaped planform were about 1.8 m (6 ft) in diameter. The pilot was located in the central frame with the powerplant in front of him. This unit drove the screws through a system of belts and pulleys. The operator held on to a wheel control. From the figure there appear to be extra screws aft, which could be used to incline the craft.

There are no records of tests. However one can predict he had belt drive problems, and it is unlikely he broke contact with the ground. A sec-

Figure 3.30   Whitehead multi-rotor prototype (1911).

ond machine was built but not completed due to a disagreement with his financial backers. As for his airplane, he may have flown, bouncing along the ground, as some helicopters did in the 1920s, with a possible still photo taken between bounces.

The attention given Whitehead's "first flight" claim disguises the fact he was a practical technician. Figure 3.31 shows a 1910 advertisement run by a distributor of Whitehead engines. Two of his (static) powerplants are listed for sale: 40 and 75 hp (29.8 and 56 kW) units, types used in

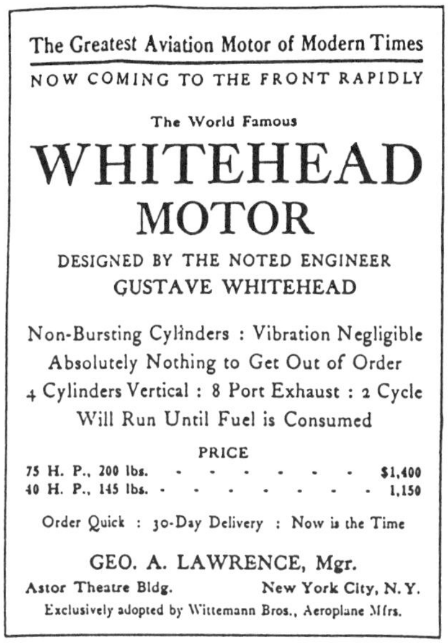

the popular Wittemann airplanes. (The Wittemann brothers in 1917 opened a factory at a field in New Jersey adjacent to what was to become Teterboro Airport.) From the ad the unit engine weights are 2.2 kg/kW (3.6 lb/hp) for the 29.8 kW (40 hp) powerplant and 1.64 kg/kW (2.7 lb/hp) for the 56 kW (75 hp) engine. Values approaching those of the rotary engines cited previously which weighed 1.34–1.52 kg/kW (2.2–2.5 lb/hp). The costs quoted in the ad ($1,150–$1,400) were in the annual salary range of a skilled draftsman.

1911 Toles

Justin K. Toles of Stockton, California invented a type of lifting rotor that was to be the basis for a helicopter (Patent 988,523). The inventor described his principle a "revolving disk for inherent stability, and peripheral alary lifts as a means to overcome a dead load" (Figures 3.32, 3.33, and 3.34). Figure 3.2 is a general arrangement of his rotorcraft, consisting of lateral rotors and a cruciform tail. Figure 3.33 shows Toles' whirl arm test rig balanced by an electric motor. The propeller is visible in this rear view. Details of the revolving disk (Figure 3.34) are from his patent.

Toles believed the stability of a spinning top could be reproduced in other rotating devices, revealing his interpretation of "gyroscopic stability".

> "The function of revolution compels the disk to assimilate balance. Nor is this phenomenon of

---

The Greatest Aviation Motor of Modern Times

NOW COMING TO THE FRONT RAPIDLY

The World Famous

WHITEHEAD MOTOR

DESIGNED BY THE NOTED ENGINEER
GUSTAVE WHITEHEAD

Non-Bursting Cylinders : Vibration Negligible
Absolutely Nothing to Get Out of Order
4 Cylinders Vertical : 8 Port Exhaust : 2 Cycle
Will Run Until Fuel is Consumed

PRICE

75 H. P., 200 lbs. - - - - - - $1,400
40 H. P., 145 lbs. - - - - - - - 1,150

Order Quick : 30-Day Delivery : Now is the Time

GEO. A. LAWRENCE, Mgr.
Astor Theatre Bldg.   New York City, N. Y.
Exclusively adopted by Wittemann Bros., Aeroplane Mfrs.

Figure 3.31   Whitehead engine advertisement (1910).

Figure 3.32 Toles helicopter design general arrangement (1911).

equilibrium destroyed, or in the least impaired by the impulse of forward movement given it." [3.50]

Today the logic of this point would be seen in tossing a Frisbee.

The rotor consisted of a central disk covered with fabric, serving also as a parachute. Small blades were attached to this disk (Figure 3.34). The blades, called *alaries* or *alary lifts* were not for "screw action", which the disk itself was to provide. The alaries considered "perfect stabilizers", were to produce a denser wake serving as an "air road" over which the air travels. Stability was to be obtained from the gyroscopic properties of the disk.

Toles built half scale models of his ideas including a four-disk version. The complete model included a tractor screw (Figure 3.32). One unit consisted of a 6 foot (1.83 meter) disk to which were connected the alaries. These were 16 inches (40.6 cm) long with an 11 inch (27.9 cm) chord. For tests the model was attached to an arm with a 50 foot (15.3 m) radius. Statically ("hovering"), with the disk turning 200 rpm the

unit thrust developed was 21.0 lb/hp (12.8 kg/kW). With an arm tip speed of 167 fps (51 m/s), the loading was calculated to be 36.5 lb/hp (22.2 kg/kW). Effectively he was determining the variation of power loading with speed. For a unit power his results show an increase in thrust with speed, which agrees with current theory. For a given weight (as helicopter gross weight) it means a reduction in power with speed. However this applies up to a point. The tip speed tested was probably the lowest before he would begin to measure increasingly less thrust per unit power, because the drag would begin to dominate. (See also discussion with Figure H.7.)

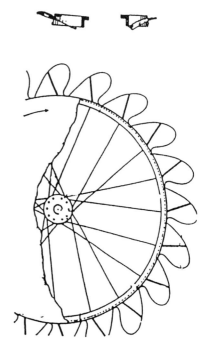

Figure 3.34 Toles concept, plan view showing "alars" (1911).

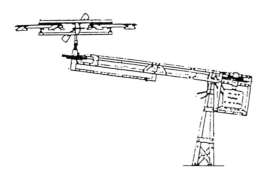

Figure 3.33 Toles whirl arm test rig (1911).

To be of any practical value for an aircraft, Toles believed the system should produce at least 50 lb/hp (30.4 kg/kW) of "burden" beyond its weight with the operator. Compared with to-day's values his predicted requirement is very high, demanding a highly efficient rotor, and therefore it is a highly optimistic expectation.

1913 Bartha and Madzer

The patent (Figure 3.35) to Hungarians Bartha and Madzer is of interest because it is an early disclosure of the need for a blade flapping hinge. The patent also shows a delta-three angle, used today to suppress flapping (as with a tail rotor), and an application to a coaxial rotor system. Note also the hinge offset which as remarked with Figure 1.17 and elsewhere, provides a mechanical control force that is independent of the air load on the rotor.

British patent 16,621 of 1913 was granted in the name of their attorney, K. Pollasek, however it was issued in Germany and elsewhere in the inventors' name.

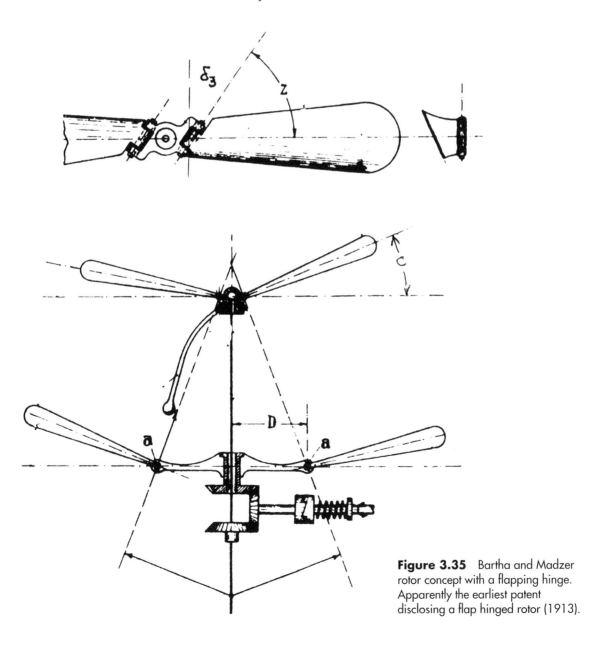

Figure 3.35 Bartha and Madzer rotor concept with a flapping hinge. Apparently the earliest patent disclosing a flap hinged rotor (1913).

Figure 3.36   Bissell helicopter concept revealed in a running advertisement (1913).

1913 Bissell

Figure 3.36 is a copy of an advertisement that ran in issues of *Aircraft* in 1913. The compound helicopter design was the idea of Joseph E. Bissell of Pittsburgh, Pennsylvania. [3.51] The inventor identified his concept with the name *Gyro-fly-wheeli-cop-ara-chute*, one that at least entitles him to some kind of prize in onomastics.

The pilot of this rotorcraft sat on a saddle, straddling an engine cylinder. The rigid rotor, about 8.5 m (28 ft) in diameter featured collective pitch control. (See small diagram to the right.) Bissell's patent (1,049,758) emphasizes the control and drive system of his invention. The long shaft from the pilot's position leading to the propeller axis of rotation, is used to swivel the propeller and the triangular vane to the left or right. The propeller is driven from a pulley at the upper end of the powerplant. The steel wire drive passes over an idler pulley (below the propeller) before it reaches the driving pulley. The powerplant apparently is an original design, and obviously static. The small diagram to the left suggests the engine is a two-stroke cycle unit.

Figure 3.37 is an earlier ad run by Bissell in *Aircraft* (1910). The inventor marked two characteristics on the patent drawing: rotor diameter 26 feet (7.9 m) and engine power, 20 hp (14.9 kW). Estimating the machine gross weight at 500 lb (227 kg) minimum, yields a figure of merit of 0.83. This assumes all the power is delivered to

FOR THOSE INTERESTED IN

AERONAUTICS

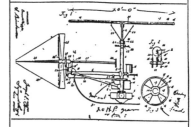

For particulars in regard to this combined

Helicopter, Parachute and Gyroscope

Apply to the undersigned

IT requires little, if any, more expenditure of gasolene to operate the combination herewith than it does to drive any other style of monoplane, as will become evident after a few moments' examination. However, the foregoing arrangement possesses a number of very important advantages peculiar to itself which cannot be over-estimated by prospective aviators—i. e.

The above machine can be easily operated by any novice; it can be started up without regard to locality by a single operator; it cannot be upset; it will come down like a feather should anything go wrong with the engine, and should it alight on the water it will float right side up. In case of wreck, the operator is less apt to be injured in this machine than in any other because he cannot strike the ground until after the machine has first given way, thereby breaking the force of contact.

JOSEPH E. BISSELL
P. O. Box 795
PITTSBURG, PA.

Figure 3.37   Bissell earlier advertisement (1910).

the rotor. (It would not be, unless there is a clutch in the propeller drive.) A realistic figure is 0.50, and for that power the rotor diameter should be 32.6 feet (9.9 meters). Bissell counted on rotor gyroscopic effects for stability.

Bissell's claim to fame as a "first" relate to his design for crashworthiness. (See text of Figure 3.37.) This is a design concern of modern interest in both civil and military helicopters. (See also Cordy—long stroke landing gear, Figure 3.110—and costs in the Glossary.)

The inventor's playfulness was picked up by the editor of *Aircraft* in writing of Bissell's appraisal of a certain aeronautical promoter.

> "Mr. Joseph E. Bissell of Pittsburgh, Pa. says that a certain Washingtonian who is attracting considerable attention through his connection in the aeronautical movement reminds him of the British general caught by the Yankees in the War of the Revolution. Says Mr. Bissell "The Yankees sent him back for fear the enemy might get a good one in his place!" [3.52]

1914/1904 Anonymous

The period 1920 and later was the era of interest in the "baby aeroplane" or "flying flivver", names for "everyman's" airplane. (See also the 1931 Nelson helicopter.) There is a helicopter report of Carr E. Booker of Raleigh, North Carolina, builder of such an airplane. In a statement believed to be written in the late 1940s, Booker is quoted as saying:

> "In the year 1904, I was employed as a machinist, not the screw-driver and plier variety. The firm with whom I was employed built for a college professor a helicopter of his design; yes, it was completed as far as we are concerned by the blueprints furnished. It did actually lift the pilot about ten feet (3.1 meters), as many ventures of such, finances gave out and in order, further development of this helicopter ceased."

The hovering claim is not credible, nor the date [3.53]. There is nothing to suggest the designer understood the fundamental problem confronted by all the early experimenters: hovering instability and its controllability. Only with divine intervention could he have risen to 10 feet—and hover there.

1917 Crocker-Hewitt

A helicopter intended for use in the First World War was conceived by Francis B. Crocker and Peter Cooper-Hewitt. (Patents 1,350,454 1,350,455 1,350,456 1,378,112 and 1,378,114.) [3.54] The project had popular appeal as revealed by a full page treatment in the magazine section of the *New York Sun*. [3.55] The configuration chosen was a coaxial rotor system with two blades per rotor (Figures 3.38–3.41). The idea was to attain high tip speeds at low angular velocity, using a large diameter, with action more like a *rotating wing* (as they put it) than a

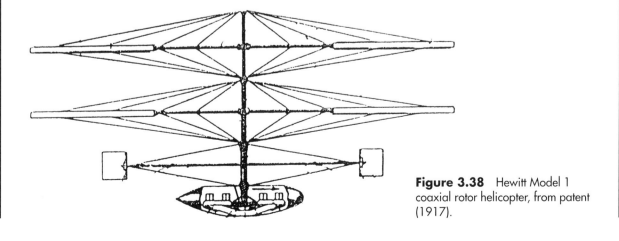

Figure 3.38 Hewitt Model 1 coaxial rotor helicopter, from patent (1917).

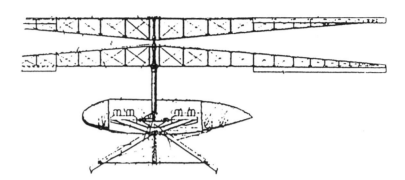

Figure 3.39 Hewitt coaxial helicopter showing variant with cantilever blades (1917).

propeller. The blades and profiles were shaped like an airplane wing.

A rig was built and tested in Ampere, New Jersey in 1918. The rotors with a 2.14 meter (7 foot) gap had a 7.8 meter (25.5 foot) radius and a 76.2 cm (30 inch) chord. The aerodynamic surface (wing) started at 41 percent radius. These were connected to the hub by steel tubes. To avoid "chattering" (i.e., flutter) the blades were attached to the arms forward of the center of pressure. This feature also allowed some automatic variation in incidence due to blade (chordwise) elasticity. There was no provision for autorotative flight. The rig was powered by two 74.6 kW (100 hp) electric motors.

At 70 rpm the lift developed was 10.0 kN (2250 lb), using 94.4 kW (126.5 hp) or 134.2 N/kW

(20.2 lb/hp). With full 149.2 kW (200 hp) delivered, the maximum lift produced was 17.8 kN (4000 lb).

The Crocker-Hewitt activities reveal an understanding of the fundamental aerodynamic principles of a rotor. The experimenters also may be the first to use the term *rotating wing* for a helicopter rotor. In the engineering world, helicopters are commonly referred to as *rotary wing aircraft*.

The helicopter work of these pioneers, particularly that of Hewitt, reveals historically the first awareness of the theoretical (hovering) principles that govern modern helicopters. Their theory was qualitatively sound, though the numerical values assigned to the parameters were slightly off, or optimistic. The theory described in Hewitt's patent 1,350,454 of 1920 used figure of merit, but put no name to this parameter. As mentioned above, he recognized the need for large diameter rotors, turning at low tip speeds, and added this view was a:

> "distinct departure from all prior attempts known to me in helicopters or aeroplanes. Heretofore propellers have always been of relatively small diameter, driven at high peripheral speed and at high angular velocity, acting upon a relatively small jet of air put into rapid motion and greatly disturbed."

Regarding rotors. Hewitt specified the following:

1. A diameter equal or greater than that derived from the term $(0.7/17)(T/hp)(T^{0.5})$, where T = thrust (lb) and T/hp = power loading (lb/hp). (This version of figure of merit solves for diameter in feet.)

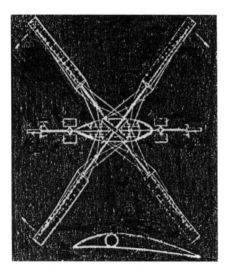

Figure 3.40 Hewitt coaxial helicopter plan view including blade profile (1917).

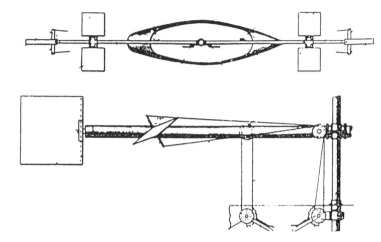

Figure 3.41 Hewitt longitudinally symmetrical control system (1917).

2. The power loading (T/hp) to be 12 lb/hp or more.
3. The rotor aspect ratio to be 5 to 1.
4. The ratio: blade area/disk area to be less than 0.12.
5. The engine, rotor-speed reduction ratio to be 8 to 1. For "high powered" machines the value to be 30 to 1.
6. The actual blade (wing) surface to start at 20 to 40 percent radius.
7. The rotor pitch axis to be ahead of the center of pressure (so pressure variations do not cause pitch divergence).

What follows is a comparison of figure of merit with Hewitt's parameters which imply it. The equations are solved for diameter along with a numerical example (sea level air density).

Figure of merit (M):
$$D = (1/33.7\,M)(T/hp)(T^{0.5})$$
Hewitt's parameter:
$$D_{min} = (1/24.3)(T/hp)(T^{0.5})$$

Hewitt presumed the maximum figure of merit (M) is (24.3/33.7) = 0.72, a high value implying a very clean rotor. In fact 0.72 is a good practical value for modern helicopters; however Hewitt suggests actual values will be lower. (See also figure of merit in the Glossary, and Appendix G.) His test results very likely in ground effect (IGE) yield M = 0.59 to 0.74 for the two measurements. OGE the values are estimated to be respectively 0.39 and 0.47, which are realistic for his time.

Overall, Hewitt's work would satisfy Item 2 (adequate hovering thrust) of the priorities listed in the present introduction. Crocker and Hewitt were definitely on the right track, revealing a good understanding of power requirements and rotor design. They had the professionalism to carry their work further, but did not. If with a little patience, and looking over Cierva's shoulder, they could have made history.

1919 Berliner

Shortly after World War I Emile Berliner was engaged in the development of his version of a coaxial rotor helicopter (Patent 1,527,666 and Figures 3.42 and 3.43). The effort was undertaken with the aid of his son Henry, who was to take over the work of his father.

The rotors consisted of two fixed-pitch propellers driven by a rotary engine. Variable vanes in the slipstream were used as wake spoilers for pitch control, and also to counteract any residual torque of the counterrotating rotors. [3.56]

Characteristics:

Rotor diameter	4 m (13 ft)
Blade chord	25.4 cm (10 in)
Rotor speed	600 rpm
Weight empty	280 kg (617 lb)
Best thrust (IGE)	4 kN (900 lb)

Evaluated in the 1919–1920 period, the machine hovered but with the aid of an assistant on the ground who steadied it (Figure 3.43). This configuration was then abandoned for development of the lateral rotor principle, still with propeller-like rotors.

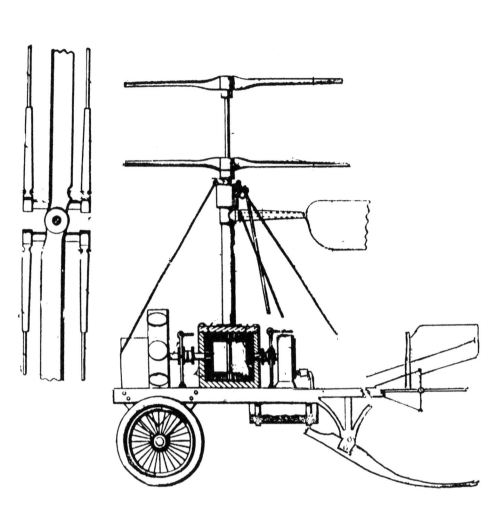

Figure 3.42   Henry Berliner coaxial rotor concept (1920).

Figure 3.43   Henry Berliner coaxial rotor prototype apparently requiring ground contact for steady hovering (1919).

1920s Young

The illustration of an early coaxial rotor helicopter (Figure 3.44) was published in an issue of *Air Beat* (Journal of the Airborne Law Enforcement Association). [3.57] The pilot was identified as Oklahoma City police officer-pilot J. J. Young. The configuration is similar to the 1919 Berliner coaxial. The rotors consisted of carved propellers driven by a rotary engine. From the design it appears it was built in the early 1920s.

The project is of interest not only for revealing the early appreciation of law enforcement possibilities of the helicopter, but (aside from practicality) it represents a simple, clean, and logical concept for its time. The design as shown may not be complete. There are no visible provisions for hovering control, and no evidence of a fuel tank of any size. Judging from the wide track landing gear, the inventor anticipated some hovering instability problems.

1920 Beach

In 1920 William J. Beach, an Australian living in Manhattan, had underway a helicopter project. [3.58] He believed his concept had a good chance of winning the forthcoming Michelin competition and the $1 million prize.

The novel feature of the lateral rotor helicopter (Figure 3.45) was the means for driving the ro-

Figure 3.44 Young coaxial rotor helicopter prototype (1920s).

Figure 3.45 Beach lateral rotor model. Compressed air drive (1920).

tors. One of the lateral units consisted of a set of coaxial, counterrotating rotors. Each unit had two rotary engines below it. The engine traveled around the rotor axis of rotation in a path resembling planetary gears. The inventor believed by mounting the engines away from the rotor axis, the power to drive the rotor was reduced.

A 2 foot long model was built (Figure 3.45) and demonstrated to potential investors. For power the model used a group of compressed air engines fed by a flexible hose connected to a ground-based power supply. During a demonstration the model hovered about 0.6 meters (2 feet), but had to be steadied by hand. Beach announced plans to build a full scale helicopter using motorcycle engines, but the machine did not materialize. Beach's idea introduced two flywheels to the system. Each one would add a gyroscopic couple to its rotor assembly as the case for a single propeller airplane in pitching, for example. However the force effect on the helicopter itself would be cancelled out by the counterrotation.

1920–1933 Exel

George Exel of Clifton, New Jersey on his own spent over 45 years in helicopter development. Yet he is little known as a helicopter pioneer. [3.59] In this interval he built seven machines or major variants, in three configurations. In chronological order the types were coaxial, corotor, and tail rotor.

Machine No. 1 was built and tested during 1920–1922. Figure 3.46 shows the helicopter under construction. The two-blade coaxial rotors were powered initially by a 20 hp (14.9 kW) Buick engine. Longitudinal control was by CG change, using a sliding seat. A surface in the rotor wake served for yaw control. During indoor tests, rotor vibration proved excessive and the power insufficient for hovering. The Buick was replaced by a more powerful rotary engine.

Characteristics:

Rotor diameter	6.6 m (21.5 ft)
Rotor speed	130 rpm
Gross weight	440 kg (968 lb)
Empty weight	297 kg (654 lb)
Powerplant, Gnôme rotary	37.3 kW (50 hp) @ 1400 rpm

The new variant was tested at Teterboro Airport. Without the pilot on board it was barely able to hover, and the control system was ineffective. Exel found the type of blades used were difficult to balance. He then abandoned the simple coaxial configuration for the corotor system. This machine No. 2 (Figure 3.47) was built and tested during 1923–1924.

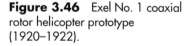
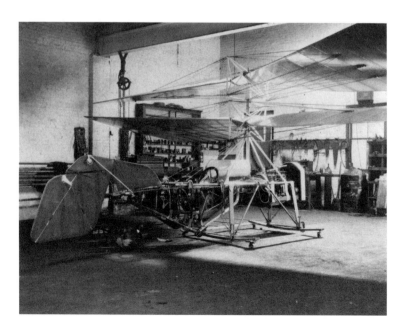

Figure 3.46 Exel No. 1 coaxial rotor helicopter prototype (1920–1922).

Figure 3.47 Exel No. 2 corotor helicopter (1923–1924).

The corotor system refers to the idea of reacting shaft torque of an engine-driven propeller or screw by the crankcase, to which the reacting rotor is attached. With the rotary engine (crankcase drive), the idea most likely suggested itself. In Exel's arrangement the crankcase drives the lifting screw (propeller) while the otherwise stationary shaft of the rotary, drives the rotor in counterrotation. Considering hovering only, the basic analytical equalities are the following.

The total power of the two rotating elements is the sum of the powers of the lifting screw and the rotor. This total power is theoretically equal to the engine *static* (one element fixed) power. The torque of the lifting screw is equal to the (reactive) torque of the rotor, and either is equal to the static torque of the engine. Because the torques are equal, and the total power a sum, and by definition of power, the static speed of the engine is the sum of the speeds of the screw (propeller) and the rotor. With these givens, the preliminary design can proceed with two considerations:

1. The total (uninstalled) power beyond hovering must account for losses, as well a vertical climb power.
2. The rotor must be sized to permit power-off, autorotative descent.

Note that the corotor principles just described are modern, and apparently, Exel worked out his system by trial and error unaware of these principles. In either case, the system compels the propeller to carry most of the helicopter weight, as described below.

Machine No. 2 (under construction, Figure 3.47) shows the lifting screw (an ordinary propeller) driven by the crankcase of the rotary engine located in the rotor hub. The engine shaft drives the rotor. With this system the gearbox of No. 1 was eliminated. The controls were the same as on the earlier helicopter.

Characteristics:

Rotor diameter	7.3 m (24 ft), 4 blades
Propeller diameter	2.5 m (8.33 ft), 2 blades
Powerplant, Le Rhône rotary	59.7 kW (80 hp) @ 1200 rpm

Late in 1923 tests were conducted indoors in Passaic, New Jersey. With full-throttle and the operator standing beside the machine, it barely lifted one wheel off the ground. After several tests the engine was replaced with a 110 hp (82.1 kW) Le Rhône rotary. Tests showed little improvement. In hindsight the redistribution of power with the larger engine gained him little, very likely because of the corotor principle.

Around this time Exel entered his machine in the British helicopter competition of 1925–1926, and was probably one of the few entrants with

Figure 3.48   *Exel No. 3 Triaxial helicopter (1924–1925).*

the semblance of a real helicopter on hand. At this point in the development Exel decided the rotor system needed a reduction gear. He introduced to machine No. 2 an intermediate rotor, making it No. 3 (Figure 3.48). This variant he called *triaxial* because of the three rotating members. Development took place during 1924–1925 (Figure 3.49).

Machine No. 3 had a new lifting screw with a diameter of 1.8 meters (6 feet), while that of the two-blade intermediate rotor was 4.3 meters (14 feet). The latter included in its hub a planetary gearbox. The triaxial design is disclosed in Exel's patent 1,561,424. Tests were conducted in Montville, New Jersey. This variant was able to lift off the ground but the control system proved to be of little use. Machine No. 4 (Figure 3.50) is a modified version of the previous one. The engine shaft was lengthened 51 cm (20 in.) to lower the CG of the helicopter. The intermediate two-blade rotor was replaced by a four-blade rotor with a 4.9 meter (16 foot) diameter. Lowering the CG did not improve controllability, however the thrust was improved with the new intermediate rotor.

Late in 1926 a severe windstorm destroyed the helicopter (Figure 3.51). Exel salvaged the engine, and this was used in machine No. 5. At the time of the accident he was working on a method of cyclic control using ailerons on the main rotor blades. This system along with a swashplate were introduced in his No. 5 variant (Figure 3.52 and 3.53). The helicopter was a corotor without the intermediate rotor. The swashplate accounted for both cyclic and collective control of the main rotor, which now looked like the modern high aspect ratio type.

Characteristics:

Upper rotor diameter	2.9 m (9.5 ft)
Upper rotor speed	1100 rpm
Lower rotor diameter	10.4 m (34 ft)
Lower rotor speed	90 rpm
Powerplant Le Rhône rotary	82.1 kW (110 hp)
Engine speed	1175 rpm

Tests (1930–1933) showed the rotor to be responsive to the cyclic and collective system used. However vibration was excessive, and the machine was incapable of hovering. Exel concluded a speed reduction gearbox was necessary, but the one he had was destroyed with machine No. 4. With this program he abandoned helicopter work for development of a two-stroke cycle engine.

Shortly after World II, and the emergence of the practical helicopter, Exel renewed his interest in rotorcraft. At this time (1946) he built his sixth helicopter, the Model 100. This machine with swashplate controls was flown about 70 hours.

Figure 3.49 Exel Triaxial side view drawing from patent (1924).

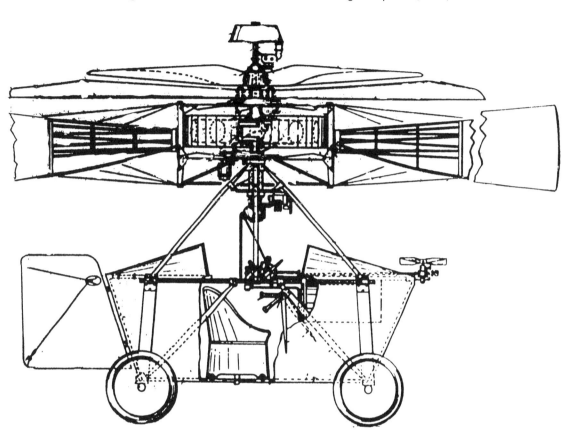

Figure 3.50 Exel No. 4 Triaxial helicopter variant (1925–1926).

Figure 3.51 Exel No. 4 wrecked by a storm (1926).

Figure 3.52 Exel No. 5 corotor with a swashplate (1930–1933).

Figure 3.53 George Exel with No. 5 helicopter (1930–1933).

Figure 3.54 George Exel in his seventh and last helicopter (1956). The sixth (Model 100) was a conventional tail rotor helicopter built in 1946.

Lack of funds terminated the project. However in 1967 at age 74, he built his seventh and last helicopter (Figure 3.54).

The corotor concept had its appeal to others as well. The system is inefficient because it puts the main support of the helicopter on a small, highly loaded propeller. The disk loading on this screw (propeller) can be as high as 10 times that of the rotor. In this example hovering thrust on the propeller is 68 percent of the total required. A reasonable conclusion is the main rotor is there mainly to satisfy autorotation. Considering speed, 82 percent of the static value is in the propeller, with 18 percent in the rotor. Exel's rpm values for No. 5 (above) do not add up probably for practical reasons that could be related to the engine rating or his readings. Exel's rotor speeds of 1100 and 90 add up to 1190, while the engine rating is 1175 rpm. It is also possible he oversped the engine to get more power out of it, a logical move but not a wise one with the corotor. As suggested previously, most of the power increase would go into an inefficient propeller,

and the performance improvement would be marginal.

Theoretically the optimum corotor exists when both rotating elements have the same diameter and rpm. Exel was heading in this direction with introduction of the intermediate rotor and a planetary reduction gearbox. It appears the most efficient corotor is a conventional coaxial rotor helicopter.

Judging from his work, Exel was one of the few who went far beyond the "one-off" stage in helicopter development. Exel's objective in all this activity never appeared to surpass the personal challenge of producing a practical helicopter. An unassuming, candid individual, he is worthy of recognition as one of America's dedicated pioneers.

1921 Leinweber

The Leinweber helicopter prototype was a Chicago project of Victor H. Leinweber, sup-

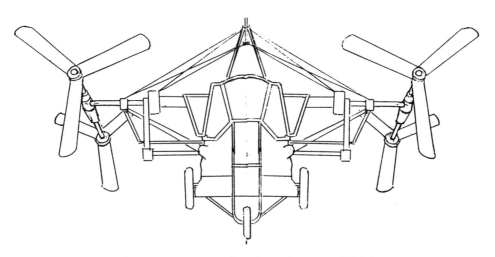

Figure 3.55 Leinweber tiltrotor front view (1921).

ported by three family members. The machine, a result of 16 years experimentation is disclosed in patent 1,344,640 (Figures 3.55 and 3.56). The prototype was built during 1920–1921 with the aid of Glenn Curtiss. The configuration was an early application of the tiltrotor configuration. Each of the lateral rotor units consisted of a set of coaxial counterrotating screws located at either end of a mast. This mast pivoted to incline the rotor assemblies. [3.60]

The screws resembled ships' propellers, especially designed by Leinweber. Two Gnôme rotary engines of 74.6 kW (100 hp) each pow-

ered the machine. The machine weight was 681 kg (1500 lb) and the rotor diameter approximately 5.5m (18 ft). The helicopter used a compressed air system for "automatic" control, along with a conventional rudder. There was no provision for power-off safe descent. Little has been published on the tests except that it failed to fly.

The Leinweber approach to screw design was one favored by others. The focus in minimizing hover power appears to be on efficiency through planform shape and twist, rather than on disk loading.

Figure 3.56 Leinweber tiltrotor prototype (1921).

1921 Hall

In 1921 the Hall Airplane Company of Los Angeles had under construction an airplane-helicopter (Figure 3.57). Called *vertical lift*, the aircraft was intended for operations in Mexico in areas not accessible by other means. The concept was developed by Chris Mathews and C. S. Hall (Patent 1,307,826). [3.61]

The biplane had circular openings in the middle of the wings. The upper opening contained a fixed-pitch lifting propeller, while the lower wing opening, about 20 percent greater in diameter, allowed the propeller wake to clear the aircraft. The rotor appears to be inadequate for anything more than an improved forward climb rate, which they claimed would be 18,000 feet (5490 meters) in 10 minutes.

With this design a significant amount of thrust would be lost in the wake-drag or download on the fuselage. Considering the steep takeoff, the wing area (relatively lower) is selected for cruise flight. Even so, the large openings would suggest an inefficient wing with regard to overall lift-drag ratio. The designers would have a problem in deciding the operating modes of the lifting screw and tractor propeller, and the drive system. While the screw would operate in the steep climb, they probably expected it to operate in cruise as well. Hence both propeller and screw would be directly connected.

The power-off (engine failure) condition involves a different design consideration. It is preferable to declutch the engine and lock propeller and lifting screw, to prevent rotation and drag increase. Considering the reduced wing area and high-drag configuration it is likely the power-off landing speed would be very high, probably 65–70 percent of the maximum speed of contemporary airplanes. One could take off from a confined area but could not land there safely in an emergency.

The designer C. S. Hall is apparently the same individual who formed the Cunningham-Hall Aircraft Corporation in Rochester, New York, in 1928. In the late 1930s the company produced some advanced, conventional airplanes.

1922 Pittsburgh

Advocates of vertical flight in the early 20th century chose at least three approaches to rotor design, some of which have been described. One was to use a propeller (airplane or specially shaped), the second was to view it as a kind of marine screw where every element

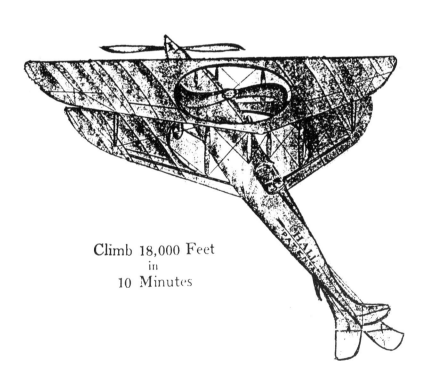

Climb 18,000 Feet
in
10 Minutes

Figure 3.57 Hall "vertical lift" airplane-helicopter concept (1921).

(section) must operate at its highest efficiency (as in Leinweber's case) or a highly twisted helix, while the third approach saw it as a rotating wing of high aspect ratio. Only the last was sensitive to diameter, lack of which is practically a theme in this book.

A propeller specially designed for helicopters was built by Pittsburgh Airplane and Motor Company in 1922. The laminated ash propeller with square tips had a diameter of 2.0 meters (6.5 feet) with a constant chord of 27.7 cm (10.9 in). The screw to be used on a three rotor helicopter, was designed to absorb 1/3 the power of a Liberty 12 engine. The output of this powerplant was 298–313 kW (400–420) hp.

The screw was whirl-tested at the Wright Field Propeller Laboratory (Dayton) in 1922. [3.62] A conclusion revealed it was no better than a conventional propeller. From test results the figure of merit calculates to be 0.53–0.61, confirming the conclusion.

1922–1923 Berliner

After abandoning the coaxial rotor principle (1919), Henry Berliner produced a lateral rotor prototype that underwent substantial modifications. He retained the fixed-pitch propellers for lift (Figure 3.58). The machine was a pure helicopter built around a Nieuport biplane fuselage. Its nose-mounted rotary engine was turned to point aft to drive the rotors.

Hovering pitch control was by a small variable pitch propeller mounted at the rear top surface of the fuselage. Vanes in the rotor slipstream provided lateral control. Roll was accomplished by closing the vanes on one side (like a shutter). Closure spoiled the thrust on that side and the resulting differential thrust rolled the machine. The design did not account for power-off safe landing.

The rotors with a diameter of 4.5 meters (14.8 feet) were driven by a 110 hp (82.1 kW) Le Rhône rotary engine. With the pilot the total weight was 613 kilograms (1350 pounds), and 568 kilograms (1250 pounds) empty.

The machine was demonstrated at College Park, Maryland in June 1922. It made a few flights, hovering up to 3.7 meters (12 feet). At 2.1 meters (7 feet) the machine covered 91.5 meters (100 yards) at about 24.1 km/h (15 mph). Overall performance was unsatisfactory and Berliner dropped the pure helicopter for the helicoplane configuration. First as a triplane [3.63] and then as a cleaner biplane. [3.64] The problem of power-off flight was treated by adding the wings.

The triplane (Figures 3.59–3.63) used the same pitch and roll controls as the helicopter. In addition to its normal use, the rudder bar introduced a yaw moment in hovering. This yaw was obtained by differentially tilting the rotor axes in the longitudinal direction (Patent 1,570,121).

Figure 3.58 Henry Berliner lateral rotor helicopter (1922–1925).

Figure 3.59   Henry Berliner triplane helicopter in flight (1923).

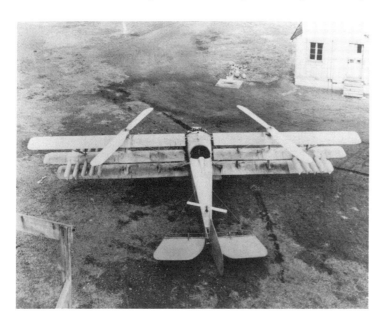

Figure 3.60   Henry Berliner triplane-helicopter showing lateral control vanes below airscrews and longitudinal control propeller at tail (1922–1925).

Figure 3.61   Henry Berliner triplane-helicopter side view (1922–1925).

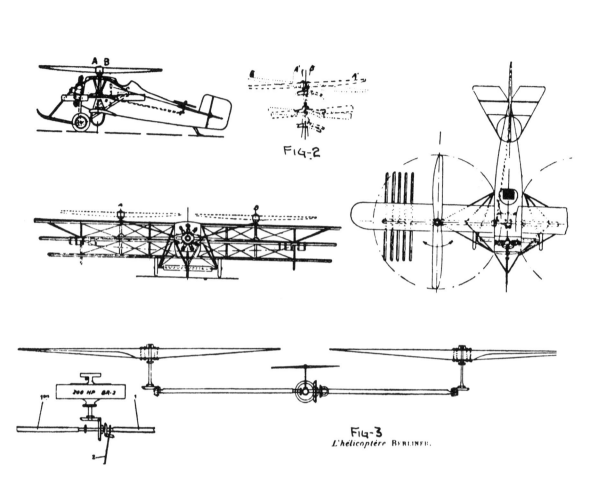

Figure 3.62   Henry Berliner triplane-helicopter three view arrangement (1922–1925).

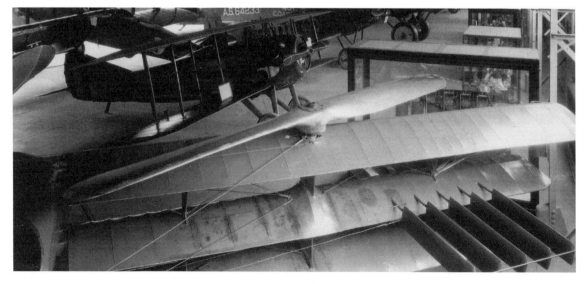

Figure 3.63   A 1950s photograph of the Smithsonian exhibit revealing details of the wing, airscrew, and vane assembly of the Berliner triplane-helicopter.

Characteristics:

Wingspan (maximum)	11.6 m (38 ft)
Wing chord	56 cm (22 in)
Powerplant Bentley rotary	149.2 kW (200 hp)
Rotor diameter	4.6 m (15 ft)
Blade chord	35.6 cm (14 in)
Blade twist (nominal)	8.7 degrees
Rotor spacing	5.2 m (17 ft)
Rotor speed	550 rpm
Tail rotor diameter	122 cm (48 in)
Tail rotor speed	700 rpm
Weights	
Empty	749.1 kg (1650 lb)
Fuel (20 minutes)	27.2 kg (60 lb)
Oil	3.7 kg (8 lb)
Pilot	90.8 (200 lb)
Total	870.8 (1918 lb)

The blades of laminated spruce used special profiles and pitch distribution. With the engine pointing inward, it was hand-cranked by a box in the tail rotor shafting. Use of the high-speed tail rotor drive for starting required less cranking effort. While starting torque was lower, more crank turns were required. An unpowered model was wind tunnel tested to establish the best gliding performance. The best lift-drag ratio measured was 4.0

A number of controlled flights with the triplane were made January–March 1924. A report by Harold Harris of the Army Air Corps revealed the following: The taxiing speed of 50 mph (80.5 km/h) was considered high. The machine was unable to fly free of ground effect. At 15 feet (4.6 meters), the maximum flight duration was about 1½ hours. In a crude calculation of the height-velocity point, the craft was considered capable of a safe landing from 800 feet (244 meters) at 56 mph (90.1 km/h). (A comparable height today at that speed would be about 150 feet (45.8 meters). There were no lateral or longitudinal oscillations in flight, and the yaw tendency was within control limits. The pilot believed the weight could be reduced about 200 pounds (90.8 kilograms). This machine is now in the Smithsonian.

Figure 3.63 shows the triplane on exhibit there in the 1950s. This view reveals the lateral control vanes. Apparently lateral control was one of Berliner's major problems, since different arrangements were tried, first with controls on the propellers, which proved ineffective. The triplane was flown initially without slipstream spoilers (Figure 3.59), then with vanes (Figures 3.60–3.63). The vanes, mainly for hovering, were located in the slipstream of most the propeller radius.

The biplane (Figures 3.64–3.66) shows a different approach to improve the airflow, by using a

Figure 3.64 Henry Berliner helicoplane with staff in conference.

Figure 3.65 Henry Berliner helicoplane in flight.

Figure 3.66 Another view of Berliner helicoplane in flight. Best performance was 64.4 km/h (40 mph) at 9.2 meters (30 feet) (1925).

shorter upper wing. He abandoned the vanes for controllable wing tips (ailerons) with their own flaps. Apparently the intent of the flapped wing tips was to obtain high lift coefficients for yaw control in hovering. However this arrangement also introduces a rearward component to the lift, which in hovering had to be corrected by forward tilt of the propellers. Compared with vanes, this system would give better control in forward flight, since the former was optimized for hovering. Overall Berliner probably had better lateral control, but he did not have a helicopter. He had developed a STOL aircraft. This simpler helicoplane (Figures 3.64–3.66) appeared in the summer of 1925.

Characteristics:

Rotor diameter	6.1 m (20 ft)
Rotor speed	360 rpm
Gross weight, 1 hour fuel	840 kg (1850 lb)
Powerplant Bentley rotary	149 kW (200 hp)

In that year the machine was flown out of ground effect at a height of 9.2 meters (30 feet). It was maneuvered laterally 366 meters (400 yards), and attained a forward speed of 64.4 km/h (40 mph).

Berliner entered a helicoplane in the British helicopter competitions of 1924 and 1925–1926. This machine was a monoplane with a wing area of 16.7 square meters (180 square feet), the screws rotating below the wing panels. At the time the lateral control system was undefined. The entrant was considering three options: slipstream blocking, differential rpm, and pitch variation. (His best choice would have been pitch variation.) For this design the main rotor diameter was 6.1 meters (20 feet), and that of the lifting tail rotor, 1.4 meters (4.5 feet). The weights of the machine were 613 kilograms (1350 pounds) empty, and 831 kilograms (1830 pounds) loaded. Berliner's entry noted the machine was to be completed in September 1924.

Combining the work of father and son there was no greater persistence than their effort to produce a successful helicopter. The persistence is evident in the number of configurations and variations tried, all leading to a compromise to get something that worked. But the principle is unforgiving, if it cannot hover it is not a heli-

copter. Ideas that started out simple as the lateral rotor helicopter, ended up with wings and appendages. It is curious that Berliner's last configuration (the single wing) was the one J. C. Johnson in 1929 started with (Figure 3.94). The complexity plus poor performance as either helicopter or airplane would lead any rational individual to question the tractability of such a thing as a helicopter. Berliner himself must have come to this conclusion for he gave up the search for vertical flight in favor of the proven fixed-wing aircraft.

In retrospect he was on the right track with lateral rotors, as demonstrated by the Focke FW-61. What is difficult to explain is why he (or others) did not abandon the propeller rotor when Cierva in 1923 demonstrated the value of a flapping hinge rotor. This idea could have started Berliner in a new direction of investigation.

1922 DeBothezat

George DeBothezat (1882–1940) was one of the more prominent and successful pioneers of the early helicopter era. His interest in lifting screws dates to 1916 in Russia. Among his works was a detailed theory of this system of propulsion. In 1917 Saint Petersburg he conceived the design of a helicopter. However the Revolution compelled him to leave the country and eventually emigrate to America.

At the end of the First World War DeBothezat proposed to the U.S. Army Air Service construction of a machine of his design (Patent 1,573,228). The Flying Section of the Material Division agreed to support the program, eventually to the amount of $2 million. [3.65] Work began on a prototype in January 1921, with the first flight occurring in October 1922. The helicopter (Figures 3.67 and 3.68) was a single-seat quadrotor. The airframe consisted of an open structure of aluminum alloy tubing in the form of a cross, with one main and one set of transverse (lateral) frames. Each of the four ends supported a rotor system. The axes of the rotors were inclined inward toward each other, and each was provided with collective pitch control. At their ends, the two lateral beam-frames supported thrusting screws. These "control propellers" featured variable pitch. There was also a

Figure 3.67   DeBothezat helicopter in flight (1922).

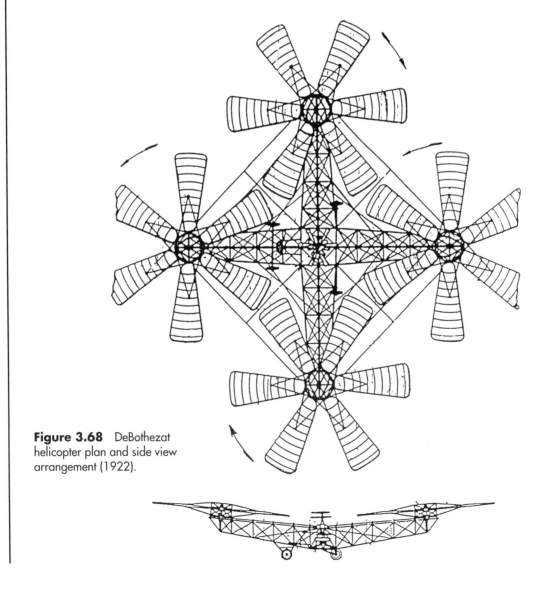

Figure 3.68   DeBothezat
helicopter plan and side view
arrangement (1922).

small auxiliary lifting screw at the intersection of the beam-frames. Located below this screw was the rotary engine powerplant with its output flange facing upward.

All the screws were turned by a mechanical drive system. The latter consisted of a main gearbox at the engine with shafting to each of the main rotor gearboxes. The lateral rotor boxes included an angled shaft leading to boxes at the two control propellers. There was no free-wheeling device in the rotors.

The pilot's controls consisted of a stick, pedals, and a coaxial handwheel system. Typical actuation consisted of sprockets, chains, cables, and pulleys. The stick was used for lateral and longitudinal control of the helicopter, a sense now common with the helicopter cyclic pitch system. The inclination was produced by differential thrust of the corresponding two rotors. The pedals differentially operated the two control propellers to yaw the machine. The larger of the coaxial handwheels actuated main rotor collective pitch, while the smaller one controlled the pitch of the auxiliary lifting screw (at the frame center). These screws were part of the system for optimizing power-off descent. Power-off, the main rotor pitch was reduced to a low angle, continuing rotation in its original sense. Increasing pitch of the auxiliary screw (using the small hand wheel) prevented overspeeding the system. Added functions of this central screw were to cool the engine and provide some lift. This auxiliary screw, described in DeBothezat's patent, was later removed.

To hover, the pilot set the desired collective pitch with the large handwheel. The throttle opened to increase rotor speed until the machine lifted off. The pilot then concentrated on flying the helicopter with the stick and pedals. Separating the throttle from the collective pitch (large) handwheel increased the pilot's workload, an idea avoided today.

Characteristics:

Lifting rotors (four, six-bladed)
Diameter	8.1 m (26.5 ft)
Blade tip chord	1.53 m (5 ft)
Rotor speed	90 rpm
Diameter, control propeller	61 cm (24 in)
Speed, control propeller	1000 rpm

Powerplant	Bentley BR-2 rotary
Engine power	149–164 kW (200–220 hp)

(Replaced a 112–127 kW (150–170 hp) Le Rhône rotary.)

Weights	
Gross, including pilot and fuel	1680 kg (3700 lb)
Empty	1544 kg (3400 lb)
Disk loading	8.3 kg/m^2 (1.7 lb/ft^2)
Power loading	10.4 kg/kW (17.1 lb/hp)

Flight evaluation was undertaken at McCook Field, Dayton, Ohio. The test pilot was Art Smith, a well-known exhibition flyer, with two Army pilots also flying the machine. Over 50 test flights were made from the first (October 1922) to April 1923. Overall these totaled 100. The flights were conducted in ground effect. On the latter date the helicopter lifted the pilot and three men hanging on the airframe to about 1.2 meters (4 feet) for a few minutes. The machine also hovered at 4.6 meters (15 feet). The contract called for a 91.5 meter (300 foot) hover ceiling which the machine failed to attain.

The Army's official summary report on the program included the following comments:

Favorable features
1. Inherent stability. DeBothezat fulfilled his claims of securing restoring moments in a helicopter comparable to those of airplane stability.
2. The control arrangement is similar to that of an airplane.
3. Controllability. More positive response than in many other types of helicopters. Only the time lag is objectionable.
4. Lifting capacity. Low ceiling due to overweight rather than lifting screws.
5. General design principles. A complete helicopter fulfilling at least theoretically all the requirements for a helicopter.

Unfavorable features
1. Mechanical failure of any one of the screw elements results in a loss of control and stability, due to dissymmetry. Pilots experienced gear and blade failures. Units not reliable, particularly the bearings. The transmission too complex, with inherently low reliability.

2. Control sensitivity. A fine adjustment required to change pitch, and the response much slower than that of an airplane.

3. Power-off descent. The principle is sound, but the time to operate the controls to convert the ship is too long. Wheel control for overall pitch had to move against air loads and friction. The time involved considered the main difficulty.

4. High structural weight.

5. Mechanical complexity makes construction (i.e., erection) and maintenance lengthy.

6. Rotary engine location is extremely dangerous with respect to the pilot. Plane of rotation passes directly through pilot's chest.

7. A problem is involved in abandoning the machine in the air. Provision is made for a backward somersault through the fuselage truss. (See Figure 3.67.)

8. Blade alignment. If not aligned properly, different thrusts occur on all four rotors. This can be corrected with the pitch control, but it results in large torques which are difficult to control. Impossible to secure directional stability, even with constant movement of the foot pedals.

9. Structural detail defects. Screw blade-spiders (holding the pitch controls) tend to fail under air loads. Several have failed and it is feared one will give way under tests. The main frame experienced weaving.

During tests the pilot was too busy maintaining hovering equilibrium to venture into a transition. Generally, the report emphasizes flying qualities and human factors with additional commentary on the structure. It is interesting that many experimental configurations of the 1950s revealed similar general problems. Even today any helicopter maintenance chief will confirm as perpetual, the bearings problem.

The report was prepared by W. F. Gerhardt, Chief, Flight Research, and Harold Harris, Chief, Flying Section. Gerhardt later (1926) conducted helicopter model experiments on his own at McCook with the assistance of Paul Stanley. Stanley later joined Pitcairn Aircraft (1929), and became Chief Engineer of Autogiro Company of America in 1941. (See also 1924 Pitcairn.) The helicopter was flown by Thurman H. Bane of the Air Corps. Not only was he the first military helicopter pilot, but a strong supporter of the project. (See also 1924 Bane.)

The problem of maintaining hovering balance close to the ground resulted in addition of bumpers to each of the beam-frames. (Compare Figures 3.67 and 3.69.) Figure 3.69 also shows DeBothezat by one of the control propellers, which were vulnerable without the bumpers.

Published data, including whirl tests with a single rotor, yield an unrealistic figure of merit. In one test at 100 rpm, rotor thrust was 6.7 kN (1500 lb), absorbing 41 kW (55 hp). The combination yields a figure of merit of 1.18. The anomaly may be attributed to absence of accounting for ground effect.

The project was dropped in January 1924. For years the DeBothezat helicopter was in storage at Wright Field. The demands of the Second World War resulted in its demolition to make room for other material. A rotor system was salvaged and it is preserved in the Smithsonian.

While DeBothezat is the individual usually associated with the helicopter, Ivan Jerome (Eremeef)

Figure 3.69 George DeBothezat beside helicopter, showing control rotor (1922).

Figure 3.70 Cartoon celebrating rotary wing pioneers showing Jerome sharing credit with DeBothezat (ca. 1953).

deserves recognition as the co-designer and construction head. Jerome saw DeBothezat as the mathematician, co-designer, public relations, and publicity man for the project. [3.66] Figure 3.70 a cartoon (ca. 1953) by C. H. Guischard of Massapequa, New York (Jerome's home town), is a tribute to all the major rotary wing pioneers. The list leads off with the "U.S.A.F.-Jerome-DeBothezat" name (1922), giving equal credit for the quadrotor helicopter to Jerome.

During 1937–1940 DeBothezat produced a single seat, coaxial rotor helicopter under the name of the Helicopter Corporation of America, of Long Island City, New York. [3.67] Two variants were developed, the last being the GB-5 (Figure 3.71). The interairscrew engine was a modified 63.4 kW (85 hp) Franklin. Control was obtained by shifting the CG of the fuselage relative to the rotors, and differential collective pitch was possible. The idea of the "suspended blades" was to produce inherent stability (Patent 2,116,334).

The 295 kg (650 lb) machine was flown by Boris Sergievsky, a long time associate of Igor Sikorsky as well as captain of his flying boats. Early tests resulted in a rollover, breaking a blade. As flown, the helicopter exhibited a high level of stability to the extent the pilot could observe its behavior while standing beside the machine. With subsequent modifications this characteristic was lost. On its last flight with the pilot the machine rose to its maximum height and rolled over.

The observed stability was likely due to the design fact the powerplant location brought the helicopter CG closer to the plane of rotation. The observation could have been in calm air, and no mention was made of drift. That the pilot stood beside the machine (without his CG-lowering weight) raised the CG even more. The configuration always would be more unstable with the pilot in the helicopter. The best that could be accomplished with this design was a demonstration of near-neutral stability. (See stability in the Glossary, and Figure H.8.)

Figure 3.71 DeBothezat GB-5 prototype with interairscrew engineer (1939).

DeBothezat patented (2,180,922) a strap-on version, shown in Figure 3.72. The strap-on idea has appealed to other designers as well, using rotors and rockets, Buck Rogers style. The practical problem is one rarely travels while hanging from supports (discounting parachuting), and human legs do not make good alighting gear in a forced landing, not to mention the possibility of serious injury. Such designs if developed eventually appear with the individual seated on some kind of landing frame.

1923 Perry

Thomas O. Perry was an inventor holding over 60 patents. One in 1904 was for a windmill

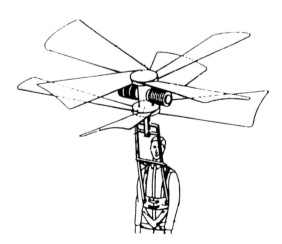

Figure 3.72 DeBothezat strap-on helicopter concept (1936).

whose blade design figured in his helicopter project. From 1914 Perry had ideas for helicopters that were patented between 1918 and 1920 (1,272,846; 1,345,101; and 1,524,309). Chicago Helicopters Limited was formed to promote his ideas, and in particular to raise money for a project. [3.68] A prototype was built in 1923 by Plamondon Manufacturing Company of Chicago. Around this time Perry entered the helicopter in the forthcoming British helicopter competition of 1924, and later in the 1925–1926 contest. The helicopter (Figure 3.73) featured coaxial counterrotating rotors. Like the 1918 Crocker-Hewitt, the inventor saw the blades as wings, and literally used them as fixed wings. The two rotors were attached to a simple, open-frame car carrying a crew of two.

A vertical tube ("spinal column") connected the rotor to the car. Below the floor were fuel tanks and a rotary engine. The engine pointed upward driving the rotors through a reduction system of spur gears (Figure 3.74). Rotor drive and rotor control actuators were located within the column. Variable pitch blades were attached to two hub-drums (sleeves) freely turning on the column. In his helicopter patent the inventor emphasized the need for a cambered blade section, an idea derived from his windmill patent.

The operator's controls consisted of three movable rings around the column at hand level (Figure 3.74). The rings served the separate functions of collective pitch change, cyclic pitch change (longitudinal only) and "steering" (yaw

Figure 3.73 Perry (Chicago Helicopters) prototype (1923).

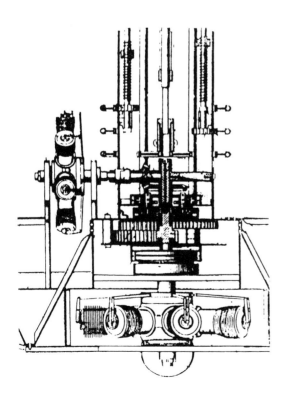

Figure 3.74 Perry helicopter control and drive system details (1923).

control). A horizontal tail surface mounted on a boom could be added if required for "soaring" or "volplaning".

The word *volplaning* is today a quaint aeronautical term that went out of use in the early 1920s. It appeared in 1909–1910, referring to aeroplane travel in general, but more commonly to "a dive descent or downward flight at a steep angle on the part of an aeroplane under control and with the engine shut off". Today this maneuver is called *gliding*. The word of French origin, a source of aeronautical terms, combines *vol* (flight) with *plané*. The latter suggests the way a bird extends its wings in a plane when soaring.

Figure 3.73 shows the ring locations and also the two collective pitch swashplates, just below the hub drums. Note as distinct from Exel, Perry's swashplate did not provide full cyclic control. The inventor appreciated the need to use collective pitch control as the way to change rotor thrust, while maintaining constant rotor speed. Differential collective pitch produced the yaw. Perry had a novel approach to power-off descent, his volplaning. By means of a handcrank with a gear at one end, the operator could engage the rotor drive system. Accordingly the blades became "fixed" wings lined up the flight direction. With this arrangement and the tail, the pilot could glide to a landing.

In his patent the inventor postulated the presence of continuous "wind waves" that would provide extra lift to the helicopter. Based on this concept he expected to stretch the power-off glide. Also power-off he envisioned reducing the "weather angle" i.e., reduce the "wing" angle of attack, through pitch control (depitching the blades) at the same time the blades were locked at right angles to the flight path.

Characteristics

Rotor diameter	14.3 m (47 ft)
(Replaced a 11.6 m–38 ft-rotor.)	
Blade chord	1.22 m (4 ft)
Rotor speed	60–80 rpm
Powerplant Le Rhône rotary	82.1 kW (110 hp)
	at 1250 rpm
Gross weight	1271 kg (2800 lb)
Empty weight	811 kg (1787 lb)
Height	4.9 m (16 ft)
Maximum speed (estimated)	113 km/h
	(70 mph)

Perry tested three models of his machine, including a "falling model" for power-off drop tests. The latter was launched from an airplane at 305 meters (1000 feet), descending at a rate of 229 m/min (750 fpm). Perry calculated the rotor thrust of the full scale machine to be 13.9 kN (3125 lb) under the following conditions:

Rotor diameter	11.6 m (38 ft)
Rotor speed	80 rpm
Blade pitch angle	8 degrees
Rotor power	64.2 kW (86 hp)
Disk loading	13.5 kg/m^2 (2.76 lb/ft^2)
Power loading	20.1 kg/kW (36.3 lb/hp)

Tied down with iron weights, the machine was tested at Lombard, Illinois. The results were not publicized, but apparently were unsatisfactory. Typical of many of these machines, it could have met with an accident in attempting to hover. The project was dropped due to lack of follow-on financing.

Overall, the inventor had some advanced ideas about rotor design and pitch control. Like others, he did not appreciate the criticality of time in pilot control response, probably in tests, and particularly in his approach to power-off descent. The calculated figure of merit is 1.59, indicating problems with lift, beyond the others concerning mechanical reliability and instability, common at the time.

1924 Pitcairn

The noted rotary wing pioneer (and benefactor) Harold F. Pitcairn was involved in helicopter development before his better known work of introducing the autogiro to America. [3.69] Assisting in this rotary wing activity which took place in the Philadelphia area was Agnew E. Larsen. He fixed Pitcairn's interest in 1920 with a state of the art study. Pitcairn tested models configured with frame-mounted, slipstream vanes used to react the single rotor torque (Figures 3.75 and 3.76). With this arrangement a plurality of narrow-chord, high aspect ratio blades were evaluated. Figure 3.75 shows a two-blade rotor model with adjustable vanes outboard of the 70 percent radius. These vanes filled an annular sector in the strongest part of the rotor wake. Attached to a central post was a rotatable motor housing, to which the vanes were attached. This meant the vanes were effective if the frame did not rotate relative to the ground. Torque reaction would be evaluated by altering the vane incidence angle. Figure 3.76 shows a four-blade rotor with a full frame of antitorque vanes. Most likely the multiple, high aspect ratio vane configuration was chosen to avoid the ground effect problem. (See 1936 LePage for a discussion.)

Model tests also were conducted using a Magnus-effect rotor for torque reaction. In retrospect this concept is similar to the (Boeing owned) McDonnell-Douglas Company Notar system in that circulation is induced to create a (lateral) force. There is "lift" circulation also around a conventional rotor blade radial axis.

Through his meetings in England with Cierva in 1925, the year may be taken as the date Pitcairn became formally interested in the autogiro. While there and through Larsen a design entry was submitted for the British helicopter competition. (See also Larsen in Appendix C.) The configuration included the antitorque vanes and a single, gyrocontrolled rotor.

Figure 3.75   Pitcairn helicopter model with partial complement of antitorque vanes (1924).

Work continued with helicopter models using hinged rotor blades, an idea indicating Pitcairn was in tune with the successful autogiro rotor system. The vanes were dropped in favor of a jet-driven rotor. Along the way, a rubber band driven tail rotor was evaluated, apparently with the jet rotor. The jet power was provided by a tank of carbon dioxide, driving a three-blade rotor. Four and five foot (1.2 and 1.5 meter) diameter rotors were evaluated, showing an improvement over the vane system.

By 1928 a 12 foot (3.7 meter) model using the same propulsion concept, was drop-tested from a balloon, the object being the evaluation of transition to autorotation. The test apparently was influenced by Cierva's work and of a type ignored by their contemporaries. Even so, no forward flights were attempted. The appearance of the autogiro led Pitcairn in this year to enter into negotiations with Cierva, and helicopter activity was dropped. However, as a licensor he maintained an interest in helicopters. (See below.)

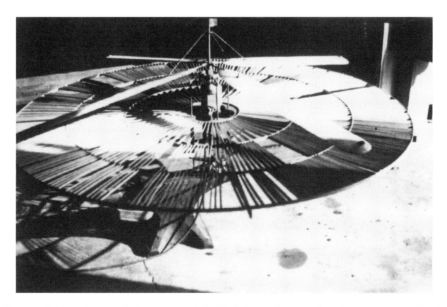

Figure 3.76   Pitcairn helicopter model with full complement of antitorque vanes (1924).

It was not until 1945 when Firestone, successor company to G & A (a licensee), produced its first helicopter. Two or three were built designated Model 45. It was a well designed machine for its time. Despite Army evaluation as the XR-9, the machine went nowhere, being preempted by the Sikorsky XR-4.

In 1929 Pitcairn obtained American rights to Cierva's inventions, and in the process emerged the Autogiro Company of America (ACA). This organization became the licensor, developer, and promoter of rotary wing (autogiro) flight in the United States. Autogiro construction was licensed to Kellett (1929) and Pitcairn, the airplane company (1929). In time there were several hundred ACA-patented ideas, some of which were directly applicable to helicopters (legally demonstrated after a lengthy lawsuit).

With Pitcairn's activity, the Philadelphia area became the cradle of rotary wing flight in America, also the logical place in the eyes of Jules Verne. In addition to Pitcairn and Larsen, other pioneers behind the rotary wing activity of the 1930s in this venue were Paul Stanley (ACA), Harris Campbell (ACA), Richard H. Prewitt (Kellett, and mentioned previously), Paul Hovgard (Kellett) and R. B. C. Noorduyn, who later formed his own airplane company. The leading pilots included James G. Ray (ACA), John Miller (Kellett), Fred "Slim" Soule (ACA), Dave Driskill (Kellett), and Lou Leavitt/Levy (Kellett). (Levy added two t's to his name in the spirit of the two Kelletts and a Prewitt in his company. He later became an Alaskan bush pilot.) The Kellett brothers went on to build helicopters.

Ultimately Frank Piasecki established his company in the Philadelphia area, [3.70] developing the tandem rotor helicopter, now Boeing Helicopters. The early work of Arthur M. Young (1931, described later) evolved into the Bell helicopter configuration. [3.71] Kellett sold its business to Hughes Aircraft in California, and engineers went with it. Finally, E. Burke Wilford of Pennsylvania Aircraft Syndicate (PAS) was identified with gyroplanes in the 1930s and later became an advocate of large transport helicopters. [3.72]

1924 Nemeth

In 1924 S. P. Nemeth of Chicago produced a helicopter design consisting of a single main rotor and a tail rotor for torque compensation. At the tail was a propeller for forward and rearward flight as well. The two-blade main rotor used aileron controls. This 6.1 meter (20 foot) diameter rotor turned 200 rpm, belt-driven by a 11.2 kW (15 hp) at 2000 rpm Harley-Davidson engine. A single seat design, it weighed 177 kg (390 lb) gross, and 100 kg (220 lb) empty. Maximum thrust was estimated to be 2.8 kN (450 lb). The auxiliary rotors had a diameter of 61 cm (24 in). The design was not built, but in 1944 Nemeth tested the NH-2. This 48.5 kW (65 hp) machine had a 7.9 meter (26 foot) diameter rotor. It was followed in 1945 by a variant with engine-propeller units mounted on arms at right angles to the blades. He later dropped this approach to torque elimination for research with jet-driven rotors. Nemeth's sequence of configuration investigations could almost be generic.

1924 Lux

In 1924 W. Lux had under construction a machine entered in the British helicopter competition of that year. [3.74] The design featured coaxial rotors with provisions for feathering the blades. The concept permitted pitch change of one or both rotors, and included cyclic control for propulsion. The rotor diameter was 12.2 meters (40 feet), with a fuselage length of 6.1 meters (20 feet). Apparently the project was dropped for Lux was not an entrant in the 1925–1926 competition.

1924 Anonymous (Williams)

A helicopter project was underway in Connecticut around 1924, and the only information on it are two photographs (Figures 3.77 and 3.78). [3.75] The configuration is similar to the Williams 1908 design (Figure 3.11) and most likely his follow-on project. As mentioned before, Williams was a Connecticut resident.

Figure 3.77 Static view of helicopter test stand, attributed to Williams (ca. 1924).

Figure 3.78 is an illustration from Williams patent 1,076,803, and the resemblance verifies the above supposition. Most likely the helicopter was a precursor to Williams' entry in the 1925–1926 British competition. The two illustrations are a hovering test stand version of the patent. However it could be the complete machine as Williams envisioned it, but a tail would have been helpful. Focus of the patent is on a form of pitch and yaw control, using blade warping and rotor differential torque. An unusual feature of Figure 3.77 and 3.78 is the application of a rotor ("wing") warping system.

Despite the lack of published information, a considerable amount can be deduced from the two figures. (Some information was derived from enlarged photographs of the two shown.) The discussion that follows assumes the helicopter is a Williams project. In general the account covers description, derived characteristics,

handling, and operation of the machine. By this extended account, one can appreciate what serious helicopter engineering of the early 1920s was about.

Description

Figure 3.77 is a static view of the machine which can be seen as a helicopter or a test stand, while Figure 3.78 shows it with the rotors turning. The machine consists of a coaxial, contrarotating rotor system driven by a rotary engine through a set of bevel gears. The unit is mounted on a platform on which the operator sits. Located at the platform corners are four, thick castering wheels. Visible on the frame are slots, presumably for handling the stand.

The inventor chose the rotating wing approach to rotor design. The two-blade rotor wings (or blades) are attached rigidly to an elongated hub

Figure 3.78 View of Figure 3.77 (Williams) helicopter in operation. Note curve of the rotor shaft.

using two, offset spars. Restraining cables extend from the rotor shaft to either side of the wing leading-edge.

The rotary engine is likely a popular war surplus Le Rhône of 59.7 kW (80 hp) at 1200 rpm. Unlike some other rotaries, which were either on or off, The Le Rhône could be throttled to half its speed. It lacked a fuel pump and the tank had to be maintained under pressure. Starting was by handcrank. The engine, shown running in Figure 3.78 drives two ring gears by a pinion between them. The gears are exposed (visible as the parallel members at the level of the engine driveshaft), showing each ring gear attached to its hub by six arms. Design practice did not include putting large gears in a box. The upper gear drives the lower rotor, while the lower gear drives the upper rotor. The upper rotor driveshaft is inside the lower rotor shaft. There are two supports for the shaft system. One is on the plat-

form, and the other at the end of four diagonal struts that meet almost halfway up the shafting (Figure 3.77).

The control system consists primarily of a throttle and a kind of blade-collective pitch control. Collective pitch (in this case incidence angle) is increased in warping the wings by pulling on control cables attached to the trailing edges. The leading edge restraining cables define the pivot. Relaxing the control cable pull brings the flexible wings back to a low (or zero) pitch or incidence angle. Note the operator in both figures has only one hand on the control. With the other he grips a strut for his own balance.

The operator's right hand (Figure 3.77) is on a vertical push-pull stick. The stick operates the throttle and blade pitch by means of parallel rods attached to this stick. (See Figure 3.77 which shows the rods parallel.) At the engine end, the lower rod (a push-pull rod) is connected to a bell crank and a diagonal link leading to the throttle. The operator's stick can also pivot left around the throttle, push-pull rod. Pivoting to the left (apparently) actuates the upper parallel rod. This rod is a drag link that pulls on the wing warping cables. Figure 3.78 shows the upper link out of parallel, indicating the operator pivoted the stick to his left and is holding blade pitch. This lateral movement pulls on the drag link which through a rod leading upward to the driveshaft, pulls on cables (attached to a slider) that increases the pitch of the blades collectively.

The operating rotor in Figure 3.78 has a definite air load on it, though the platform has not lifted off. By design or accident, the blade spars are very flexible. This is evidenced by comparing the tip-path plane in both photos.

An unusual (and early) approach to helicopter control was provision for CG shift by weight shift of the operator (kinesthetic control). Both figures reveal the operator's seat is elongated fore and aft (Figure 3.79). The feature permits him to shift his weight by sliding along the seat. Figure 3.77 shows his legs fully extended, with feet braced against the platform. This location was likely his "full aft" CG position. In Figure 3.78 he is seated forward on the bench with the rotor operating. Most likely if the test stand were to tilt forward excessively, he could slide back rapidly to restore balance. Note in both positions the operator maintains his equilibrium by holding on to a strut. Probably he needed that support if lateral CG shift (body pivoting laterally) was to be used for lateral control.

This kinesthetic control elicits two observations and one judgment. The control approach compelled the operator to rely on one hand for all mechanical control manipulation. As a pilot he would be very busy shifting and pivoting (including cross coupling) his body to hold it in a "trim" position. As suggested later this machine did not hover or fly, and this is fortunate. The kinesthetic control concept in combination with the inventor's many other problems would make it a dangerous machine to fly, and guaranteed to be demolished on its first flight. Risks of this type to life and structure would never be tolerated today.

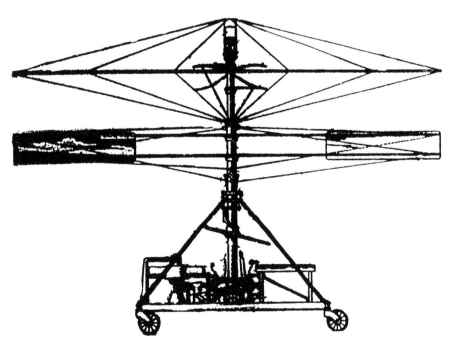

Figure 3.79 William patent showing resemblance to Figure 3.11 and Figure 3.77. His novel feature was pitch control using blade warping (1913).

Characteristics (estimated or derived)

Rotor diameter	5.5 m (18 ft)
Rotor speed	200 rpm
Tip speed	61 m/s (200 fps)
Gear reduction (approximate)	6:1
Height overall	4.3 m (14 ft)
Weight empty	318 kg (700 lb)
Operating weight	409 kg (900 lb)
Rated power	59.7 kW (80 hp) normal
	69.3 kW (93 hp) maximum
Engine speed	1200 rpm normal
Fuel consumption	30.3 liters/h (8 gal/h)
Oil (castor) consumption	4.7 liters/h (1.25 gal/h)

Handling

The test stand was auto towed to the test site. At this point the unit could be spotted using the grips on the frame. Four men would be required to move the 346 kg (700 lb) stand and shift it in place. The castering wheels (which seem inappropriate for flight) allow ground movement using rotor propulsion with the operator seated forward. (Helicopter CG slightly forward of shaft axis, will pivot machine on its front wheels.) For assembly, the rotor was installed on its shaft along with the support and control cables by tilting the 4.3 meter (14 foot) high platform on its side.

Operation

One assumes testing was done in calm air. In operation, the engine is started by an assistant on the ground, using the handcrank. Without a clutch, the engine is run up to idle (600 engine and 100 rotor rpm) with blades in relaxed (zero) incidence. Initially the operator is seated in "neutral" (midbench) to balance the engine and fuel weight. (the position in Figure 3.78). The operator holds the lever, the functional equivalent of a collective pitch stick of today's helicopters. Instead of up-and-down motion (collective pitch motion) and twist (throttle motion on the collective stick) the lever is moved forward and aft (throttle motion) and toward himself laterally (collective pitch motion). When the operator releases the grip the warped blades automatically revert to zero pitch.

In the 1908 machine (Figure 3.11) Williams also provided a blade warping (collective pitch) con-

trol system. Note the long rod to the operator's left running close to the diagonal strut. For this design the pitch was introduced when the operator held the control rod in contact with the strut. At the same time he was steadying his weight. Releasing the grip would put the blades in zero pitch. In the 1924 design Williams combined collective pitch and power in the same control lever, thereby anticipating the modern convention.

Using the figure of merit equation one can check the rotor thrust available. The value is 0.53, and ground effect would increase the thrust about 4 percent. The value 0.53 may be optimistic, but it is reasonable to assume the stand could lift off the ground. If it did break contact with the ground it was just the beginning of the designer's real problems. However there appears to be a problem that kept the stand on the ground.

As noted in the 19th century introduction, there was a progression in testing relative to problems encountered. First on the list were structural problems on the ground. The present machine apparently followed this progression, because the initial, inhibiting problem was shaft vibration. Figure 3.78 shows the part of the rotor shaft above the upper support is curved. The curvature or bending produced a whirl misalignment radius of about 5.1 cm (2 in) at the shaft tip. The estimated unbalance is equivalent to a 114 gram (¼ pound) added to the tip of one blade. An alert operator would cut the engine before serious damage occurred. The vibration (swirl) radius may be amplified by its frequency (once per revolution at 200 rpm) being close to the natural frequency of the slender shaft with its concentrated weight of the rotors (63.6 kilograms-140 pounds) at the upper end. The problem resembles the "sprung shaft" reported in the 1908 Williams account. The slender shaft problem very likely affected other experimenters, and could be the reason often the test results were not made public. (See also ground resonance in the Glossary.)

1924 Newbauer

Valentine Newbauer of Los Angeles was engaged in helicopter work in the 1917–1927 period. His ideas are covered in patents, 1,446,718; 1,569,669; and 1,743,378. He entered his design

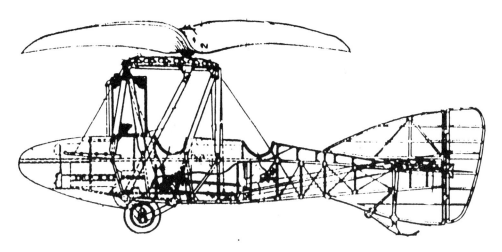

Figure 3.80 Newbauer helicopter concept from patent (1924).

in the 1924 British helicopter competition, requesting the evaluation be conducted in the United States. Newbauer cited patent 1,446,718 in his application (Figure 3.80), but apparently this was not his entry. One of his designs was a monoplane with a two-blade rotor mounted in the midsection of each wing panel. The British entry was a biplane variant with a 13.4 meter (44 foot) wingspan, powered by a 112 kW (150 hp) Curtiss engine. Newbauer's patent 1,446,718 featured a novel rotor. He shaped the undersurface of the blades so the ends curved downward. The inventor claimed that the air moved is crowded inward and rearward and "compressed, forming an intensified air shaft giving much greater lift". He expected the concept to produce 30 percent more lift than a plane

surface, but this performance improvement is highly improbable.

By 1927 Newbauer was working on a simpler system, a compound helicopter consisting of two propeller-type rotors and a tractor propeller. [3.76] Figure 3.81 is a model of his design. With a 1.12 kW (1.5 hp) engine he claimed it lifted 27.2 kilograms (60 pounds). The full size machine was to use a 448 kW (600 hp) engine. The weight the model could lift is very optimistic. The resulting figure of merit is 2.0, a value not physically attainable. Ideally with 1.12 kW (1.5 hp) the maximum thrust is around 134 N (30 pounds). Perhaps the inventor measured the thrust of one rotor and erroneously assumed he could lift twice as much with two rotors, using the same power.

Figure 3.81 Newbauer compound helicopter model (1925).

1924 Oriol

One of the more unconventional approaches to VTOL is that of Ramon Oriol. [3.77] Oversized, coaxial counterrotating propellers were tiltable relative to the fuselage (Figure 3.82). The tilt was produced by a compressed air system. The propellers were driven by means of a gearbox and two rotary engines facing each other in the nose of the fuselage. It was expected the two-row rotaries would provide a degree of "gyro-scopic stability" with both engines turning in the same direction. The lower sets of figures show the aircraft attitudes for takeoff and landing. A bumper at the tail served as a pivot for both these maneuvers.

The rotaries of the size considered produced 104 kW (140 hp) at 1200 rpm, while the empty weight is likely to be in the 908 kilogram (2000 pound) range. The purpose of the configuration was not stated but it seems more a military concept than a commercial one. However passengers were likely to be more adventurous and daring in those days.

1924 Brown

W. E. Brown of New York City proposed an unusual concept for the 1924 and 1925–1926 British helicopter competitions. The configuration was based on a conventional tractor biplane with short wings. His idea was to convert the lift

Airplane-Helicopter Flyer

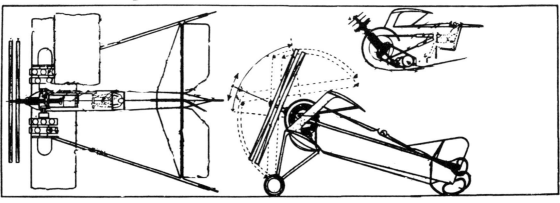

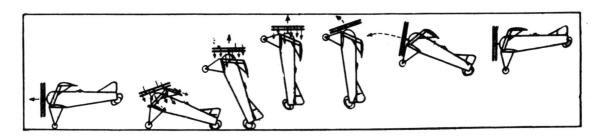

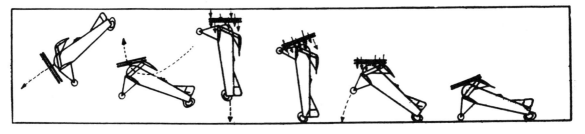

Figure 3.82   Oriol VTOL concept (1924).

of a propeller to lift on annular wings, through use of the airscrew wake.

Two assemblies of the novel rotor system were mounted on the fuselage. Each assembly consisted of an airscrew whose wake flowed down a conical deflector, turning 90 degrees, passing through two sets of annular wings. A centrifugal fan surrounded the inner annular ring. The design, 12.8 meters (42 feet) long was to be powered by three 108 kW (145 hp) engines.

Brown also had a patent for a compound helicopter with coaxial rotors (1,500,572). The rotor drive consisted of two steam turbines each with a pinion driving its own gear, with the latter turning counterrotating rotors (Figure 3.83). [3.78]

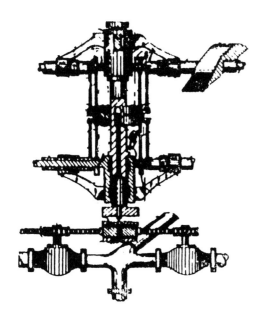

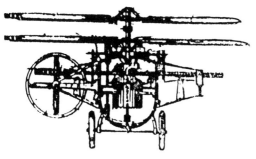

Figure 3.83 Brown compound helicopter concept (1924).

1924 Bane

Thurman H. Bane noted before as a pilot of the DeBothezat helicopter (1922) and also the Army's first helicopter pilot, [3.79] patented a compound helicopter (1,557,789). The design (Figure 3.84) consisted of main lateral rotors with two auxiliary lifting rotors at the tail. There is no evidence the design was built.

1924 Keefer

Like some others of this date, the only information on the project is based on an entry in the British helicopter competition. The C. H. Keefer design was a helicoplane featuring biplane wings with a 7.6 meter (25 foot) wingspan, powered by a 74.6 kW (100 hp) engine. The concept was still in the design stage in early 1924, and very likely a prototype was not built.

1924 Begg

Apropos of the above, one A. C. W. Begg had an entry in the 1924 British competition. The rotor consisted of a group of radial arms, and to each arm was hinged a triangular vane forming the blade. Vane angle control used a system of levers and sliding collars.

1925–1926 Hollander

M. Hollander submitted a design for the 1925–1926 British competition. The concept is covered in patents 1,453,283 and 1,466,901. His invention relied on a suction-lift principle, whereby a high velocity airstream acted on the upper surface of the craft. The idea appears to be a special application of the Bernoulli effect to a hovering aircraft. [3.82]

1925–1926 Larsen

Agnew Larsen [3.83] noted previously with Pitcairn was one of the more prominent rotary wing designers of the autogiro era. Larsen had an entry in the 1925–1926 British helicopter competition. A drawing was submitted, taken from British patent application 11,074 of 1925.

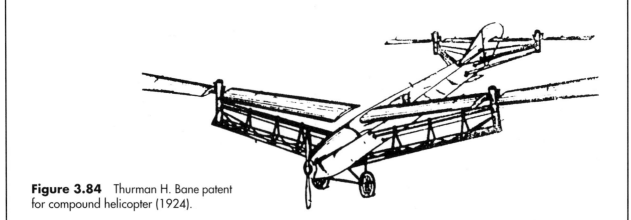

Figure 3.84   Thurman H. Bane patent for compound helicopter (1924).

The configuration consisted of a four-blade rotor using adjustable vanes in the slipstream for torque reaction, a concept he worked out with Pitcairn. The 9.8 meter (32 foot) diameter rotor was universally mounted, and by inclination a propulsive component was obtained. The power-plant was a 149 kW (200 hp) Wright engine. This design was not built, probably set aside with the promise of the autogiro.

1926–1926 Ford

In 1925 A. S. Ford had under construction a prototype entered in the 1925–1926 British competition. This design is an early 20th century application of the steam turbine proposed by Hargreave (Figure 2.7). As today the major problem is to provide a practical, airborne steam-condensing system.

The machine powered by a 1306 kW (1750 hp) steam turbine engine was propeller-driven and it featured a novel lift system. This had to be a large flying machine. Using a unit weight of 1.6 kg/kW (2.63 lb/hp) with condenser, Ford's powerplant would weigh around 2088 kilograms (4600 pounds). [3.84] Using a power loading of 6.1 kg/kW (10 lb/hp) the gross weight amounts to 7495 kilograms (17,500 pounds). The weight seems excessive for a proof of concept design. Such a high weight would only complicate unnecessarily a development program. (Consider the weight of the Wright Flyer of 1903.)

One possible explanation is Ford found the least power for his design came to a large figure, and everything else followed. This approach resembles a common and basic design problem today

of determining the smallest aircraft that will satisfy a specified (military) mission. It is also possible he envisioned a large commercial machine as his "first-off" project.

Even so, such a high weight would not give him much of a useful load. Compared with one of the largest piston engine helicopters built, his useful load would be only about 36 percent of that of the piston helicopter. Compared with a modern gas turbine powered helicopter of the same gross weight, the Ford design would carry a crew of 1 and 12 passengers at most. The turbine machine capacity would be a crew of 2 and 22 passengers.

1925–1926 Pusterla

Another entrant in the 1925–1926 British competition was A. Pusterla. His monoplane-helicopter design had a 15.3 meter (50 foot) diameter rotor, and was powered by two 74.6 kW (100 hp) rotary engines. Pusterla cited his British patent 205,841. [3.85]

1925 Beach

Stanley Y. Beach, an airplane builder (1909) and mentioned in conjunction with Whitehead (1911), entered a design in the 1925–1926 British competition. The concept 18.3 meters (60 feet) long consisted of four, two-blade lifting screws powered by 597 kW (800 hp) Packard engines. Two of the screws were tiltable for propulsion.

In 1940 Beach figured in a revived investigation of the claim Gustave Whitehead had flown before the Wright brothers. Beach asserted "Whitehead never got off the ground with his plane". [3.86]

1926 Myers

George F. Myers of Jackson Heights, New York was an inventor of helicopters, gyroplanes, and helicopter airplanes. His interest in helicopters dates to 1897 when he filed a patent for a helicopter, [3.87] and a prototype was built in 1904 (Figure 3.85). It consisted of three lifting screws and two laterally disposed tractor propellers, each driven by a two-cylinder engine. Diameter of the lifting screws was 4.1 m (13.3 ft) and the propellers, 1.8 meters (6 feet). Several years later it appeared as part of a machine with multiple annular surfaces mounted above the helicopter (Patent 1,226,985 issued in 1917).

Myers' major effort relates to a coaxial rotor machine patented in 1926 and built under the name Myers Flyers Inc. Beyond this, two configurations were entered in the 1924 British competition. One a helicoplane and the other a design for a craft with three rotors in tandem. It appears neither was constructed. The entry remarked $2 million was spent on flying machines.

The 82.1 kW (110 hp) helicoplane used a four-blade lifting airscrew and a tractor propeller, both of variable pitch. The wings featured

valves that opened for vertical ascent. The tandem triaxial design had inclined screws for lift and propulsion. Control vanes were located in the slipstream of each screw. This version used three 298 kW (400 hp) Liberty engines.

The coaxial rotor machine is shown in two variants, a tiltwing in Figure 3.86, and a pure helicopter in Figures 3.87–3.90. The prototype was built around the fuselage of a Thomas-Morse airplane, many of which were war surplus. The two 5.5 meter (18 foot) diameter lifting propellers were driven by a 74.6 kW (100 hp) Gnôme rotary engine. The drive consisted of a clutch and a 2.3 :1 bevel gear reduction system. A group of vanes was used for control. These were located on booms on either side of the fuselage, and at the aft end. Two additional vanes were mounted forward of the nose powerplant. All these were actuated by the pilot's stick.

Construction was supervised by Vincent Burnelli who was also the pilot. Burnelli an airplane designer, through the years was identified with

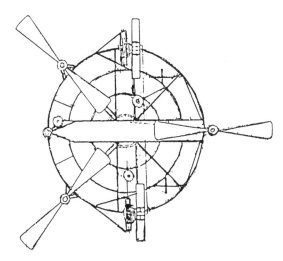

Figure 3.85 Myers triaxial prototype (1904).

Figure 3.86 Myers tiltwing prototype (1926).

Figure 3.87   Myers coaxial rotor helicopter prototype (1926).

Figure 3.88   Myers helicopter being towed out for tests (1926).

airplanes in which the fuselage was an airfoil-shaped lifting body.

Initial hovering tests were made with the machine restrained by weights. Forward flight tests were conducted at Curtiss Field, Long Island in September 1926. The machine flew a distance of 305 meters (1000 feet) at a height of about 3.1 meters (10 feet). However at intervals it

touched the ground, suggesting inadequate controllability. Another flight covered 915 meters (3000 feet).

Following this effort Myers dropped his helicopter development to perform services as a patent attorney. In the late 1940s "Doc" Myers appeared at helicopter forums, honored as the oldest living helicopter pioneer.

Figure 3.89 Myers helicopter rear view (1926).

1928 Pitts

The Pitts helicopter prototype was built around a novel rotor invented by John W. Pitts of Detroit (Patent 1,602,778). [3.88] The unusual feature of the rotor was its ability to axially reciprocate and rotate at the same time (Figures 3.91, 3.92, and 3.93). Each blade of the 60 blade rotor had a full-radius vane attached to it. The vane, twisted 90 degrees root to tip, was free to flap about its radial hinge by impressed axial motion. Rotor rotation caused the drooping vanes to swing out, closing the space between the blades, forming a solid rotor disk.

Figure 3.91 appears to be the first variant of the helicopter or "umbrella plane". The large drum below the rotor contains the reciprocating and rotating mechanism. (See also Figure 3.92 from his patent.) Figure 3.91 shows a conventional airplane fuselage revealing the engine bed-rails at the front. In this design the engine driving end would face inward. Apparently Pitts abandoned the airplane fuselage approach and adapted the rotor and propulsion system to a truncated structure, large enough to hold the operator (Figure 3.93).

Figure 3.90 Myers helicopter hovering with restraints (1926). Lack of photo clarity of helicopter in flight suggests the era when it was difficult to get a picture off the ground of an unwilling helicopter.

Figure 3.91 Pitts helicopter prototype, early configuration with conventional airplane tail (ca. 1920s).

Rotor action was as follows. As the rotor turned, its shaft moved downward, creating a puff of air. On the upstroke the hinged vanes drooped allowing air to pass between the blades. It was in-

tended this action would produce the thrust to lift the machine. The 1226 kg (2700 lb) craft was powered by a 67.1 kW (90 hp) Curtiss OX engine.

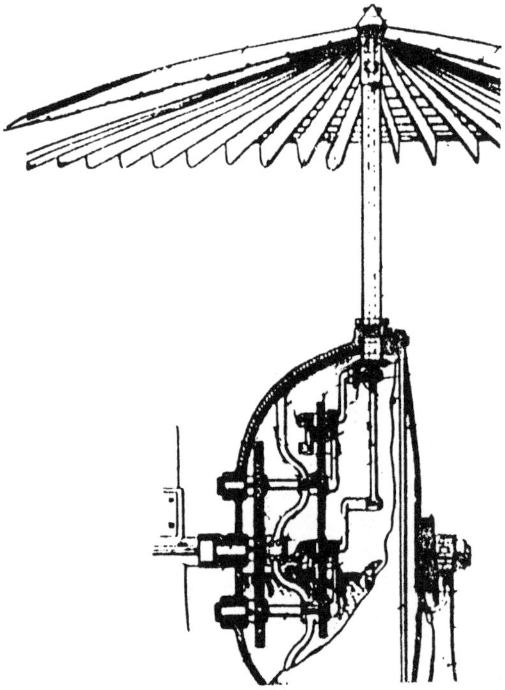

The machine was tested but only succeeded in shaking itself off the ground. A motion picture record of the flight attempt has appeared in film clips of odd flying machines, including one produced by the British Shell Company. Anyone who saw this film would recognize which one was the Pitts. It appears to be the first helicopter in which vibration was designed into it.

In 1931 there was a report on a helicopter built by Pitts and W. P. Kindree, most likely the machine described above.

1929 Johnson

A typical airplane-helicopter configuration intentionally so designed (i.e., one the helicopter designer did not resort to in default) was built by J. C. Johnson of West Palm Beach, Florida (Patent 1,485,269 of 1924, also 1,713,874). [3.89] A monoplane was fitted with two 5.8 meter (19 foot) diameter, propeller-type rotors, each mounted below a wing panel (Figure 3.94). The airplane was a production Hamilton Metalplane

Figure 3.92 Reciprocating and rotating system arrangement for Pitts helicopter.

Figure 3.93 Pitts prototype as tested shorn of its tail (1928).

Company monoplane built in Milwaukee. (The Hamilton name survives in the Hamilton-Standard company, for the designer developed a metal propeller as well.)

The machine was flown in the latter city by Victor Allison. It was reported the craft took off after a short run of 23 meters (75 feet). In the helicoplane mode, power to the tractor propeller was halved and the lateral screws started. The combination produced a steep angle climb. Johnson called the tests "ninety percent perfect".

A practical reason for locating the propellers below the wing, which Berliner (1922–1925) also disclosed in a proposal, concerns airflow through the propeller and blockage. With propellers above the wing, blocking the focused wake is more detrimental to thrust due to the accompanying vertical drag on the wing. (See also the Berliner triplane discussion.) Even today there is a tiltrotor VTOL tradeoff in the choice between tilting the rotors alone or the rotor and wing combination.

Below the wing as in Figure 3.94, the inflow to the propellers affects thrust less because the oncoming air before the turn is drawn into the propellers from an infinite reservoir, and this air

does not impinge on a surface. Hence the propellers operate in a better aerodynamic environment. However being close to the ground at takeoff creates its own hazards.

The Berliner projects and the Johnson configuration reveal the frustration in the trial-and-error approach to obtaining an optimum vertical flight aircraft. As noted before, after many variants Berliner arrived at the configuration Johnson started with. Both settled for a monoplane with steep climb ability derived using a complicated system, a performance better served using a wing-flap system, today identified with steep takeoff and landing STOL aircraft.

Another important observation is modern methodology does all its "trial-and-error" work in the design stage through tradeoff studies thereby avoiding costly development costs and time. This methodology is part of *systems engineering* which is discussed in the Glossary.

1930 Curtiss-Bleecker

As an aeronautical engineering student at the University of Michigan, Maitland B. Bleecker became interested in the torqueless rotor heli-

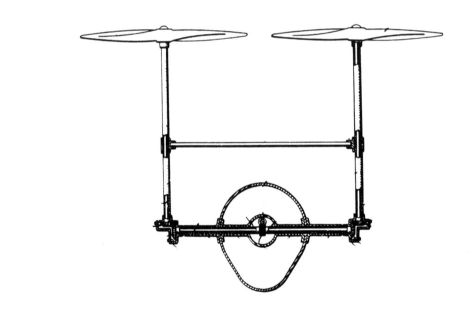

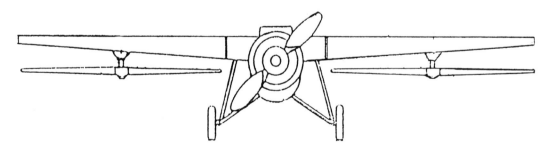

Figure 3.94   Johnson helicoplane prototype (1929).

copter. Later an employee of NACA (Langley) he conducted some experiments that led him to a propeller-driven rotor prototype. In 1926 Bleecker proposed to the Curtiss Company of Garden City, Long Island a design which the company agreed to construct.

The object of his design was to provide a torqueless, rotating wing system, driven by rotor-mounted propellers. A craft that had a certain amount of gyroscopic stability, capable of autorotative flight. The invention is disclosed in patents 1,819,863 and 1,934,399. [3.90]

The prototype appeared publicly in 1930 (Figures 3.95–3.99). It was a two-seat helicopter with a single four-blade rotor. The paint job consisted of a blue fuselage and silver and yellow blades. The blades were free in pitch, but otherwise rigidly mounted to the hub. The four, blade-mounted tractor propellers were driven by a central engine (shaft upward) that turned with the rotor. The fuel tank also was part of the rotating mass. Electrical power was transferred from the airframe to the engine by means of a slip-ring assembly (Figure 3.98 detail). This unit consisted of copper rings and carbon brushes. A separate copper ring served to provide boost

power for starting. The throttle control (Figure 3.98 detail) involved a gear, pinion, and cam arrangement transferring motion from the airframe to the rotating engine. The transfer unit used a rotating, cylindrical cam driven off the main gear through two pinions. The cam had two spirals each in a sense opposite the other. Through throttle motion, the cam in moving vertically rotated one or the other pinion. This rotation drove the main gear, which in turn actuated the carburetor throttle lever and its valve.

Blade cyclic and collective pitch control utilized vanes called *stabovators* trailing behind each blade. Yaw control was obtained by a vane aft of the fuselage, pivoting about a horizontal axis; the vane acting in the rotor wake, where the blade chord was widest. To enhance lift, Bleecker apparently shaped the blade planform to have a wider chord in the wake of the propellers.

The pilot's controls consisted of a conventional stick for longitudinal and lateral control, and a rudder bar to activate the aft vane. A lever beside the pilot varied collective pitch. The stick connected to the stabovators through a novel mechanism for blade cyclic control (Figure 3.98

Figure 3.95 Curtiss-Bleecker prototype (1930).

Figure 3.96 Curtiss-Bleecker prototype overhead view (1930).

detail). The swashplate equivalent, consisted of a rotating spider with its axle attached to a ball and socket joint (a spherical bearing) that is part of the airframe. The spider assembly could be raised vertically for collective pitch or inclined for cyclic pitch changes. The spider and bearing unit is connected to the cyclic control stick through a system of cranks and rods. Four rods hinged on the spider lead to the four stabovators through individual rod and crank systems. It was necessary to balance the weight of the pilot

Figure 3.97 Maitland Bleecker in cockpit of helicopter.

(seated forward) with a passenger or ballast in the aft cockpit.

Characteristics

Rotor diameter	14.4 m (47.3 ft)
Blade chord, inboard	170 cm (66.8 in.)
Blade area, total	34.4 m^2 (370 ft^2)
Airfoil section	GO-387
Pitch range, degrees	-12.5 to $+27.5$
Rotor minimum speed, hovering	60 rpm
Rotor maximum speed, flight	120 rpm
Powerplant	Pratt-Whitney Wasp
Powerplant rating	313 kW (420 hp) @ 2100 rpm
Fuel capacity	113.6 liters (30 gal)
Cooling fan diameter	81.3 cm (32 in.)
Stabovator area	1.2 m^2 (12.5 ft^2)
Propellers	Hartzell
Propeller diameter	2.1 m (6.75 ft)
Propeller maximum speed	1530 rpm
Gross weight	1544 kg (3400 lb)
Empty weight (approx)	908 kg (2000 lb)
Useful load, % gross weight	20–30
Maximum speed, calculated	113 km/h (70 mph)
Rate of climb, calculated	305 m/s (1000 fpm)

The machine hovered under control in a hanger, and made about 15 flights "when and where desired". The public appearance in June 1930 failed to materialize in a flight, due to a lubrication problem. It appears the helicopter was later damaged in hangar tests. Critics of the machine deemed it unstable and the vibration excessive. Later that year the project was dropped, after an expenditure of $250,000. No pictures of it hovering have been released to the public.

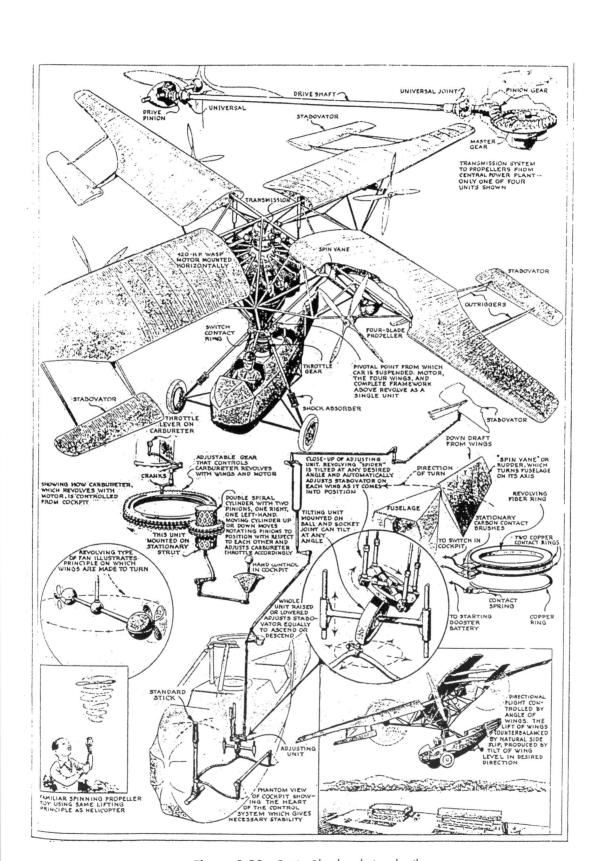

Figure 3.98 Curtiss-Bleecker design details.

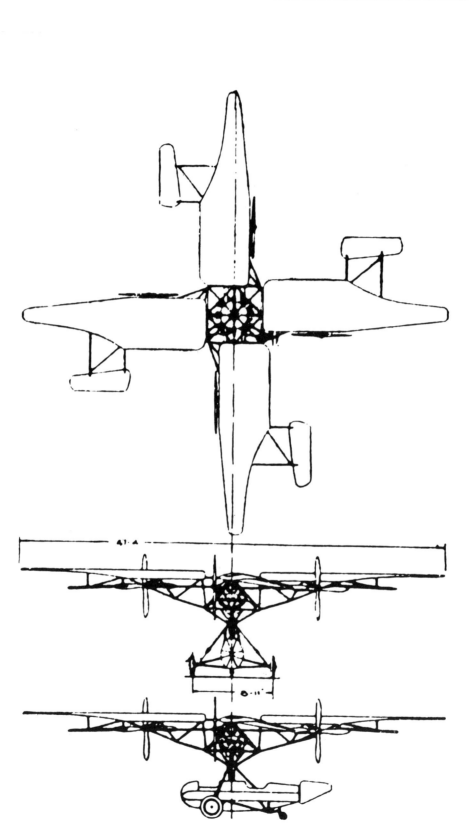

Figure 3.99 Curtiss-Bleecker three-view general arrangement (1930).

Bleecker believed the machine was basically sound. He thought the real problems were in detail design and maintained that the work should have continued. Another view attributed cancellation to its complexity, and to the national economic depression which caused many such projects to be cancelled. Bleecker accounted for all the controls in his design, and they appear to be effective, except for yaw, which probably was marginal. But he apparently could not control the machine's instability, a problem worsened by mechanical failures.

In Europe nine prototypes were built using the propeller-driven rotor system: Isacco (1928–1935) who built four (France, England, Russia); Hellesen-Kahn (1923, France); Brennan (1925–1925, England); Josephson (1937, Russia); and Nagler (1940–1941, Austria). Anton Flettner in Germany tested a 30 meter (98 foot) rotor version in 1934. From its appearance he called it *schwange ente* (pregnant duck). During hovering trials it was destroyed by a gust.

Basic design problems concern radial placement of the propellers on the blade, and where to locate the one or more powerplants. Seven prototypes featured propellers at the blade tips, while three including Bleecker put them near the mid-radius. With six prototypes the powerplants were located at the blade tips, direct-driving fixed pitch propellers. Two others, Bleecker and Brennan, put the engine at the rotor hub. The latter used a rotary engine and Bleecker a static radial turning with the rotor. The Hellesen-Kahn and the Nagler had the engines and propellers for the two blades mounted near the mid radius. Josephson experimented with electrically driven helicopters, and in his case the three motors mounted at the blade tips, directly drove the propellers. The different approaches to propeller and engine placement reveal individual ideas as to which parameters were most important. At the same time, each choice created other problems related to design, function, and rotorcraft operation.

The following summarizes the tradeoff aspects in developing the propeller-driven rotor in hovering and forward flight. Note first the power required to drive the basic rotor blades is independent of the location of the engines or the propellers. However the drag of the propulsion

unit itself and propeller inefficiency will increase overall engine power required.

Engine location affects its operation as well as the structure and weight of the rotor system. One general problem concerns propeller ground clearance, more so if the propellers are located at the blade tips. As a result, propeller diameter is limited. Four blades are used to provide sufficient area to produce the relatively high thrust required.

For a selected design rotor speed, rotor power available is proportional to the propeller thrust times the radial dimension to the propeller. Thus propeller thrust required is twice as high at mid-radius compared with tip placement Most of the prototypes listed above use tip-mounted propellers to keep the thrust requirement as low as possible. The same thrust argument applies to jet-driven rotor prototypes. All these locate the thruster at the blade tip rather than inboard. Location will affect propeller efficiency. Propeller power loss in producing thrust (the measure of propeller efficiency) as suggested above, must be added to rotor power required to obtain the necessary engine power. Considering the Bleecker design (Figure 3.99), with propellers at 40 percent radius, the ideal efficiency is only 54 percent, compared with 95 percent with the same propellers at the tips. (The actual efficiency is about 80 percent of the ideal value.) Compared with a blade tip drive, about 76 percent more power is required in locating the propeller at 40 percent radius. Considering hover capability of the Bleecker as derived from the listed characteristics, it is unlikely the machine could hover out of ground effect at the weight listed (assuming it was controllable). The estimated engine power would be abut 35 percent greater than the value 313 kW (420 hp) given above. Overall, a high price was paid to avoid a tip propeller.

The jet driven rotor systems that came later all favored tip jets because of the greater propulsive efficiency. In the recent quest for a flyable, human-powered helicopter, one concept is to use tip propellers (to relieve the initial starting torque effort). However the design must deal with the problem of propeller efficiency (increased power required) and vulnerability.

With tip propellers and engines, rotor gyroscopic effects and rotor inertia are high. High inertia means slow, sluggish rotor response to speed changes. Particularly because the propellers lack pitch control. However the arrangement gives a high degree of gyroscopic stability that aids in controllability.

There are also fuel and lubrication problems due to engine operation in a centrifugal field, most likely one of Bleecker's problems. Centrifugal force causes fluids (fuel, oil) to collect at the outer walls of system components. This effect increases fuel consumption and starves surfaces of oil. Such functional and fluid problems also apply to blade tip-mounted jet engines of recent prototopes. These include turbojets, ram, and pulse jets.

Particularly in the early designs, the tip engine approach required more blade reinforcement and weight to limit blade static droop, and to avoid propeller pitch or roll damage in a marginally controllable helicopter. Locating the engine at the rotor hub introduces drive system problems dealing with blade deflections and maintenance.

None of these helicopters flew through transition to forward flight. One obvious problem concerns flow through a propeller that is turning in a circle and simultaneously translating. At design maximum speed the Bleecker propellers undergo an angle of attack variation of 20 degrees either side of the face, in one rotor revolution.

There is no reverse flow because the peripheral (rotor) speed of the propellers is about three times that of the forward flight speed. There are also propeller side force effects but these do not appear to be significant. Gyroscopic forces on the propeller blades and shafting can be catastrophic if there are inadvertent, rapid changes in helicopter pitch or roll. (Regarding the last, see also 1931 Young.)

1930 Sikorsky

The work of Igor Sikorsky in Russia and the United States is well known in both accomplishment and literature. His early rotorcraft work is described in *The Aviation Careers of Igor Sikorsky*. [3.91] In 1925 Sikorsky considered the jet-driven rotor principle, but dropped it for the shaft drive system. The first tail rotor concept appeared in 1930 (Figure 3.100). Prototype development began with a test stand in 1938. The prototype tail rotor helicopter (VS-300) was first flown in 1939. However inadequate control led to the revised, interim configuration, the VS-300A (Figure 3.101). This machine became the first successful helicopter in the United States.

With this helicopter in 1941 Sikorsky established a world record for endurance of 1 hour and 32.5 minutes. In Figure 3.101 note rotor direction of rotation, a sense opposite modern American convention. (See also rotor rotation in the Glossary.)

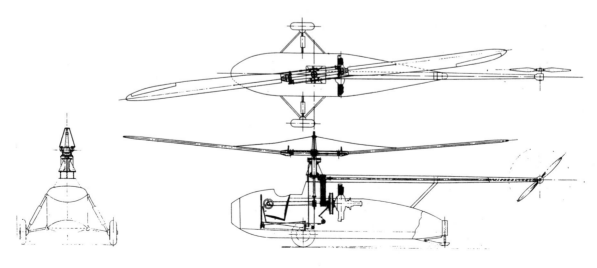

Figure 3.100   Sikorsky tail rotor design (1930).

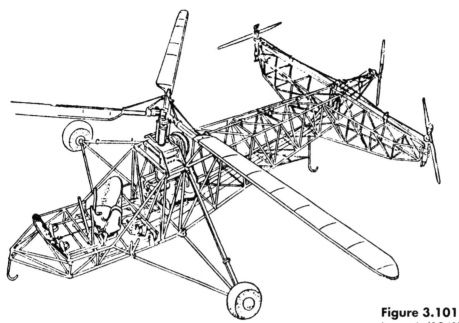

Figure 3.101 Sikorsky VS-300 isometric (1941).

The most common configuration today, the tail rotor, is an old idea. It is interesting in retrospect so many of the entrepreneurs described here favored the coaxial rotor system. Relative to the latter the tail rotor idea is a more subtle, less obvious design solution. The first to reduce it to practice was the Russian Boris N. Yur'ev. [3.92] Figure 3.102 shows two variants of the helicopter, along with design details that include a swashplate control and belt-driven tail rotor. Figure 3.103 is a model of his configuration.

In 1912 a prototype was built around a 18.7–22.4 kW (25–30 hp) Anzani engine, the only one available to Yur'ev (Figure 3.104). During ground trials the main rotor shaft failed. As often remarked here, this failure was a common one with the large diameter rotor prototypes. The accident terminated the project. The designer considered the helicopter underpowered, and a 52.2 kW (70 hp) Gnôme rotary concept followed (Figure 3.102, lower helicopter). Unlike the prototype this design shows the engine mounted off the rotor axis of rotation. Compare the upper and lower helicopters of Figure 3.102. Presumably Yur'ev chose the offset arrangement to give him freedom to select rotor speed.

1931 Young

The helicopter activities of Arthur M. Young are of particular interest because his work led to series production of very successful helicopters by Bell Helicopter, later a division of Textron. [3.93] His work began around 1928 in the Philadelphia area using models. In 1931 he tested a remotely-controlled 14.9 kW (20 hp) machine. The three blade rotor of 4.6 meter (15 foot) diameter featured propeller-driven blades, as part of a torqueless system. It was destroyed in flight, apparently due to the gyroscopic forces acting on the propellers. (See also the Curtiss-Bleecker, 1930 entry.) Figure 3.105 from Young's patent 2,082,674 (filed 1933) discloses his concept for a propeller-engine unit mounted at the blade tip behind which is a controllable tab. The tab is used for blade pitch control. The torqueless model was followed by one with coaxial rotors. Figure 3.106 shows a remotely-controlled model that was in the direct line of development to his final rotor system. This variant consists of a teetering rotor with a gyroscopic mass mounted above it. Young's final configuration used the flybar concept (Figure 3.107).

Work on his full scale tail rotor prototype began in 1941. As the Bell Model 47B it was the first helicopter to receive CAA (FAA) certification, in March 1946. During this period Bartram Kelley worked with Young to realize the practical teetering rotor system, one that has become a Bell trademark. Kelley was a long-time friend of Young's and later became head of engineering at Bell. An important component of the rotor was addition of dampers to the stabilizer bar (flybar). These served to extend the hovering os-

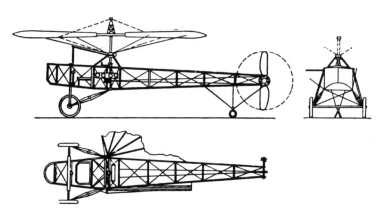

Проект вертолета Б. Н. Юрьева под двигатель в 50 *л. с.*

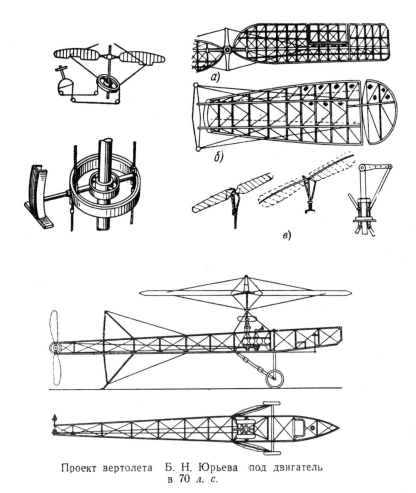

Проект вертолета   Б. Н. Юрьева   под двигатель
в 70 *л. с.*

Figure 3.102   Yur'ev tail rotor design and control concepts (1909–1912).

Figure 3.103 Yur'ev helicopter model (1909–1912).

Figure 3.104 Yur'ev prototype with 18.7 kW (25 hp) Anzani engine (1912). B. N. Yur'ev is at the extreme left.

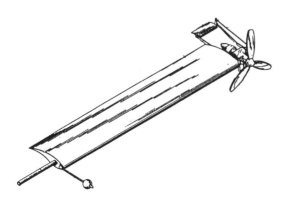

Figure 3.105 A. M. Young propeller-driven rotor, (1931).

Figure 3.106 A. M. Young remotely-controlled tail rotor model.

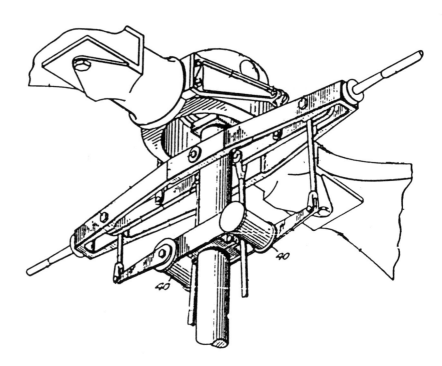

Figure 3.107 Bell-Young rotor stabilization system as finally evolved (1941).

cillation of the helicopter by delaying the following rate of the fuselage.

Figure 3.107 from patent 2,646,848 discloses the rotor system complete with dampers (part 40) critical to success of the system. This figure shows the rotor plane in the same plane as the universal joint, teetering unit. An alternate feature utilizes underslinging for control relief, and blade preconing. The last is a common technique for relieving blade stresses in teetering rotors, and propeller blades as well. With preconing the center of mass of each blade is in a plane above the hub universal joint. Underslinging the rotor brings the masses into the plane of the universal joint. This arrangement reduces the otherwise excessive vibration in the controls (Young patent 2,497,429).

Young's work at Bell involved two pioneering helicopter pilots, Joe Mashman and Floyd Carlson. The latter was the first to hover an untethered Model 30 (1943). Mashman was Bell's first demonstration pilot. His biography is in the book *To Fly Like A Bird* (1992).

The inventor had a very philosophic view of life. Apparently a metaphysical philosophy striving to integrate the material world with human consciousness into a continuum, a seamless whole. [3.94] This suggests an updated version of Tao-

ism. In everyday contemporary life, one comes close to this continuum in the experience between the individual and one's car.

1931 Nelson

In 1931 W. Nelson of Colorado made public his work on a lateral rotor *Aerocar* (Figure 3.108). [3.95] Helicopter tests were conducted but with unpublished results. The craft was then dismantled for "further patent protection". The design weight was 204 kilograms (450 pounds). Nelson claimed the helicopter could fly 161 km/h 100 mph, consuming 18.9 liters/h (5 gal/h) fuel. Rotor windmilling was to account for power-off descent.

Nelson believed a three-place helicopter weighing 545 kg (1200 lb) would require only 22.4 kW (30 hp), or 24.3 kg/kW (40 lb/hp). He reasoned the blades move faster through the air than the comparable wing of an airplane at the same flight speed. The lift per square foot was considered higher for the rotor.

Nelson's power appears optimistic. For a lift-drag ratio of 6 to 7 at 160 km/h (100 mph) the power required would be more like 41 to 33.6 kW (55 to 45 hp) respectively. Even so the higher power required for hovering was not accounted for.

Figure 3.108 Nelson Aerocar concept (1931).

Designed to sell for $500, the *Aerocar* was a typical concept for "everyman's helicopter" an idea that extended into the 1940s and 50s. The plywood Landgraf H-2 of 1944 resembled the *Aerocar*. Landgraf's machine weighed 386 kg (850 lb) gross with 63.4 kW (85 hp), giving a power loading of 6.1 kg/kW (10 lb/hp). The latter is ¼ the power loading predicted by Nelson. The maximum speed of the H-2 was given as 137 km/h (85 mph) with cruise at 113 km/h (70 mph). [3.95] The Landgraf data provides a realistic comparison with Nelson's projections.

1931 Langdon

In 1931 Jesse D. Langdon of Bell, California produced a machine he named *helio-gyro-copter*. [3.96] The idea was to combine the features of the helicopter, gyroscope, and airplane (Figure 3.109). The novel part was the rotor. This unit was attached to a wingless tractor airplane. From the figure the fuselage appears to be from a Curtiss JN-4 (*Jenny*), a common war surplus airplane. The rotor with its shaft mounted in the front cockpit had a diameter about 9.8 meters (32 feet). It resembled a bicycle wheel, which may have given him the idea. A 0.31 meter (1 foot) wide rim attached to the

hub by many steel cables was to provide the gyroscopic stability. Four sets of the cables were fabric covered, forming individual, twisted blades. The intent was to reduce twist as the rotor speed increased. The helicopter which weighed 749 kilograms (1650 pounds), was powered by a 243 kW (325 hp) Hispano-Suiza engine. A gearbox was avoided by a use of a friction disk drive, a concept also used in some early automobiles.

From the illustration it appears the engine driveshaft was pointed inward, suggesting Langdon intended to fly the machine initially as a pure helicopter, or at least hover it in this configuration. During initial tests it was reported the machine lifted off the ground a few feet (about a meter). But there is no account of his dealing with rotor torque. It is possible the stored energy in the rotor aided in its lift-off, and it is unlikely a stabilized hovering condition was established.

Langdon was granted some patents but these do not cover his prototype. Patent 1,694,880 discloses a four-rotor helicopter featuring helical screws, combined with a tractor propeller. Patent 1,791,597 applies to a VTOL driven by a propeller within a cylindrical fuselage. A third patent 1,932,702 shows a rotor with jets at the rim.

Figure 3.109 Langdon prototype (1931).

1934 West

In 1934 Paul F. West of Elmer, New Jersey patented a novel rotor and control system (Patent 1,942,888). [3.98] He envisioned a lateral rotor helicopter with rotors attached to a tractor airplane fuselage and tail.

West used a novel rotor control arrangement that permitted automatic pitch change for flight in the helicopter or autorotative modes. The effect was based on sensing rotor deceleration. The mechanism consisted of a system of pulleys and cables to change pitch, by virtue of the inertia

effects of braking the hub. Differential hub-braking produced the lateral control, and a cam system at the hub suppressed flapping.

In the late 1930s West tested a rotor system, and it appears he did not build a complete helicopter. Considering the complexity including pulleys and cables in the blades, the invention does not seem to be a clean way to approach the problem.

1934 Hays

Through models, Russell Hays of Lawrence, Kansas conducted experiments on various

Figure 3.110 Cordy jet-lift helicopter (1934).

Figure 3.111 Cordy prototype overhead view (1934).

modes of flight. [3.99] In the late 1920s he built models that attempted to imitate the flight of insects. In 1931 he designed a single rotor helicopter that used an inclined surface for torque reaction.

In the following years Hays evaluated small models of novel design weighing up to 0.68 kilograms (1½ pounds) (Patent 1,977,724). By 1934 20 models were flown. In 1935 he patented a means for pitch differential actuation, applicable to lifting propellers (2,045,355).

1936 LePage

In the mid-1930s W. Laurence LePage of Philadelphia had a helicopter project that featured the vane system for single rotor torque reaction (Patent 2,265,193). [3.100] Associated with this work was Havilland H. Platt a rotary wing engineer who in the 1930s also held a patent on a cyclogiro (2,004,961).

The following discussion has a dual purpose. Not only does it review their project but it dramatizes the problem in using vanes to react torque. Often throughout the narratives individu-

als propose vanes and the ensuing shows they invariably underestimated the surface area required to react this torque. With the torqueless rotor system (as Curtiss-Bleecker) much less area is required. But even here modern, practical experience reveals the vane idea is inadequate, and a small tail rotor proves more effective. Figure 3.112 shows a wind tunnel model revealing the extensive area required for torque reaction. To increase reactive force to the desired level, the vanes were fitted with adjustable flaps at the trailing (lower) edge. The model also shows the need for additional surface area (aft fins) necessary for directional stability.

Model wind tunnel tests were conducted in 1936. The basic and initial problem with the vane concept is the fact torque-reacting surfaces are less effective in ground effect. This fact calls for more (or greater) vane area than otherwise necessary. The significant parameter is the ratio of rotor-head height above the ground to the rotor diameter (h/D). With the model surface area shown, the full rotor torque is compensated for when h/D = 0.5, that is, the hovering torque is fully compensated when the hub height is above the ground a distance equal to or more than the rotor radius. With the model on the ground (h/D

Figure 3.112 LePage-Platt wind tunnel model of antitorque vane helicopter (1936).

= 0.42 approximately), torque compensation is about 80 percent of that required for hovering. The configuration tested had a vane to rotor disk area ratio of 0.135, a relatively low value in view of the following.

Design for a full scale two seater with a 5.2 meter (17 foot) rotor diameter required four vanes, each with a span of 3.0 meters and chord of 0.92 meters (10 and 3 foot span and chord respectively). Vane profile was the NACA 2412 section. A calculation reveals the required area ratio, vane to disk area is 0.53, which means the vane area required is about half the disk area.

It appears the design was never built, for LePage joined with Platt to produce the XR-1 lateral rotor helicopter (1940–1941).

1936 Dixon

Around 1936 Jess Dixon of Andalusia, Alabama built a roadable "100 mph" machine called *auto-helicopter* (Figure 3.113). [3.101] The single seat, coaxial rotor system featured two large

auto-type powered wheels for ground travel. The small forward wheel was steerable, while the aft one served as a bumper.

The rotor control consisted of a kind of swashplate-slider arrangement operated by two vertical rods directly handled by the pilot. The rods are connected to what appears to be a ring surrounding the rotor shaft. This ring is manually operated by the pilot in horizontal (cyclic control) and vertical (collective pitch control) directions. Foot pedals actuated a hinged vane on the tail, counting on rotor downwash for yaw control. With coaxial rotors his yaw control force would be small. Even so, in modern designs this configuration requires large tail surfaces particularly for autorotation.

The helicopter used a four cylinder, 30 kW (40 hp) aircooled engine pointing inward, driving the rotor through belts. The fuel tank was located above the engine.

It is obvious the auto wheels and drive added excess weight to the flight mode and increased complexity. During 1934–1936 The Autogiro

Figure 3.113 Dixon roadable helicopter prototype (1936).

Company of America developed the AC-35 roadable autogiro. The roadable part used a single "bull wheel" at the rear of the fuselage, driven by the engine located behind the pilot. The roadable components (wheels, drive, brakes, clutch, and steering) proved to be too much a penalty for the added performance, and the project was dropped.

Referring to Figure 3.113, the forward steerable wheel puts the CG of the machine ahead of the rotor shaft. In hovering the CG location would require aft cyclic control and the CG would shift aft as fuel is consumed. The engine appears to lack a cooling fan. The hinged vane angle emphasizes hovering. As a rudder for forward flight, a greater angle would be more effective.

During the Second World War Dixon was associated with Twin Coach Company of Kent, Ohio in the design of another coaxial machine.

1936 Focke

To complete this account of frustrated efforts, it is fitting to conclude with the success of Heinrich Focke (Figure 3.114) in Germany. He deserves the credit for the first practical helicopter, the FW-61, after which there were many to come throughout the world, including America. To the end of 1949, 1100 helicopters were sold by U.S. manufacturers.

Prior to Focke's narrative it is fitting to mention the pioneers who were instrumental in creating rotary wing flight in America. The most prominent are Igor Sikorsky, Arthur M. Young, and Frank Piasecki. Others are Charles Kaman and Stanley Hiller, all entrepreneurs as well as designers. Special mention is given to Frederic B. Gustafson and the NACA (NASA) organization for contributing the theoretical and practical base for today's helicopters. This kind of information if it existed a century ago would have spared many of the pioneers of the narratives their fruitless groping for a solution.

In 1949 there were about 2600 individuals involved in the design and manufacture of complete helicopters. In its broadest sense they were all pioneers. The following is by no means a complete list of engineers and their early affiliations who were part of the above total.

Ralph Alex (Sikorsky)
Newby O. Brantley (Brantley)
Harris Campbell (ACA)
Elliot Daland (Piasecki)
Glidden S. Doman (Doman)
Lee Douglas (Piasecki/Boeing)
Jerome Friedenberg (Sikorsky)
Michael E. Gluhareff (Sikorsky)
Serge E. Gluhareff (Sikorsky)
Robert Head (McDonnell)
Harold Hirsch (Hughes)
Kurt Hohenemser (McDonnell)
William E. Hunt (Sikorsky/Teicher)
D. K. Jovanovich (McCulloch)
David H. Kaplan (Convertawings/Bell)
Edward F. Katzenberger (Sikorsky)
Harold E. Lemont, Jr. (Lemont)
Boris Labensky (Sikorsky)
Robert Lichten (Bell)
Ralph B. Lightfoot (Sikorsky)
Don Myers (Piasecki)
Allen Price (Platt-Le Page)
Charles M. Seibel (Seibel/Bell)
I. I. Sikorsky (Sikorsky)
Gerhard Sissingh (Hiller)
Wieslaw Z. Stepniewski (Boeing)
Joseph Stuart III (Hiller)
Miller Wachs (Sikorsky)
Robert Wagner (Hiller/Hughes)
Wayne Wiesner (Kellett/Hiller)

As remarked above the FW-61 was the first practical helicopter (Figures 3.115–3.117). [3.102] that is, the first after which the helicopter became a useful flying machine with unique capabilities. The first free flight (FW-61 V1) occurred June 26, 1936. In the following year, world's records were established with the FW-61, piloted by Ewald Rohlfs. Records include an endurance of 1 hour and 20 minutes, a distance in a closed circuit of 80.5 kilometers (50 miles), a speed of 122.3 km/h (76 mph), and altitude of 2440 meters (8000 feet). Aside from the records the decisive feature of power-off autorotation was demonstrated. (The rotor had only two collective pitch positions, one for powered flight and the other for autorotation.) The first autorotative flight was performed May 10, 1937 from an altitude of 400 meters (1310 feet).

Two machines were built. In 1938 Hanna Reitsch [3.103] in the V2 created an international sensation by flying it in the Berlin Sports Palace. However Carl Bode was Focke's test pilot in the pioneering years. [3.104]

Figure 3.114   Heinrich Focke with model of FA-223 helicopter.

Characteristics

Rotor diameter	7 m (23 ft)
Rotor speed range	150–400 rpm
Powerplant	Bramo SH-14A
Rated power	119.4 kW (160 hp)
Weights	
Gross	949 kg (2090 lb)
Empty	779 kg (1716 lb)

The world press acknowledged the primacy of Focke's helicopter, but he had critics. One of these was Oscar Asboth, mentioned previously. In their time his early machines set informal world's records. One of the pilots of an Asboth machine was RAF Captain R. N. Liptrot who also flew Isacco's *hélicogyre* in 1928.

Figure 3.115 Focke-Wulf FW-61, the first successful man-carrying helicopter (1936).

Figure 3.116 FW-61 showing engine cooling fan, mistaken by critics as a propeller.

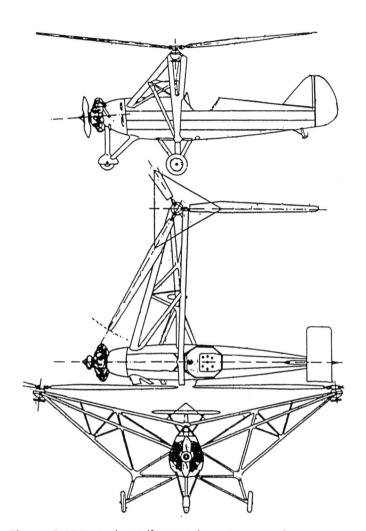

Figure 3.117   Focke-Wulf FW-61 three-view general arrangement.

In 1937 Asboth published an analysis that concluded the Focke machine could not reach the altitude it did as a helicopter, but as an autogiro. Asboth supported this argument by claiming more development on lifting propellers was necessary to make a practical helicopter than that suggested by Focke's work. Asboth concluded "The machine . . . is an autogiro which also can fly vertically to a degree, due to having a second rotor attachment". (He was referring to the "autogiro's" "propeller." [cooling fan].)

In an article in Luftwissen (1938), as if to enlighten Asboth, Focke described his detailed and systematic work since 1934, in arriving at the successful helicopter. [3.105] (His paper recognized the contribution of Cierva

to the practical helicopter, as later did Sikorsky.)

Focke concluded by taking exception to Asboth's ". . . . thinly disguised accusation of fraud" particularly regarding the altitude flight. He went on to state Asboth's calculations were based on misinformation, and the FW-61 alone demonstrated the ability to transition into autorotation, something Asboth was not able to do. On the performance of his machine he concluded.

"Nobody, myself included, would have thought such a performance possible, considering this is the first model and has relatively small power reserve. The success however illustrates in a brilliant manner the great future possibilities of helicopter flight."

Chapter 4
EPILOGUE

In view of the consistent failure of the helicopter entrepreneurs before Focke, it is of interest from an engineering viewpoint to examine what made the Wright brothers succeed compared with the designers of prototypes described here, and why the Wright Flyer (also Flyer I) was the first successful airplane. This when the Wrights were faced with the same set of problems confronted by other flying machine adherents.

Below is a technical analysis, of the Wright design approach contrasted with the helicopter equivalent in the early 20th century. [4.1]

The mere fact of successful mechanical flight in December 17, 1903 was in time so overwhelming subjectively, that technical analysis of why it succeeded became of minor interest. Technical

factors usually recounted concern the early gliding flights, use of a modest wind tunnel, and the (decisive) invention of wing warping for lateral control. Subsequent copying of the machine by others was not a technical analysis but an endorsement of the design.

In the first years of the 20th century the major problems faced by all addressing mechanical flight relate to the following: stability (i.e., instability), controllability, power, structural integrity, and weight. Nominally, all but power and weight involved safety of flight.

As mentioned before, a certain amount of instability can be tolerated if controllability is positive and effective. Both conditions, especially in the case of helicopters, prevail without taxing the pilot's human limits. The wings alone of the

Wright Flyer were very unstable but invention of wing warping (effectively, ailerons), along with a simple rectangular wing platform and forward placement of the elevators, resulted in an airplane manageable by the pilot.

An important corollary is that the Wright design minimized power, weight, and structural integrity. The installed engine power, and consequently weight and high speed, were minimized by launching the airplane into flight. This approach avoided the higher power required for takeoff, even though low power compromised flight speed, in order to favor the goal of practical flight itself. The choice reflects the Wrights' understanding of priorities.

Even the environment was factored in. For men from Dayton, Ohio to select Kill Devil Hills (Kitty Hawk), North Carolina for its steady winds does not come to mind immediately. Steady headwinds would reduce the power required by taking advantage of the energy in the wind, and this favors controllability in its smoothness (like a wind tunnel). However this favorable wind would discourage them from making a turn to fly downwind. The first complete circle was flown in 1904 with the improved Flyer II. Flyer III flown in June 1905, was the first "practical" airplane, a year and a half after the success with Flyer I.

Elimination of a wheeled landing gear not only reduced weight but its high drag (and power increment) as well. Equally drag-reducing was the prone position of the pilot, which in turn reduced weight by eliminating seating and other unessential equipment. The last for example would include an elaborate control actuating system required with upright seating, as well as airborne instruments. Minimization extended to leaving wood surfaces unpainted.

Use of two, large diameter, chain-driven propellers not only balanced torques but provided greater disk area, giving greater thrust per available power. (The disk loading effect also described for helicopter rotors.) Their own propeller design of carved wood is by mere inspection more efficient than the tube and fabric type (Figure 3.1) used by others. The Wrights recognized the propeller as a wing flying in a circle, a concept later accepted in helicopter rotor

analysis. Choosing two propellers rather than one large one of the same area and locating them between the wings, probably resulted from choice of short (skid) landing gear and a prone, centrally located pilot. Actually the pilot was off center, balancing the engine weight.

A single central propeller set higher than the engine, which was mounted on the plane of the lower wing, would be a hazard to the pilot. Hence in a tradeoff, two propellers were used either side of the pilot, mounted high enough to clear the ground, and at the same time providing a favorable airflow past the biplane wings.

Structural integrity concerned three main factors: wing loads in maneuvering, the propeller drive system, and powerplant operation (i.e., powerplant reliability) itself. Most likely the Wrights learned wing strength and minimum wing weight from their glider experience. The bridge-like rectangular, biplane structure that is wire-braced, is the simplest and strongest for the wing area desired. Wire-braced monoplane wings were more of a challenge and appeared 6–9 years later. The unsuccessful contemporaries favored the more difficult monoplane wings, probably because there were no biplane birds around to copy.

In flight demonstrations there is no evidence that the Flyer I developed high load factors. Aerodynamically they probably could not pull high "g's". For example they avoided turns that would develop load factors. This was unlikely in any case since the plane flew only a few feet above the ground, and in ground effect (another minimum).

A less obvious consideration is the fact the Wrights were further into development and solved problems (reflected in the design) not confronted by their contemporaries because flights of the latter were marginal or bound to the ground.

Powerplant reliability was verified by bench tests with an engine of their own construction, a design emphasizing low weight and functional simplicity.

Overall one can conclude the design of the Wright Flyer I was marginal in all respects but the decisive one of controlled flight. It was a highly integrated design, with a well defined priority, serving a single and successful purpose. It was the first aeronautical "proof-of-concept" design, and could not be used for anything else, including repeated flying.

The Wrights' contemporaries though they accomplished "something", failed to a major extent because they missed the point of leaving on the ground every thing and every idea but the essential ones for practical flight, and in not knowing there was only one crucial factor: adequate control of instability. The latter they did not learn empirically, for few machines left the ground into free flight long enough to deal with the problem. The Wrights' sophisticated totality of the pre-flying tradeoffs and design integration along with minimization and focus are not evident features when analyzing contemporary flying machines. This lack of evidence applies to the early helicopters as well.

For a helicopter, the problems are more demanding because it must hover. On the ground or in the air, a helicopter is always alive. Of a modern helicopter as a design problem it is said the creature is a flying fatigue machine, one that resists being what the engineer insists it must be. This aphorism reflects an appreciation of the uncompromising problem prototype builders of the early 20th century were willing to take on, despite the failures around them. A corollary aphorism: "nature is a jealous mistress".

Weight control even today is a greater requirement, again because of the hovering feature. In prototypes, the light weight, self-cooling rotary engine was found good-fortune. Hovering cooling became a development problem in the 1940–1945 period when the lighter, airplane piston engines were adapted to helicopters.

Some of the early entrepreneurs chose the propeller-type rotor accepting weight for strength, but at the same time settling for a reduced diameter, both associated with higher power required. As described in the Glossary, selecting a larger rotor of wing construction reduced weight and power, but this choice introduced vibration problems in the blades and slender shafting.

Helicopter structural integrity was more demanding. Everything was vibrating whether on the ground or briefly in the air. Structural fatigue, a fundamental consideration in all modern helicopters, was little understood in aircraft until the late 1930s. Rotor blade fatigue, with the blades bending cyclically as they rotate, first appeared as a problem in the autogiro era. It was not until the late 1950s that analytical techniques were developed to deal with blade fatigue and service life (flight hours before retirement) of blades. The object is to design blades with "infinite life".

Relative to fixed wings, the conflict in early machines between stability and controllability was more severe, and there was a misunderstanding of rotor design and behavior. None of the experimenters produced a control design that could be considered effective, nor did they understand rotors except as a simple, but perverse, lifting devices. The Wrights understood fixed wings before the first powered flight. Contrary to 19th century belief, they rejected the notion stability was achieved by some pendulous mass below the machine. The helicopter experimenters showed no sense of priorities as did the Wrights, and bundled all the development problems in one grand trial and error effort with prototypes. However they were only acting in the spirit of the age (particularly in America). Few were as deliberate as Robert Fulton. Only Hewitt had a grasp of rotor performance and only Rochon understood blade articulation and elastic flexure. Focke, consistent with the Wrights' approach reduced the helicopter to practice. Like the Flyer I, the FW-61 as a design was just enough to prove helicopter flight was feasible and not much more.

The systematic approach, as remarked before, is known elaborately today as systems engineering. It is the fundamental methodology in taking on vast problems (particularly, one of a kind) in aeronautical and space engineering. The methodology has spread to other field as well, commercial architecture for example. Ultimately the systematic approach was the common quality that Fulton, the Wrights, and Focke demonstrated in common.

If there is a general lesson from their work it is this: work methodically, seek out the critical element, and minimize everything else. What results is not optimum but it proves the point. With this particular methodology one is compelled to update that almost forgotten 19th century remark critical of flight: "If God wanted man to fly He would have given him wings". Or brains.

Considering the previously noted good ideas (of Veyrin, Rochon, Hewitt, and Cierva in particular), a provocative thought is why historically, these progressive ideas on helicopters were not followed up. The assumption here is that "progress" moves in a straight line, that good ideas are immediately picked up to enhance the process of innovation. There are at least three explanations for this.

1. Fixed wing was demonstrated by the Wrights as the proven approach to mechanical flight. This marginalized helicopter investigations. A machine with a questionable future, in the light of its unsuccessful past. [4.2]
2. There was no useful, analytical engineering base, i.e., theory initiated or extant on such concepts as performance and stability. The lack was recognized by Chanute in 1894, and it applied nominally to helicopters until the late 1920s and 1930s. It is very desirable to have a theory first to know what is important in observations, and to know the rational avenues of research. Part of the problem here was individuals who could contribute were more interested in fixed-wing principles.
3. A corollary of the second explanation is the general absence of analytical sophistication in this particular field, in contrast to pure mathematics, for example. Invention, intuition, and accident were the ways of creativity. A well-known example of "reverse theory" applies to thermodynamics. It emerged as a discipline only after steam engine development proved itself in practice.

With regard to modern, evolving helicopter technology, the trend is toward augmenting knowledge by extensive and detailed analyses. (Such an approach is more American than European.) One relies less on deliberate invention and more on sound, interacting analytical and experimental methods. This view does not minimize scientific discovery but there is less possibility of this in helicopters today. Today, rela-

tively more and varied intellectual energy can be brought to a problem. The modern effort is based on extensive use of computers in analysis, design, and manufacturing, computers for example have made possible an entirely new approach to structural analysis: the finite element method. This method applies to such complex components as rotor blades and airframes as well as simple parts (e.g., critical bolts).

In sum, ideas can be ahead of their time because the environment for appreciation or understanding is simply not there. The only "fault" here is using today's knowledge to judge that of yesterday's.

In view of the erratic technological way to the successful helicopter as discussed above, one can reflect on the public and professional response to such an advanced idea as a flying machine in general, and the helicopter in particular. [4.2]

As described before, this activity followed both inventive and scientific directions. Remarkable to the helicopter itself was the prolonged duration in public view of the mostly unsuccessful efforts to make it practical. For an ultimately successful and unusual product as a flying machine, one may postulate five discrete stages to both the public and professional response to the work of its adherents.

1. On introducing the idea of human flight by mechanical means, the initial reaction is to see it as impossible. Only in mythology, fantasy, and religion did humans have wings.
2. In time, the dogmatic view softens as the notion develops a life of its own. Disputation involves broad philosophic principles and claims.
3. In the third stage the concept is deemed impractical. Criticism is now on specific technical or barrier problems that inhibit feasibility.
4. The idea is taken seriously in the fourth stage. Technical problems are discussed. There is tentative, and at times skeptical acceptance.
5. Finally there is general acceptance. Because the concept (the flying machine) has been reduced to practice; an accomplished fact. Nothing makes things so obvious as a detailed explanation.

Not every critic or adherent necessarily ran the full course. One could enter the discourse at any stage.

For helicopters and flying machines in general, the first three stages are identified here with the 19th century. Recall the *Scientific American* criticism of 1848 and its attitude change in 1869. Other (French) criticism was described in the 19th century summary.

The fourth and fifth stages apply to the early 20th century. The success of the Wrights in 1903 ultimately removed doubts abut flying machines, but not immediately, for there were skeptics. That consummate aeronautical engineer Igor Sikorsky witnessed those early years and recounts in a paper in 1971 initial skepticism toward the 1903 flights. He recalls a newspaper article headlined "Fliers or Liars". Below this was the editorial comment:

> "When a man of profound scientific wisdom has demonstrated with unassailable logic why a man could not fly, why should the public be fooled by silly stories about two bicycle repair men who have never been to college. . . .".

Sikorsky witnessed the initial flight demonstration of the Wright machine in Europe (France, 1908) and wrote in the same paper . . . . "the impression and enthusiasm were tremendous". [4.3] With this demonstration the world accepted the airplane as here to stay. [4.4] About 30 years later one could say the same about the helicopter.

In the 1920s and 1930s, the helicopter went through its own third and fourth stages of reaction. Such took the form of both personal and technical criticism. The limited publicity on the Beach (1920) model dwelt on his novel approach to using "planetary engines" that whirled in circle-like gyroscopes. Editorial comment on the idea concluded with the remark that apparently there was a ". . . . total eclipse. . . ." of the system.

Exel, who worked on many variants (1920–1923) was considered a "nut" and chronic "tinkerer", a typical character of that era. He married late, preferring to spend his time and funds (he ran a garage) courting the helicopter.

During World War II helicopter development was at a low level. After the war, American engineers could not dump the autogiro and deprecate its prominent engineers fast enough for the helicopter. This put the latter on the defensive, even though they were not anti-helicopter. This technological drift was a resounding and lasting statement of the importance of hover capability. Enthusiasm peaked in the early 1950s when about 120 American companies and entrepreneurs were involved in its development. [4.4] Today one could count 10 at most.

After the war the author had conversations with the pioneer Isacco, then a resident of Paris, and the Italian D'Ascanio, on their treatment in the early days, before they were justified in their beliefs. Isacco was invited to the Soviet Union to build a giant helicopter with a 24.4 meter (80 foot) diameter rotor, which he produced in 1935. He was deported when construction was completed not knowing the fate of his machine. Years later it was revealed the craft never flew, due to rotor problems.

In 1930 the D'Ascanio helicopter in Italy set a world record. After the war he visited the United States to follow up on current helicopter activities. Considering the vindication of belief in the helicopter, he was asked what bothered him most in those early days. It was the public head-shaking in his presence, implying he was foolish and mad to get involved in such crazy idea. (His second problem was the constant contention with the financial backers.)

Another aspect of the last two stages is the professional, or scientific approach to the helicopter. In the United States, NACA took the lead as suggested before. If one includes its autogiro work, rotary wing aircraft got fair treatment before World War II. The first NACA report on helicopters was released in 1920 (Technical Note 4). Aside from other reports on European activities, this document was followed by one in 1925 by Alexander Klemin. [4.6] The author was an early proponent of the helicopter and an early educator on the subject. Within this time interval, the only testing at NACA involved a propeller-type rotor in forward flight. All helicopter work was dropped with the advent of the autogiro in the early 1920s, but it was revived in the 1940s. Practically all the basic helicopter theory and testing emerged from work by this organization.

In general, the criticism directed at mechanical flight in the 19th century was not differentiated. But there was divergence toward the end of the century and into the next one. Certainly the drift was due to the positive progress with the fixed wing principle. In contrast rotary wing proponents still had to endure criticism and apparently rely mostly on faith that the machine could be made practical.

Considering the variety of prototype flying machines and their powerplants, comment is sparse on the noise signature such devices make, something that becomes very evident even to its creator on the first runup of these unique devices. Noise pattern can be reviewed from both historical and contemporary aspects. The latter is a problem of increasing concern.

Noise as a positive value was mentioned in conjunction with James Watt. Chalmers (1908) vividly described the sound of his rotor system. A contraption that looked suspect to begin with could easily sway public to ridicule by the sound it made. The notion of unanticipated acoustical phenomena extended into the 1950s when blade tip engines on jet-propelled helicopters were first run up. In one case the noise of a two-seat pulsejet helicopter with its tip-mounted (buzz bomb) engines could be heard about 7 kilometers (6 miles) away. The pulsejet emitted an organ-trumpet sound while the ramjet produced a high pitch sound due to the high tip speeds necessary for operation.

With the modern, tail rotor helicopter one could anticipate the tail rotor noise because it is a kind of propeller. But it is unlikely anyone expected the "blade slap" sound characteristic of helicopters under certain flight conditions. Blade slap is due to rapid air pressure variations on the main rotor blades. The phenomenon is strongest (loudest) when the helicopter is descending in its own wake (air vortecies), particularly in the 113–145 km/h (70–90 mph) speed range. However the slap is not always very loud. The movie *Apocalypse Now* had a long helicopter sequence featuring as much blade slap as helicopters. As suggested above, helicopter noise has become a major design problem regarding wider, close-in public acceptance.

The specifics described immediately above do not suggest the underlying social view of science and technology that is spotted throughout this book. 19th century attitudes were highly favorable of their benefits, ignoring the human consequences. A general optimism and faith that science and technology could solve all problems was strong in America in the last half of that century. Aspects of the view are touched on in different parts of the book: the New York Crystal Palace Exhibition of 1853, steam power, the telegraph (with ". . . . the cycle of invention complete. . . ."), interest in balloons and aerial fight in general, and the periodical, *Scientific American* created (1845) to record this spirit. The truth is technical solutions do not solve social problems, but they can create them.

The turn of the century revealed an attitude change. There emerged skepticism that all science in conjunction with a pliable and abundant Nature produced nothing but good. Science fiction writers, particularly the later Verne described here, and H. G. Wells wrote of the dark side of this benevolence. It is curious a similar skepticism is emerging at the turn of the 20th century, a subject fit for a new, revealing book on social philosophy. Even so, there is no stopping the evolution of technology.

The foregoing accounted for public reaction to the helicopter of the past. There is also a public reaction to the helicopter of the present. While there seems to be a general acceptance of the helicopter as an appealing and useful aircraft, there are significant numbers who perceive this machine in negative ways, implying fear and dread, at least as a result of presentations in TV shows, in films, and in the print media, i.e., novels, science fiction, and comics. (Use for TV news reporting tells a different story.)

The helicopter is seen and presented as a lethal instrument devoid of accountability, representing law and order, arrogance, and power. Advertising offers its own image, exhibiting the helicopter as a symbol of status, privilege, and wealth. Mysterious government activities, with potential for destruction devoid of credible explanation reinforce even further this negative view. These perceptions are hardly the ones of its early visionaries, way back to Mortimer Nelson (1865). Nonetheless it is a practical statement of the uses of technology when released to the public.

The proper response to these unfavorable views is for its sources to present a balanced picture, ultimately favorable to what the helicopter is about. This response is unlikely so long as sensationalism sells. The helicopter today is a novelty, a ready subject for this exploitation. It is important for individuals to understand the helicopter is far more than the fantasies created by various forms of entertainment.

Consider the following. Combining military and civil versions, there are about 38,000 helicopters flying today, the world over. Roughly half are in civil operations. All these helicopters are doing work less desirable or not feasible by other means, work that is not often brought to public attention in the news or via the entertainment media. Some such as emergency medical services (EMS) when shown are taken for granted.

Military operations include extensive flight training, combat simulation, field exercises, and others of a utility nature (transport, search and rescue, EMS). Civil operations are more varied, covering training, corporate services, charter work (logging, crop dusting, EMS, aerial photography-including filming evil helicopters, fire-fighting), and scheduled transport, as oil rig servicing.

One possible explanation for the subjective, negative view of many, is the general public has little personal contact to date with the helicopter and no control of it, unlike the association with fixed-wing aircraft. Whatever are the failings of the latter, these are kept in perspective because of airplanes' utility in daily life. As a prospect, the more people are familiar and involved usefully with helicopters the more control they will have over them. The less will be the alienation and speculation over the true role of the helicopter in their lives.

The concluding part of this account of early rotary wing ideas and projects is a reflection on this activity in a wider context. Specifically, the part considers the work in relation to technical progress in general, today's counterparts of the early entrepreneurs and inventors, the military

and civil systems that have emerged, the political and international environment, and finally an overview of what the pioneers of the 19th and early 20th centuries were all about.

Here technical progress has two features. One is the time-lag between the idea and its practical application, commented on previously in specific cases. The other is progress itself in technology creation.

Considering the time-lag first, it was noted that heated activity in mechanical flight began in the middle years of the 19th century, about 70 years after the first manned balloon flight. A second lag in this period concerns the initial development of the internal combustion engine, with its delay in aircraft application of about 40 years. A third lag refers to the practical rotor for a helicopter, including the flapping hinge (along with low disk loading). The idea of a flapping hinge was published as early as 1911. A hinge patent existed in 1913 and in the early 1920s the autogiro demonstrated the practical need for the hinge. Yet it was not until the late 1930s that the idea was incorporated in the successful helicopter.

These lags are acceptance anomalies that have diminished with time into the present era. That is, today the gap between a new concept (or problem) and its practical application (or resolution) is much narrower. A new idea seems to find spontaneous applications. Most likely the receptivity phenomenon is due to the effects of global mobility and communication. Both are brought on by technology itself. This dispersion has been called "stimulus diffusion". [4.7] People catch on faster today than they did years ago.

The interest in mechanical flight in mid-19th century took place during the Industrial Revolution. But such is not an explanation. Most likely it involves a system of circumstances. Supporting a previous remark, a reason the balloon preempted other ideas is that it worked, becoming the accepted way to travel through the air. As Robur discovered, progress in manned flight was then merely a matter of improving the idea, by adding propellers and shaping the bag.

The dominance of the balloon for such a long period revealed its shortcomings and limitations, important preconditions for change. The deficiencies reinforced the view of advocates of mechanical flight, even though some others believed the quest was in the same category as perpetual motion.

Refuting the negatives were measurements with lifting surfaces that demonstrated feasibility, followed by manned glider flights. Now the focus was on fixed wings. There was obvious progress in this approach, and the reasoned view put priority on this form of flight. While there was convergence toward practical fixed wing flight, helicopter advocates had to wait longer to show comparable progress.

The second feature listed above referred to technical progress itself in technology creation. In the long view technological innovation has proceeded along a line that can be seen as logarithmic. There were "bursts" of innovation along the way, and periods of stagnation. (One author postulated "geniuses" through history appeared in clusters.) "Stagnation" refers to periods when the status-quo resisted such progress. Even so, such a curve describes the general trend. Until the Second World War the creation and diffusion of knowledge was relatively slow. That war represents the bend in the curve that shoots upward (the eminence of stimulus diffusion). One could argue the bend existed in the First World War. In terms of human history the 25 year difference is not significant.

The idea of the wheel is at least 5000 years old, and carts and four wheel wagons are just as old. However it was not until about 800 A.D. that wagon builders introduced the pivot for the front wheels useful for making tighter turns. Today the idea is one that would almost immediately suggest itself. The Romans thought of it but chose the short wheel base wagons instead, apparently an early example of an army favoring mission and maintainability over maneuverability and vulnerability. (An army of maneuver would have made the opposite choice.) The steam and windmill ideas of Heron mentioned earlier in conjunction with toys, also had no followup until centuries later. It took a millennium for the helicopter toy to travel from China to Europe, if it came that way at all.

The notion of "progress" itself is relatively new. Most likely in old times before the "bend", tech-

nology responded to immediate needs. People lived by tradition, a solidifying concept. Aside from religion, they had little else to go by. Their vision was limited to the seasons, not technology. Innovation implies a break in the traditional way of doing things. Today progress, being "modern", is a value in itself regardless of the worth of the output. Needs are created in a consumer economy. Consistent with the location of this bend is the remark by a 19th century historian (Henry Adams), anticipating the oncoming 20th century. "The American boy of 1854 stood nearer the year 1 than the year 1900."

Today, evolving technical innovation is different because it affects social human factors and the individual's very biological structure, with a concurrent impact on values. (A value attached to an object becomes an attitude.) "Technology", critical as it is, still lacks the status or focus of, for example "the economy". Often technology is subsumed by it even though technology has a separate existence, and is driving society. The availability is such that priorities must be established in the specific technologies through its social value. The view impacts on helicopters as well as other forms of technical innovation. Progress in this field is not defined by the technology itself, but by the social value and politics it engenders.

A characteristic of the 21st century is the concern for placing limitations on technical progress not by technology but by a new social, environmental, and global consciousness that will impose moral values and priorities on it. The helicopter with its simple and significant hover capability will always be part of this progress. The question is, how many?

The introductions and narratives revealed two types of investigators termed inventive and scientific (or technical). The former described one who relies more on intuition than formal technical discipline, in undertaking helicopter work. The latter applies a trained, systematic approach to this activity. One can identify the current counterparts of these advocates.

Except possibly for patents, the (helicopter) inventive type has disappeared from public notice. As mentioned before, in the 1950s there were numerous helicopter projects in the United

States. (A repeat of fixed-wing builders after the First World War.) Many were independent, inventive individuals who worked with models or prototypes. Their disappearance is attributed to the success of the helicopter itself, the complexity in defining current problems, the development costs, the lack of investor interest, and the idea the hovering problem was "solved".

Today these inventive individuals are replaced by amateur technicians (home or kit builders) interested in constructing their own helicopters of a proven design. Those who design the kits are innovators but work at a different level from those who searched for the practical helicopter. Equally significant is the difference in available knowledge, materials, and components.

The scientific counterpart is found mostly within the helicopter industry itself (often including academia). The maturing process leads to specialization. Now specialists are the foundation of the industry. This specialization leads to projects led by a program or systems manager. One replaces the independent entrepreneur of earlier years, but they are not interchangeable.

The modern manager should have both the tenacity of the entrepreneur ("defending the design") and a technical understanding of one's subject. The earlier scientific type showed more interest in technology than management. The specialized approach depersonalizes the program. With large programs (or large companies) visibility is lost, except for the few at the top level. The systems engineering concept in the present sense does not create, for it deals with process or methodology. An organization will have a special creative staff, typically the "advanced design" group. Here is the place for today's technical entrepreneur. Methodology itself as a discipline is an important characteristic of modern engineering, replacing the "groping" of earlier years. Today in industry there are both "technical engineers" and "systems engineers."

The startup technical entrepreneur in the helicopter field is scarce today, in contrast to software applications designers, for example. As suggested above, the scarcity is due mainly to the costs involved and the lack of venture capital interest. A more subtle point concerns the fact a hovering rotor is a very simple, unsophisticated device, once

they got the parameters right. As a result there is little room for a breakthrough in hovering systems, except in simplifying the helicopter itself. Further, there is a limit to how fast a rotor can be flown edgewise through the air. For these reasons the VTOL is the direction for major changes but at the sacrifice of hover capability.

Technology always had two branches, military and civil. In fact military engineering was one of the first technical professions. Except for the ephemeral, Civil War activity and the DeBothezat helicopter project, the full span of the narratives reveal no military influence. Since the advent of the practical helicopter, the military have been the driving force behind helicopter development. This branch of technology has lived up to all the expectations put on the military idea of the helicopter, and in a relatively short time. From the historical viewpoint this is a remarkable achievement by the industry, yet one taken from granted.

In reflecting on the number of good ideas the early entrepreneurs advanced that were ignored, one can appreciate the value of urgent military necessity in forcing positive development. This notion is exemplified in the dramatic difference in aircraft quality before and after two world wars, and in today's progress in military helicopters versus commercial ones.

One can conclude it is an aspect of human behavior passed down in history that the absence of war is an opportunity cost to technology, not made up by the "commercial spirit". Being "lean and mean" by definition creates nothing. It means withdrawal and consolidation. The kind of technology described here requires patrons. Often with technology, the government is the biggest patron of all. In recent times the military role has been in a state of flux as is its financial support of the helicopter. The prospects are for integration of civil and military requirements and technology. International trends indicate a widening of the use of helicopters in matters of prominence in the 21st century: conservation, ecology, inspection and peacekeeping, these in addition to humanitarian missions. Oddly enough, the last is not free of hostile resistance.

In recent years the civil (commercial) branch benefited from the military developments. The two, fundamental vehicles envisioned by the early rotary wing advocates have yet to be realized. These are the personal or private helicopter and the scheduled intercity or feeder helicopter. Success in both these areas would increase use far beyond the present operations. Despite progress in the technology itself, the helicopter today is a special purpose vehicle. Its strong suit waits to be played.

In the 1940s a well-known helicopter pioneer predicted in a decade or so, people would be visiting each other in their private helicopters. Toward the end of World War II many articles were written on the privately owned helicopter to come (Figure 4.1). Now the concept is given little thought. In the light of today's helicopters, the notion is fanciful. Aside from the vehicle design problem itself, such a concept (the private helicopter) cannot exist except as part of a vast system of its own.

The common motor vehicle, a modern utensil, is part of a system so extensive that a substantial part of the population is employed in the field of transportation. The environment has been altered in many ways, first to accommodate it, but now to its disadvantage. Today its negative impact is increasingly in public consciousness.

The problem of introducing a new system concerns not only vehicle design, but it encompasses the new, extensive system itself, one that must compete with the old existing vehicle system. Even though there is a case for the private helicopter, the technology requires development, and there is always room for optimism. Humans used the horse for at least 4000 years, yet it was wiped out by the motor vehicle in about 40 years. By doing nothing the latter will get its four thousand year run. Think of it.

The technology does exist for the commercial, short haul transport helicopter. Considering "public convenience and necessity", ground and air traffic congestion, limited airport space, and noise, the helicopter offers more in new possibilities than the fixed wing aircraft, when moving goods and people over short distances.

Like the private helicopter, the early vision remains unfulfilled (Figure 4.2). The industry has failed to capitalize on the inherent advantages of the transport concept, the very reason historically individuals aspired and strived to produce a craft that could hover and fly vertically. Once the helicopter was created, this idea was set aside.

Figure 4.1   The private helicopter of the future from the viewpoint of 1945.

Figure 4.2 The commercial passenger helicopter of the future as envisioned in 1946.

A basic problem is the craft attempts to compete with the fixed-wing counterpart on the latter's terms. The helicopter (in studies at least) tries to fit into the fixed-wing system that pervades the country. Needed is a new philosophy for an independent heliport system, a national grid taking in the whole country, dedicated to intercity (including small city) transport and shuttle service. City-center operations and airline through traffic, physically are not part of this concept. Integration with the latter would require future reshuffling of the total concept of air travel.

The heliports are scaled down, unique versions of airports created in uncongested areas. Each is paired to another city and assigned its own "catch region". The philosophy resembles that in creating a modern mall, but not in imitation of it. The venue suggests the idea behind location of industrial parks, which imply the same geographical purpose. Such heliports are accessible by surface vehicles (autos, busses, taxis, limousines) via new roads, away from today's traffic flow.

A pilot system would spot the heliports near New York City and Washington. The vehicle should carry around 100 passengers, with noise attenuation and all-weather capability as major design requirements. The useful load to include passengers, mail, and express goods. To the benefits of public transportation are those related to new forms of employment including one that maintains a skilled technical pool.

Funding for such a system is accounted for in phases. The startup activity is a joint venture including government, industry, and capital (venture, debt, equity). The initial shortfall is made up in (federal, state, local) subsidy.

It can be noted the airlines were originally subsidized. The above financing approach makes more sense than the endemic, periodic bailout of private ventures, a kind of unwitting subsidy paid retroactively. With responsible regulation, the money would be put to use in serving useful social ends.

In general it is likely every public transportation system worldwide requires a subsidy, either visible or invisible. It is inherent in any public transportation system that the more people who are served, the more inefficient the service is. The

most efficient government provides no service at all. Aside from being anarchic consider the following. Many people do not fly, but pay their share of the national airway system. If only fliers paid, the air fare would include a substantial, pro-rated portion of the airway operation and maintenance costs. To argue the non-flier benefits indirectly is correct. But this presumes two classes of citizens. Ultimately the decision is one of the cost-benefit to society of this new mode of travel.

The civil-military boost should come from a basic, purposeful national industrial policy. A concept of increasing need in view of the intense competitiveness of the modern, interdependent global economy.

The 1950s bend in the curve described previously has a peculiar American significance. Around that time there was a coarse rule (the author's) regarding technology. Whatever were the fruits of it, the United States owned 40–50 percent of the world total. A check of an almanac will verify this. (History is repeating itself today with computers.) Since that period the rest of the world is rightfully gaining an increasing share. Even so, the wealth of a country is not what it owns, but what it produces and exports.

Without a vision as described above, the worldwide helicopter industry is greater than is the demand for helicopters. Added to this problem is the large number of military surplus helicopters on the market. Devoid of vision the industry implodes rather than explodes. In view of the increasing global interaction and interdependence, people of all nations are questioning their identity and the limits of nationalism. If history teaches anything it is that change is normal, that we have not reached the rotary wing End of Technology, that the goal of social expenditure is now only to support its entropy.

An industrial policy should not only support the helicopter industry but aviation in general. For its aeronautical achievements have benefited world commerce, and at the same time upgraded the technology and methodology of other disciplines. This wider support should involve the ultimate transportation concept (terrestrial, at least). Such a concept implies activity well into the 21st century.

Two voids in this ultimate spectrum refer to global mass travel (GMT), and the previously noted personal helicopter. The automobile will continuously amplify its qualities as both a boon and bane to society.

The boon is in low cost global travel by means of Atlantic and Pacific car ferries, traveling over water at high speed using the air cushion principle. Such giants will carry thousands of cars in a roll-on, roll-off mode. The powerplant system is in the thousand megawatt range. With fusion energy as the power source, electricity is supplied to superconducting motors, used for both lift and propulsion. (Verne's *Albatross* of the 21st century.)

Considering the bane, the private auto is in a Malthusian bind. The number of cars keeps increasing (even with possible population control) but the number of new, desirable urban venues is practically constant. This bind results in increasing congestion, gridlock, quality time loss (in engine-idle), exhaust pollution, and emotional dysfunction.

By default people will be compelled to take to the air, opening up more desirable land in the process. The helicopter is the only vehicle that can meet this need. When the need becomes a necessity, the public will accommodate the new aerial system that will one day be as comprehensive and pervasive as the present automobile system. Recall the horse and the improbability

of the auto replacing it. The total concept involves more than travel. The new technologies will provide work for women and men in a stream for generations. There is little doubt of the enduring social value of these concepts.

Such ventures require leadership, possessing inspired vision combined with the drive and resources to follow through. These ventures can and should be defining features of the 21st century.

Viewing in retrospect the helicopters and variants of the 19th and early 20th centuries, it is unusual for an ultimately successful technology to unfold such consistent inappropriateness even though the components for success were being revealed with time and in parallel. One cannot conclude the helicopter "evolved" in this period, as did the airplane. In truth the helicopter "mushroomed" in the late 1930s. These early efforts were a chaotic collection of ideas and activities, all sharing a common objective.

Hindsight is good vision, and hindsight teaches something. While of little significance to evolution, one values in these helicopter pioneers the dedication, seriousness, enthusiasm, and entrepreneurial spirit. One recalls an Italian saying "the results were indifferent, but the performance was spectacular". They knew what they wanted but overall, they were a group whose reach exceeded their grasp.

Appendix A

OTHER PROJECTS

The following list of activities are not covered in the narratives, mainly because little information is available on them to warrant narrative treatment. Some feature illustrations only, and for these the figure number is given below along with the reference.

Key: C-concept only, P-patent information, M-model, T-tests, V-vehicle (prototype built or under construction).

1849	Porter and Robjohn	C	*Revoiloidal spindle aeriod* [A.1]
1862	Luther C. Crowell West Denis, MA	P	Steam-powered tiltrotor Early convertiplane concept [A.2]
1886	John Wooton Boonton, NJ	C	Rotor-parachute [A.3]
1871	S. Trudell New Orleans, LA	M	Coaxial rotor helicopter Drop-tested from a balloon [A.4]

Figure A.1　Lateral rotor helicopter concept of W. D. G. (1874).

1874	W. D. G. New York City	C	Steam-powered lateral rotor helicopter Empty weight (68 kg (150 lb) (Figure A.1) [A.5]
1879	John J. Greenough Syracuse, NY	P	Fans in wing, component tests (Figure A.2) *Aerobat* [A.6]
1880s	Dudgeon	T	Lifting screws
1885	J. S. Foster	C	Human-powered, lateral rotors Diameter 2.44 m (8 ft) [A.7]
1888	Edward P. Johnson	C	Multi-rotor, Six propellers for lift and thrust [A.8]
1892	J. C. Walker Texas	P	VTOL, blowers for lift [A.9]
1908	Rudolph Dressler	V	[A.10]

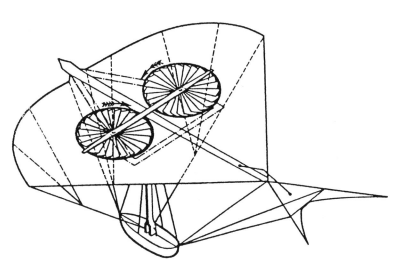

Figure A.2　Greenough Aerobat (1879).

1908	H. T. Keating	T	Twin screws inclined inward
	Columbus, OH		35 degrees [A.11]
1909	L. S. Dorland	P	[A.12]
	San Francisco, CA		
1909	J. Potts	P	Biplane-helicopter, four airscrews
	Winchester, OH		22.4 kw (30 hp) [A.13]
1909	Wade	P	Air sucker (jet-lift) [A.14]
	Chicago, IL		
1909	Klassen	V	*gyroplane*, chain-driven rotors
	San Francisco, CA		(Figure A.3) [A.15]
1909	Baptiste	P	[A.16]
	Saint Louis, MO		
1909	H. La V. Twining	P	Two lifting screws, Aero Club of California [A.17]
1910	W. L. Green		Flapper (ornithopter)-helicopter [A.18]
	Monroe City, MO		
1910	Irvine		Cyclogiro [A.19]
1910	Lacour		Helicopter-biplane [A.20]

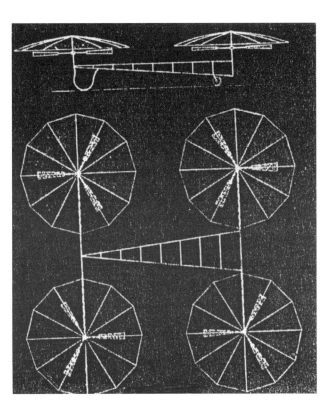

Figure A.3 Klassen quadrotor prototype (1909).

1910	J. Muckle Kansas City, MO		Air sucker (jet-lift) [A.21]
1910	F. O. Cates	P	[A.22]
1910	C. H. Buckbee Selwood, OR		Four screws, boat-shaped body [A.23]
1910	G. W. Calvert Acheson, MO		Multi-screw, universally jointed [A.24]
1910	A. H. Freidel Baltimore, MD	V	Twin screws [A.25]
1910	A. H. Hettinger Bridgeton, NJ	V	Powerplant by the designer [A.26]
1910	Etienne Planche Trenton, NJ		[A.27]
1910	Lefevre brothers Smyrna, DE	V	[A.28]
1911	Lincoln Beachey	C	Popular exhibition flyer [A.29]
1919	J. E. McWorter Saint Louis, MO		*Autoplane* [A.30]
1925	C. Q. Payne	C	
1926	Shaw	P	Prop-driven wing, (Figure A.4) [A.31]
1930s	E. A. Stalker Ann Arbor, MI	T	Jet-driven rotor, Univ. of Michigan to the 1940s, (Figure A.5) [A.32]

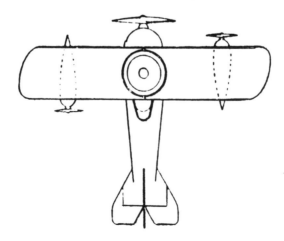

Figure A.4 Shaw propeller-driven rotor concept (1926).

Figure A.5 Stalker jet-driven rotor test rig (1945).

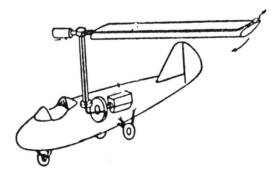

Figure A.6 Knight single-blade jet-driven rotor concept.

Figure A.7 Knight single-blade rotor test rig (1940s).

1930s	Montgomery Knight Atlanta, GA	T	One blade, jet-driven rotor [A.33] Georgia Tech (Figures A.6, A.7)
1931	John Buczkowski Great Neck, NY	M	[A.34]
1934	Harry Cordy	V	Jet-lift, (Figures 3.110, 3.111)
1938	Halligan brothers Beardstown, IL	V	Two-blade propeller-driven rotor marginal hover [A.35]
1939	Lawrence W. Brown Clinton, MO	P	[A.36]

Appendix B

COMPETITION ENTRANTS 1924

The following is a complete list of the entrants to the British helicopter competition of 1924. This list and the one for the 1925–1926 competition were supplied by the pioneer helicopter pilot and RAF Captain, R. N. Liptrot. He later authored a book *Rotorcraft* with J. D. Woods (Butterworth, 1955). It appears both lists have never been made public before. The references are from other sources.

Key: AA-Austria, AU-Australia, BR-Great Britain, DE-Denmark, FR-France, GE-Germany, IT-Italy, NE-Netherlands, US-United States, DE-Design, MO-Model, PA-Patent, PR-Prototype, UC-Under construction.

J. W. Waite and Col. Turner-Clarke	BR	UC	Paddle rotors
F. DeGrosse	AU	DE	Concept only
V. Newbauer	US	PA	1,446,718 [B.1]
Chicago Helicopters (T. O. Perry)	US	PR	Coaxial rotors [B.2]
C. M. Brune	BR	UC	Modified biplane, British 154,929

A. C. W. Begg	US	DE	Novel rotor
J. R. Porter	BR		Novel lift system [B.3]
British Helicopter Co. (Purton and Purton)	BR		British 168,732 and 201,989
G. F. Myers	US	PR	[B.4]
W. Lux	US	UC	
Hellesen-Kahn	FR	PR	Propeller-driven rotor [B.5]
E. Berliner	US		[B.6]
F. Samide	BR		Paddles [B.7]
M. Fitzgerald			No work on prototype
A. G. Von Baumhauer	NE	UC	Helicopter-biplane. [B.8] British patent application 9821/1924
W. E. Brown	US	DE	[B.9]
C. H. Keefer	US		Helicopter-biplane [B.10]

Appendix C

COMPETITION ENTRANTS 1925-1926

Key: AA-Austria, AU-Australia, BR-Great Britain, DE-Denmark, FR-France, GE-Germany, IT-Italy, NE-Netherlands, US-United States, DE-Design, MO-Model, PA-Patent, PR-Prototype, UC-Under construction.

E. D. Haworth	BR		Three rotors and wings
G. Spurgeon and Chapman	BR	DE	
F. F. Greenaway	BR	DE	Ten, 7.5 kW (10 hp) engines
J. Westaway	BR	DE	Concept only
J. Westaway and Skelt	BR		Three 7.5 kW (10 hp) engines and 3.1 m (10 ft) diameter rotors
C. M. Brune	BR	PR	Helicopter-biplane
W. Scotter	BR	PR	British 16,494/1924 and 17,981/1915

A. G. Von Baumhauer	NE	PR	Helicopter-airplane [B.8] British patent application 9821/1924
E. T. Buckley	BR	MO	Model tests
M. B. Bleecker	US	DE	Prototype not yet built [C.1]
J. R. Vernon-Venables	BR	DE	Propeller-driven blades, biplane
A. Pusterla	US	DE	Helicopter-airplane [C.2] British 205,841
R. Chillingworth	GE	DE	Convertiplane [C.3] British patent application 2930/1925
F. Samide	BR	DE	Paddles, lacked financing [B.7] British patent application 8214/1925
A. E. Larsen	US	DE	[C.4] British patent application 11,074/1925
Chicago Helicopters (T. O. Perry)	US	PR	Coaxial rotors [B.2] 1,272,846 and 1,354,101
G. F. Myers	US	DE	Three inclined airscrews [B.4]
G. F. Myers	US	PR	Helicopter-monoplane [B.4]
J. R. Porter	BR	DE	British 209,895 [B.3]
J. N. Williams	US	PR	Coaxial rotors [C.5] 1,023,233 and 1,076,803
N. Hollander	US	PA	1,453,283 and 1,466,901
N. S. Muir	BR	MO	Multiplane
G. Exel	US	PR	Corotor [C.6]
A. S. Ford	US	UC	[C.7]
C. J. Moller	DE		Two 6.7 kW (9 hp) engines
F. Aldovrandi	IT	PA	Coaxial, seeking funding [C.8] Italian patent 228,510
H. P. Wheeldon	BR	DE	Concept
A. J. Mawbey	BR		Four Westaway propellers
C. Q. Payne	US		
J. E. Noeggerath	GE	PA	Tilt-screw monoplane 1,786,545

W. E. Brown	US	DE	Two lifting screws and propeller 328 kW (440 hp) [C.9]
Hellesen and Kahn	FR	PR	Propeller-driven rotor [C.10]
E. and H. Berliner	US	PR	Monoplane-helicopter [C.11]
H. Pittner	AU		
B. L. V. Kay	BR		Ten, 7.5kW (10 hp) engines and Westaway propellers
B. L. V. Kay	BR		"Three deck" machine, 11 engines
S. Y. Beach	US	DC	Convertiplane [C.12]

Appendix D
PATENT LIST

The first section lists U.S. patents, these are followed by the foreign ones. Originally British patent numbers were repeated every year, each number accompanied by the year. Later (ca. 1920s) they were numbered consecutively, as are U.S. patents. The patents are tabulated in numerical order along with the inventor's name.

Key: BR-British, IT-Italian, SP-Spanish, GY-German, A-application number

32 378	Nelson
106 862	Oakes
214 546	Badgley
447 284	Del Valle
902 859	Cornu
908 794	Metcalf
970 616	Edison
988 523	Toles

1 023 233	Williams
1 028 781	Purvis
1 049 758	Bissell
1 076 803	Williams
1 096 045	Mees
1 155 485	Ellehammer
1 145 388	Rochon
1 226 985	Myers
1 272 846	Perry
1 307 826	Hall
1 344 640	Leinweber
1 345 101	Perry
1 350 454	Hewitt
1 350 455	Hewitt
1 350 456	Hewitt
1 361 222	Berliner, E.
1 378 112	Hewitt
1 378 114	Hewitt
1 446 718	Newbauer
1 453 283	Hollander
1 466 901	Hollander
1 472 148	Berliner
1 485 269	Johnson
1 500 572	Brown
1 524 309	Perry
1 527 666	Berliner
1 557 789	Bane

1 561 424	Exel
1 569 669	Newbauer
1 570 121	Berliner
1 573 228	DeBothezat
1 590 497	Cierva (flap hinge)
1 602 778	Pitts
1 605 327	Chillingworth
1 694 880	Langdon
1 713 874	Johnson
1 743 378	Newbauer
1 786 545	Noeggerath
1 791 597	Langdon
1 818 116	Cordy
1 819 863	Bleecker
1 843 643	Kimball
1 932 702	Langdon
1 934 399	Bleecker
1 942 888	West
1 977 724	Hays
2 004 961	Platt
2 045 355	Hays
2 082 674	Young
2 156 334	DeBothezat
2 162 794	Asboth
2 180 922	DeBothezat
2 209 879	Focke
2 265 193	LePage

2 318 259	Sikorsky (tail rotor)
2 497 429	Young
2 584 516	Young
2 614 636	Prewitt
2 633 924	Young
2 646 848	Young

Foreign

1 921/1861 BR	D'Amécourt
2 930/1925 BRA	Chillingworth
8 214/1925 BRA	Samide
9 821/1924 BR	Von Baumhauer
11 074/1925 BRA	Larsen
12 469/1896 BR	Davidson
14 455/1910	Wojciechowski
16 621/1913 BR	Bartha and Madzer
16 494/1924 BR	Scotter
17 981/1915 BR	Scotter
18 768/1903 BR	Bourcart
154 929 BR	Brune
168 732 BR	British Helicopter Co.
201 989 BR	British Helicopter Co.
205 841 BR	Pusterla
209 895 BR	Porter
249 702 GY	Bartha and Madzer (1912, flap hinge)
81 078 IT	Crocco
228 510 IT	Aldovrandi
81 406 SP	Cierva (flap hinge)

Appendix E
ROTARY WING HANDBOOKS AND HISTORY

The 18 volumes of the Rotary Wing Handbooks and History series covering the technology from its origins to 1950 were prepared under contract to the Air Materiel Command, U.S. Air Force by Prewitt Aircraft Company of Wallingford, Pennsylvania. The author was editor and prepared some of the volumes, while the others were prepared by specialists. The completion date was 1950. Some of the documents were published by the Office of Technical Services (OTS), U.S. Department of Commerce. The complete work, totaling about 5000 pages was reproduced on microfilm. Copies (on three spools) were donated to the American Helicopter Society and the National Air and Space Museum of the Smithsonian.

Material for the present book is based on research originally undertaken for the above project, drawing on the early American efforts contained therein. For the book, this effort is augmented by introductions, additional narrative and illustrations, a topical glossary, a critique of these early projects in the light of current technology, an epilogue, and the addition of Systeme Internationale (SI or metric) units to the numbers.

The volume numbers and short titles are listed below. Volumes published by the OTS include a PB number in parentheses. The letter (A) indicates those prepared by the author. For other volumes the specialist's name is in parentheses. [E.1]

1   History to 1900
     (A) 55 pp. illus.

2   Development 1900–1938
     (A) 207 pp. illus.

3   Development 1939–1950, USA
     (A) 256 pp. illus.

4   Development 1939–1950, Foreign
     (A) 129 pp. illus.

5   Weights and Balance
     (A) (PB 129 097) 98 pp.

6   Aerodynamics and Performance
     (I. A. Sikorsky) (PB 121 097) 71 pp.

7   Vibrations
     (R. A. Wagner) (PB 111 289) 73 pp.

8   Mechanical Design and Description
     (Harris Campbell and A) 273 pp. illus.

9   Rotor Blades
     (A) 115 pp. illus.

10   Stability and Control
     (W. E. Cobey) (PB 111 521) 65 pp.

11   Special Types of Rotorcraft
     (A) (PB 111 633) 131 pp. illus.

12   Autorotating Wings (Description)
     (A) 190 pp. illus.

13   Convertible Aircraft
     (A) (PB 111 288) 79 pp. illus.

14   Rotary Wing Industry
     (A) (PB 111 391) 71 pp.

15   U.S. Patent Abridgments
     (A) 1815 pp. illus.

16   Foreign Patent Abridgements
     (A) 927 pp. illus.

17   Subject and Inventors Index (Patents)
     (A) 212 pp.

18   Bibliography of Rotating Wing Aircraft
     (A and Elizabeth S. Zimmerman) 403 pp.

About half the total number of pages relate to patents, which are classified under 920 subjects. The bibliography includes a cumulative index of all the volumes. It lists about 5000 titles worldwide and books, classified under 15 subjects.

Appendix F
MODERN ORGANIZATIONS

The introduction to the first period (19th century) mentioned the need for a Mechanical Bureau to disseminate information based on "sound mechanical principles". What was only a suggestion at the end of the 18th century, today is a significant activity in its own right, devoted to promotion and promulgation of helicopter knowledge and the helicopter experience. The idea is a major element of a function that resembles a system but without central direction. The top level elements of this pseudo-system are design and manufacturing, operations (civil and military), and support. The last is the subject of this appendix. Obviously there is interaction among the top three elements.

What follows describes individual organizations that are dedicated fully or partially to sustain and advance the use of the helicopter. These organizations consist of societies, educational institutions, laboratories, and museums, each promulgating its activities through publications and other mediums.

The principal technical society is the American Helicopter Society (AHS); for civil operators it is the Helicopter Association International (HAI). The first is described immediately below.

The AHS (a not-for-profit organization) was formed in 1943, dedicated to furthering research, development and application of helicopters and other vertical flight machines. Today it is an international organization representing all aspects of the industry. The membership is drawn from corporations (engineering and management staff), government (military and regulatory individuals), operators (owners, pilots, maintenance workers), and from people in education (teachers, students). Members also include corporate entities as well as entrepreneurs and consultants.

Nonprofessionals from the general public also are eligible for membership. Individuals interested in vertical flight are encouraged to join the AHS.

> American Helicopter Society
> 217 North Washington Street
> Alexandria, Virginia 22314
> Phone 703/684-6777
> e-mail: ahs 703@aol.com

AHS activities involve meetings, committees, programs and others dealing with education. The biggest activity of the year is the annual forum, held in different cities. In addition to presentation of forum papers, there is a technical display of helicopters (What would Mortimer Nelson think of this?) and components. It is the largest show of its type in the world. The society also cosponsors meetings with other domestic organizations as the American Institute of Aeronautics and Astronautics, Helicopter Association International, and NASA, as well as foreign ones.

Local (regional) chapters hold monthly meetings covering technical and historical subjects, and feature inspection trips. There are also specialist meetings encompassing all the major disciplines of vertical flight. The principal committees are technical. Their purpose is to establish and maintain a high quality to the technical information released to the members through its publications. There is also a committee that presents to the public the formal AHS position on research and development, safety, rotorcraft technology, and other factors of public interest.

Special programs include the Vertical Flight Foundation which grants student scholarships, and a student design competition to produce a helicopter preliminary design. Beyond these there is an annual awards program that recognizes individual accomplishment. The society is also involved in promoting academic and student interest in vertical flight. There are over 30 student chapters. Schools strongly identified with this activity are Georgia Institute of Technology (with interest dating to the 1930s), Pennsylvania State University, University of Maryland, and Princeton University.

The AHS serves as a "clearinghouse for vertical flight worldwide". The society publishes its own documents, and provides a library service covering its own publications, tapes, videos, and reprints of external documents. The principal periodicals are the *Journal of the American Helicopter Society* (containing original papers on the theory and practice of vertical flight), and *Vertiflite*. The latter is a magazine featuring semi-technical articles, business activities, and historical subjects. The AHS also publishes an *Annual Directory* consisting mainly of membership identification, but includes a helicopter design survey as well.

As mentioned above, the principal operator's organization is the Helicopter Association International, located in Alexandria, Virginia. The organization is for civil helicopter operators. It publishes *Rotor* magazine which represents its members in matters concerning aviation and small business in general; and *Helicopter Annual*. The latter presents an overall view of the industry. It includes a membership directory, buyer's guide, and helicopter statistics e.g., safety trends, and heliports in the United States (which number around 5000). The HAI holds a major, annual trade show (HELI-EXPO) which includes several hundred companies exhibiting the latest in helicopters, products, and services.

Another not-for-profit facility is the American Helicopter Museum and Education Center (AHM & EC) in whose name are the functions of the organization. Founded in 1993, it is located in the cradle of rotary wing flight in America. It is the leading organization of this type. The AHM & EC accepts membership from the general public.

American Helicopter Museum and Education Center
   1220 American Boulevard
   Brandywine Airport
   West Chester, PA 19380
   Phone 215/436-9600
   e-mail 73641.100@compuserve.com

A special program of importance in maintaining a flow of engineering manpower into the industry is the U.S. Army-funded Centers for Rotorcraft Education and Research. "Centers of Excellence" are supported at three schools: Georgia Institute of Technology, Pennsylvania State University, and the University of Maryland.

In addition to the foregoing activity, two independent publications of note are *Rotor & Wing* magazine of Potomac, Maryland, a periodical in tune with its readership, and *Rotor Roster* of Hilliard, Florida. The latter is an annual listing of the world's civil helicopter operators totaling over 20,000, classified by manufacturer, serial number, country of registration, and owner/operator.

In retrospect one can wonder how far an advocate two centuries past could go in envisioning the totality of the helicopter activity described above. This helicopter world represents a small fraction of today's complete "Mechanical Bureau". The vision needs to account for the global interaction as well as the "stimulus diffusion" mentioned in the Epilogue. The latter suggests a *pari-passu* effect whereby other technologies are also progressing, and in so doing contribute ideas that can be adapted to helicopter technology.

This notion also works in reverse. It is very likely the systematic, fatigue analysis procedure and prediction so important to rotor blade life was adopted by the fixed-wing industry.

As suggested in the introduction to this appendix, the totality of the interaction is an example of how human activities in a particular field of endeavor tend toward formation of a loosely connected system. In this case one centered on the helicopter. The resulting interaction provides tremendous leverage in knowledge relative to the lone, isolated entrepreners who populate this historical account. This interaction is merely a restatement of the Epilogue discussion of the logarithmic nature of progress in modern times. And like the curve itself, there can be no end to it. At this point one enters the domain of philosophy for there is technology that can manipulate the very human genetic structure. The meaning of this is all technology valued for itself, progressively evolves into a political issue, and then into one of morality, the ultimate standard to judge the social benefit of this technology.

Appendix G
SYSTÈME INTERNATIONALE UNITS

G.1 GENERAL

The trend toward globalization of all affairs in general, and in particular the gradual adoption of the Système Internationale (SI) units in technology in the United States (including helicopter engineering), compels one to include this system in any new work. [G.1] The SI units are added in this book jointly with the traditional British system (feet, pounds, seconds, degrees Fahrenheit). The comments of the appendix apply to one exclusively familiar with the British system and this point of view is taken to interpret the SI system. The latter is also identified as the "metric system" however the SI system reduces the number of units and most likely even those familiar with the common metric system will find some of the derived units strange.

The SI units as a standard are limited to meters, grams, seconds, and Kelvins (the "Base units"), and their fractions and multiples. There are ambiguities and subjective decisions regarding rigorous usage of the Base units exclusively, even though the system itself is logical and simple. Obviously another concern is in developing a "feeling" for the numbers in the new system. For example a rotor thrust loading of 5 pounds per square foot has a significance not evident in its SI equivalent of 239.5 newtons per square meter. Simple conversion factors in calculating SI units from the British ones are not the problem. However comprehension initially may be elusive in dealing with equations and derived units. In the present case this refers to using helicopter concepts that apply to thrust (as a force), weight, air density, and other that involve concepts of force and weight.

Certain coefficients are dimensionless and therefore numerically the same in either system. This applies here to figure of merit, thrust coefficient, and lift coefficient, among others, assuming proper or consistent units are used.

The terminology elicits some explanation from the British system viewpoint. This refers to the meaning and use of "mass", expression of all power in kilowatts (usually thought of as applying to electricity only), use of joules for energy terms, pressure equivalents, terms related to absolute temperature (Rankine to Kelvin), and the concept of time.

For notation in the ensuing explanations of these concepts, the equations utilize units (abbreviated) instead of symbols. This simplifies comprehension and permits focus on the dimensional aspects of the equations that follow.

G.2 LENGTH, HEIGHT AND DISTANCE

The Base unit is meters, where meters = (0.305) (feet). There are common variations. Nominally, large numbers are in kilometers, with altitudes in meters, and inch units expressed in centimeters or millimeters. Fractions of an inch are in millimeters.

G.3 MASS AND FORCE

In the SI system "mass" is used exclusively in the general sense of "something having substance", the amount of matter the object contains, an item having "weight". This usage differs from the British system in which both weight and force are given in pound units. The SI approach uses different units for each. Units of force are in newton(s). (The plural is to be avoided in SI units, even so, they are used in some cases.)

In the British system, mass has the specific meaning of a weight (pounds) divided by gravitational acceleration (feet per second per second). This mass unit has the name "slug". The word is attributed to professor John Perry of what is now part of Imperial College, London and coined around the turn of the 19th century. [G.2]

In SI units (properly in the singular) newton equal (kilogram of force) times (acceleration due to gravity). In this case the value of acceleration is 9.806 meters per second per second. Note in subsequent comments, plurals will be used where convenient. Thus either rotor thrust or centrifugal load on a rotor blade, for example are expressed in newton(s), while helicopter weight is in kilogram(s). Where in hovering the thrust equals weight, the choice of newtons of kilograms becomes arbitrary. One tends to use kilograms except where force is obvious, as in rotor thrust measurements, which would be in newtons. In SI units air density (rho) is in kilograms per cubic meter.

The thrust coefficient is:

C_T = thrust /(rho)(tip speed squared)(disk area)
C_T = newtons/(kg/m^3)(m/sec^2)(m^2)

Standard atmospheric tables give air density (rho) in kilogram/m^3 units. (Reference G.7, for example.) At standard sea level conditions the value is 1.225. Dimensionally gravitational acceleration does not appear in the above equation. However newtons = (gravitational acceleration, in meters per second per second) (kilograms), with (rho) in kilogram per meter cubed units. (See also C_T in Part G.11.)

G.4 POWER

In the SI system watts or kilowatts replace metric horsepower, giving watts a more general meaning. As mentioned above, watts (a word introduced in 1882) has been identified exclusively with electrical power. The new use of watts for mechanical power (as well as electrical) restores the historical relationship between James Watt and power. The conversion factor is:

KW = (0.746)(hp)

Thus a 1000 hp engine is rated in SI units 746 kilowatts.

G.5 LOADINGS

Following the foregoing reasoning, thrust (disk) loading is measured in newtons per square meter. Similarly, the associated power loading is in newtons per kilowatt when the numerator is a force. (See also pressure, below.)

G.6 ENERGY

The unit of energy is the joule. It is related to the British Thermal Unit (BTU) as follows:

joule = (1054.4)(BTU)

Specific fuel consumption (SFC) conversions use the joule or kilowatt.

(micrograms)/joule = (169.4)(lb/hr)(1/hp) also:
newtons per hour per kilowatt = 5.964 (lb/hr)(1/hp)

G.7 PRESSURE

The name of the SI unit of pressure is pascal, which is measured in newtons per square meter. In pounds (here a force) per square inch (psi) the relationship is:

pascals = newtons per square meter = (6895)(lb/in^2)

Often newtons per square meter results in a large number of digits. These are reduced by expressing pressure in kilonewtons per square meter:

kilonewtons per square meter = kilopascals = (kN/m^2) = (6.89)(lb/in^2)

To reduce the number of digits further it is preferable to use bars:

bars = (newtons per square meter)/(10^5), for conversions:
bars = (0.069)(lb/in^2), for disk loading:
newtons per square meter = (47.88)(lb/ft^2), also:
kilograms per meter squared = (4.88)(lb/ft^2), for power loading:
kilograms per kilowatt = (0.608)(lb/hp)

The helicopter loadings (disk, power) are taken to refer to weight, not force. In these cases, the last two equations would be used for conversions.

G.8 TEMPERATURE

The temperature in degrees celsius = (absolute temperature in kelvins) minus (absolute zero in kelvins), where absolute zero in kelvins is = 273.5.

G.9 TIME

The Base unit for time in both systems is seconds. However as applicable, hours and minutes are sometimes used (i.e., tolerated) for the derived units of flight speed (kilometers per hour), and climb rate (meters per minute). Frequency in cycles per second is measured in hertz.

G.10 FIGURE OF MERIT

As mentioned before figure of merit (M) is dimensionless. Nevertheless, the units must be consistent in either system. Below are the units first for the British system and then the SI system.
British units:

$$M = [(lb)/(ft\ lb/sec)][(lb/ft^2)/(2\ rho)]^{0.5}$$
$$ft\ lb/sec = (550)(hp)$$
$$(rho) = slugs/ft^3 \qquad the\ mass\ density\ of\ air$$

As defined in the narratives:

$$M = [(PL)(DL)^{0.5}]/[(550)(2\ rho)^{0.5}]$$

For Sea Level Standard Day:

$$M = (PL)(DL)^{0.5}/(38.0) \qquad PL\ in\ lb/hp$$
$$DL\ in\ lb/ft^2$$
$$(rho) = 0.002378\ in\ slugs\ per\ ft^3$$

SI units:

The force may be expressed in newtons (N), as below, or in kilograms (kg), where N = (9.806)(kg). As noted before, the constant is metric acceleration due to gravity, and the mass density of air is given in kilograms per cubic meter. Expressing power in kilowatts results in the following:

$$M = [(N)/(1000)(kilowatts)][(N/m^2)/(2\ rho)]^{0.5}$$

For Sea Level Standard Day:

$$M = [(PL)(DL)^{0.5}]/(1565) \qquad PL\ in\ newtons\ per\ kilowatt$$
$$DL\ in\ newtons\ per\ square\ meter$$
$$(rho) = 1.225\ in\ kilograms\ per\ m^3$$

Sample comparison:

$$DL = 5.22\ lb/ft^2 = (9.806)(4.882)(5.22) = 250\ in\ N/m^2$$
$$PL = 12.5\ lb/hp = (9.806)(0.608)(12.5) = 74.52\ in\ N/kW$$
$$British\ units \qquad M = (12.5)(5.22)^{0.5}/(38) = 0.75$$
$$SI\ units \qquad M = (74.52)(250)^{0.5}/(1565) = 0.75$$

Expressed in kilograms instead of newtons and using the relationship newtons = (9.806)(kg) the constant becomes $(1565)/(9.806)^{1.5} = 50.9$

G.11 THRUST COEFFICIENT

In British units the thrust coefficient equation is:

$C_T = (T/A_D)/(rho)_o[(rho)/(rho_o)](V_T{}^2)$
$C_T = (420)(DL)/[(rho)/(rho_o)_o](V_T{}^2)$
      T = thrust in pounds
      $(rho)_o$ = Sea Level Standard Day density of air
      = 0.002378 in slugs per cubic foot
      $(rho)/(rho)_o$ = air density ratio
      V_T = rotor tip speed in feet per second
      T/A_D = disk loading in pounds per square foot

SI units:

Thrust is a force and therefore expressed in newtons. As before, disk loading is in newtons per square meter. However air density is always in weight or kilogram units, and here both kilograms and newtons are used in the same equation.

$C_T = (0.816)(DL)/[(rho)/(rho)_o](V_T{}^2)$
      DL in newtons per square meter
      V_T in meters per second
      $(rho)_o$ = 1.225 in kilograms per meter^3

G.12 FUEL RATE AND SFC

      Using liter units the fuel rate is:
            liters/hr = (3.79)(U.S. gallons/hr)
      Specific fuel consumption (SFC) is in micrograms per joule units:
            micrograms/joule = (169.4)(lb/hr)/(hp)

Note in this equation the left side apparently lacks a time unit. In fact the time unit cancels out on either side of the equation when viewed as follows:

      micrograms/joule = $(0.432)(10)^6/[(BTU/hr)(hr/lb)]$

Jane's annuals use this unit. In some texts [G.7] the following is used:

      newtons/kilowatt hr = (5.96)(lb/hr)/(hp)

G.13 REPRESENTATIVE APPLICATIONS

The following are comments on the use of SI units in some representative texts. Current texts differ in treatment. Some (not on this list) use the British system exclusively. Others incorporate only the SI units, or in this transition period, present both systems as does this book. Still others include the SI system in varying degrees of emphasis. It is obvious the treatment for references containing descriptive data (as this book) is less complicated than in textbooks involving equations, curves, and tables.

Reference G.3 presents a concise summary of SI units, and along with G.4 makes the distinction between force and mass (i.e., weight) units. Reference G.5 includes a summary of the SI standard [G.1]. Reference G.6 gives numbers in both systems with the British system in parentheses, the case for this book as well.

Reference G.7 uses both systems. Numerical calculations are in SI units with the solutions given in both units. (British system in parentheses.) Here newton is for both force and weight, however atmospheric density is in kilograms per cubic meter (to make it consistent with use of newton). Hence air density in this reference is expressed in units of weight rather than the familiar "mass density" used with British units.

Reference G.8 is directly applicable to helicopters. Both systems are used. Numerical calculations are in SI units, while curves show both systems. Reference G.9 presents SI units exclusively, while G.10 basically uses the SI system with some figures in both systems.

Reference G.11, a style manual, summarizes the SI system. It comments on the different units for mass (weight) and force, and the preferred numbers for use with SI units.

G.14 CONCLUDING REMARKS

Application of SI units in current and future literature and education is a relatively simple effort. A problem arises in the retrospective conversion (or subsequent referencing) of all past scientific and engineering documentation existing in the British system. Typically conversion would include redoing all the tables and curves into the new system. The conversion effort most likely will be highly selective insofar as past information fits into present and future work. What is not, in effect no longer exists except for certain scholars interested in the material for other than its content. Even so, conversion of selected past documentation will be a significant increment in labor in literature research. In the future conversions likely would be undertaken by professional societies or under government contract.

The change suggests the Chinese introduction of *pin yin* (romanized, Chinese phonetic alphabet, or CPA) into modern education and writings. It is not likely most of the old works in Chinese characters will be transcribed. They are in a lengthy transition as Europeans were when national literary languages began to appear in writings, replacing Latin, the universal language of scholars. This transition began around the 11th century ending in the time of Columbus, the navigator who (through transportation) put an end to both Scholasticism and the medieval era.

Appendix H
GLOSSARY

The encyclopedic definitions given here relate to terms and concepts used in this book. The definitions include inputs from both the historical and current points of view.

actuator disk

As noted before, the notion of an actuator disk is a simplifying concept introduced by Hermann Glauert as an aid in calculating the velocity effects of a hovering, lifting rotor (or airscrew) producing a jet of air. Conceptually, there is no physical structure producing this jet of air. Therefore it is a system requiring the least power to do so, making the notion an ideal construct. (No viscous or other drag effects are included.) This least, power-required concept is used for comparison with the actual power-required, suggesting a kind of efficiency standard. *See also* figure of merit.

articulation (rotor)

Beside blade pitch control, a "fully articulated rotor" features blade hinges near the hub in both the vertical (flapping) plane, and the plane of rotation (lead-lag or chordwise plane). The implications of a lag hinge are described with *ground resonance*. Full articulation was discussed with Rochon (1911).

Figure 3.35 shows a rotor with a flap hinge only. This hinge provides the stability characteristic described in the 19th century introduction. The radial location of the hinge is significant to helicopter control. It is desirable to locate this hinge outboard of the center of rotation (see D, Figure 3.35), with an offset distance equal to 4 to 12 percent of the radius. This offset, in combination with the blade centrifugal force and blade flapping (when produced by the pilot's cyclic pitch application) produces a mechanical control moment, in addition to the aerodynamic moment of the cyclic pitch application. Availability of this mechanical control is particularly useful in a pushover maneuver, a condition in which there may be little air load (aerodynamic moment available) on the rotor to incline the helicopter.

The flap hinge may be skewed by introducing a "delta-three" angle (Figure 3.35). This angle causes the blade pitch to reduce when the blade flaps upward. The effect applies to both main and tail rotors. It is particularly useful with the latter where excessive flapping is undesirable, and effectively, the tail rotor requires collective pitch control only.

A rigid rotor, i.e., one without hinges at the hub, features blades that are capable of changing collective pitch only (Figure 3.2). The early, lifting propellers were in this category, but they usually lacked the pitch control of modern equivalents which some experimental helicopters used. In a few current, rotor head designs, the flap "hinge" is actually a flexible or elastic, mechanical part.

A modern teetering rotor (usually with two blades) has a second type of rotor articulation. The cantilever blades are rigidly attached to a universal joint (i.e., gimbaled) hub. This design is also termed a semi-rigid rotor, meaning the rotor is free to teeter (flap) but the blades are rigidly attached to the hub in the chordwise direction. For this design, the blade chordwise stiffness must be relatively high because varying aerodynamic drag forces introduce a once-per-revolution, chordwise impulse on each blade. Accordingly the blade must be designed to avoid a resonant condition in the operating range of rotor speeds. Alternatively, the gimbaled rotor blade may be designed to be very limber chordwise if this avoids resonance in the rotor speed range. Though the blade would be lighter in weight this approach is not taken with modern rotors. *See also cantilever blades in* structural integrity.

Practical application of the flap hinge began in the autogiro era of the early 1920s. The teetering rotor appeared in the late 1930s on helicopters designed by Arthur M. Young, later in conjunction with Bell Aircraft Corporation.

autogiro

Autogiro was originally a proprietary word coined by its inventor Juan de la Cierva. [H.1] Today it has become the generic name for a class of rotorcraft that rely on the autorotation principle to support itself in the air. Any unpowered rotor can be made to autorotate for the right conditions of rotor attitude relative to the flight path. The attitude is established by inclining the rotor by means of hub tilt or by applying cyclic pitch (feathering) control. (Aerodynamically, one is equivalent to the other.) Blade pitch angle also is important, and it is usually zero or a few degrees positive. Autorotation at high pitch angles is possible. The rate of descent is lower, but there is less rotor energy available for the landing flare and for braking descent rate.

For a powered rotor with power off, the pitch must be rapidly decreased to the autorotative value. This in order to avoid the hazardous reduction in rotor speed if the power-on, high pitch angle is maintained. (See also discussion with Figure H.7.) The low pitch in autorotative descent also allows the rotor to speed up, increasing its useful energy. Overall, the low pitch approach is preferable because of the two features mentioned above.

autorotation

Autorotation is the aerodynamic phenomenon generally described above that drives the freewheeling autogiro rotor, or unpowered helicopter rotor. The ability to land a helicopter safely with engine failure was the absolute requirement for a practical helicopter. This ability was first demonstrated by Focke. *See also* invention (helicopter).

The specific aerodynamic effect is as follows. For an autorotating rotor blade-element (or section) near the tip, there exists a resultant, aerodynamic force vector at such an angle that a small component of this vector is pulling the blade around sustaining its rotation. (Most of the resultant force is to support the helicopter.) The helicopter autorotative condition (or autorotation) is established by the pilot by proper blade-pitch reduction and rotor angle of attack (i.e., gliding angle) by means of cyclic pitch control. To establish this small "pulling" component, the autogiro rotor (or helicopter rotor in autorotation) is inclined aft so the air flows up through it. This direction is opposite the airflow through a helicopter rotor in powered, forward flight. This difference in flow direction in normal flight is one of the features that distinguishes an autogiro from a helicopter. (Also, an autogiro needs a propeller to pull it forward, and it cannot hover.)

Note the blades are pulled, not "blown" around. In the autogiro case with the rotor inclined away from the flight direction, the resultant force vector also has a drag component. The propeller overcomes this drag and the drag of the rest of the autogiro. Typical values of lift-drag ratio (at maximum lift coefficient) are 4.0–6.0 for the complete machine, and 7.0–9.0 for the rotor alone.

Autorotating wing aircraft not of Cierva origin are called "gyroplanes". The term should include autogiros, but it is used mainly to distinguish between Cierva products and others. Particularly because at one time noted before, "autogiro" was a proprietary name.

A rotorchute is the rotary wing version of a parachute (Figure 3.28). Like nature's seed pod, a rotorchute may have just one blade, for a single blade also will autorotate. (See Figures A.6 and A.7.)

In autorotation the energy of the fall keeps the rotor turning. The more profile (or other) drag the rotor has, the faster it will fall to maintain autorotation. The best a rotor can do in minimum rate of descent approaches that of a parachute. For the same disk loading, a rotorchute has less drag than a parachute, which means the latter has a higher drag coefficient, and a lower rate of descent.

Helicopters with blade tip engines as ramjets or pulsejets, will have more rotor system drag resulting in greater descent rates (power off) relative to a conventional helicopter. For a ramjet, the descent rate is increased by factors of 1.75 to 2.2, which are very high. The first value applies to a steep descent (not desirable), while the second refers to a normal glide and landing flare. Pulse jet engines have less "cold drag" (i.e., power-off drag). In autorotative descent its ratios are about 85 percent of those listed for the ramjet. As a partial compensation, tip engine helicopters have more rotor energy for the landing maneuver. In some past designs there was enough energy available to hover briefly before touchdown. A design treatment to compensate for high rotor system drag is to use low disk loadings, under 10 kg/m^2 (2 lb/ft^2), suggesting a small helicopter with a large rotor. Even with this technique, the high descent rates mentioned above prevail.

A ramjet engine produces no static thrust. The rotor must be turned up (started) to tip speeds of 183 m/sec (600 ft/sec) for it to func-tion. The necessary pressure rise depends on ram air exclusively. Ramjet blades carry internal fuel and ignition lines.

A pulsejet is an elongated engine that has less frontal area (and less drag) than a ramjet. The former produces static thrust but compressed air for starting must be injected at the inlet. This design requires fuel, air, and ignition lines through the rotor head, inside the blade to the tip engines.

For both engine types, though simpler, fuel consumption is very high compared with the turboshaft engine. Noise and high fuel rates are two factors inhibiting acceptance of these helicopter configurations.

In the 19th century the idea of autorotation was unknown. Though a falling maple seed or the windmill itself (originally with the rotor turning almost parallel to the ground) should have set someone thinking in the right direction. It is curious that some conceptualists saw the falling seed as a helicopter rather than what it really was. Their preferred solution to power failure was the addition of a parachute or fixed wings. The former was no answer to failure close to the ground where free fall of a few hundred feet are required for the parachute to fully open. In the early 20th century autorotation theory was understood but ignored in practice for there were more important problems in getting the machine off the ground into controllable flight.

Bernoulli theorem

The Bernoulli theorem (or equation) is a concept applicable to the flow of air. It is named for the work of Daniel and John Bernoulli, later developed mathematically (around 1755) by Leonard Euler. All three were of Swiss origin.

This theorem is as fundamental to the flow of fluids (air, water, and other) as Newton's is to gravity. The theorem is a natural "given" just as is Newton's "gravity". Bernoulli seeks to hold the rotor or wing up, while Newton seeks to pull it down. In steady level flight one equals the other. Lift equals weight.

Considering flowing air as an "incompressible fluid", which it is at low Mach numbers, the theorem states in its simplest form, the total energy along a streamline is constant. At a point in a streamline where the velocity of an air particle is "high", its pressure will be lower than the surrounding (atmospheric or other) static pressure. Conversely, where the velocity is "low" the static pressure will be high. Stated as an equation, the total pressure at a point in the streamline is equal to the sum of its static and dynamic (velocity) pressures. Each streamline is identified with a specific total pressure. In uniform flow all streamlines approaching a body have the same total energy (or total pressure).

From the above it follows to produce a suction on the upper surface of an airfoil (the aerodynamic term for a wing or rotor blade cross section), the velocity (dynamic pressure) over it must be high. On the lower side the static pressure must be high, to constitute the total lift on the airfoil. The shape of an airfoil and its angle to the velocity vector are selected to satisfy these conditions. The oncoming air of many streamlines each with the same total pressure approaches and passes over the airfoil. In so doing it is compelled by the airfoil shape and angle (nose up to the wind) to continually trade static and dynamic pressure until the air passes downstream where (theoretically) it resumes the same flow condition as far upstream.

The Bernoulli theorem is theoretical because it does not represent real flow conditions which account for skin friction and turbulence drag (reflecting energy losses) as the flow passes around an object in its path. Nor does it account for *compressibility* (Mach) effects when the speed is near sonic speed. If the object is being powered through the air (i.e., not in a wind tunnel), the powerplant must make up the energy loss to keep the object in flight. The presence of this drag, which is part of the total for a flying machine, is the need for thrust to overcome it. In normal level flight, the total drag equals the thrust to overcome it. Overall, the horizontal and vertical forces are in equilibrium. *See also* Figure H.7.

It should be noted the Bernoulli equation is usefully applied in conditions where streamline flow exsists around a body. A simple example beyond aircraft application is in establishing the static pressure and dynamic velocity relationship for a pitot-static tube (the flight velocity sensing instrument attached to aircraft).

The Bernoulli theorem leads to aerodynamic notions of air flowing from high to low pressure areas, i.e., circulation. Consider a rotor blade tip in hovering. If a high pressure exists on the lower surface and a low one on the upper surface, it is obvious air will flow around the tip from the low to upper surface, forming a vortex. The vortex is continuously shed because the blade is rotating. This tip flow and that along the full length of the blade, form the rotor wake. The vortex or circulation is the manifestation that the blade is producing lift. This vortex is sometimes visible if the rotor is operating in a smoky or foggy atmosphere. *See also* helicopter power curves.

In the narratives Pennington (1828) recognized the Bernoulli phenomenon but was unable to express it analytically. The effect was also noted with Hollander (1925–1926). Until recent years most airfoil data was obtained from wind tunnel tests. Today with data processing the discipline of computational fluid dynamics can predict analytically characteristics of an object in the airstream, augmenting use of a wind tunnel.

blade and rotor design

In the 19th century rotor design was based mainly on the dual, offset spar system using two blades (Figure 3.1). In some cases this approach continued into the early 1920s (Figures 3.11 and 3.77). A variant is shown in Figure 3.8 (Berliner). Here a single spar tube extends from one blade tip to the other. The "wings" are mounted on the tube at the desired pitch angle. In the Berliner case the wings are smooth on the under surface, while the upper surface contains a set of ribs holding the surface to the spar. The exposed ribs suggest the inventor expected most of the lift to come from the lower surface, where in fact most of the lift comes from the upper surface. Such an arrangement increases drag in forward flight because at some angles of rotation the air velocity has a component flowing radially along the blade.

A single tube approach also was used by Hewitt (Figure 3.38). Here the ribs were covered on both sides like a contemporary airplane wing. In planform the constant chord Perry design (Figure 3.73) resembles modern blades. The Exel design (Figure 3.47) showed rotor wings with several radial members connecting the blades to the hub.

Most likely the rotating wing approach followed from the decision to reduce rotor weight relative to the equivalent lifting propeller. Unlike the cantilever propeller blades, use of wings entailed the fitting of many guy wires above and below the blades (Figures 3.38 and 3.89).

After the First World War variations of the common, wood airplane propeller were used on helicopter prototypes. (Figures 3.43, 3.44, 3.60, 3.64, and 3.89). Another propeller-like approach, of carved wood, emphasized efficiency rather than diameter, the real power reducer. The blades were highly twisted with more surface at the root than at the tip (Figures 3.56, 3.71, and 3.80). The idea was to approach the ideal, uniform (induced) velocity described here with figure of merit. Aside from underestimating the value of diameter in power reduction, the concept apparently deemphasized the effects of forward flight. In this mode the inboard parts of the blade are of little use to lift no matter the configuration. Today the blade root end can start at 10 percent radius or more, without detriment to lift. Most modern blades have a constant chord selected for reduced cost and manufacturing ease. The twist is moderate, being 8–10 degrees, root to tip.

The earliest practical blades for helicopters appeared with Focke (Figure 3.110) and Sikorsky (Figure 3.97). These blades outmoded today, generally had their antecedents in the autogiro. Blade materials have been transformed from solid wood, wood and fabric, and plywood (the last two with steel spar tubes) to adhesively bonded metal blades a type pioneered by Prewitt. (The critics believed glued metal blades would not hold together in flight; they did.) The most advanced blades today consist of molded (plastic) materials combining Kevlar or carbon filaments (or both) with Epoxy resins.

The earlier wood blades absorbed moisture and were constantly in need of rebalancing before flight. The latest blades constructed of composite materials were influenced in design by Army requirements to reduce radar reflectivity. For lightning strikes, composite blades must be "grounded" by a metal circuit to the rest of the helicopter otherwise a strike could explode the blade by delaminating it. This is avoided by bonding within the blade contour a metal conductor such as wire mesh.

A blade can be preliminary-designed in about a week but it will take years and millions of dollars to substantiate the design as airworthy. Unlike propellers, rotor blades are designed for a specific helicopter and become an intimate part of it. (See next entry for the detailed design approach and the reasons for this intimate relationship.)

blade structural integrity

While all components and systems of a helicopter are equally important from the safety viewpoint, the rotor blades are more equal than the others. What is described here is the care that goes into the detailed analysis of an airworthy rotor blade and system. Yet this is only the first step in the program to substantiate it. Others include extensive component and blade bench-fa-

tigue tests, ground whirl tests, and flight tests, all accompanied by test instrumentation. The elaborate attention to the rotor system reveals the fact a rotor is a dynamic structure, unlike the static structure of a wing. In fact an airplane (airliner) wing does flex in flight of necessity to maintain a reasonable design weight, but nevertheless the point above still holds. What follows are three major considerations in analyzing the rotor system: ultimate (static) loads, fatigue and service life, and vibrations. First the historical view.

In earlier years the probable approach to hingeless blade strength analysis and design was to simply combine the centrifugal and air load forces and calculate the stresses as if it were a simple cantilever beam, the root area taking the highest stresses. Beyond this, treatment was by trial and error, reinforcing the weak points. For the propeller type rotors, the inventor's probable approach was to rely on the propeller manufacturer's experience to make a blade of one's own design.

The autogiro era of blade design was a transition period. Blade structural analysis became more elaborate. With flight experience, blade fatigue problems had to be addressed but in very simple ways, mostly by avoiding or accounting for stress concentration, particularly in steel spar tubes, as the result of holes, weldments and manufacture. Design was conservative, resorting to trial and error, resulting in heavy blades. At the time there was no methodology to predict blade life. This came later.

The ensuing comments on blade static loads considers first the hinged blade, followed by the cantilever (teetering rotor) type, both in hovering and maneuvering flight. The load factor discussion applies to both types of blades.

In hovering the vertical forces on a hinged blade are due to the airload and centrifugal force. The former is zero at the hub, reaching a maximum at about ⅔ radius, then dropping off to zero at the tip. In steady hovering, the airload on a blade is (obviously) equal to the gross weight divided by the number of blades. (Downward drag effects on required thrust are neglected here.) With a hinge, the blade will rise to an angle such that the moments of the airload and centrifugal force are in equilibrium. *See also* coning angle. The blade can now be treated as a beam with a hinge at one end operating in a centrifugal force field. What has been described is the static, 1G condition which is not a condition for static strength analysis. (It is for fatigue analysis.) Load factors in maneuvering are higher, and a factor of 3.5 G is arbitrarily used [H.2] as the highest expected in flight. This is conservative for the highest in actual flight is around 2.75 G obtained in a rolling pullout. Early on, one helicopter was lost in attempting to develop this load factor.) Note the helicopter load factors are much less than those of fixed wing, combat aircraft which are in the 8 to 10 G range. For stress (strength) analysis a factor of safety (1.5) is superimposed on the above values, which are "limit values"; i.e., the highest expected in flight. The arbitrary, limit negative load factor (as developed in a pushover maneuver) is minus 1 G, although even half that is ever attained.

The elasticity (stiffness) of a blade must be accounted for in calculating blade stresses. Recall in the Rochon (1911) discussion that recognized practical blades can be very limber as well as stiff, meaning stiffness itself is not a measure of strength, for a limber blade can experience lower stresses than a stiff one. The actual bending moments (and stresses) in a typical, flexible blade can be ¼ those for a blade that is extremely rigid. Centrifugal force "relief" makes the difference. If the blade was extremely flexible (as Figure 3.28) the blade bending stress would be negligible and the centrifugal stress alone would be present. In general the total stress at a point on the blade is the sum of the relieved bending stress (plus or minus) and the stress due to centrifugal force.

Forward flight introduces periodic, blade air loads and flapping about the hub hinge. Consequently, there is periodic blade bending, a form of vibration that must be accounted for in the analysis and design. Blade flapping motion produces periodic inertia loads, and the centrifugal force at a blade element is also periodic. While a rotor speed control device will keep the centrifugal force constant, the normal component of this force will vary because of the blade both flapping and bending as it rotates.

Once all the stresses at a point on the blade are known for each flight condition and are analyzed, the total stress summation is then compared with the allowable stress of the blade material. If they are equal, the "margin of safety" (MS) is zero. If the allowable stress is higher the MS is positive, meaning the design is conservative. Obviously there can be no negative MSs, for this means the amount of blade material is insufficient for the design stress put on it. In some cases where the anticipated loads are not

well understood, the criterion is for all analyses to show very high positive margins. If they understood it, this criterion should have been used in the early prototypes, but they were more likely to rely on trial and error.

The second consideration identified previously relates to blade fatigue and service life prediction. Service life is given in the number of hours the blades can be flown before they must be retired. The object is to design blades with "infinite life". (An unusual case of infinite life relates to the Douglas DC-3 originally built in the 1930s. Enough of them are still flying that the airframe is considered to have infinite life.)

The first step in an analysis is to identify the blade critical areas subject to fatigue. The blade is divided into 10 to 20 elements (strips) for purposes of determining the fatigue critically of each element or point on the blade.

In the preliminary design phase of a new helicopter the investigation is a theoretical analysis. That is, the complete characteristics (structural, performance, flying qualities and other) are predicted before a machine is available for evaluation. Ideally, all the subsequent testing on the ground and in the air serve to verify (substantiate) the original predictions. More likely, the process is one of iteration.

Running in parallel with the analyses are static and fatigue bench tests of both blade materials and representative samples of the actual blade. These test results follow the laws of probability. Prior to application in life prediction the results must be processed statistically (mean values, deviations, confidence levels). The output of this treatment is then conservatively applied to stress-cycle design charts. When complete blades are available they are installed on a rotor head and ground whirl-tested for structural integrity substantiation and other purposes. This type of tests serves to assure the initial experimental helicopter flights are structurally safe.

Ideally four helicopters are used in the flying phase, all with the necessary test instrumentation. One is exclusively for structural testing, fitted with strain gages on the blades at the elements marked off. Both helicopter load factors and blade stresses in all the anticipated maneuvers are measured. A second machine is for performance and flying qualities measurements. Another one evaluates systems related to the powerplant, controls, hydraulics, fuel, electrical and other, including auxiliary equipment. The fourth is a standby helicopter, also used as a flight demonstrator or for marketing purposes. (One is reminded here of the apparently elusive concept of "roll out". An interpretation defines it as the point when the helicopter or other aircraft is formally transferred from manufacturing to the flight test group. One group builds it, another flies it.)

There is an apparent paradox regarding the overall approach in that helicopters are flown before they are fully substantiated. However iteration also applies here. The flight envelope is widened carefully and progressively as more is known of its flight characteristics.

This systematic approach to helicopter evaluation evolved after the Second World War. The inventors of the early 20th century were more heroic in constructing a prototype and then attempting to fly it with little foreknowledge of the outcome. Fortunately few were fully airborne and for any length of time that would induce structural failure.

Once all the blade information is available from bench and flight tests, an analytical procedure is followed to define its hours of service life. The principles of this methodology are described below. [H.3] The procedure applies to commercial helicopters however it is applicable to military craft as well. The principal difference is in the definition of the missions and maneuvers required for the helicopter to sample the fatigue "damage" anticipated when in service.

The methodology is based on the "cumulative damage hypothesis". [H.4] This presumes every steady, vibratory, or impact stress on a blade accumulates and combines to determine the service life of the blade. (This fatigue or damage accumulation also applies to autos and other dynamic machinery.) As suggested above, a set of maneuvers is defined and each maneuver is assigned a percentage of the total flying time, or total life (still unknown, in actual hours). Samples of each of these maneuvers are performed by the helicopter (with the strain-gaged blades) to obtain a sample of the steady and alternating stresses produced along the blade radial elements.

As mentioned earlier bench fatigue tests on blades and components are part of the program. These samples, which are used to correlate cycles with flight hours by way of rotor rpm, also are strain-gaged and fatigue-tested under a preestablished range of steady and alternating stresses. At different steady load levels the blades are subject to various levels of cyclic

bending. The intent here is to obtain a family of practical values of cycles-to-failure of the blade material, and at different levels of steady and cyclic stress. Consider the paper clip. With the common habit of bending a paperclip to failure, there is no steady stress applied to the wire, only an alternating one. If it were possible to also supply a steady tension stress, the wire would fail in fewer cycles of bending. Obviously if the steady tensile strength was at the failing strength of the wire, no bending cycles could be applied to it, and it would have no fatigue life.

Available at this point in the procedure, are both the stresses sampled in flight and those resulting from the bench fatigue tests along with cycles to failure or "runout". The last term refers to combinations of steady and alternating, bending stress levels that are of such a magnitude that no amount of cycles will cause failure. (The remark applies to the paper clip as well if bent slightly and cycled.) Runout also means a particular blade element has infinite life at that level of steady and alternating stress. About 60 percent of helicopter flying (cruise, steady hover) produces stresses at this level. The remaining 40 percent of the maneuvers cause the most damage and govern blade service life.

The third major step in life determination is a mathematical manipulation to obtain the actual calculated life in hours of the most fatigue-critical part (or parts) of the blade. This equation sums up ratios of the percent time for a certain maneuver to the fatigue life in hours at the maneuver stress level. Such applies to the fatigue-critical point on the blade, and it defines the theoretical fatigue life in hours for the blade. The actual service (retirement) life is usually taken conservatively to be 75 percent of the theoretical life. Service life values of 4000 to 5000 hours are customary. For a helicopter that flies 1000 hours a year, this means the blades are retired after 4–5 years of flying.

If the theoretical life is much lower than the range given above it is desirable to redesign the blade or part of the blade to increase its life. Obviously it is desirable to design a blade with infinite life. However it is the nature of a vehicle that hovers, to be extremely weight, productivity, and operating-cost sensitive. Unless infinite life is easy to attain, in a tradeoff it is preferable to produce a blade with an acceptable finite life.

The third basic blade consideration mentioned initially relates to blade vibration. For a helicopter, vibration has different meanings, all related to the fact flight is with rotating, not fixed wings. The major ones deal with comfort level, vibration effects, and blade vibratory stresses. A fourth, ground resonance is a separate subject here. Another involves blade torsional vibrations (flutter) a problem that can be avoided through design.

Airplane flight is smooth from the comfort viewpoint because in steady level flight the lift magnitude on the wing does not fluctuate. A rotor in steady level flight experiences combined rotational and translational aerodynamic forces that are periodic and instantaneously different for each blade, and these lift forces increase with flight speed. Such forces affect both comfort levels and blade vibratory stresses. The dominant vertical vibration on a helicopter, which affects passenger comfort, has a frequency related to the number of blades on it. The more blades the smoother the flight. There are horizontal, periodic forces in the plane of rotation that also affect comfort. Where excessive, the design solution to alleviate these in-plane rotor vibrations is to isolate the rotor assembly from the rest of the helicopter. Normally the vertical vibrations are tolerated. More blades are preferred to fewer when the number does not compromise the design approach. However these vertical vibrations are of concern to blade vibratory stresses.

Of interest here is the effect and treatment of the varying blade stresses resulting from the periodic aerodynamic forces. The foregoing methodology on determining service life did not dwell on the nature or magnitude of these stresses. The intent of the design technique described below is to minimize the level of vibratory stresses a blade will experience, before it is studied for service life. Essentially the technique involves establishing blade properties that avoid resonance (and consequent stress amplification) in the operating speed range of the rotor. In theory blade resonance will always exist at some rpm, because the periodic aerodynamic forces (the fundamental or a harmonic) will be in tune somewhere with one or more of the blade bending natural frequencies. Therefore the technique becomes a game of shifting the points of resonance away from those that could occur in the rotor operating speed range. In this game there are two major players, the periodic (exciting or forcing) aerodynamic forces and the blade natural frequencies that respond to these excitations.

As suggested above the dominant vertical vibratory force is in the order of the number of blades. Thus a three blade rotor has a strong three-per-rev vertical vibration acting on the helicopter and on each of the blades. The blade under consideration is essentially a hinged beam held out by centrifugal force. For a given bending mode, its natural frequency is the static value plus an amount due its speed of rotation, a stiffening effect. A study of this vibration problem begins with determination of blade static natural frequencies for the different modes of bending.

Appreciation of bending mode (static) natural frequencies easily can be demonstrated with a plastic, flexible straightedge having the following nominal dimensions: length 30 cm (12 in), width 2.5 cm (1 in), and thickness 1.6 mm ($\frac{1}{16}$ in), maximum. (It should be thin enough to have a slight static deflection when held horizontally.) In gripping one end it becomes a small cantilever blade. By shaking the model blade rapidly without moving the hand, (about 180 cycles a minute) the first bending mode appears, which is a uniform bending of the blade, root to tip. A more vigorous shaking reveals a node near the middle of the blade. This becomes the second, natural bending mode (static) of a cantilever beam. Higher, natural bending modes are not possible with the hand, but a higher shaking would reveal the third bending mode with two nodes on the blade.

It should be obvious if a full scale blade experienced aerodynamic forces of a frequency in resonance with the blade (equivalent of one's hand motion), the blade would be undergoing severe alternating, bending stresses. These are unacceptable because they shorten blade life.

A hinged blade produces similar mode shapes except for the first natural mode which is a simple swinging back and forth (or up and down for the full scale blade). Grip the model blade at one end with two fingers and swing it. The natural frequency is about 100 cpm and there is no bending (the motion is like half a seesaw). In this hinged case the second mode of vibration is the first bending mode.

In preliminary design, given a particular blade, either hinged or cantilevered, it is desirable to obtain a big picture of both the blade modes of vibration and the (theoretical or potential) forcing frequencies that can result in resonance, or in unacceptable proximity to it. This big picture is in the form of a blade frequency diagram (Figure

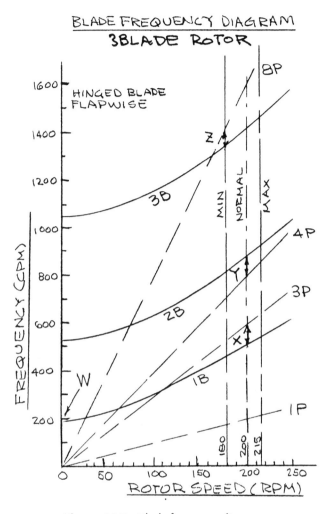

Figure H.1   Blade frequency diagram.

H.1). [H.5] The diagram is an example for a hinged blade in the flapwise (vertical) direction. Chordwise bending is normally not critical from the resonance viewpoint. However a lag-hinged blade will experience fatigue bending from the damper that snubs the lead-lag motion in flight. Blades without a lag hinge also require in-plane analysis to avoid a resonant condition.

Referring to Figure H.1, the plot shows calculated blade natural frequencies vs. rotor rpm for the first three bending modes of the sample, hinged blade. Point W is the static value for the first bending mode and the curve shows the effect of rpm. Also plotted are radial lines (spokes) that represent forcing frequencies (arbitrary and undefined as to origin) of one-per-rev (1 P), 3 P, 4 P and 8 P. The three vertical lines represent the rotor operating range (limits),

marking minimum, normal, and maximum speeds. Points of resonance are those where the radial lines intersect the natural frequency lines. The design game is to avoid resonant conditions in the rotor speed range.

Referring to the figure, consider normal rpm first, assuming the helicopter has three blades, meaning there is a strong 3 P vibration present. The gap X indicates the 3 P vibration is in near resonance with the blade first bending mode. The actual resonance point (the intersection) is below the operating speed range. The gap X introduces a choice of accepting the cyclic stress amplification and factoring it into the fatigue analysis, or to change the blade properties so the gap is much wider, yielding an acceptable vibratory stress.

Gap Y shows there is near resonant condition with a 4 P excitation acting on the blade second mode of bending. The design choice is as above. In the fatigue analysis the fourth harmonic of the airload introduces an amplification factor that is applied the normal rpm bending moment (increasing the periodic stress). Gap Z shows an 8 P aerodynamic excitation is in resonance with the third mode of bending at minimum rotor rpm. In this example the bending moment increase is likely to be very small and unimportant to the overall fatigue life of the blade.

In general the amplification factors associated with the gaps X, Y, and Z to be applied to the bending moment analyses are in the form of transmissibility equations associated with all types of vibrating machinery. [H.6] Such factors typically are in the range of 1.5 to 2.5 times the bending harmonics they are associated with. The inference is, a certain amount of stress amplification is unavoidable in practical blade design. Even so, the increments still yield the service life range discussed previously.

The foregoing discussion on blades is a sample of the great care taken to assure the structural integrity of the rotor system for literally and figuratively, everything hangs on this. The trend today is to combine all the helicopter problems of weights, performance, stability, control, aerodynamic, blade properties and other, into individual or combined computer programs. It appears however the more elaborate the program the fewer are those who understand it.

Brayton cycle (gas turbine)

The Brayton, Joule, or constant pressure cycle is the thermodynamic cycle applicable to the gas turbine, [H.7] just as the Otto cycle is identified with the piston engine. In 1872 F. Stolz designed a powerplant resembling the modern gas turbine. The efficiency was low and the unit was not able to sustain itself. In the same year Hiram Maxim (1872) was alert enough to introduce the powerplant into one of his designs.

Apparently the first experimental unit in the United States was built at Cornell University in 1902. However European industrial turbines were first to go into service. Practical aircraft gas turbines were emerging in the late 1930s, but production versions did not appear (in Europ) until the Second World War.

The turboshaft form is the modern type used in helicopters Figure H.2. It differs from a turboprop engine used in regional airliners mainly in the magnitude of the output shaft speed. The turbine can be the same unit except the turboprop includes a gear reduction stage (a bolted-on gearbox) to drive a propeller. Shaft output speed is in the 1200 to 2200 rpm range. The turboshaft version lacks the gear reduction and its output speed is in the 6000 rpm range. Not only is this engine lighter but the high output speed is there to accommodate the helicopter designer. It gives one freedom to pick a reduction-speed gearbox (a custom unit) that satisfies the preselected, design rotor seed. Reduction ratios are around 15 to 1 for the main rotor and 2.5 to 1 for a tail rotor.

Referring to Figure H.2, the cycle action is a constant, through-flow process from the air inlet end to the jet discharge at the exhaust end of the turbine. The intake air is first compressed, flowing into the combustion chambers (burners).

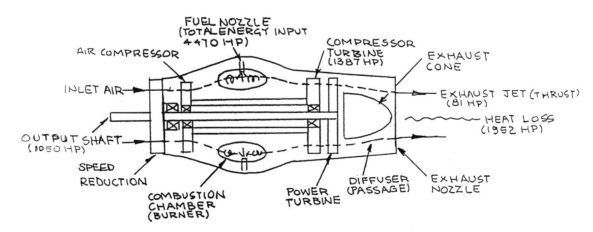

Figure H.2 Schematic of helicopter turboshaft engine. Energy data for 783 kW (1050 hp) turbine.

Fuel is injected at the burners and combustion initiated at constant air pressure. (Combustion in the Otto cycle is initiated at constant volume.) The high energy combustion gas flows through a first stage turbine wheel that drives the compressor, thereby sustaining the operation. Some energy is lost in this stage. The gas then flows through a second turbine wheel (the power turbine) that drives the output shaft. The residual energy of the gas is discharged as exhaust. This exhaust produces a small amount of thrust that may or may not be used for propulsion.

For a typical shaft turbine of 783 kW (1050 hp), the horsepower energy in the fuel is distributed as follows (the percents are of the total fuel energy):

Item	kW	hp	%
Shaft (useful) power	783	(1050)	23.5
Power to drive own compressor	1035	(1387)	31.0
Exhaust (useful as thrust)	61	(81)	01.8
Thermodynamic (heat) losses	1456	(1952)	43.7
Total fuel energy available	3350	(4470)	100.0

If the exhaust energy is included in the useful amount, about 25 percent of the total energy in the fuel is converted to useful work. This percent is defined as the thermal efficiency of the powerplant. The turbine problem in the late 19th and early 20th centuries may be stated using the above example. Given the total energy available in the fuel, the thermodynamic loss and compressor-drive energy requirement were equal to or greater than the available fuel energy. Hence there was no useful output. An analogous problem exists today in the effort to produce useful, fusion energy.

There seems to be little public reflection that the exhaust from an airliner's jet engines is not noxious, in view of the carbon monoxide problem with piston engines. Carbon monoxide is a product of incomplete combustion. For jets, combustion occurs with excess air (i.e., oxygen) and the combustion is complete. The exhaust is mostly smelly hot air, including carbon dioxide. With concern for the environment, automotive fuel has been oxygenated. This results in combustion products that contain more carbon dioxide and less of the monoxide. The process is a way to introduce "excess air" into this fuel.

Engineering thermodynamics, the use of heat to produce work and power, as indicated in the epilogue evolved mainly by the practice-to-

theory route. The early, ingenious use of heat is attributed (by the author, at least) to China. Ancient Chinese applications refer to special utensils for cooking, in particular the use of a heat-focusing wok, the boiler-steamer combination to cook a complete meal with a minimum of heat, creation of porcelain by special manipulation of heat, and heating of the brick bed.

In Europe the steam turbine toy of Heron was mentioned previously. The closest idea to an early shaft turbine is revealed in the work of da Vinci (Figure H.3) and of Venetian Bartolomeo Scappi (1570), Figure H.4. The intent was to turn a spit using convection heat. Figure H.5 shows his concept drawn horizontally for comparison with Figure H.2. However the idea did not kindle further interest in the principle. In the 19th century extensive use of steam power compelled theorists in a form of second guessing to explain it and heat in general.

Nevertheless from the late 18th century thermodynamic principles were evolving independently as a scientific phenomena, (i.e., devoid of application). [H.8] The basic theory developed in the latter part of the 19th century was important in the development of the internal combus-

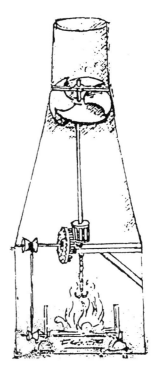

Figure H.3 Da Vinci hot air mill driving a roasting spit (ca. 1480–1482).

Figure H.4   Venetian dual fan roasting spit (1570).

tion engine and the gas turbine. With the advent of the former, the steam powerplant through retro-naming was classified as an "external combustion engine".

compressibility

Compressibility and Mach number are related concepts. The latter is a numerical indicator of the phenomenon. These are important concerns in the effort to increase the maximum speed of high performance helicopters. *See also* helicopter power and performance, *and* rotor, ABC type. Attention is on the airflow at the tip (or outermost part) of the advancing blade in high

speed flight. In this area the total air velocity at a section is the sum of the rotational speed and the flight speed.

Mach number is the ratio of a velocity to the speed of sound in air. Here in particular it is the ratio of the total tip velocity of the advancing blade to the speed of sound at the flight altitude. From theory, the sonic velocity in air is determined only by the local temperature. At sea level in the standard atmosphere the ambient temperature is 15 degrees celsius (59 fahrenheit) and the speed of sound is 340.3 m/sec (1116.4 fps). This value decreases with altitude as the air temperature decreases.

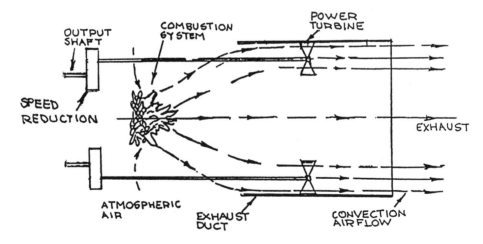

Figure H.5   Figure H.4 redrawn horizontally.

Compressibility is a characteristic feature of air such that at a certain Mach number, the drag of the air flowing over the blade begins to increases rapidly to values far beyond what incompressible flow would predict, i.e., drag proportional to the square of the velocity. This sudden drag rise leads to substantial increase in rotor (profile) power required. The effect also introduces blade pitching moments as well as twisting and vibration, and it worsens the noise level. At low Mach values (around 0.6 or less) air is "incompressible" in the sense that it flows freely around a body, the blade contour or profile in this case, according to the Bernoulli relationship described previously. Obviously air can be compressed but an external, not a natural force is applied to it.

There is a specific sonic velocity of interest. It is the local value in the airflow at some point on the blade where, by virtue of blade shape or angle of attack, the air is moving faster than the total velocity as defined above, and at the local speed of sound. The value of total tip velocity Mach number as defined above, exists when a point on the blade attains sonic velocity. This particular Mach number is defined as the critical Mach number. The particular value is taken to be the one where drag divergence begins to occur. It is desirable to design a blade for high speed application to have as high a critical Mach number as possible. Affecting this critical value are blade thickness (adversely) and local lift coefficient (the higher the more adverse). The low drag direction is toward very thin blades, mainly near the tip, operating at low lift coefficients.

In the design stage there are different approaches to minimizing the Mach effects. If not excessive, the drag increment is accepted as an increase in profile power. Considering thickness alone an 18 percent thick (thickness-chord ratio) section at a free stream Mach number of 0.8 will produce a profile drag increment of 60 percent, which is excessive. The corresponding increment for a 12 percent thick blade is 5 percent. However thin blades introduce aeroelastic (flutter) problems and adverse control forces both of which require design accountability. High performance rotors feature modified planforms as well.

Under certain flight conditions it is possible to produce the Mach drag rise on the retreating side of the rotor disk. This is due to the associated high lift coefficients which produce low

critical Mach numbers. Note this discussion of compressibility applies to high performance fixed-wing aircraft as well.

configurations

Rotorcraft configurations (variants) identified in this account are described below. *Autogiro* and *helicopter* (configurations) are separate entries. Collectively the present group may take the name vertical takeoff and landing (aircraft) or VTOL. In a narrower definition VTOL applies to machines that utilize jet engines for lift, and the engines may be used for propulsion as well. Separate jet engines may be selected for each function.

In the early years recounted here, concepts included jets of air generated by blowers, or jets produced by propeller airstream deflection. As mentioned in the 19th century introduction, such a configuration without the combustion feature was called "air sucker", and earlier by Chanute, "air blast" (machine).

1. Compound (aircraft or helicopter)

The compound configuration includes both a rotor and a fixed wing, plus a separate propulsion system (propellers or jets). In forward flight the rotor is free to autorotate at a minimum-drag pitch angle. Variants include an arrangement where some of the lift remains in the rotor, or the rotor itself is folded and stowed for forward flight. In the early years the rotor-wing-propeller combination was called "helicoplane". In modern helicopters it is not necessarily a good idea to add wing area "for added lift". That lift, subtracted from rotor thrust, can reduce the total rotor thrust available for control of the helicopter. The stub wings found on some (military) helicopters are not for lift but serve as platforms to carry weapons. The incidence setting of these wings can be fixed at a zero lift angle in normal flight. In fact the angle is actually selected (upward) such that when the helicopter is tilted forward (nose down) in the firing attitude, the weapons are launched from a level position. Otherwise they would fire toward the ground, shortening the range.

2. Convertiplane

This configuration with a fixed wing provides for conversion of the hovering, rotor lift-system to a propulsion mode by tilting the complete rotor system forward. The wing then supports the craft in forward flight. With the tiltwing variant, the wing and rotor are integral, both tilting forward for forward flight. The idea here is to avoid the download on the wing in hovering. Modern versions of the convertiplane use two rotors laterally arranged. With this configuration the total fixed wing area is sized for cruise flight. Less wing area is required compared with the equivalent airplane, where total area is determined by the desired minimum landing speed.

With some early prototypes adding a fixed wing helped in forward flight, but in hovering it was a hindrance because of the download mentioned above. Most likely the Berliner triplane (Figure 3.62) with its three, high-aspect ratio wings was configured to provide sufficient wing area for low-speed flight, simultaneously minimizing the download on it. Even so, there will be wing and airscrew mutual interference.

3. Aerostat-helicopter

The aerostat-helicopter (or helicostat) combines a kind of elongated balloon (or pressure airship) with a helicopter. Such a concept was favored by some of the inventors in the 19th century, and used with some prototypes in the early 20th century. However the combination appears to be for different reasons for each period, though in both cases they may be called default solutions.

As remarked before in the Jules Verne account and elsewhere, the 19th century view was characterized as conservative if it started with something already known, and therefore more attainable. But as the 20th century prototypes reveal, the helicostat had its own set of problems. In the latter era, adding a gas bag to a helicopter appeared more a sign of experimental desperation than optimization. Presumably the balloon would relieve some of the instability, allowing evaluation of lift and control without the complexity in stabilizing it.

4. Heligiro

A heligiro combines the features of a helicopter and a wingless autogiro. The craft hovers as a helicopter and flies forward as an autogiro. Depending on the powerplant arrangement there also may be a heligiro mode of flight. In this case one engine continually drives the rotor and the other the propeller. This variant permits all the power available to be used for propulsion, but only one powerplant is available for hovering. The arrangement does have a kind of marginal dual engine reliability. A heligiro with a single engine implies a mechanical drive system in which power is shifted from the rotor to the propeller. The heligiro had possibilities in the early 1940s when autogiro speeds were higher than helicopter speeds. Overall, the concept carries too much machinery and complexity to satisfy its intended purpose.

5. Corotor (helicopter)

The corotor principle was described with Exel (1930–1933). With this configuration the engine is located between two counterrotating airscrews, one a rotor and the other a propeller (or ducted fan). As noted before the piston engine crankcase at the lower rpm, drives the rotor. The crankshaft at the higher rpm drives the propeller or fan. Considering control, the upper rotor which is lightly loaded may feature a large flap hinge offset to obtain an adequate control moment. The latter augments the reduced aerodynamic moment on the rotor.

coning angle

The coning angle is the steady angle formed by a hinged rotor blade relative to its plane of rotation. The angle is defined by the equilibrium of two principal forces, aerodynamic lift and blade centrifugal force. This angle is a measure of the thrust on the rotor. With a helicopter on the ground prior to takeoff, the blade pitch is such there is little lift on the blades. The coning angle is close to zero degrees. An observer on the ground will see the rotor turning in a plane parallel to the ground. At takeoff the rotor carries the full weight of the helicopter and the blades will be seen to "cone up" and remain at a certain angle (a few degrees).

In forward flight with full weight carried by the rotor, there exists a mean or average coning angle. The blades flap around this mean angle, thereby defining an inclined, tip-path-plane (and thrust vector). Rotor inclination is in the direction of flight, but the fuselage attitude for the flight condition depends on other factors. These are mainly the fuselage drag, presence of a tailplane, and CG location. The last varies for each flight, depending on the quantity of fuel on board, and the amount and distribution of payload.

It is important to maintain rotor speed within the design limits. Turbine-powered helicopters feature a rotor, constant-speed control. Small, piston-engine versions usually do not. In general, rotor speed must be monitored particularly to keep it above the minimum rpm value (Figure H.1). Low rotor speeds lead to excessive coning creating problems with control, blade stresses, and safety of flight.

Heavy-lift helicopters which lift 18 to 27,000 kilograms (20–30 tons) of useful load have a particular design concern in avoiding excessive coning angle. This angle is preferably below 10 degrees. Other design considerations drive toward a high lift-load per blade and low centrifugal force, the last determined by the need to maintain an acceptable, blade tip speed. For this reason heavy-lift machines appear with many blades (often five) to favorably control coning by balancing airload against centrifugal force. In addition, more blades makes each one lighter, desirable in ground handling.

The helicopter designs and prototypes of the narratives lacked a flapping hinge. With the flexible spar-type cantilever blade, the rotor loads likely produced a virtual hinge and coning angle, despite the reinforcing guy wires. The effect is evident in comparing Figure 3.77 with 3.78. An overlay study showed the turning rotor had a tip-path-plane 20.0 to 25.4 cm (8 to 10 in) above the static (reference) position. Unlike the propeller type, the large gap between rotors of the rotating wing variants (Figures 3.3, 3.11, 3.73, and 3.77) very likely was established with this clearance in mind. To be effective, the guy wires required high angles, another reason for the gap.

control system (helicopter)

Modern helicopters feature rotor collective and cyclic pitch control. As mentioned elsewhere and in conjunction with Figure H.7, collective pitch is used in all flight modes because it is the power-level control. As such it also defines the mean *coning angle*. The cyclic pitch control inclines the rotor thrust vector, and hence the helicopter in the desired flight direction.

For yaw, i.e., directional control, the single rotor helicopter uses a tail rotor, also required to counteract main rotor torque. In serving the latter, tail rotor thrust is not symmetrical in either direction. In one direction rotor torque aids in the turn, in the other the tail rotor thrust must overcome the torque as well.

A jet-driven rotor has little rotor torque. Yaw control is produced by rotor downwash impinging on a surface (usually not very effective), or by deflection of the exhaust jet from turbine. Power-off, the jet-rotor helicopter lands under control as an autogiro, while the mechanical

drive system still has use of the tail rotor. In some cases a jet rotor helicopter will feature a mechanically-driven tail rotor, mainly required if it is designed to hold a heading with a side wind. However the rotor also will be necessary to overcome the torque of accessories required to be driven off the main rotor. Accordingly, the design tail rotor thrust is selected by such factors as yaw-rate desired, sidewind forces in hovering and autorotation, and accessories torque. All yaw control systems are actuated by pilot's rudder pedals.

The control actuating mechanism for the main rotor is divided at the rotor head swashplate bearing. The "upper controls" turn with the rotor, while the "lower controls" are attached to the airframe. The system which may contain a hydraulic boost, includes rods and cranks connecting the rotor controls to the pilot's cyclic and collective pitch sticks. Since collective pitch also establishes power, the throttle is a twist grip on this stick. (See also discussion of helicopter attributed to Williams (1924)). The pilot's cyclic pitch stick includes a trim control button called "coolie hat". Figure H.6 shows the original one which has the same contour as the button.

In the 19th century, control if considered at all consisted of shifting a weight to incline the craft, and to actuating a rudder for yaw. Rotor thrust variation was by speed control, however there were a few other possibilities. In 1871 one pitch control idea was proposed by Wenham in Britain. He devised a screw capable of pitch variation. The invention consisted of crossbars as in Figure 3.1, covered with fabric. However each bar was attached to its own hub. Pitch

Figure H.6 The original "coolie hat," the name of the trim button on the cyclic pitch stick.

could be changed by axial movement of the lower bar. [H.9] Presumably as with Williams, the relaxed position was zero pitch (or less). Recall also the novel idea of hydraulic pitch control proposed by Croce-Spinelli (1871), Figure 2.25.

costs (life cycle)

Historically the notion of cost if formally considered at all was centered on an initial budget for a prototype, followed by the inevitable quest for funds as a result of development snags. As suggested before "ran out of money" the common explanation was a deferential expression meaning loss of faith in the project by the investor. In retrospect it is highly unlikely those early entrepreneurs grasped the magnitude of the work and cost to produce a viable commercial helicopter partly because they failed to understand the magnitude of the problem itself. (In their defense, it is often preferable not to know the full problem, otherwise little innovation would ever occur.)

Today, starting with a simple requirement or operating concept, a preliminary design is generated. One that permits an iterative costing procedure with the following sequential form:

> development costs
> production prototype costs
> series production costs, and marketing
>   costs if commercial
> operating costs

For a military helicopter program, the life cycle costs encompasses all costs from the initial concept to the final disposal of the aircraft and its support equipment many years hence. This approach to costing involves an initial estimate of the present cost of future money, since the life cycle may be 20 years or more.

Development costs include preliminary and final design of the helicopter, manufacturing costs, including test helicopters, as well as costs of component and prototype test programs and support items (maintenance, training and other). As mentioned before, it is preferable to have four helicopters for tests. A fifth is mainly an airframe for static and dynamic tests (as drop tests).

Along with development a helicopter specification is created and updated. This activity combined with formal design changes and tradeoff studies are part of configuration management (CM), which in turn is part of the overall systems engineering procedure or methodology. The overall principle behind CM is to assure the specification, the drawings, and the helicopter are each an exact statement of the other. Such a philosophy guarantees the outcome will be what is required and paid for. (A concept that should filter into general society.) In modern times the trend is toward a complete, computer-oriented development program suggesting the Boeing 777 project. Using the computer there is a high degree of real-time integration of all the functions (computer aided design and manufacturing, test, evaluation, subcontracting, etc.) required to complete work through series production.

The costs of a commercial program through FAA certification can be as high as $100 million for a medium-sized twin turbine helicopter. The base (sales) price of a sedan-sized helicopter can amount to $1 million or more. A rotor blade can cost as much as $10,000 and be subject to retirement in 4–5 years. Inflation is also a significant factor in the base price of the helicopter. Its price will increase at a much greater rate (possibly three times or more) than the Department of Commerce Price Index for transportation equipment. However one must consider the relatively low production rate relative to autos. Even so, production rates will not make so much a difference as would a new design philosophy.

As identified above and elsewhere in the discussions, elements of this philosophy include low disk loading, inherent stability (or its automatic, fail-safe equivalent), forgiving flying qualities, crashworthiness, low noise levels, and automobile-competitive costs. Considering performance, hovering, vertical takeoff, and autorotative capability are mandatory. High maximum speed should not govern the design. As a vehicle, the fewer the parts for both the helicopter and its powerplant, the better. This concept puts the personal or private helicopter far beyond the forseeable future. But one cannot presume the goal is unattainable. Humans will not be ground-bound forever, and it will always be cheaper to hover above the ground than to shoot off into space to visit a neighbor.

There is a relatively new cost element that significantly affects base price, namely the cost of product liability insurance. Despite the exhaustive programs for design, development, and production leading to FAA certification as briefly described here, a manufacturer remains liable to negligence lawsuits. Even when no-fault is found, a considerable amount is spent in the defense litigation.

Sone legal action, e.g., declaring the Piper Cub a "defective product" is absurd. The FAA has presented itself as a friend of the court declaring design approvals are the province of the FAA not the courts. While not easily determinable, the amount allotted to this insurance can be 15–20 percent or more of the base price. From the manufacturer's viewpoint such insurance, defense judgments, and settlements are all excessive. These costs inhibit both innovation and production of small aircraft, including helicopters.

Nonetheless some recourse or fault-finding is necessary. The problem of negligence emerged with the Industrial Revolution when technology and its products were held in awe. Recall the comments here regarding the Atlantic Cable, and in the Verne narrative. What human damage it caused was ignored because the social benefits were overwhelming. The victims of this philosophy showed up in 19th century novels and manifestos. Also very likely, in those days (and in some underdeveloped countries today) such injuries were accepted as one's own carelessness and fault. Until recent years auto accidents were similarly treated. The concept of legal negligence evolved after the Civil War when objective standards of negligence of "fault" appeared. The notion "no fault = no liability" was as close to an equation that a legal concept could attain.

As identified before, the crashworthiness requirement introduces an additional cost element to the helicopter base price. Special design features also add around 4–6 percent to the empty weight of a military helicopter. The crash mode for a helicopter is mainly vertical. (For airplanes and autos, it is horizontal.) Certain structure must be highly energy-absorbing. Seats and landing gear are designed to travel or "stroke" vertically to absorb impact energy.

Operating cost is the last in a chain of costs dealing with a marketable helicopter. Generally costing formats will differ for military and commercial helicopters. In the initial design stages determination of this cost is most elusive because it depends on the cumulative effect of all the analyses and assumptions that went before. The latter refer to such items as realism of the base price estimate, maintenance including retirement schedule, and annual utilization. Main-

tenance costs have always been a major concern with helicopters. Regarding early, Army helicopters there was a truism that each helicopter had three transmissions: one in the helicopter, one in transit, and one in overhaul. Today no one would accept this in an automobile.

Just on the cost basis alone, the personal helicopter (Figure 4.1) is a long way off.

cyclogiro

The cyclogiro is a rotorcraft capable of hovering but based on a rotor principle different from a helicopter. [H.11] The rotor assemblies (usually two) replace the wing panels of an airplane, serving as both the lift and propulsion means.

Each rotor assembly resembles an elongated cage rotating about its spanwise axis. The vanes or blades, usually three or four, are part of the cage, turning parallel to the axis of rotation. Each vane is articulated about its spanwise axis in two senses, suggesting those of a helicopter rotor. The pitch of all the vanes on a rotor can be increased collectively to increase the resultant lift force vector. The vanes also can be varied cyclically (hence "cyclogiro") to tilt the resultant vector forward or aft and positions in between. The resultant vector is included forward to support the craft and propel it.

The sense of rotation is fixed so the uppermost vane position faces the flight direction, producing the most lift. The vane at the bottom of the revolution (180 degrees later) is moving away from the flight direction, producing less lift. This variation in lift per revolution suggests there is an optimum peripheral speed relative to the design horizontal flight speed.

Most the prototypes appeared in the period 1910 to the late 1930s. Some were misidentified as "helicopter". With the advent of the successful helicopter the cyclogiro along with the autogiro lost their appeal. The former was too complicated mechanically and its lift-drag ratio was relatively low, and as remarked before, the autogiro could not hover.

density ratio

Density ratio is the ratio of air density at a given altitude to that of the standard air density at sea level. This parameter is of fundamental importance in aerodynamic and performance analyses. At sea level the standard density is 1.225 kg/m³ (0.765 lb/ft³), and the density ratio is 1.0. Unless atmospheric conditions are specified (pressure, temperature), the value here in the calculations is taken to be 1.0.

disk loading

Disk loading is the ratio of the design gross weight of the helicopter to the swept (disk) area of the rotor. It is measured in kilograms per square meter (pounds per square foot). On a test stand, rotor thrust loading in the British system of units also is in pounds per square foot but in SI units it is in newtons per square meter.

Disk loading is an important design concept because of its effect on power required (lower is better), power-off rate of descent (lower is slower), and high-speed forward flight. For the last, a low disk loading normally inhibits high speed due to retreating blade stall. Helicopters emphasizing speed and high performance use disk loadings in the 34–49 kg/m^2 (7–10 lb/ft^2) range. For small training or light helicopters the range is 20–24 kg/m^2 (4–5 lb/ft^2), although lower values are feasible.

The analogous concept for airplanes is wing loading. A low value signifies low induced power (as for a helicopter) and low, power-off landing speed. Similarly high performance airplanes use high loadings. The intent is to maintain a minimum wing area, (and drag), desirable for long range flight. A high wing-loading also implies a long takeoff ground run, and wing flaps are used to reduce this to a design or required value. For comparison, typical wing loadings in kilograms per square meter (pounds per square foot) are from 29.3 (6) for a sailplane through 83 (17) for a small single engine airplane to 683 (140) for a long range airliner. Even with flaps, takeoff ground run of the airliner is around 1373 meters (4500 feet).

As noted before, most the early investigators failed to appreciate or show awareness of the importance of disk loading. Today its importance is physically demonstrated in the very large diameter rotor required for a human-powered helicopter.

drag (aerodynamic)

Drag has three components applicable to helicopter preliminary design. Parasite drag, rotor induced drag, and rotor blade profile drag. Each represents a power loss to be made up by the powerplant. (Total power accounting is discussed under helicopter power and performance.)

Parasite drag refers to all kinds of drag that do not contribute to lift. These include pressure and form drag, which streamlining aims to minimize. Direct impact of air on an object causing the aerodynamic pressure is part of parasite drag. Form drag is evident by the turbulent wake behind a body in an airstream. The drag of the rotor head, landing gear, and tail surfaces are part of a parasite drag.

Induced drag (and power) is the price the rotor pays to produce its lift or thrust. This power loss manifests itself in the jet of air (the downwash or wake velocity) it produces while hovering. *See also* figure of merit *and the Crocker Hewitt (1917) discussion.*

Blade profile drag is of importance because it is a particular case of one of the fundamental parameters of an airfoil (wing). It is primarily skin friction drag, which in turn is determined by the boundary layer of air flowing around an airfoil. Considering aerodynamics, a certain depth or thickness of air flowing past a surface has properties unlike that of the free stream air. At the front part of the blade this layer is laminar in that the air flows smoothly around it. Over the aft part of the blade the flow becomes turbulent and the layer thickens. For the laminar part, the velocity gradient is zero at the blade surface increasing smoothly to the free stream value. A representative thickness of the laminar layer near the blade tip in hovering is in the 5–10 millimeter (0.2 to 0.4 inch) range. As the blade rotates, there is a friction-shearing in this boundary layer because air has viscosity, and this shearing action results in the blade profile drag. Broadly interpreted, the profile drag of a blade (or wing) is due to the natural presence of a boundary layer (both laminar and turbulent) in flight. There is an additional profile drag increment caused by compressibility, a phenomenon described under that heading.

Considering the relative magnitude of drag, the rotor head and (fixed) landing gear exhibit high parasite drag. The bare fuselage is usually streamlined and its drag is relatively low, in the form of skin friction drag, a notion applicable to tail surfaces as well. The subject of drag is discussed further in conjunction with Figure H.7.

ducted tail rotor

Some helicopters feature a tail rotor enclosed in a well-defined duct or shroud. From the static thrust viewpoint and yaw control, there is a distri-

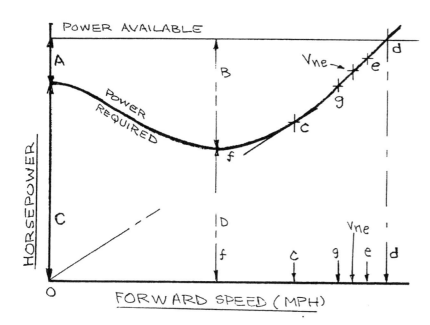

Figure H.7 Helicopter power curves.

bution of total thrust between the rotor itself and the shroud. As an approximation, the equivalent-free rotor diameter (thrustwise) is equal to the outside diameter of the shroud. Shroud thickness is a compromise. A thick shroud is a better thrust producer, but it creates more drag. The same thrust is obtained by a smaller rotor within the duct, with thrust sharing ideally as high as 50–50. Ducted propellers avoid fin blockage of the tail rotor. They tend to be noisier, but with proper blade and rotor design an acceptable sound can be attained. The rotor is actually a multi-blade fan and the shroud protects it from ground strikes. The idea of "flying the tail rotor" suggests the importance of protecting it in maneuvering flight.

figure of merit

The concept of figure of merit was defined in the 20th century introduction. It resembles an efficiency applicable to a hovering rotor, assumed out of ground effect (OGE). Figure of merit (M) as used here applies to rotor thrust measured or assumed, whether the machine or test rig is on or off the ground. In evaluating rotor performance using M, account is taken of ground effect, because OGE the efficiency would be less.

Figure of merit presumes there is a minimum (ideal) horsepower required of the rotor to support the helicopter, or to produce a certain amount of static thrust on a test stand. This min-

imum value is the power required to produce a volume of air having a diameter equal to the rotor diameter, with a uniform wake or downwash velocity from blade root to tip. For this minimum (ideal) value M = 1.0.

A fictitious actuator disk having no physical presence is assumed to produce this airflow because anything physical moving the air would have a (profile) drag associated with it, making the system less than ideal. In a real system, the velocity along the radius is not uniform (but blade twist helps), and the actual rotor has drag. For modern rotors M = 0.70 to 0.76. (Figure of merit is dimensionless, see Appendix G.) Static thrust of a modern airplane propeller gives an M = 0.62, lower than the above. Design of this airscrew is not optimized for static thrust, favoring instead climb rate and maximum speed. In both applications the constant speed, variable pitch design-approach is taken.

The concept is useful in preliminary design, and it serves as a check on efficiency of a tested rotor. From experience, practical rotors yield a maximum figure of merit at a mean lift coefficient of around 0.60. This knowledge permits one to establish the total blade area required to produce the desired hovering thrust with the greatest efficiency.

Use of figure of merit in the narratives is to check the realism of the design approach or the test measurement. For actual rotors (or airscrews) used in the 19th century the attainable value was likely to be 0.50 or less, and probably a little higher in the early 20th century. Some calculated values in the narratives yield an M greater than 1.0, which by definition is physically not attainable.

flapping wing aircraft

The configuration of a flapping wing aircraft is also known as a "flapper" and ornithopter. The latter word is based on Greek *ornis* (bird) and *pteron* (wing). The idea of a flight by flapping wings is probably as old as the first human who witnessed bird flight. The idea is familiar in the world of mythology and in ancient notions of mechanical flight. The earliest in writings is the wooden pigeon of Archytas of Tarentum (Taranto), at that time a Greek city. Archytas (ca., 400–350 B.C.) was a philosopher, scientist, and mathematician who among other ideas is credited with originating the pulley. Da Vinci is well known for his designs of a man-carrying ornithopter, a design that took considerably more of his time than the helicopter.

Serious efforts in producing a practical one occurred in the first quarter of the 20th century. There were many prototypes. [H.11] Only one is described here in the narratives—the Green flapper helicopter of 1910. In the early 1900s many studied and dissected birds in the futile effort to uncover clues to mechanical flight by any means.

Ideas also came from the Bible. One Reverend B. Cannon had a revelation that encouraged him to form a company to construct a flapper. His first machine Ezekiel I did not work and in 1910 he began construction on an advanced version Ezekiel II. Cannon apparently connected ornithopters with Ezekiel, the birdman of the Bible. The latter had visions of four-winged, human-like creatures and giant eagles. No illustrations are available of Cannon's work but it is possible Cannon conceived a four-wing flapper suggesting a dragonfly.

One noteworthy ornithopter was the prototype of Leonard W. Bonney. He was a popular exhibition pilot in the years before World War I. The *Gull* took five years to construct. On May 4, 1928 he attempted to fly the machine at Curtiss Field, New York. The craft climbed to 31 meters (100 feet) and out of control, fell to earth. Bonney lost his life and the machine was demolished. [H.13]

The ornithopter always has its advocates even to this day. But now the object is different. It is a challenge to human ingenuity to make one work. Most likely someone eventually will demonstrate mechanical bird flight in hovering or forward flight. But it is unlikely to be with the mechanism of true bird flight, that is, the way individual, interacting feathers are involved. As the mechanical ones have demonstrated, ornithopters attempt flight using the gross motion of bird's wings consisting of solid surfaces. Bats have sold surface wings which are closer to the mechanical version.

As with helicopters, the ornithopter design must account for power-off flight and vibration. Power-off, a glide could be established in forward flight but not as a flapper. There is no equivalent to autorotation. With the wings fixed, some incidence or aircraft adjustment would be required. Power failure in hovering would be more critical. Like the helicopter the machine would fall a distance before establishing the power-off control mode which is gliding flight. The problem is critical when the machine is hovering within a hundred meters (300 feet) of the ground.

The flapping motion in flight induces fuselage vibrations related to the flapping frequency. These reactive vibrations can be alleviated somewhat by double-jointing the wing panels. Additional design problems concern the weight, function, and mechanical integrity of the flapping mechanism, particularly because the wings are loaded as cantilever beams.

gas turbine (See Brayton cycle.)

ground effect

A helicopter hovering close to the ground, in ground effect (IGE) causes the wake airflow to be affected by its proximity to the ground. The effect appears for any size helicopter when the rotor is operating at a ground height equal to or less than its radius.

At a rotor hover height equal to half the rotor radius, the thrust will increase about 15 percent. For a specific helicopter weight, the power required is sensibly reduced. This reduction is greater at lower hover heights. Close to the ground, there is also a thrust gain (or power reduction) in forward flight. As a procedure the technique is useful when an overloaded helicopter is operating under emergency conditions. Practical use of this running takeoff occurred in the evacuations during the war in Vietnam.

A second effect of the ground is present when the rotor is very close to it but not in contact with it. The helicopter becomes an air cushion vehicle (hovercraft) aligning itself to the slope of the ground. In this case rotor control is required to keep the craft from drifting downslope.

ground resonance (vibration)

Ground resonance was explained in general in the 20th century introduction. It was noted "ground resonance" is not apt when applied to the instability phenomenon. Nonetheless, the term has come to be accepted in identifying a certain type of helicopter ground instability. The phenomenon is of mechanical origin and aerodynamics does not enter into the problem.

Considering mechanical vibrations in general, there is a significant difference between an instability and resonance. Instability refers to a condition in which the vibration once initiated, reinforces itself with increasing violence until destruction stops it, providing there is no human intervention to stop the action in its early stage. Instability is a divergence, there is no equilibrium condition as for resonance.

Resonance as a characteristic of blade vibration was discussed under blade structural integrity in conjunction with Figure H.1. In general, resonance exists when an exciting or forcing frequency, as the varying aerodynamic forces on a rotor blade, are in tune with one or more of the natural frequencies of the structure (blade) the dynamic airload is acting on. Equilibrium exists between the applied force and responding reaction. An unbalanced rotor turning at a given rpm on the ground may cause a gentle rocking of the helicopter. This is a form of benign resonance with the forcing function of the rotor in tune with the damped natural frequency of the landing gear.

In discussing the subject one must separate the behavior of lag-hinged rotors with three or more blades from those with two blades. Both arrangements can produce motions when coupled with landing gear properties that may cause damage to the rotor or the helicopter itself. The three or more blade system is discussed first, initially assuming the blades are without dampers.

The ensuing gives an example of the frequency relationships for a damperless, three-blade rotor. The example is followed by a simple test procedure to check for the instability, and a personal account of what can happen when the instability takes over, unchecked. These accounts precede discussion of two-blade rotor systems. Finally, the vibration experience with the historical rotors is reviewed.

A certain helicopter on the ground has a roll natural frequency of 135 cycles per minute (cpm). For comparison a Honda Civic in its (damped) "roll" mode has a natural frequency of about 90 cpm, measured by rhythmically pushing down on a fender. (This makes the helicopter much stiffer in the roll mode.) At a rotor speed of, say 180 rpm (the minimum value in figure H.1) the blade lead-lag natural frequency (without dampers) is calculated to be 45 cpm. From theory, the out-of-pattern forcing frequency of the rotor is $180 - 45 = 135$ cpm. Since this frequency is equal to the roll natural frequency, the rotor speed of 180 rpm puts the helicopter at the center of its ground resonance condition.

One design solution to avoid resonance is to alter the roll natural frequency so it is far above or below the rotor operating range. For the example of Figure H.1 this means well above a rotor speed of 215 rpm (say 240 rpm) or well below 180 rpm (say 120 rpm). However for practical reasons it is desirable to introduce damping in the blades and landing gear. As remarked earlier, the damper solution is a product with the design distributing the damping equally between the blades and the landing gear.

Despite the design care there are conditions of incipient resonance with operational helicopters. These refer to uneven landings, or if the helicopter lingers light on its landing gear as it lifts off. The latter cases cause reduced damping in the gear. Rapid corrections avert an undesirable outcome. One extreme case is described below.

During a test program, one simple method of determining the tendency toward this instability is to explore slowly the rotor speed range from low to high, while measuring the roll frequency. In this case the helicopter is tied down with slack cables, to allow some roll freedom. If the roll frequency is the same as the rotor speed the shake is caused by simple rotor unbalance. (As mentioned above, this motion is a form of true resonance.) But if it is at an "odd frequency" relative to rotor speed, the vibration is emergent ground instability. For the above example, when the rotor turns 180 rpm, the "measured" odd frequency would be 135 cpm. At the first hint of a problem the engine is shut down. But sometimes nature has its own procedures.

The author was involved in a program with an experimental helicopter that had a rotor head designed without blade dampers and fitted with interblade struts intended to prevent the blades from falling out of pattern. (The forcing function in an instability.) To check its effectiveness the test procedure was to gradually increase rotor speed measuring the fuselage vibrations for presence of the odd frequency. The procedure was started with a test engineer seated at the controls in the cockpit, the helicopter tied down with the slack cables, and the author standing by the helicopter at the rotor center of rotation ready to measure the vibration with a stopwatch. Upon a signal the test engineer opened the throttle on the piston engine. Entry into the resonance was sudden, unexpected, and violent. The instant impression was like one who came prepared to check for a drumbeat with a stethoscope. The vigor of the motion caused the test engineer's seat to collapse throwing him away from the ignition switch. He had a prolonged struggle against the motion that was forcing him backward toward the rotor, and with effort finally was able to cut the engine.

Meanwhile the author saw the tiedowns were holding as the helicopter violently rolled, tugging and letting upon the tiedowns as it did. It was considered prudent (and a rule) to remain close to the helicopter in resonance for there was no telling where the flailing blades reinforced by a rolling helicopter were in relation to the ground.

On assessing the damage, beside the collapsed seat, cooling fan blades in the vertically-mounted engine fatigued off (due to the violent roll and gyroscopic bending). These pieces flew out of the cowling above the author's head. One of the aluminum blades chewed itself off at the hub and took off like a javelin.

More happened. A technician positioned himself in front of the helicopter to take motion pictures of the machine's behavior. The ground in the area of the helicopter had a slight grade such that the plane of rotation pointed forward to the ground where the cameraman was standing. The potential problem was obvious and he was advised to film from the side not the front. However he insisted on the front to get a better view of the rolling action. The technician started shooting film as the helicopter went into resonance. Fortunately, he moved to the side just as the blade separated and landed in the spot he had just left.

There is nothing subtle about ground resonance if allowed to develop. In this case the (damperless) linkage system did not work because the overall, the chordwise flexibility of the blades and their restraint defined a virtual lag hinge. The damage was severe because of the inadvertent delay in cutting the power. It should be emphasized this was an experimental helicopter. For a conventional production rotor with dampers, if vibrations do emerge, followed by immediate corrective action, the worst that could happen would be some bent parts at the root end of the blades.

In theory and practice the ground vibration problem is less tractable for a two-blade rotor with lag hinges, and the system is not seen on modern (single rotor) helicopters. However in the past this knowledge did not prevent some from trying it out, more out of ignorance than experience. In one case a small rocket-driven rotor used two, damperless, hinged blades mounted on a test pylon. The blades were made of adhesively bonded sheet stainless steel. On the first runup the rotor went into resonance, popping the bond of the inboard trailing edges. In another case a two-blade rotor with lag hinges was tested in autorotation mounted on a truck facing the wind. In this case to avoid coupling, the truck was firmly supported off its tires so there could be no feedback.

The alternate two-blade solution is to use the semi-rigid teetering rotor system as described with Young (1931). The hub is universally jointed (gimbaled) and the cantilever blades are designed to be very rigid in the plane of rotation. Such a design introduces in flight a different type of vibration in the plane of rotation that is of aerodynamic origin. The varying drag impresses on each blade a once-per-revolution force in the plane of rotation. The high chordwise stiffness is to avoid resonance in the operating rpm range. Note with reference to Figure H.1, the design problem is similar except for the two-blade rotor the dominant excitation is in the plane of rotation, while for the hinged rotor it is in the vertical plane. The (two-blade) vibration produces a twice-per revolution cyclic force in the plane of rotation at the rotor head. The latter vibration requires some form of mast isolation to avoid transmitting to the fuselage and the passengers a substantial periodic force.

In practice the shaft vibration problem first appeared with the Bell-Young rotor system. The solution was to suspend the complete engine-rotor unit in its own vibration isolation package (Young-Kelley patent 2,615,657).

Overall, from the vibration viewpoint, the two essential design features of a two-blade teetering rotor system are a stiff blade chordwise, and a rotor vibration isolation system. In modern versions only the rotor system (not the engine) is shock mounted. This is also the case for jet-driven rotor versions. For a teetering rotor system with three or more blades, the in-plane aerodynamic forces cancel out, and there is no mandatory requirement for rotor isolation.

Regarding the historical prototypes, there was likely a common vibration problem with the coaxial rotating wing approach that was not present with the coaxial propeller arrangement. The former featured flexible blades on elongated driveshafts, necessary for rotor clearance. (As noted, they probably favored this configuration because it was lighter and it permitted better control of blade design.)

Williams (1908 and Figure 3.12) commented on the "sprung shaft" that ended his tests. Figure 3.78 (Anonymous/Williams) definitely shows a form of shaft whirl. Yur'ev (Figure 3.98) had a shaft problem, and Luyties (Figure 3.3) as well as Purvis-Wilson (Figure 3.23) most likely experienced this. In these cases one can attribute the problem to inadequate drive-shaft rigidity, the weight taken out of the rotor should have gone into the driveshaft; and the fact it was difficult to maintain a truly balanced rotor. One senses a standoff between the rotor and propeller approaches, which in hindsight produced only negative knowledge.

helicopter power and performance

Helicopter power determination involves two basic concepts: power available and power required. (The notion also applies to fixed wing aircraft but the resulting curves are different because they cannot hover.) The following outline procedure is part of the preliminary design (PD) process. The output of PD includes a preliminary specification for the helicopter. "Final design" is an iterative and tradeoff procedure involving detail design and analysis, test and evaluation of the experimental helicopter and its components. Some of this procedure is described under blade and rotor design, and blade structural integrity, and overall, under systems engineering. [H.10] Performance can be calcu-

lated once the two powers are known by using a simple plot of two power curves (Figure H.7).

Power available refers to the rating of the powerplant allowing for adjustments. This is compared with the helicopter power required for a given set of conditions and assumptions. Calculations for both result in the characteristic curves of Figure H.7, the form of which applies to all helicopters.

Generally there is one hovering condition that sizes the powerplant. A typical military condition requires the helicopter to hover (OGE) at 1220 meters (4000 feet) with an air temperature of 35 degrees centigrade (95 fahrenheit). (This ambient temperature taxes the powerplant.) At this point the helicopter is to be capable of a vertical climb of at least 137.3 meters per minute (450 feet per minute).

With turboshaft engines, the rating is related to the duration of the power level used, and at what altitude. This suggests the importance of getting the most out of a shaft turbine of a given weight, without damaging it. Damage here refers to the pilot's indirect control of combustion temperatures, with their consequent effect on turbine blade integrity.

Because of its hover capability, helicopter weight is more critical compared with fixed-wing aircraft. Most professionals consider introduction of the turbine to helicopters the most significant development since the practical helicopter itself. Even nature recognizes the difficulty in creating hovering flight. The heaviest creatures weigh only a few ounces, after a day's activity they are exhausted and often slip into a torpor.

The rating of the powerplant prior to installation is the point of departure for matching power curves. As installed in a particular helicopter there are certain power losses charged to it that are necessary for a turbine (in particular) to operate satisfactorily. These components (with power losses) include ducts, filters, and particle separators for the ingested air; cooling systems; and ducting and obstructions at the exhaust end of the engine. The total losses amount to 5–10 percent of the uninstalled rating. The net power available is then the plot of Figure H.7. As shown, this rating is assumed constant with forward speed.

Helicopter power required is based on calculations when plotted give the bowl-shaped curve of the figure. Some of the conditions and assumptions are listed on it. There will be a set of these characteristic curves for selected altitudes, including sea level, initially for the standard atmosphere (or standard day). In addition to this standard or "model atmosphere" there are also standards for hot, cold, polar and tropical atmospheres. Once both curves are calculated a considerable amount of performance information can be derived.

In its simplest form the power-required curve is calculated by a summation in steady level flight of rotor power required, parasite-drag power of the rest of the helicopter, and some other losses (transmission, tail rotor). Numerical calculations proceed by assuming a series of flight speeds from zero mps (mph) to beyond the anticipated maximum speed, and solving the equations that go with calculating power required. A sophisticated analysis would use an extensive computer program tailored to the specific helicopter or company involved. Fortran has been a favored software for engineering calculations. An established company will have set up an aerodynamics and performance manual describing among other things the standard procedures for this analysis.

The power absorbed by the rotor itself consists of induced and (blade) profile drag power. These values were described in figure of merit. When corrected for non-ideal conditions the ideal power becomes the predicted induced power required. Profile drag power calculations include accounting for rotor blade properties (airfoil section, profile drag coefficient, mean lift coefficient, critical Mach number), tip speed, rotor solidity, and air density ratio. A significant aspect of the properties of the atmosphere is that only the density of air normally enters into aerodynamic and performance calculations. Nonstandard atmospheres specifying ambient temperature and altitude (pressure) are converted to the standard air density at that altitude before use in the calculations. However high temperature definitely affects turbine power output (available) adversely.

Parasite power is required to overcome the drag of all the non-rotor parts of the helicopter. Such parts include the rotor head, fuselage, tail items, landing gear, antennas and other appendages, as well the drag caused by mutual interference of these parts. Analytically the drag of all these parts is summed up, giving a drag conveniently equated to that of a flat plate with a specific "parasite" area. This area times the dynamic pressure at the specified flight velocity gives the total parasite drag of the helicopter for that speed. The parasite power is then the product of this drag and the flight velocity. The total parasite drag also can be determined through wind tunnel tests.

In recent years to conserve power and weight, the automotive industry has been publicizing auto drag coefficients, which are actually parasite drag coefficients. Drag reduction is reflected in the contours of modern autos. The depressed front end and design of the overall shape also keep the vehicle from taking off into free flight. At least, the shape inhibits the lift that reduces tire tractive force. Based on the frontal, cross sectional area, an auto drag coefficient of 0.28 (Lexus LS 400) is considered good. The comparable value for a five-place helicopter is about 43 percent greater. Though it is streamlined, the helicopter fuselage has, as listed above, many draggy things sticking out of it.

Like the uninstalled powerplant, there are other losses charged to the helicopter itself. The main one being the tail rotor power. These are included in the power required curve. The summation is plotted as the lower curve of Figure H.7. As explained before, the shape of this curve versus velocity is an indicator of the pilot's collective pitch stick angle as well as the blade collective pitch angle itself.

The characteristic shape of this curve is due to induced power decreasing with forward speed, while the profile power tends to remain constant with speed, with a value much lower than the induced power in hovering. The latter is true until such a flight speed is reached where the blade compressibility power increment increases substantially. Parasite drag power is zero in hovering and this (drag) power increases as the cube of the velocity. By point d (Figure H.7) most of the power required is derived from this drag. The trade between induced power and parasite power results in the dip in the middle speed range where lies the least amount of power to fly the helicopter.

The power curves as plotted give much information useful in performance determination. Referring to Figure H.7 and recalling that a set of curves applies to a given gross weight and altitude, the following can be derived.

1. Gap A is the excess power available for vertical climb. For the military requirement this power will be the value to produce at least the

specified rate of climb for the given ambient temperature. Gap B permits one to calculate the maximum rate of climb. The speed for maximum climb is f. In general climb rate is proportional to the excess (available) climb power divided by the helicopter gross weight.

2. Point d, where power available equals power required is the maximum speed. However considering retreating blade stall and attendant flight roughness, calculations may limit the maximum speed to the value at point e, which is before the speed the helicopter would run out of power. However there is a maximum speed limit that overrides both the above limitations. It is the "never-exceed speed". This can only be established experimentally with a flight test. The limit is not directly related to power but to controllability. Any helicopter has limits to its rotor speed range, center of gravity travel, and pilot's control travel. The last implies limits to rotor inclination (cyclic pitch control) in any direction.

Theoretically it is possible for a helicopter at high speeds to have such a combination of forward rotor tilt and forward CG location that puts the helicopter in a condition from which the pilot cannot recover. The problem manifests itself in severe vibration in the helicopter and cyclic pitch stick and a pronounced pitching tendency. The effects are violent, and up to 35 percent of the rotor disk may be stalled. To avoid this problem each helicopter model or significant variant must be flown experimentally to seek out the speed at which this trouble will occur. The exploration itself is hazardous and the effort requires a skilled test pilot. The defined never-exceed speed is taken to be 90 percent of the velocity at which the roughness was encountered. This speed value decreases with altitude. Once established the never-exceed speed becomes part of the operator's manual.

3. Point c, the tangent from the origin approximates the flight speed for maximum range with minimum power required and fuel consumed. However the operational speed of the helicopter may be taken at a higher value, as point g. This speed may be used to calculate helicopter range. Unlike an auto where normal weight change is not significant, helicopter range calculations take into account the fact the consumption of fuel reduces the gross weight with time. This reality will predict a greater range than one based only on the gross weight at the start of the trip.

4. Gap D determines the minimum power to

remain aloft, and point f then represents the speed for maximum endurance.

5. Power-off, autorotative performance also can be estimated considering gaps C and D. The assumption here is the loss of altitude (power produced by gravity) is used to overcome (or is equivalent to) power consumed in hovering, or other flight conditions. In general the rate of descent in autorotation will be proportional to the power-on power divided by the gross weight. Note the similarity in analytical approach between powered climb and autorotative descent. The first relies on engine power while the other the fall energy (power). *See also* autorotation.

Historically two aspects of the power required curve are of interest. The first was discussed in connection with the L'Aérophile 1909 correspondence exchange, concerning rotor induced and profile powers, and need for both in the analysis. Later when induced power theory was developed it seemed a little difficult to envision it took increasingly less induced power (or overall power) to fly forward than to hover (point h versus point f). Considering that it is the jet of air that supports the helicopter. One explanation is the oncoming airflow which appears to be free, makes up for what the rotor is not producing in induced flow.

There was a third controversy in the 1930s unrelated directly to power. With Cierva favoring rotor control through hub tilt and hinged blade flapping, there appeared a competitive group that provided rotor control by a different mechanism, specifically by blade feathering. Analytically the former was demonstrated by J. A. J. Bennett and the feathering approach, by Raoul Hafner. Eventually it was accepted that aerodynamically one is equivalent to the other. Today helicopters fly with a mix of flapping and feathering blade and control motions.

helicopter toy

It is interesting to examine the language of helicopters toys and the word *helicopter* itself, viewing them both from the West and East. Typically the West relied on Graeco-Roman words in naming, while the East used metaphors.

The earliest word *whirigig* dates to the 15th century applied to pinwheels. It has been applied to any gadget that whirls or spins, and in the time of the Wrights it was used for the helicopter toy.

In the early years after World War II the full size machine took this name as a byname, but it has gone out of fashion. Currently the full size helicopter has the familiar or slang name *chopper*. In planning, the Army uses *helo(s)* while engineers as often as not call them *rotary wing aircraft*.

As mentioned before, D'Amécourt (1863) coined the word *hélicoptère* and he took the traditional Western approach. The names *stropheor* (1846) and *spiralifer* (1860s) also follow this style. Helicopter is a compound of the Greek adjective *elikoeioas* (spiral, winding) and the noun *pteron* (feather, wing). Thus rotating wing, a picture that must have seemed unusual at the time.

Stropheor takes for its root the Greek *strofao* (turn, spin), also found in the word catastrophe. The combining form "-or" changes a verb to a noun indicating an agent (thing or person). The suffix is found in other words as compressor and liberator. *Stropheor* may be translated as "a thing (toy) conveying rotation".

Spiralifer, a French creation, consists partly of the French noun *spiral* (spiral), ultimately the Latin *spira* (coil, twist). The word suggests both turning and rising. The suffix "-fer" is from Latin *ferum* (to hold up, support, carry). This is found in other words as transfer and refer. Accordingly the translation may be taken as "a thing (toy) that spins and climbs". The word toy is from German *zeug* (thing).

As mentioned above, the Eastern interpretation of the toy is metaphoric identifying it with the dragonfly. This insect has two sets of wings that remain extended when at rest. The wingspan varies but it is mostly in the 5.1 to 10.2 cm (2 to 4 in) range. It is capable of hovering and darting about with vigor, attacking its prey (mosquitos, aphids) in flight. This fact has earned it the nickname "mosquito hawk".

Traditionally, the Japanese had a fond, special relationship with their many dragonflies. In ancient times Japan itself was referred to as the "land of dragonflies". The insect has figured in poetry since the 5th century so much so that a Western observer in 1910 was moved to write about the poetry (mostly haiku): ". . . . the poems on dragonflies are almost as numerous as the dragonflies themselves in early autumn". [H.14]

Figure 1.13 is an illustration from a Japanese source. Alongside the toy are two sets of Japanese characters read vertically. The two characters to the left are Chinese borrowings among the many that are collectively called *kanji*. They are read vertically in Japanese as two syllables *tom-bo* (also *ton-bo*), meaning "dragonfly". The vertical characters to the right are from one of two Japanese syllable-scripts. The characters shown are written in the script *katagana*. The syllables read *to-n-bo-u*, also "dragonfly". (The romanized version of Japanese words is *romaji*.)

The two characters to the left also can be read in Chinese which is their source. As two pictures they read vertically *qing-ting*, "dragonfly". The top character alone also means "dragonfly". The two Chinese characters are compounds, the right side (called the "phonetic") gives the sound of the character, while the left character (called the "radical") suggests its meaning. The left hand part (the radical) is the same for both because it suggests among other things, the insect family. The right hand sides of both produce the sounds *qing ting*. The romanized spellings (script) used in this book are in the modern style called *han yu pin yin*. The first two syllables mean "Chinese language" while the last two "convert sounds into syllables". *Pin-yin* is also called the "Chinese phonetic alphabet" or CPA.

To complete the Asian study, dragonfly in Korean is *chamjari*, and in Vietnamese *con-chuon-chuon*. Recall also in Cayley's time (mid 19th century) the European name for its version was "Chinese top". However in the literature available, no distinction is made between the palm type and the pull-string helicopter toy.

In modern times the dragonfly together with the hummingbird have been used as proper nouns for specific helicopter models, for example Hoverfly, Dragonfly, and Libellula. The last is the scientific name for a genus of dragonfly.

Any bird can hover briefly especially in a headwind. What makes the hummingbird unique is that it feeds while hovering. This is a strange phenomenon among birds, apparently manifestation of some unknown fact of evolution (or lack of it). It is known the bird is constantly feeding. Even so, at the end of the day it may have insufficient food energy to survive the next day without entering the torpor mentioned previously. In this state the bird's metabolism drops to about $1/50$ of its value when awake, and it takes about an hour to recover, rendering it very vulnerable. Sometimes it does not awaken. Hovering may be a way to speed up the process of storing food energy, which is tiring in itself. At the end of the day there apparently is a net gain in energy but not enough to respond overnight as other birds do. This condition raises a philosophical question regarding hummingbirds. Considering the millions of years they have existed, and the idea of natural selection, one can question why they have not evolved out of this marginal existence.

helicopter types

The difference between a helicopter and autogiro was explained under the latter entry. Helicopters are classified basically by rotor arrangement and by powerplant type. In some cases as with jet driven rotors the special feature is identified first.

Use of two or more rotors was to account for torque reaction of one rotor by a second one. This idea had general appeal in the two periods narrated here. The following are common helicopter configurations.

1. Tail rotor helicopter

The single main rotor with a tail rotor is an old idea (Figures 3.98 Yur'ev and 3.96 Sikorsky). It was Sikorsky who reduced the configuration to practice, followed by Piasecki, Bell (Young), and Hiller. This arrangement has become the principle one for helicopters today. It is produced in sizes from a single-seater to a heavy load-lifter capable of lifting a sling load of 11,000 kilograms (24,250 pounds).

2. Tandem rotor helicopter

In the United States the system with one rotor behind the other is the second most common configuration. It is associated with larger helicopters originally developed by Piasecki and now produced only by Boeing (Philadelphia). It is a military helicopter with a singular advantage over the tail rotor type in its wider range of allowable CG travel. The largest today can lift an external load of 12,700 kilograms (28,000 pounds).

3. Coaxial rotor helicopter

This is the historical arrangement, particularly in the 19th century, and many in the early 20th century entrepreneurs favored this. None are produced in the United States today however they are still operational in Russia, in applications where low speed and hovering are important.

4. Lateral rotor helicopter

The configuration of the first practical one (Figures 3.110, Focke). None are produced today because the tandem type has the CG travel advantage. In the 1940s two prototypes were evaluated for military application, one by Platt-LePage Aircraft and the other by McDonnell Aircraft. However the largest helicopter ever built was the Russian Mil-12 prototype, with a gross weight of 105,000 kilograms (231,483 pounds). In 1969 it lifted a load of 40,204 kilograms (88,634 pounds).

5. Intermeshing rotor helicopter (synchropter)

The two rotors are arranged laterally to intermesh. The axes of rotation are angled away from each other and intersect below the helicopter. It is a compact form of the lateral rotor system. The configuration was first reduced to practice and in production by Flettner in Germany in the late 1930s. The FL-282 served in World War II, and in its time it was the best helicopter flying. In the U.S., Kaman Aircraft has been identified with this configuration in production. The largest operational one is designed for an external lift of 2724 kilograms (6000 pounds).

The idea itself is old. The earliest patent of record is to Frenchman Max Bourcart (British 18,768 of 1903). Bourcart came from a family of aeronautical researchers that dates back to 1800. Another intermesher invention (1910) is the patent of Guatav Mees (1,096,045). After a visit to Flettner in Germany Richard H. Prewitt Chief Engineer at Kellett Aircraft initiated in the 1940s two prototype helicopter evaluation programs. These were followed by the Kaman production versions.

6. Multi-rotor helicopters

Helicopters with three or more rotors do not exist today, although they had their adherents in the past. One trirotor prototype was built in 1948 but it went nowhere. The DeBothezat (1922) helicopter (Figure 3.68) was a quadrotor, and one was built in France in 1907.

For this design the rotor head is simplified because only collective pitch is required. This arrangement will produce pitch, roll, and yaw moments. In theory the system has favorable CG travel in the longitudinal and lateral directions. As noted with the DeBothezat narrative, there is a problem with pitch adjustment for trim and heading whereby the consequent torque compensation is difficult to balance out for the selected heading. Overall the single and tandem rotor systems have shut out the quadrotor configuration, apparently for good. [H.15]

Historically, multirotors are as shown in Figures 3.13 (Kimball) and 3.30 (Whitehead). The rationale for using many small diameter rotors is not explicit. It may be related to safety, ease of control, uniformity of wake flow or producibility. However malfunction of the complex drive system would preclude satisfactory operation, even before the machine left the ground.

invention, helicopter

A fair question is: who invented the helicopter? In its common sense, invention involves a "flash of insight" evident to the inventor and others in the same field. "Combinations" also are invention. If anything the helicopter followed the second route. A more immediate question is: who was "first" with a helicopter? Consider the second question initially.

Being first is a mystique in itself, often no more significant than being the precursor to a practical solution created by others. From the inventor's viewpoint being second is sometimes better. The creator, if on the right track, may exhaust oneself emotionally and financially before the payoff, and the successor becomes the beneficiary. A reasonable criterion for the claim of being first is the object (here a vehicle) demonstrated to be technically practical, repeatable (in production) and ultimately, useful. Such an inventor deserves general and official recognition. The other claimants should be satisfied in being honored as local visionaries.

With this rationale the Wright brothers were the first to create a viable airplane. They knew what an airplane looked like and the other contenders did not. Likewise Cierva created the first autorotating wing aircraft (the autogiro), and Focke the first practical helicopter in the world. This was followed by Sikorsky as first in America. Sikorsky also set the common configuration of a single main and tail rotor. Just as the common airliner is a low wing monoplane. The configuration is so common that to call it a "monoplane" sounds quaint.

The idea of inventing the helicopter requires a more detailed analysis. The *World Almanac* records Sikorsky invented the helicopter in 1939 in the United States. [H.16] Some modern, benighted writers on helicopter history take the work of Focke as inconsequential despite the narratives here revealing the difficulty in creating a practical helicopter. In the insightful sense, no one "invented" the helicopter. Focke reduced it to practice by virtue of the right combination of components demonstrating hover capability, vertical flight, and autorotation. Autorotative

ability was the critical, decisive element. Again, the narratives reveal both its importance and elusiveness. Today this feature is rarely in public consciousness and therefore not an important condition for invention. In fact some still believe power failure results in catastrophe. Since most helicopters flying today have tail rotors, Focke's lateral rotor machine suggests a dead-end project and therefore inconsequential.

It is interesting this view did not hold for the Wright Flyer I which was a fixed-wing dead end very unlike modern airplanes. The Flyer I featured biplane wings, horizontal planes forward, vertical planes aft, skid landing gear, and a prone pilot.

By parallel argument, if Focke's machine was not the first practical helicopter, neither was the Wright Flyer I the first practical airplane. By 1908 the world accepted the machine demonstrated human flight as feasible, even though the Flyer I design was not worth repeating. The critical element to its success was the introduction of a lateral control system adequate to deal with the wing instability. For the helicopter the critical element was demonstration of practical, safe power-off flight in autorotation. If credit is to be given for creating the first practical helicopter, it must be based on the first to demonstrate autorotation. This after other conditions were met.

There are four individuals to be considered in this analysis: Focke, Flettner, Sikorsky, and Young (Bell). All had practical prototype helicopters but chronologically, their autorotation demonstrations were sequential. Focke had two FW-61 prototypes. On May 10, 1937 a machine demonstrated autorotation from 397 meters (1300 feet) altitude. Technically, he was first. Equally important he demonstrated to the world the helicopter was a viable flying machine. In its time it was a technical and political sensation.

Anton Flettner was second with the FL-265 intermesher, of which six were built. The first transition to autorotation occurred in August, 1939. In June 1941 for the first time ever a helicopter (FL-265) transitioned from helicopter flight to autorotation, and reversed to powered flight. [H.17] Years later, Flettner recounted to the author the anxiety behind the demonstration by both the pilot and those on the ground considering it was the first time.

It is curious that published information on Sikorsky and Bell prototypes do not make a point of autorotation. The dates given here are estimates. The Sikorsky VS-300A (Figure 3.96) rotor arrangement consisted of a single main rotor with two lifting rotors aft and an antitorque rotor. This configuration was the first successful Sikorsky, setting an endurance record in 1941. It is apparent such a design was not intended for autorotation, and flying was near the ground. Variants with the single main and tail rotor appeared later. This version may have performed autorotation in the 1941–1942 period. In January 1942 the XR-4 made its first test flight. The first systematic tests of this machine in autorotation were conducted by NACA around 1947. [H.18] Chronologically Sikorsky was third in demonstrating autorotation. He can claim to be first with a practical tail rotor helicopter, but this was not the world's first practical helicopter.

The Bell helicopter prototype designed by Young made its first formal flight in July 1943. As noted before, in March 1946 the Model 47B was granted the world's first commercial helicopter license by FAA. The first autorotation probably took place in the 1944–1945 period, since safe autorotation had to be demonstrated for certification. These dates put the Bell fourth in the string of successful helicopters.

In his *Bell Notes* Young makes the remark: ".... even seeing my designs copied by Sikorsky (i.e., the tail rotor) does not ... affect me." [H.19] This observation is not correct for the narratives show Sikorsky had the tail rotor idea in 1930 (Figure 3.100) and probably even earlier. The initial configuration of the prototype in 1939 was a clean tail rotor machine. Young's tail rotor tethered model was tested in the early 1940s. [H.20] Beyond these, one can trace the tail rotor to the Yur'ev prototype of 1909–1912 (Figure 3.102), and even earlier to 1874 with the Achenbach concept in Germany. Apparently and credibly, Igor Sikorsky had no knowledge of the work of Yur'ev. [H.21]

As pioneers of helicopter development in America, Young deserves equal stature with Sikorsky. What gives Young this stature is not simply the stabilizer system, but the complete rotor concept, one based on the universal joint mount, and the teetering rotor system. This successful design was an entirely new approach, and not derivative as were the systems with articulated blades. Historically the Young design was a complete departure from the many rigid-rotor concepts described in the narratives, as well as from the autogiro-based blade articula-

tion ideas on other helicopters. Of the American pioneers only Young's name is not a company name. (It is like crediting a daVinci painting to his patron.) Considering Young's philosophy, this lack would mean little to him.

The discussion here focused on seniority in autorotation. Regarding successful helicopters the Piasecki PV-2 was the second practical helicopter flown in the United States. The three mentioned here (Sikorsky, Young, and Piasecki) along with entrepreneurs Hiller and Kaman, are clearly the founders of the helicopter industry in America.

kinesthesia

Kinesthesia is the sensation of movement, weight resistance, and position in the muscles and joints of the body. Active kinesthetic control was a feature of the 1924 helicopter attributed to Williams (Figures 3.77, 3.78, and 3.79). Others with this feature are Kimball (Figure 3.13), Exel (Figure 3.46), and the stand-on helicopter (Figure H.8).

Small helicopters (usually single-seaters) fitted with regular controls also respond to body shifts by the pilot. In general, pilots passively use kinesthetic cues to recognize incipient malfunctions.

lift coefficient

Lift coefficient is an aerodynamic parameter applicable to an airfoil or wing derived from test data for a given wing shape and profile. The concept is adapted typically to a hovering rotor by theoretically determining the average (or mean) value of lift for all the rotor blades acting as a lifting disk. Averaging is the result of the fact lift on a blade varies from root to tip. In structural studies this lift distribution is the air load acting on it.

The mean value is significant because it has been found the maximum figure of merit will occur in a band that can be represented by a mean (rotor) lift coefficient of 0.6. The value is related to *solidity* (sigma) as follows:

$$C_{lm} = (6.0 \ C_T/\text{sigma}) \quad C_T = \text{thrust coefficient}$$
$$\text{sigma} = \text{solidity ratio}$$

Knowing the mean lift coefficient and thrust coefficient as design inputs, one can calculate the required blade solidity (total blade area) required.

Figure H.8   De Lackner *Aerocycle* helicopter with CG above the rotor (1950s).

The 19th century introduction discussed a possible way the inventors established rotor blade area. There was then no theoretical-empirical approach as the above to establish this area. The approach then and in the early 20th century appears to be based on trial and error, and in some cases by testing a family of rotors. There is no specific information on how these investigators arrived at the full scale geometry. A subtle aspect of hovering helicopter theory is the development of an analytical approach for determining optimum blade area.

power loading

Power loading is the ratio of helicopter weight to power input to the rotor, in kilograms per kilowatt (pounds per horsepower). This interpretation is used in determining figure of merit. There is another power loading concept of nominal interest. It is the ratio of helicopter weight to total (uninstalled) engine power available. While the power loading term was not used, it was the main parameter of concern to the entrepreneurs of the narratives. They were interested first of all in how much horsepower it took to lift a given weight.

Today, power loadings for the rotor alone, i.e., power delivered directly to the rotor are in the range of 4.9–6.1 kg/kW (8–10 lb/hp) for high-performance helicopters, and 8.5–9.7 kg/kW (14–16 lb/hp) for small training helicopters. Based on uninstalled engine power available, the range is 1.8–2.4 kg/kW (3–4 lp/hp) for military designs, and 5.5–6.1 kg/kW (9–10 lb/hp) for trainers.

As noted in the earlier discussion on 19th century powerplants, steam powerplants alone weighed 36.5–103.4 kg/kW (60–170 lb/hp).

Practical rotary engines of the early 20th century weighed 1.3–1.5 kg/kW (2.2–2.5 lb/hp). For comparison the weight of helicopter turboshaft engines varies from 0.15 to 0.24 kg/kW (0.25–0.40 lb/hp).

pressure jet helicopters

The pressure jet principle focuses on use of compressed air or combustion gas to drive the rotor. The drive is from nozzles at the tips of hollow blades. Unlike tip jet engines (pulsejet, ramjet) the powerplant is in the fuselage and the air or gas is ducted to the blade tips. The intent of the pressure jet design is to avoid use of complicated, high maintenance mechanical drive systems as well as the tail rotor for torque-compensation of the main rotor. However jet rotor systems always have some main rotor torque, the result of driving accessories off the main rotor. As the case for tip-mounted engines, a small tail rotor is added to account for this torque. There have been four main design treatments to pressure jets. These approaches are: tip burning, hot cycle, warm cycle, and cold cycle. [H.34] In each case prototypes or test stand units have been built.

1. Tip burning (compound helicopter)

With this arrangement burners are fitted in the blade tips. Combustion takes place there in a chamber containing the flow of compressed air and fuel. The resulting gas is discharged from nozzles, driving the rotor. Fuel consumption is very high, and the sound level excessively high. As a result the process was used only for short duration hovering and transitional flight. The forward flight mode relied on fixed wings and propellers. The rotor continues to turn but it is not (normally) powered. The Fairey Rotodyne prototype was flown during 1959–1962. At the latter date the project was abandoned in favor of the conventional helicopter. McDonnell Aircraft built the XV-1 pressure jet and this project did not go beyond the evaluation stage that ended in 1957.

2. Hot cycle rotor helicopter

In this system the exhaust gases of jet engines are ducted through the hub to blade tips and discharged there. The low pressures associated with jet exhaust and the high gas flows gives this rotor system a bloated look. The high gas temperatures presented a design problem for the rotor blades. Compared with the tip burning pressure jet (above) the hot cycle fuel consumption is

about half. The Army evaluated one, the Hughes XV-9A built in 1964, but nothing followed, except investigation of the warm cycle as a replacement.

3. Warm cycle helicopter

This concept was similar to the hot cycle except the gases are at a lower temperature obtained from a mixture of jet exhaust and compressed air. The source being a fanjet engine. Only a test stand version was built. The system was intended for very heavy-lift helicopters in the payload range of 18,160 kilograms (20 tons) to 24,440 kilograms (52 tons). The test stand version was evaluated in Germany in 1965 but nothing followed. The above three concepts ended after the evaluation phase, most likely because there was no military requirement for a heavy load-lifter beyond those currently available, and the mechanical drive advocates presented a strong case for its viability in any size helicopter.

4. Cold cycle pressure jet helicopter

No combustion is used in this system, just compressed air drives the rotor. Of the types, this is the only version that was produced in series. The two-seat helicopter was built by Sud Ouest Aviation in France and designated SO-1221 *Djinn*. About 180 were produced in the 1953–1960 period. A 1990 commercial helicopter register listed 23 as still accounted for. This configuration is the most promising of the group, and some private venture versions were built in the 1970s and 1980s but the major manufacturers appear to be committed to the mechanically driven rotor.

rotary engine

A rotary engine is an air cooled, piston powerplant (Figure 3.5) in which the crankcase drives the airscrew while the crankshaft is fixed. [H.22] Propellers of the time had a low, rotational inertia. A heavy flywheel was necessary for smooth operation of the engine. (The static engine of the Wright Flyer I required one.) With the rotary this component was not required. The rotating cylinders served this purpose. Even so, the rotating mass introduced a high, gyroscopic couples in maneuvering flight. The rotary gave a lower weight per power compared with automotive adaptations. As stated before, other advantages to prototype helicopter application were the self-cooling property and its surplus availability after the First World War.

The air and fuel were fed to the cylinders through a hollow crankshaft. In functioning like a two stroke (cycle) engine, the fuel and oil were mixed. To avoid lubricant dilution castor oil was used because it did not mix with the gasoline. Fuel and oil consumption were high, and overhaul cycles were as low as 15 hours.

Some rotaries operated only "on" or "off" and power was coarsely controlled by "blipping" the ignition switch. The engine was noisy because the rotating cylinders precluded use of a muffler exhaust system. Anyone who has seen aviation movies of World War I will recall the constant on-off buzz of the rotaries as the planes were ready for takeoff, or when coming in for a landing. Some makes as the Le Rhone could be throttled, offering better power control. Hence it was favored in helicopter applications.

The rotary arrangement was designed specifically for airplanes, and in its time was a popular and successful powerplant. The period extended through the First World War, after which the surplus engines became available. By this time it was being replaced in production by the static radial air-cooled engine.

rotor, ABC type

This concept is of interest because it was an attempt to attain high flight speeds by reproducing fixed wing air loads on a rotor system. Physically it was an advanced concept for a coaxial rotor helicopter using the historically preferred rigid propellers. An Army project, it was experimentally evaluated on the XH-59A (Sikorsky S-69) helicopter. The rotor idea called Advancing Blade Concept (ABC) was flight tested during 1975–1981. [H.25]

The rigid propeller S-69 focused on increasing flight speed by use of rotors flying edgewise. The approach was to overcome deficiencies common to single rotor and conventional coaxial configurations. In either configuration, high speed flight is limited both by retreating blade stall and advancing blade *compressibility*. The ABC design approach is to reproduce in the coaxial rotor system a form of spanwise lift distribution resembling one on a fixed-wing aircraft. For the latter, each wing panel is aerodynamically like the other, with no inherent rolling moment present in steady level flight. Attention is on control of the advancing blade angles of attack through a special kind of pitch variation.

Such a control also permits the advancing blade to operate more efficiently.

The ABC helicopter requires stability augmentation, and the concept uses a higher harmonic control (HHC). This replaces the conventional swashplate, a mechanism giving just one pitch-change cycle per revolution, which is simple harmonic motion. The HHC alleviates the significant vibration inherent in the ABC system. The vibration alleviation treatment is complicated because it must be responsive over a wide range of rotor speeds. This variation is required to control the tip Mach numbers of the advancing blade, and to maintain the rotor angle of attack efficiency for flight speeds from zero to over 547 km/hr (340 mph).

While the prototype demonstrated the high speed potential of a rotor in edgewise flight, it also revealed the complexity of the system to accomplish this. The favored high speed configuration is the tiltrotor realized in the Navy-Bell V-22 Osprey program.

rotor head

In the 19th and early 20th centuries, what may be called the rotor head was a simple component whose sole purpose was to hold one or two cantilever blade spars fixed to a vertical driveshaft. Features as pitch control, hinge offset, and articulation (flap, lag hinges) were yet to appear. The cantilever idea also applied to the common propeller as a rotor.

There were some attempts at collective pitch control in prototypes (Figures 3.38, 3.69, 3.73, 3.77, and 3.94). In the United States, a swashplate for cyclic and collective pitch control was a feature of the Exel prototype of 1930 (Figure 3.53). The earliest concept in Europe is associated with the 1909 Russian design of Yur'ev (Figure 3.98).

rotor moments

The engineering concept of a "moment" refers to the product of a force acting at the end of a lever arm. It is measured typically in meter-newtons (foot-pounds) when referring to rotor moments. Moments are the phenomena that incline the helicopter in pitch, roll, and yaw, introduced by the cyclic pitch control, and the tail rotor. These three modes represent three degrees of freedom (DOF) for the helicopter. Totally there are six DOF. The other three motions are produced by forces, not moments. These are the motions in the vertical, lateral and fore-and-aft directions. All of them are important in the analysis of helicopter stability and control.

Another application of moments is in structural analysis, discussed here in blade structural integrity. In the case of a rotor blade, a simplified example of bending moment would be the product of the air load (force) times the radial position (length) where the total air load is assumed to be concentrated. The units also are in meter-newtons (foot-pounds). The bending moments produce bending stresses in the blades, which when added to the centrifugal stress give the total stress at a radial point on the blade.

rotor rotation sense

On a single rotor helicopter there is no technical preference in which direction a rotor turns. When viewed from above, i.e., as seen on a drawing of the plan view, the rotors of American-built helicopters turn counterclockwise. So do British, German, and Italian rotors. French and Russian rotors turn clockwise. Thus rotors have nationality.

The dominant counterclockwise convention is believed (by the author, at least) to have its origins in the 1920s in conjunction with the aerodynamic and structural analyses of the autogiro rotor. Helicopter rotors which came later simply continued the tradition, since its rotor analyses are extensions of the autogiro theory. How the autogiro analysts decided on rotation is not known but it must have been a conscious decision. Airplane propellers viewed from the front turn counterclockwise. Possibly the American convention extended this to rotors viewd from above (on paper).

Some French helicopters are flying in the United States. These easily can be identified in low altitude flight by observing the direction of rotation from the ground. From below, French rotors will be seen to turn counterclockwise while American rotors and some German ones in the United States turn clockwise as viewed from the ground.

solidity ratio

Solidity ratio or solidity, designated by the Greek letter sigma, is the ratio of the total blade area to the (swept) disk area of the rotor. As discussed with lift coefficient, solidity is an important output of analysis permitting one to establish the optimum total blade area. It should be noted the final choice of solidity involves gen-

eral considerations as hovering at altitude, high speed, and maneuvering with high load factors.

The designer is free to apportion total blade area among a number of blades. The actual number is set using other criteria. Some specific factors in selecting this are the following:

1. Increasing the number of blades reduces aerodynamic vibration, producing a smoother ride.

2. The design preference may be for a specific number of blades as two for a teetering rotor, and three or more for blades with actual or virtual hinges. Note a teetering rotor can be designed with three or four blades.

3. The blades may be taken from a previous product of the manufacturer, either as-is, or as modified. This would not be the case for high-performance helicopters where the blades are practically tuned to the rest of the machine.

4. Blade weight as it relates to ground handling becomes a consideration as the helicopter size increases. For heavy-lift machines the blades can number six or more.

5. With gas or compressed air driven rotors (pressure jet helicopters) the fewer the blades the lower the duct losses.

6. Blade cost, rotor weight, and rotor head complexity (e.g., blade folding) may influence selection.

Most of the lifting propellers on early 20th century prototypes had two wood blades because of common propeller availability, and for special shapes, ease of fabrication. In cases where the inventor had multi screws in mind (Figure 3.56), wood remained the preferred material to work. Normally, the special shapes started out as rough cut, bonded laminations. These were then hand-carved to the final contours. The wing form of rotors also featured two blades but three and six blade rotors (Figure 3.68) were used as well.

stability (helicopter)

Hovering stability was discussed with Veyrin (1892) and in the 20th century introduction. The investigators of both periods failed to examine why a hovering rotor has a mind of its own. With the fuselage hanging below it (CG below the rotor) the system does not respond like a pendulum or a balloon with a suspended basket when disturbed by a gust. It was pointed out previously that a hinged rotor helicopter with the CG below the rotor is inherently unstable.

Inherent stability, a feature solved early in the history of fixed-wing aircraft implies the stability is "built in" the configuration. Inherent stability does not rely on black boxes (electro-mechanical devices) or servo (feedback) control. The problem was solved in the airplane by use of wing dihedral (for lateral stability), and tail surfaces (for longitudinal stability, because a wing alone is unstable). In a few cases the inherent stability can be excessive from the controllability viewpoint. Some advanced, high-wing military transports are deliberately designed with anhedral to reduce the effect on lateral stability and consequent controllability. The word anhedral is taken to mean the opposite of a dihedral, indicating the wing panel droops from root to tip. Some helicopters use blades with downswept tips (anhedral). In this case the interest is in performance as affected by wake vortecies of individual blades interfering with each other. The anhedral improves hovering figure of merit a few percent, but its value in other flight modes is mixed. In addition there is a structural problem with such tip treatment.

In theory, an inherently stable helicopter is easier to fly and more forgiving. Inherent stability is attained with the CG above the rotor. Apparently this was the case with Veyrin's experiments. But this relationship is undesirable for more important reasons, the main one being ground clearance. In the 1950–1960 period there were patents and machines featuring this concept, but they did not go beyond the prototype stage. Figure H.8 shows one evaluated by the Army as a vehicle for the individual soldier.

The design preference with all modern helicopters is the high rotor and low CG, which are controllably unstable. This choice created a viable helicopter but along with cost and maintainability, the required high skill-level inhibits wider acceptance of it. A personal or private helicopter should at least show inherent stability before its other problems are attacked. A very forgiving machine is essential.

There is one design for inherent stability with the low CG configuration. This was conceived by the author. [H.24] Essentially the design features a four-blade rotor, but with properties of the two opposing blades of one set, different from the other two. Considering hovering stability, one pair emphasizes a rotor property of "speed stability", and the other set, "damping in pitch". Equally important is the requirement

each pair deemphasize the properties of the other pair. No servo or black box is involved. The concept requires more power than the conventional four-blade rotor, but that is the price paid for inherent stability.

What follows is a general discussion of hovering helicopter stabilization that relies on feedback systems. In a gross sense, forward flight stabilization requires simple solutions, as surfaces and the tail rotor itself. Whether they are mechanical, aerodynamic, or electronic the concepts introduce devices that are proportional to helicopter attitude and time rate of change of attitude. For a single rotor helicopter the moment of inertia in pitch is much greater than in roll by a factor of 3 to 5. (These properties also were discussed with ground resonance.) Discussing the stability in roll will also account for its behavior in pitch. The great inertia difference makes lateral control more sensitive to cyclic stick motions.

In modern times, each practical prototype exhibited different degrees of hovering instability and controllability. [H.25] In general without feedback devices, the significant stability parameters include blade-hinge offset and angle, rotor flap inertia, fuselage moment of inertia, and the slope of the curve of blade section-lift (coefficient) versus angle of attack. The last parameter (slope) is important because some airfoils respond to a gust more "sluggishly" than others. An airfoil with a shallow sloped curve is slower to respond than a steep one. A specific combination of all the parameters mentioned above permit an inherently unstable helicopter to be controllable.

The first feedback concept introduced was the idea of Young (1931) described previously. This concept involved a gyroscopic flybar that came to be a trademark on all but the most recent Bell helicopters. [H.26] Essentially, the flybar permits design control of the rotor following-rate independent of the behavior of the rest of the helicopter. [H.27] Three patents reveal chronologically the evolution of the design to the final one used on Bell helicopters.

Patent 2,384,516 (Filed 1941) shows a simple flybar linked directly to the hub of a universally jointed, semi-rigid rotor. In this case the coupling is direct, and flybar angle equals pitch angle. Patent 2,633,924 (1948) introduces a horizontal link in the flybar system serving as a control mixer. The outboard end of the link is a pivot attached to the flybar. The inboard end is connected to a vertical control rod leading downward to the swashplate. Between these two pivots is a vertical rod connecting the flybar to the gimballed hub. This system does not include the essential feature of flybar damping. The damping is introduced in Patent 2,646,848 (1947) becoming the final design for the helicopters. The damper provides the time rate of change of attitude as mentioned above. It is attached to the rotating mast below the flybar and is connected to the mixing link by its own vertical rod (Figure 3.101).

The Hiller control rotor (paddle) design serves the same purpose aerodynamically that the gyroscopic flybar does for the Young system. The paddle concept was devised by Joseph Stuart III, after a tour with Bell helicopter. [H.28] Control rotor flapping provides the necessary cyclic pitch change to the lifting rotor which in turn lowers the following-rate of the rotor.

The paddle system proved to be an essential design solution in radio-controlled helicopter models. [H.29] The model blades invariably have little flap inertia relative to the inertia of the fuselage it is supporting. This means the rotor following rate without paddles would be very high, resulting in a very unstable and uncontrollable model. With a control rotor, its flapping introduces the necessary cyclic pitch to the main rotor, lowering its following rate. The action renders the model controllable.

As mentioned earlier, two parameters of significance to stability are blade flapping inertia and airfoil lift curve slope. Both properties must be significantly different for the main and control rotors to work effectively. That is, if the system consisted of four identical blades there would be no gain in stability augmentation. Typical ratios for the Hiller UH-12 full-scale helicopter reveal the differences. [H.30]

Lift curve slope:
control rotor / lifting rotor = 0.36
Blade flapping moment of inertia:
lifting rotor / control rotor = 59.0

In the case of the Hiller Hornet ramjet helicopter, the engines as tip weights obviated need for the paddles. However they were retained, having become a trademark of the company. Once the Young and Stuart devices were practically applied, others conducted studies comparing effectiveness to different helicopters. [H.31]

Relative to historical accomplishment, what makes Young's idea special is his direct focus on the problem of hovering stability. Others before Focke concentrated on rotor lifting power, effectively ignoring stability. They depended on a marginal controllability to deal with it. De-Bothezat may have some claim to treating stability but indirectly.

It is remarkable how benighted the early experimenters were in treating stability in general. Not one of them pondered the possibility a rotor is not a horizontal airscrew. A propeller has the simple job of pulling a machine through the air, unmindful of what it is pulling. Its only feedback concerns maneuvering gyroscopic forces, torque, and propeller wake. A rotor has a fundamental influence on helicopter behavior, mainly because it can hover. This unawareness can be attributed partly to the lack of accepted analytical principles of helicopter hovering stability. The value of an analytical base is that it points out the significant parameters to deal with, which are important and which are not.

As noted before, Young's major contributions are the gimbal mount with its teetering rotor, and the stabilization system. However things change, particularly as military helicopter systems become more sophisticated, and flight itself is undertaken with more precise requirements. Today in these advanced helicopters, desired flying (handling) qualities are designed into the system and not left to chance. [H.32] This concept takes advantages of the extreme design flexibility of electronic systems and electromechanical devices. Only small and medium-sized commercial helicopters now rely on the simple parameter variations, some with aero or mechanical feedback devices. The largest ones along with military machines require electronic stability augmentation systems.

The helicopter and the precision in its flying qualities could not be imagined in the 19th century, and in fact did not hold until after World War II. Prior to that war, the airplanes that flew were defined by performance. To a great extent handling qualities were accepted as they came out. Providing the airplane demonstrated competitive performance (speed, maneuverability, climb rate, range, endurance). The controllability differences were particularly wider in the planes of World War I when a good fighter plane could have tricky handling qualities.

Today military thinking is directed toward air-to-air combat of fighter helicopters World

War I fashion. With such a mission, desired flying qualities are critical to tactical superiority.

STOL

The steep takeoff and landing aircraft (STOL) is essentially a fixed-wing aircraft with a short takeoff run and steep climb. By use of special leading edge slats and trailing edge slotted flaps, lift coefficients as high as 3.5 are attainable. A high value of this parameter is desirable for reducing takeoff distance. For comparison the takeoff value for an airplane with a plain wing is at most 1.5, while a helicopter rotor in hovering will have a mean lift coefficient around 0.6. The takeoff run to clear a 15.3 meter (50 foot) obstacle is a typical measure of STOL performance. Small and medium size STOLs will accomplish this in 152.5–305 meters (500–1000 feet). The largest versions require 366–610 meters (1200–2000 feet), the last figure being less than half the distance for an airliner. In the small ones, the climb is so steep sometimes it is not possible for a passenger to sit erect. Commercial autogiros have a difficult comeback because this type now competes with the STOL aircraft which are simpler in construction.

STOLs with lifting screws have been included in the narratives. These are Hall (Figure 3.57), Berliner (Figure 3.64), and Johnson (Figure 3.93). For added lift modern STOLS experimentally have used a form of jet lift in addition to extendible wing components.

strip analysis

Mentioned with Chalmers (1908), strip analysis is a convenient mathematical technique whereby a rotor blade is divided into 10, 20 or more radial elements (strips). Each element is assumed to have uniform air load, weight, and flexibility. The end conditions either side of the element are shared in common with the adjacent elements. Strip analysis in preliminary design is used as a starting procedure in various analyses as air load, centrifugal force, elastic properties, and weight. From the calculations one derives among other quantities, blade stresses and natural frequencies.

Experimenters in the early 20th century whether interested in wings or rotors found it convenient to measure aerodynamic properties of a surface (a panel or strip of the typical section) in motion by whirling the surface around a

fixed center to which it was attached. For wings the technique served in place of a wind tunnel as a means within the resources of the experimenter. Chalmers experimented with a few of the more important "strips" (the outboard ones) rather than with a full complement of rotor blade elements.

systems engineering

The traditional (pre World War II) elements to creation of a new aircraft involved a specification, followed by analysis, design, test, and production. If commercial it was offered for sale. If military it was deployed and integrated into the existing system for which the requirement was initiated.

After that war, it was evident a more comprehensive, total approach was required to assure the aircraft functioned as specified in its now more complex environment. The total top-down approach was easier to accomplish because of the extensive use of computers. With this new thinking emerged the idea of viewing a new aircraft not as an entity but as part of a system, thereby introducing many more elements for consideration and accountability.

The "systems" approach to procurement, as prescribed by military methodology, emerged in the late 1940s and early 1950s. The concept has evolved since then. Today, any procurement of consequence requires the systems treatment conducted within the framework of the methodology. This applies to quantity procurement of Army helicopters as well.

Of general interest is the fact "systems" of all kinds, visible and invisible are increasingly interacting with individuals in everyday life. It is no secret the world is driven by technology, and one seeks to be a participant in this world not only materially but cognitively, the last meaning the ability to think rationally about the information overload, and to respond to it with equal rationality. It is important to understand systems behavior and to adopt in society some of its formal procedures such as foresight (planning), accountability, tradeoffs, and independent review. These enable one to interact with them as equals.

What follows is an outline of the military approach to this methodology. As methodology it is a formalized procedure and design process. [H.10] It is not a substitute for creative design activity or critical thought. As understood here a system is a self-sufficient unit that when finally realized is a complex of money, skills, equipment, techniques, data, software, and facilities that function interactively for the purpose of carrying out a predesignated role. A system exhibits equilibrium, it holds itself together.

Past civil systems "just grew", the case for old established corporations and such public services as the air traffic control system. As it exists today, the latter was not designed from the top down as today's systems methodology would dictate. A grand manifestation of a system and one that evolved is the familiar automobile transportation system. This system includes the vehicles and highways and the multitude of services and things associated with these. There is no central head for this example (a subtle definition of a democracy), but modern military systems do have central control.

Systems engineering as a methodology has two primary activities, each with its own tools and techniques: the engineering process itself, and the management of this process. Below is a description of the first and it is followed by the program or project management activity.

The engineering process (an Army helicopter system, for example) accounts for all activity from the definition of a need through creation and operation of the system, to obsolescence in-

cluding disposal. The design methodology must account for the complete life cycle of the helicopter, including all its support factors, by means of a top-down investigation that is mainly a deductive process.

Figure H.9 is likely the best single, top-level diagram revealing what the system engineering process is about. [H.33] The activity begins with an analysis of operational requirements. The cost-benefit criteria of a civil system is, in the military environment, taken to be cost-effectiveness. The outer loop clockwise through requirements, design and product assurance are the main, dependent, sequential activities. The field activities of the diagram represent supporting investigations, the heart of which are tradeoff analyses.

Tradeoff studies deal with optimization of a particular object or subsystem, by selecting and critically evaluating different candidate approaches. The study result is selection of the best alternate that meets a set of preestablished criteria.

Presence of the field activities in the figure (letters A to D) result in four loops, and these are iterative. Loop A refers to defining the helicopter requirements. This is an elaborate process in itself. Loop B is the helicopter design loop and loop C refers to the interaction of design, production, and product assurance (or quality

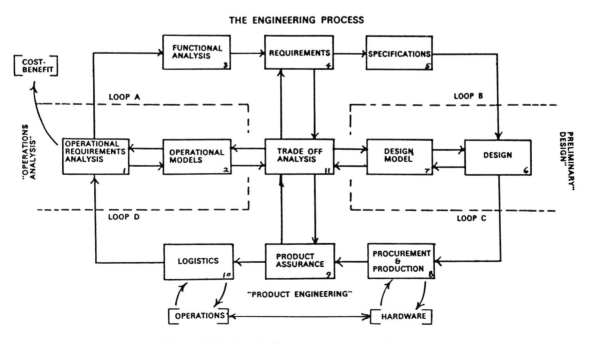

Figure H.9 Top level systems engineering diagram.

control). Product qualification is crucial to the military acceptance of the helicopter system.

Product (also qualification) assurance involves a variety of factors aimed at assuring operational suitability of the complete system. This function includes such factors as tests of components, subsystems, as well as helicopter flight tests and services; verification of predicted flying qualities and performance; structural integrity substantiation; mockup evaluation; safety verification; environmental performance evaluation; as well as procurement and procedure compliance. Also accounted for are military features such as weapons effectiveness, radar reflectivity, and reliability and maintainability.

Maintenance is measured in man-hours per flight hour. Predictions can give values as low as one hour per flight hour, but in practice can be as high as 10 to 18 hours. Using the Army format, the operating cost of the AH-64 Apache helicopter is $2700 per hour, reflecting the highest maintenance rate cited above. For the long-lived Huey (UH-1H) it is down to $209 per hour.

Referring again to Figure H.9, loop D represents the user's (the Army's) interest in the helicopter system. The broken lines show how operations analysis and preliminary design as disciplines fit into the overall process. The lower, outside loop (systems hardware delivered to operations) is an iterative function, post delivery. Such feedback represents service experience which in turn leads to helicopter (and system) modifications and changes.

With the helicopter (or other aircraft) in a continual process of improvement the concept of a learning curve is not clear, for it may be flat, and even negative. In the past there have been cases where through the years the helicopter is fully "improved" but by that time the helicopter itself is obsolete. This leads to a problem that is not only applicable to helicopters but other military systems as well. It is the decision to either upgrade old equipment or introduce a new design. The latter would start the system engineering process all over again.

The problem concerns cost effectiveness expressed separately as both cost and effectiveness. It is very likely that upgrading can be shown to be substantially cheaper than innovating. One view serves the status quo and low cost while the other serves progress and effectiveness. At this point the final choice depends on which faction in government has the last word.

A secondary problem occurs if the decision is to sell off outmoded helicopters as the Huey. Such a practice hurts manufacturers of new helicopters by competing with them. These sales affect commercial operators as well. Because they are bargains, government agencies buy them and do their own flying. This activity denies work to the commercial operators, many of which struggle to stay in business.

Each of the blocks of Figure H.9 has its own procedures. The least obvious is the functional analysis block. A functional analysis is necessary because of the variety of military missions the helicopter is required to perform, and the fact that early in the program most of the detail functions (or activities) must be identified and accounted for in the design of the helicopter and its support. Functional analysis is the practical starting point for the organization conducting the systems engineering. (Operations analysis is carried out within a government agency, or it is contracted out separately.) The main procedure consists of creating a family of functional flow diagrams. Each flow diagram will detail sequentially all the functions (actions) required to carry out one of the specific military missions. These diagrams consist of identified blocks arranged sequentially from start of a mission to its end.

The purpose of the diagrams is to identify in a logical manner all the necessary items required to satisfy the activity including possible malfunctions called for in the block. Such items are collected into requirements that eventually appear as specifications. These specifications cover all levels of equipment and services from a single electric motor, or maintenance item to the complete helicopter itself. There is no other rational way to identify the thousands of items that constitute the complete system. It should be noted there is no one, unique set of functional flow diagrams, for different companies will function the program in different ways. Even so, they all should come up with comparable sets of specifications.

The overall procedure in its first iteration phase for procurement of a helicopter is termed "contract definition". This means a few qualified companies (actually teams of companies) are contracted by the government to undertake preparation of the system specifications. In parallel, the life cycle costs are estimated. Essentially they represent the contracting team's proposal to produce the system as originally outlined by the government.

As noted initially the second half of the process concerns program or project management of the program as defined above. For any program, each of the lead contractor's main staff has its equivalent in the military. The latter includes its own program manager and staff, all serving in the interest of the government. The Army manager is particularly concerned with such items as critical design reviews, problems impacting on costs and schedules, and those affecting the baseline document (the legal, contractual obligation).

What follows applies to the lead contractor's program management procedures. Project management as for the helicopter system, involves such activities as identification (discussed above), control, review, audit, verification and integration of the complete system. Integration concerns not only the system aspects, but the activity of the many subcontractors, and vendors as well as the team members, involved in the program. Note here the program management group is active in both the contract definition phase as well as the production phase if the successful bidder. This also suggests an iteration procedure. In common with any management, the object is to deliver the specified helicopter system at the lowest cost, in the shortest time, and in the present case, using systems engineering methodology.

The driving document is the master plan, the baseline document, and the core activity is the design review. Like any contract, this document as originally written is the basis for management review of changes to it. An important secondary process is "configuration management". As mentioned previously under *costs*, the aim of CM is to assure the (helicopter) specifications, the design, and the hardware are each an exact statement of the other. The discrepancies are subject to critical design review.

Project management has its own tools, the main ones being a work breakdown structure (WBS), life cycle costing (LCC), configuration (including data) management, and dependency charts (project flow charts). The last which are important to program control and scheduling, refers to computer-oriented flow diagrams using cost or task sequencing, by means of PERT and critical path techniques. In general all the aspects of systems engineering of Figure H.9 and its management have their own computer programs.

In a simpler form for small organizations, the WBS and scheduling and dependency techniques exist in software suitable for PCs. Such include Microsoft Project for Windows, Software Publishing Company Harvard Project Manager, and Primavera Project Planner.

The management ideal, practical with computers, is concurrent systems engineering where all the functions of Figure H.9 have real-time status and feedback capability for any and all the activities. With this approach, one avoids the traditional sequential way of creating a product (the helicopter) which flows from design to manufacturing to quality assurance. The high degree of integration results in a significant saving in cost and time.

The life cycle of a system from the military viewpoint which funds it, begins with an in-house "concept formulation" phase. This leads into the operational requirements block of Figure H.9. There follows the contract definition phase described above and the rest of the functions of the figure. The helicopter system is acquired and deployed for its productive years. In parallel are the modification and improvement phases. Finally the system becomes obsolete and is disposed. Disposal costs are the last of the life cycle items.

The life cycle of a system may run around 20 years. This duration requires a specific treatment of "discounting" costs in the contract definition phase. Discounting is a mathematical technique for establishing the present value of future money. The intent is to arrive at a more realistic estimate of cost over the life cycle, when calculated at the program's inception. Discounting acts somewhat like interest on money.

To make a dollar payment 20 years hence would require a deposit of only say, 50 cents today. In today's money the dollar item costs 50 cents, and not one dollar. Items delivered in the intervening years will have life cycle discounts of their own. State and other lotteries work on a similiar principle since they too are paid off over say, 20 years. The winner receives initially a relatively small amount of the total won. The rest is paid off annually. Hence a $10 million award will cost the state a fraction of that amount. Likewise the winner does not win a lump-sum total, but an initial amount and an annuity the state takes out for the individual. If the winner sought the full winnings up front, one would receive the discounted amount, not the 20 year amount which could be say, half the $10 million. In life cycle costing there are available a selection of discount rates, and not a single arbitrary one.

As suggested before "systems thinking" will and should be part of the common conceptual language of the 21st century. It belongs in the educational system. Not as something nice to know, but as a rational tool useful and effective in personal and social life as it is in the military. Individuals are now part of many systems and they need the education focus to deal with them. Such education is feasible from the lowest grades. Even today the "project method" in schooling is considered progressive education. The new standard for the essentials now should be "three Rs and an S".

thrust coefficient

Where lift coefficient sees the rotor made up of separate blades, each producing lift, the thrust coefficient (C_T) sees the rotor as a unit or disk, producing the same total lift expressed as thrust. Thrust coefficient is defined by:

C_T = X (disk loading) / (density ratio) (rotor tip speed)^2
Where X = a constant
In SI units X = 0.816, in British units X = 420.
(See also Appendix G.)

A basic plot of test results for rotors (or propellers) is thrust coefficient versus *torque coefficient*. The latter is the dimensionless form of power input to the rotor. The following is *figure of merit* expressed in dimensionless form:

M = 0.707 (thrust coefficient)$^{3/2}$ / (torque coefficient)

thrust loading

Thrust loading is the ratio of rotor thrust to rotor power required in newtons per kilowatt (pounds per horsepower). The dimensions are the same as *power loading*, however with the interest in thrust not weight, the SI units are in newtons of force, not kilograms. (See also Appendix G.) Historically, test emphasis was on obtaining the maximum thrust for a given power input, i.e., in maximizing thrust loading.

torque coefficient

Torque coefficient is the dimensionless expression for rotor torque or power coefficient. The general equation is the following:

C_Q = C_P = X (torque) / (density ratio) (disk area) (rotor radius) (rotor tip speed)^2
Where X is the same constant as for *thrust coefficient*.

In SI units torque measured in newton-meters is equal to 9549.3 (kW) / (rpm). In British units torque equals 5252 (hp) / (rpm), measured in pound-feet.

weights

The current format for weight summation is the following:

Empty weight plus useful load equals gross weight (also all-up weight).

The weights may be estimated, calculated, or actual (measured) or a combination.

The design gross weight is what a hovering rotor supports. Typically it is equal to rotor thrust out of ground effect. In hovering the rotor thrust also must overcome the vertical drag of the fuselage, caused by rotor downwash. This makes hovering thrust equal to slightly more than the gross weight. In preliminary design this increment is often neglected, unless it appears substantial, as a rotor operating over a wing. For conservative stress analysis the design gross weight may be increased 10 percent or more. This allows for possible weight growth during the design process.

Useful load consists of the payload plus other consumable or removable items as fuel and lubricants and such items as rescue hoists, and high candlepower searchlights. What constitutes payload is at times arbitrary, but it generally consists of passengers, cargo and such equipment as litters and other removable items, individually or in combination.

In the periods discussed here there was no established format. The weight given for prototypes is often taken to be the operating weight with pilot. A problem concerning historical weights is the conflicting values given for a particular machine in different publications. The use of the word *weight* without restrictions can have different interpretations. It may refer to a design gross or design empty weight, prototype (actual) empty weight, i.e., bare weight, or, an approximate or estimated weight with a nominal value. The intent here is to present weights as accurately as the information will allow.

NOTES AND BIBLIOGRAPHY

The following combines references and bibliography. The former is the first entry. The bibliographic material where applicable follows the word "Also": The intent is to keep all the information on a single subject in one place. Most the bibliography is a selection from the author's Volume 18 described in Appendix E. This part covers the period to 1950. Only the less obvious foreign titles are translated. A full citation is given on first use. Subsequent ones refer only to the author (or other source) and publication date, along with pertinent details. The Chinese transcriptions are conversion to *pin yin* (Chinese Phonetic Alphabet). There is no official transliteration of Arabic, and the originating author's spelling is followed.

CHAPTER 1
INTRODUCTION

[1.1] Octave Chanute, *Progress in Flying Machines* (Long Beach, California: Lorenzen & Herwig, 1976), 128, and 250 on failures. Reprint of first 1894 edition.

[1.2] L. Sprague DeCamp, *The Ancient Engineers* (New York: Barnes & Noble, 1993). Presents a more detailed account of Heron's work with emphasis on his steam engine. Includes Woodcroft illustrations.

[1.3] Luciano Canfora, *The Vanished Library* (Berkeley: University of California Press,

1990). Describes the Library but no mention of Heron.

[1.4] Abbott Payson Usher, *A History of Mechanical Inventions* (New York: Dover, 1988), 98.

[1.5] Henry Hodges, *Technology in the Ancient World* (New York: Barnes & Noble, 1992), 216. Attribution is not clear, Heron may have drawn his information from others. At least he was the best technical writer of his time.

[1.6] Usher (1988), 140. Includes illustration of the organ with wind wheel.

[1.7] Usher (1988), 140.

[1.8] The usual illustrations of Heron's writings including the steam turbine are from the Woodcroft edition of *Pneumatica*, published centuries later.

[1.9] Seyyed Hossein Nasr, *Science and Civilization in Islam* (New York: Barnes & Noble, 1992), 101. The Syrian Shams al-Din al Dimashqi, a philosophical writer of the 14th century is likewise credited with mention of the windmill. His work containing this point appeared in a French translation in the 19th century that became popular. Even so it appears al-Masudi has prior claim, mainly because the latter has more stature in Islamic history. For a recent account of windmills see: Drees, Jan M. "Blade Twist, Droop Snoot, and Forward Spars" AHS *Vertiflite* September/October 1976, 4–9, vol. 22, no. 5.

[1.10] Antonia Fraser, *A History of Toys* (New York: Delacorte, and Weidenfield and Nicholson, 1966). The figure shows a 16th century stall in a Dutch market. A mother is opening her purse to purchase a doll her young daughter is pointing to, acting anxious to possess it. The figure caption works even today. "*Schoon voortgedaen is half vercocht*". In other words "beauty displayed is half sold."

[1.11] Stewart Culin, *Games of the Orient* (Rutland, Vermont: Tuttle, 1960), 21–22, pinwheels in Asia. Reprint of University of Pennsylvania publication of 1895. Needham (1965), 585–86, cites Liu Dong in an early 17th century work on things and customs of the Imperial Capital. Liu remarks kite flying was forbidden. This resulted in the appearance of multicolored pinwheels (*feng che,* "wind vehicle") extended facing the wind, or held while running. An explanation for kite prohibition may be due to kite fighting. In this contest the string was coated with a mix of fish glue and powdered glass or porcelain forming a kind of filament saw. The game was to engage the string of another kite and saw it free. Perhaps too many loose kites fell in the Forbidden City. Also: Culin (1960), 20–21, on kites. Needham (1965), 586, describes and illustrates a pinwheel-driven drum in which lugs on the driveshaft trip sticks that strike the drum. The author further remarks "Pinwheels set up to make noise in the wind are fairly common in Southeast Asia, e.g., Bali". Needham was curious to establish the date of pinwheel first use in China. He suggested studying the work of ancient artists who were ". . . . delighted to paint, namely the peddler's of children's toys". He uncovered one painting by Wang Cheng Beng, dated 1310. This work revealed three or four pinwheels in the peddler's bundles. Two vertically-mounted pinwheels resemble anemometer rotors, and a third suggests a folded paper version. In the 13th century Hangzhou was a toy-making center.

[1.12] William Theodore DeBarry, Wing Tsit Chan, and Burton Watson, *Sources of Chinese Tradition* (New York: Columbia University Press, 1971), Vol. I, 257, 258–61. Also: *A History of Chinese Civilization* (New York: Cambridge University Press, 1990), 208, 210. On Ko-Hung's words suggesting the helicopter, see Needham (1965), 582–83. From Needham, the significant words are: "Someone asked the Master the principles (*dao*, "the way") of mounting to dangerous heights and traveling into the vast inane (emptiness). The Master said '. . . . some have made flying cars (*fei che*) with wood from the inner part of the jujube tree, using ox leather (straps) fastened to returning blades so as to set the machine in motion". The jujube tree (*zao shu*) fruit is the Chinese red date, used in cuisine.

[1.13] Joseph Needham, *Science and Civilization in China* (Cambridge, England: University Press, 1965), Volume 4, *Physics and Physical Technology,* Part II *Mechanical Engineering,* 567–602 on aerodynamics. Needham comments (583) on Ko Hung "For the beginning of the 4th century (A.D.) this is truly an astonishing passage. . . There can be no doubt that the first plan which Ko-Hung proposes for flight is the helicopter top, 'returning, or revolving blades' can hardly mean anything else, especially in close association with a belt or strap. This kind of toy was termed in the 18th century Europe the "Chinese top. . . .". In support of Needham's point, taking the word translated literally as "returning" would suggest discrete rotating members as blades. A rotating wheel would have no sense of "returning". In his *Science in Traditional China* (Cambridge, Massachusetts: Harvard University Press, 1981), 52, Needham is specific in crediting the Chinese introduction of the helicopter toy to Europe. On the finer points of toy attribution he is not clear. The distinction between the palm and string types is not made. In a footnote (583) he recounts conversations with scientific Chinese friends who recall playing with them as children, presumably the palm-launch type as shown in Figure 1.13. Except for this 19th century illustration which apparently Needham was unaware of, there is no direct evidence available this toy (not a pinwheel) appeared in a print before that time. The toy of Figure 1.13 Culin (1960), identifies as of Japanese origin. He cites it as Exhibit 16,225 of the Museum of Archaeology, University of Pennsylvania. Considering the Japanese provenance and the fact Dandrieux's coaxial model was produced in Japan, it is possible the toy was introduced to China in the era of the Meiji Restoration (1868–1912). While Ko-Hung had a flying machine in mind, Needham presumes the latter was reduced to practice in China through a toy. He further extends the argument the toy (or the idea) was copied in Europe, and goes on to identify the 18th and 19th century models in Europe as of Chinese inspiration. Needham supports this transmission by referring to a scholar, Lynn White. The latter wrote that thousands of domestic servants were brought to Italy in medieval times, peaking in the 15th century, and these people could have introduced it to Italy. The hummer has such a strong history in Europe it is likely the three-part pull-string toy originated here, possibly by Cayley, the earliest identified with this version. Calling his device "Chinese top" would suggest his awareness of the palm-type to which he added European components of hub and string.

[1.14] Charles H. Gibbs-Smith, "Sir George Cayley-Father of Aerial Navigation (1778–1857)", Royal Aeronautical Society (RAS) *Aeronautical Journal* (London), April, 1974. Cayley's helicopter-airplane concept (Figure 2.16) first appeared in *Mechanics Magazine* (London), 8 April 1843.

[1.15] Culin (1960), 23.

[1.16] *Catalogue des Modèles d'Aéroplanes, Cerfs-Volants, Pièces Détachées,* (catalog of model airplane kits and parts) (Paris: L'Aéronautique, 1911), 18, *Cerfs-Volants* are kites. Also: Chanute (1976), 56; and *L'Aéronaute* (Paris), January, 1880.

[1.17] The ensuing notes and bibliography account for the da Vinci narrative. The helicopter sketch was drawn early in his design career. He dashed off the drawing and added a few comments then dropped the subject for his studies of bird flight and a human-powered ornithopter. The writing adjacent to the sketch (Figure 1.21) applied directly to his illustration. Below this (not shown) is a brief, continuing note on this form of flying machine. The original drawing is MS 2173 of Manuscript (codex) B, folio 83 verso, in the collection of the Bibliothèque of L'Institut de France (Paris). An estimated 14 of his works (codecies) contain aeronautical ideas. *Codex* in its modern meaning refers to a book or bound volume, an organized collection of works that existed before printing. There are many codices extant, and can be found facsimile in many libraries. In parchment form codex was a synonym for *liber* (book). The words originally referred to the trunk of a tree and a book made up of wooden tablets. Colloquially, *codex* signified "blockhead". In Latin, *liber* started out as "bark", became "book" and finally "free". A somewhat literal translation of all da Vinci had to say in his two separate passages beside the drawing, is given below. The translation is derived from: Ucelli, Arturo, *I Libri del Volo di Leonardo da Vinci* (Milan: Editore Ulrico Hoepli, 1942), Libro Decimo: Del Volo Strumentale, (Book ten on mechanical flight), 157–233. The writing beside the drawing in the figure translates: "The border of the screw, a filament of iron, large as a rope, and from outermost part to center being 8 braccia". One can sample da Vinci's writing style by holding up to a mirror the writing of Figure 1.21. The second line can be easily read as ". . . . sia di filo di fira grosso . . . .". (". . . . being a filament of iron, large . . . ."). The following translates the second passage. "I find (if) this instrument, shaped screw form, is well made, that is made of cloth of flax (linen) stopping its pores with starch and rotated with speed, that said screw makes female in the air (bores through the air) and climbs high. Take for example a ruler (*riga*) large and thin, and tossed with vigor in the air, you will see guided (by means of) your arm the line of edgewise (spin) of said board". Da Vinci here came close to describing the function of a rotor: a flat stick (ruler) launched like a boomerang and freely rotating in the air. He continues: "be the framework of the above said cloth (constructed of) reeds (i.e., flax, here he is describing construction of the rotor); one can make a small model of paper of which (according to the principle) using a thin sheet of iron and then twisted with force, and letting it go free, makes the screw roll up (rotate)". His model is energized by a spring. Also: Gibbs-Smith, Charles H., *Leonardo da Vinci's Aeronautics* (London: HMSO/Science Museum, 1967), 30–31 on the helicopter. Gibbs-Smith believes da Vinci did make and fly a spring model as described above: "This helicopter model . . . has the curious distinction of being the world's first powered aircraft . . . the first aircraft to become airborne with its power unit incorporated in its structure." It then is the world's first flying helicopter. Gibbs-Smith also comments on the fact da Vinci did not consider the helix with a horizontal axis for use as a propeller. Apparently pulling a flying machine through the air was not in his or any other's philosophy. The spectrum (the only possibilities) was complete with the notion of either a lifting screw or flapping wings. Ship propulsion began with steam-powered paddle wheels, which had the advantage of low draft and slow turning. This system was used by Fulton. The screw propeller required high rotational speeds a concept that did not suggest itself until the advent of steam. Constructed in Britain, the first successful screw-propelled steamboat was operated in 1838, it required step-up gearing. Also: *L'Ala d'Italia,* April/May 1953, 27, shows a third model interpreting the da Vinci design. This version has a single platform to which the helix wires are attached. Four projecting (dri-

ving) arms are on the rotor shaft but there is no evidence the shaft has a bearing housing. The interpretation does not consider a logical functioning system. Da Vinci's design is logical, except he did not account for ground friction at takeoff. For anyone dashing off a new concept, the first sketch is not necessarily the most fully thought out. In this case he never returned to his design to refine it. Contemporary criticism of him is in Giacomelli, R. "The Aerodynamics of Leonardo da Vinci", RAS *Aeronautical Journal,* 1930, 1016–38. Regarding his literary style Giacomelli quotes da Vinci: "I know very well, that not being myself a literary man some presumptive men think they may blame me alleging that I am a man without letters. Foolish people! . . . while adorning themselves with the labor of others they do not want to allow me the merits of mine". In passing, Giacomelli notes that by 1505 da Vinci renounced the idea of using human power in flying machines. He turned from ornithopters to gliding flight. The author concludes with 10 concrete principles of aerodynamics attributable to da Vinci's perceptions. Also: Ivor B. Hart, *The Mechanical Investigations of Leonardo da Vinci* (Berkeley: University of California Press, 1963), 191–92; Usher (1988), *IX Leonardo da Vinci, Engineer and Inventor,* 211–37; of the numerous publications on the man a good recent one is Bramly, Serge, *Leonardo-The Artist and the Man* (London: Penguin, 1994), 286–87, 454 on helicopters, 452 mentions his work with ball bearings, and "bicycle", both applicable to his carousel helicopter concept; Zubov, V. P., *Leonardo da Vinci* (New York: Barnes & Noble, 1996), an interpretive biography, includes listing of all his manuscripts and the repositories, and bibliography, 297–314. The author notes da Vinci knew Amerigo Vespucci (71) but none of his works mention the discovery of America, and though he was aware of the printing press did not account for it in any of his inventions.

[1.18] The author is indebted to Françoise Chaserant, Curator, Director of the Musées du Mans, Le Mans, France for supplying the information on the *moulinet de noix* (hummer). The information consists of a letter of transmittal (3 June 1997); a museum, folding postcard; and an article on the toy. The letter states the true nature of the toy (*jouet*), one intended to produce a humming sound (*vrombissement*), and definitely not a helicopter. The folding postcard represents a polytych (multipanel) altarpiece. One panel of the folding artwork is identified as: "*Vierge a l'Enfant en majesté avec St. Benôit*" (Virgin and Christ Child in splendor with Saint Benôit). Painted around 1460, the artists is identified as *Le Mâitre de Vivoin*. The work is now in the Musée de Tessé in Le Mans. The article is by Étienne Bouton: "*Un Ancien Jouet du Maine-Le Moulinet de Noix*" (An Ancient Toy of Maine-the Pinwheel-Nut). Published in *La Vie Mancelle* (Le Mans Life), Le Mans, December 1968, no. 91. The article advances the point the toy is not a helicopter nor any other thing capable of flight. One can reflect on the long period the toy persisted (ca. 1325–1560 Figure 1.24) without anyone thinking of putting pitch in the blades and launching the rotor. Cayley, [1.13] above, may have been the first to think of it. In general, misidentification as a helicopter is easy to understand when viewed from today's technical focus. Apparently there is often an ambiguity in interpreting medieval illustrations using modern thought ("presentism"). Another example concerns the windsock. There are many medieval illustrations suggesting this concept. But the earliest written evidence of a windsock-kite appeared in the late 16th century. See Hart, Clive, "Mediaeval Kites and Windsocks", Royal Aeronautical Society (RAS) *Aeronautical Journal* (London), December, 1969, 1019–28.

[1.19] A Book of Hours was a personal prayer book produced by skilled calligraphers and illuminators for an aristocratic lay person. (In this case a cavalier.) It included a calendar and many illustrations of religious and social life. The latter often included pictures of toys. The basic intent of the book was to provide prayers suitable for the monastic hours that divided the day [e.g., "matins" (3 A.M.), "vespers" (6 P.M.)]. In medieval times the monk-summoning bell-sounds served as a clock before the invention of movement timepieces. The Order of St. Michel was created in 1469 and abolished during the Revolution. It was revived and finally disappeared in 1830.

CHAPTER 2 FIRST PERIOD: NINETEENTH CENTURY

[2.1] Anonymous, *Brief History of the United States* (New York: A. S. Barnes, 1893), 93 on "flying machines".

[2.2] Kenneth T. Jackson, Editor, *The Encyclopedia of New York City* (New Haven: Yale University Press, 1995), 7. Includes a facsimile advertisement and illustration of the "flying machine". A primitive form of covered wagon with seats and no suspension system, drawn by a team of four horses. The fare was 20 shillings, probably two-thirds the weekly wage of the driver. From other sources: Common labor, even after Independence received about two shillings for a 10 hour day. By then the driver earned about one dollar a day plus room and board while on the road. In 1783 a trip from New York to Boston by the 18th century version of the shuttle, took 1 week. Horses were changed every 18 miles. Travel stopped at 10 P.M. and travelers were up at 3 A.M. the next day.

[2.3] Barnes 193, 304.

[2.4] Gustave De Ponton D'Amécourt, *La Conqûete de l'air par l'hélice. Exposé d'un nouveau système d'aviation* (Paris: Author, 24 September 1863). A 40 page monograph translated by Wolf, A. L., "The Vision of D'Amecourt" AHS *Vertiflite*, September/October 1974.

[2.5] David A. Wells, *Annual of Scientific Discovery or Yearbook of Facts in Science and Art for 1854* (Boston: Gould and Lincoln, 1854), 31.

[2.6] Silvo Redini, *Thomas Jefferson-Statesman of Science* (New York: Macmillan, 1990), 283.

[2.7] Virgil Moring Faires, *Applied Thermodynamics* (New York: Macmillan, 1940), 257.

[2.8] The information on steam powerplants and other engine configurations is from various sources, mainly the following: *Scientific American*, 13 March 1869, 169, vol. 34, Stringfellow powerplant; Wise, John, *Through the Air* (Philadelphia: To-Day Publishing and Printing Company, 1873), 158,

161, 166–68, a good survey of the state of the art; Anon, *Tableau d'aviation* (Paris: E. Dieuaide, ca. 1880), a poster 61 × 73.5 cm. (24 × 28.9 in.) with 63 illustrations of flying machine concepts from da Vinci to Edison (1880), 10 are helicopters; Faires (1940), 213–58; Dollfus, Charles, and Henri Bouche, Histoire de l'aéronautique (Paris: L'Illustration, 1942); Baumeister, Theodore, and Lionel S. Marks, *Mechanical Engineer's Handbook* (New York: McGraw-Hill, 1958), 9.56 to 9.67; Shaw, W. Hudson, "Aeronautical Works of Lawrence Hargreave", *Shell Aviation News* (London) No. 289, 1962, 2–7; Anon, *Principles of Naval Engineering NAVPERS 10788* (Washington, D.C.: U.S. Navy Training Publication Center, 1963); Sutton, Richard, "To Fly by Steam", *Light Steam Power Magazine* (Isle of Man, U.K.), September/October 1967, 224–28, vol. 16 no. 5, on Stringfellow; *Anon, The Steam Automobile* (Chicago), 1968, vol. 10 no. 3, with a compilation of articles including Rathbun, John B., "Steam Engines for Airplanes" reprint from Aeronautics, 1930 and Cadell, Alfred M., "Steam Power for Aircraft" reprint from *Aero News and Mechanics,* June/July 1930; Chanute (1976), 53, 126–27, 236, 252.

[2.9] Shaw (1962)

[2.10] *Il Novissimo Melzi-Dizonario Italiano,* II Parte, Scientifica (Milan: Antonio Vallarti, 1949), 195, Viceroy's rejection; a modern criticism of the concept is the steam generator would lack the power to operate the system. The following is an example using three pounders. Given a pounder head weight of 22.7 kg (50 lb) each with a lift of 0.76 meters (2.5 feet) in four seconds, and assume they lift sequentially as the figure suggests, the average weight lifted (though irregular) is 34 kg (75 lb). Considering the high friction in the wood gears, the power required at the turbine shaft is calculated to be 0.21 kW (0.28 hp). The design would require a weighted turbine (flywheel) because of the irregular lift. Considering their familiarity with water wheels for power the concept seems feasible but with some development. Particularly with the high rpm requirement for the turbine. The speed reduction would be more complicated than that shown in the figure; Smith, G. Geoffrey, *Gas Turbines and Jet Propulsion* (London: Iliffe, 1955) 31, illus.

[2.11] Glen D. Angle, *Aerosphere* (New York: Aircraft Publications, 1940), the most comprehensive work on aircraft piston engine description even today; *Langley's Aero Engine of 1903,* Smithsonian Annals of Flight No. 6; "Langley's Aero Work Reviewed", *Aero and Hydro,* 6 June 1914, 119, illus.

[2.12] Chanute (1976), 236, the lightest marine engine in 1889 weighed 36.5 kg/kW (60 lb/hp).

[2.13] The Steam Automobile (Chicago), 1968, vol. 10 no. 3. In its prime (early 20th century) the steam automobile which used uncondensing steam, exhibited the following values of steam consumption:

Power	Saturated Steam	Superheated steam
4.5 kW (6hp)	18.2 kg/hr	11.4 kg/hr
	(40 lb/hr)	(25 lb/hr)
14.9 (20)	15.4 (34)	10.0 (22)
59.7 (80)	12.7 (28)	8.6 (19)

The above values refer to a well-designed system, non-optimum designs have values 30 to 40 percent greater. For example a 59.7 kW (80 hp) helicopter using superheated steam and a one hour flight duration would carry 690 kg (1520 lb) of consumables in addition to fuel. This amount is more than the gross weight of the comparable, conventional helicopter. In the 1880s 1.4 kilograms (three pounds) of coal in a typical steam plant would produce 0.75 kW (1 hp) of shaft power. The thermal efficiency becomes 6 percent. This compares with 27 percent for a modern gasoline engine. Overall a consumption rate for the typical 59.7 kW (80 hp) steam plant would be:

Water	8.6 (kg/hr)	19 (lb/hr)
Coal	109.0	240
Total	117.6	259

The last compares with a rate of about 18.2 kg/hr (40 lb/hr) for this example engine using gasoline. The specific rate being 84.7 micrograms per joule (0.5 lb/hr/hp). The consumable combustion ratio favoring the piston engine is 40/240 = 0.17, roughly the same as the thermal efficiency ratio 6/27 = 0.22. Consumption of coal reveals another reason the 19th century advocates of mechanical flight had a lot to worry about. It becomes obvious the discovery of petroleum had as much to do with successful mechanical flight as did the Wright brothers.

[2.14] George P. Sutton, *Rocket Propulsion Elements* (New York: Wiley, 1949), 122–25.

[2.15] Stephen F. Mason, *A History of the Sciences* (New York: Macmillan/Collins 1962), 508. In the 1680s Christian Huygens and Denis Papin experimented with gunpowder as fuel for an internal combustion engine, but with no success.

[2.16] *Scientific American Reference Book* (New York: Munn, 1881), 129. Practically, an engine would require the slow release of the gases by addition of a substance forming a mixture serving to control the explosive pressure. Also: Chanute (1976), 23 notes gunpowder engine proposals and experiments outdated steam engines; "True Theory of Flying" *Scientific American*, 1871, 133, vol. 37, suggests gunpowder as a force to drive propelling fans.

[2.17] *Scientific American*, 1871, vol. 37, from a letter signed "C".

[2.18] Chanute (1976), 57.

[2.19] *Jane's All the World's Aircraft* (London: 1909). The first edition of this annual was published in 1909 under the Sampson and Low imprint, now under Jane's Information Group, Ltd. Henceforth listed as Jane's (with date added). Also: *Shell Aviation News* (London), no. 323.

[2.20] Gibbs-Smith (1974).

[2.21] Beaumont Newhall, *The History of Photography* (New York: Museum of Modern Art/Boston: Little, Brown, 1982), 13.

[2.22] Norman Macmillan, "Origins of Air Power" Shell Aviation News (London), 2, no. 323. Also Calder, Ritchie, *The Evolution of the Machine* (New York: Van Nostrand/American Heritage/Smithsonian, ca. 1968), 85.

[2.23] *Scientific American*, 1864, vol. 25.

[2.24] Calder (ca. 1968), 85–86. Also: Lichty, Lester C., *Internal Combustion Engines* (New York: McGraw-Hill, 1939), 2–7.

[2.25] Lichty (1939), 3–5. Also: Macmillan, *Shell Aviation News* no. 323.

[2.26] Calder (ca. 1986), 86.

[2.27] Wise (1873) on powerplant state of the art.

[2.28] Wise (1873), 137. The author refers to an article in U.S. Gazette (Philadelphia) 17 June 1828. Also: Crouch, Tom D., *The Eagle Aloft* (Washington, DC: Smithsonian Institute Press, 1983), 289–91. Pennington was a piano maker from Baltimore intrigued with human flight since childhood. As an adult, one of the first Americans to seriously address the subject. His comments here on inclined planes and flight predated his general association with lighter-than-air craft. He was persuaded by John Wise to drop flying machines for airships, particularly one with propulsive screws. Most likely Pennington can be credited with proposing the semi-rigid airship. The keel was to assist in holding the shape of the elongated bag and to support the cab. Others had the idea of supporting a suspended cab by means of cables.

[2.29] Tom D. Crouch, *A Dream of Wings-Americans and the Airplane 1875–1905* (New York: Norton, 1981), 16.

[2.30] Vadim Mikheyev, *Rozhdenie Vertoleta* (Birth of the Helicopter) (Moscow: Izdatel'stvo MAI, 1993), 33–35, illus.

[2.31] Gibbs-Smith (1974).

[2.32] *Scientific American*, 23 December 1848, 109.

[2.33] Mikheyev (1993), 37, 38, illus. Also: Edgington, Donald R., and David D. Hatfield, *The Threshold of Flight* (Inglewood, California: Northrop Institute of Technology, 1968), 9.

[2.34] Maurice Lamé, *Le Vol Vertical* (Paris: Blondel-La Rougery, 1934), Second Edition, 176–180. Also: *Flugsport* (Frankfort, a.M, Germany), February, 1921, 89 illus.; *Aeroplane* (London), 27 April 1921, 398, vol. 20 no. 17.

[2.35] *Scientific American*, 1861, vol. 18. Letter by Charles Edwards.

[2.36] *Scientific American*, 1 July, 22 1865. Also: Boatner, Mark M III, *The Civil War Dictionary* (New York: Random House/Vintage, 1988), 557. Mitchel biography.

[2.37] Paul M. Angle and Earl Schenck Miers, *Tragic Years 1860–1865*-A Documentary History of the Civil War (New York: DaCapo, 1992), 237–45.

[2.38] O. S. Nock, *The Dawn of World Railways 1800–1850* (New York: Macmillan, 1972), 171–72, illus.; Also: Sinclair, Angus, *Development of the Locomotive Engine* (Cambridge: M.I.T. Press, 1970), 231–42. The *General* was built for the Western and Atlantic Railroad. A General-type locomotive (*General II*) built in 1919 is on display in the Big Shanty Museum in Kennesaw (formerly Big Shanty), Georgia.

[2.39] Angle and Miers (1992), 237.

[2.40] Dolfus and Bouche (1942). The French were very active in helicopter promotion in mid 19th century. In the first decade after World War I, they emerged as the leaders in aeronautical technology.

[2.41] Wise (1873), 145. Also: Chanute (1976), 53–54.

[2.42] Dollfus and Bouche (1942). For Nadar's work in photography, see Newhall (1982), 66–70.

[2.43] *American Helicopter*, May, 1947, The article notes Powers was forced to hide his invention because if developed the North would have copied it. Considering the ability of the Union States to mass produce, which the South was unable to do, Powell feared its disclosure would lead to use against the South. In view of the design, his concern though patriotic, was unfounded. Also: Richard G. Hubler, *Straight Up*-The Story of Vertical Flight (New York: Duell, Sloane, and Pierce, 1961), 24; Mikheyev (1993), 60–61.

[2.44] "Another Step Toward Flying" *Scientific American,* 17 June 1865.

[2.45] Boatner (1988), 109, Butler biography.

[2.46] *Scientific American,* 1 July, 22 July, 1865. Also: Serrell, Lemuel W., "A Flying Machine for the Army" *Science News Service,* 24 June 1904.

[2.47] Harry Hansen, *The Civil War*-A History (New York: Penguin/Mentor, 1991). Butler's New Orleans reputation. Also: Angle and Miers (1992), 254, 255, Butler's General Orders No. 28, New Orleans May 15, 1862 was a notice concerning ". . . . repeated insults from women calling themselves ladies . . . ." leveled at officers and soldiers of the United States. Butler ordered for any mistreatment ". . . . she shall be regarded and held liable to be treated as a woman of the town plying her vocation."

[2.48] Hansen (1991), 166. Among the many social anomalies of a divided nation, Butler as a delegate to the 1860 Democratic Convention voted for nomination of Davis for president of the United States. Also: From Angle (1992) 91, 92, and others the following anec-

dote. In 1861 Butler had three escaped slaves under his protection who a Confederate officer demanded be returned. The Virginia secession created a technicality by which Butler felt no obligation to return the slaves to the officer who considered them their "property". Because they were "property" Butler claimed them as *contraband of war*. He held them as such; to prevent their use "against the Government of the United States". Regarding his contraband ploy, "Everybody praised its author by extolling its great use, but whether right or wrong, it paved the way for the President's proclamation of freedom to the slaves eighteen months afterwords". For a period (1866–1879) Butler served in Congress, notable for his support of the impeachment resolution against President Johnson (1868). He ran for President on the Greenback Party ticket. By this time the party was in decline. It was dissolved after a poor showing in the elections of 1884. Despite his failure, the party's progressive principles, unconventional at the time, were left for future officeholders to implement: "graduated income tax" (1913 Constitutional amendment), "woman's suffrage" (1920 Constitutional amendment), and "managed paper currency" (off the gold standard, 1934).

[2.49] Otto Eisenschiml and Ralph Newman, *The Civil War*-An American Iliad (New York: Mallard, 1991), 594, 595. The letter was from Colonel Theodore Lyman personal aide to General Meade, dated 29 November 1864. Also: Crouch (1983), 336, 343–44, 363 on Butler and balloons. Butler was one of the few generals who favored balloons for reconnaissance. Typically, in his own style. Early in the war (1861), the aeronaut John La Mountain of Troy, New York volunteered service as a civilian aerial spotter if the general would put up the cost of supplies to inflate his balloon *Atlantic*. Butler agreed to this, but only if La Mountain would give up his salary until he proved the worth of aerial observation. In general, officers were skeptical of its effectiveness. On one flight Butler flew with the aeronaut to check out the idea for himself. Ultimately five aeronauts were involved in the program, with five personal rivalries, a situation that did not help the cause of ballooning. Rejecting the tethered approach, La Mountain proposed the advanced idea of a "balloon bomber". The intent was to use the free balloon to destroy cities, to "shell, burn and destroy Norfolk or any city near our camps". By understanding air currents, one could drift out over enemy lines, at one altitude, and drift back at a higher one. Butler approved the funds to construct a bomber but the money did not materialize. Apparently the military was exasperated with the feuding aeronauts and their poor performance, meaning failure to spot significant enemy movements. In 1863 the Union Balloon Corps was disbanded.

[2.50] *Scientific American,* 1 July 1865, copied from *Journal of Commerce* (Baltimore), 1865.

[2.51] *Scientific American,* 22 July 1865, 52.

[2.52] *Mortimer Nelson's Aerial Car* (New York: Author, ca. 1865). A 16 page booklet and prospectus, illustrated. Also: Millbank, Jeremiah, Jr., *The First Century of Flight in America* (Princeton: Princeton University Press, 1943), 88–96.

[2.53] *Scientific American,* 8 April 1865.

[2.54] *Aerial Age,* 22 November 1920.

[2.55] *L'Aéronaute,* April 1870, on his ideas for propulsors and screws: Also: *L'Aéronaute,* November 1871. Croce-Spinelli produced the design of a 4109 kg (9050 lb) rotorcraft. It consisted of two lifting screws with a diameter of 7.2 meters (23.6 feet) and two propellers driven by four steam engines. Total power required was 224–298 kW (300–400 hp). Assuming all power could be delivered to the rotors the figure of merit is 1.9, which is physically unattainable. For the art of his time a realistic power requirement is 1813 kW (2430 hp) or six times more than his estimate. Also: Mikheyev (1993), 65–68.

[2.56] Chanute (1976), 71, on Maxim and Renard; 52, 252, on the Maxim steam engine. Also: Century Magazine, October 1891.

[2.57] C. Renard, "The Quality of Lifting Propellers", Academy of Sciences (Paris), *Comptes Rendu* 1903, vol. 37, 970–72; Also: *Vertiflite* September/October 1990, 48. Russian V. A. Kasjnikov in passing, calls the mathematically-same figure of merit equation the "Velmer-Zhukovskii" (i.e. the Wellner-Joukowski) formula, which he is crediting to them. Renard is likely entitled to seniority based on his 1903 work, and 19th century activity. In his paper Renard does review hovering equations of others and found them defective. In 1890 Zhukovskii wrote a paper that included prediction of rotor thrust. By attaching Wellner to the theory suggests the original theory was modified by him, whose work came later. As mentioned in this book. Zhukovskii was active in the early 1900s (1908, E. Berliner). He is one of the great figures in aeronautical science, and accepted professionally as the father of Russian aerodynamics. His complete works were published in Moscow, in 1937. [For a brief biography see Everett-Heath, John, *Soviet Helicopters*-Design, Development and Tactics (London: Jane's Information Group, 1988), 193–195, and Izakson, A. M., *Sovetskoye Vertoletostroeniye* (Soviet Helicopter Construction) (Moscow: Izdatel'stvo Maschinostroeniye, 1964), *Raboty N. Ye. Zhukovskii po Vertoletam* (Work of N. Ye. Zhukovskii in the field of Helicopters), 50–54.] George Wellner was active in airscrew research from 1893 at the Technical School of Brunn (now Brno, Czech Republic). Apparently Wellner's original equation implied a constant figure of merit of 0.53. See Hoernes, Hermann *Buch Des Fluges* (Vienna: Szelinski, 1912).

[2.58] Wise (1873).

[2.59] Wise (1873), 171.

[2.60] *Scientific American,* 24 June 1874, 407–408.

[2.61] *Leslie's Weekly,* 30 December 1876. Also: *American Helicopter,* December 1945.

[2.62] Scientific American, 1876, vol. 49.

[2.63] Chanute (1976), 64–65.

[2.64] Chanute (1976), 65.

[2.65] W. H. Pickering, *Navigating the Air* (New York: Doubleday, 1907) 112–116, illus.

[2.66] Lamé (1934), 21–23. Also: Chanute (1976), 62–64; "Le Premier appareil d'aviation a vapeur qui ait quitte le sol", *L'Aéronaute,* February 1879, 39–47, vol. 12 no. 2; "La Distribution des prix de l'institut Lombard de Milan en 1879" *L'Aéronaute* February 1880, 33, 40, vol. 13 no. 2; "L'Ingénieur Forlanini", *L'Aérophile,* January 1902, 1–4, vol. 10 no. 1

[2.67] W. Ley, *Rockets and Space Travel* (New York: Viking, 1944), 98–99; Supf, Peter, *Deutschen Fluggeschicte* (German Flight History) (Berlin: Hermann Klemm, 1935),

144–46; *Zeitschrift fur Flugtechnik und Motorluftschiffahrt* (ZFM) (Munich), 31 December 1921.

[2.68] *American Helicopter,* December 1945, vol. 1 no. 1; Harter, Jim, *Transportation*-A Pictorial Archives from Nineteenth Century Sources (New York: Dover, 1984), 141. Both have illustrations only.

[2.69] Chanute (1976), 65. Also: *Scientific American*, 1871, 402, vol. 38.

[2.70] Chanute (1976), 64. Also: "Edison and the Flying Machine" *U.S. Army Air Services,* November 1931, 15, vol. 16 no. 11; *New York World,* 7 June 1896; Magoun, F. A., *History of Aircraft* (New York: Whittlesey/McGraw-Hill, 1931), 233–34; Whitehouse, Arch, *The Early Birds* (New York: Doubleday, 1965), 31; Millbank (1943), 174–75.

[2.71] *Scientific American,* 9 May 1885. Also: *American Helicopter,* December 1945, vol. 1; no. 1; Harter (1984), 137.

[2.72] Jules Verne, *The Clipper of the Clouds* (Westfield, Connecticut: Associate Booksellers, 1962). Also: (London: Arco Publications, 1962). For a biography of Verne see: Jules-Verne, Jean, *Jules Verne*-A Biography (New York: Taplinger/Arnold Lent, 1976).

[2.73] Jules Verne, *Master of the World* (London: Sampson, Low, Marston, 1914).

[2.74] Wise (1873), 168.

[2.75] Jean Lipman, *Rufus Porter*-Yankee Pioneer (New York: Charles N. Potter/Crown, 1968), 40. Also: Porter was an early publisher (since 1834) of technical magazines as well as promoter of a "Travelling Balloon, or Flying Machine". He was particularly active in aerial navigation in the era of the *forty-niners* when the rush was on to get to California as fast as possible. Through the years Porter varied his design for a powered, spindle-shaped airship or "aerial locomotive". At his best Porter envisioned a 300 passenger ship for a transcontinental trip, with an introductory fare of $50 (including board). A round trip would take seven days. For later bookings the fare would be $200. He offered stock to investors in his venture at $5 a share, claiming "A chance to secure income of $10 to $20 per week for twenty years by the investment of five dollars in advance". (45). Porter's 150 passenger *Pioneer* was estimated to cost $15,000 to build, with operating costs of $25 a day. Construction began in Washington, D.C. in 1853. However he was beset with problems including storm damage, vandalism, and ultimately a shortage of funds, collectively compelling him to abandon the project. Even so he continued to believe this form of aerial navigation was feasible. He was correct in his faith insofar as a practical airship could be built. Frenchman Henri Giffard flew the first one in 1852, and rigid airships as *zeppelins* were operational in World War I. However they disappeared from the transportation spectrum before World War II. There is a minor revival today in the form of blimps (pressure airships) for advertising. It is curious the late 19th century powered-balloon entrepreneurs never thought of installing a propeller (or helicopter rotor) at the stern of the spindle-shaped bag. Submarines all use stern propulsion and these were fairly well-known by the 1850s, though still experimental. [See Rodengen, Jeffrey L., *The Legend of Electric Boat* (Fort Lauderdale, Florida: Write Stuff Syndicate, 1994), 11–15.] The advantage of stern propulsion is the improvement in propulsive efficiency in operating in the wake of the bag, or submarine hull. For the latter the efficiency increment is called "wake fraction". Even today there appears to be no serious thought in applying this concept. The design would likely involve a semi-rigid airship to support the stern powerplant used to drive a helicopter type-rotor. Its diameter would be about 65 percent of the maximum diameter of the envelope (bag).

[2.76] Wells (1854), 222–23.

[2.77] "Avitor" *Scientific American,* 1870, 356, vol. 35. Also: *Scientific American,* 15 January, 1870, 48, vol. 36; Crouch (1983), 331–34, Among Mariott's claims to fame is his coinage of the word *aeroplane* (330), and as one of the founders of the *Illustrated London News;* Evans, Charles, Morgan, "Steam-Powered Pioneer" *Aviation* (Leesburg, Virginia), May 1993.

[2.78] Clifford W. Tinson, *Aeroplane,* 24 December 1948, on an updated version of Verne's *Albatross.* The author estimated it to weigh 16,344 kilograms (18 tons) and carry electric motors delivering a total of 8,579 kilowatts (11,500 horsepower). With advances in fusion power development, and electrical superconductance, the electric motor may be a common powerplant for ships and other transportation systems. Even today, electric motor propulsion of naval vessels is a real possibility.

[2.79] Rodengen (1994), on Holland, 17–42, includes an illustration of Holland's invention of a tiltrotor convertiplane.

[2.80] *New York Herald,* November 1890; Chanute (1976), 68; Holland, J., "Aerial Navigation" *Cosmopolitan,* November 1892.

[2.81] James B. Means, "Man Flight" (Boston, 1891), 17 pp. Also: "Man Flight-The Last Mechanical Flight of the Century" *Boston Transcript,* 17 July 1893; Crouch (1981), 102–17.

[2.82] Chanute (1976), 68.

[2.83] L'Aéronaute, November 1892; also Liberatore (1954) Volume 1, 143.

[2.84] John Clute and Peter Nicholls, Editors, *The Encyclopedia of Science Fiction,* (New York: St. Martins/Griffin, 1995), 451, on sf magazines, see 1066–71.

[2.85] John Clute, *Science Fiction-SF*, The Illustrated Encyclopedia (New York: Dorling Kindersley, 1995), frontispiece illustration and 14, 15.

[2.86] Chanute (1976), 48–72, screws to lift and propel.

[2.87] Chanute (1976), 72.

[2.88] The false route exchange in *L'Aérophile* is in the following issues: Drzewiecki, Stefan, "Fausse Route-Simple démonstration à l'usage des inventeurs d'hélicoptères, turbines et autres sustentateurs à réaction" March 1909, 98–99, vol. 17 no. 5; "Rectification à propos de l'article 'Fausse route" 15 March 1909, 122–23, vol. 17 no. 6; Sée, A., "La Querelle des hélicoptères pour les hélicoptères. La Route n'est pas fausse. Réponse à M. Drzewiecki" April 1909, 153–54, vol. 17 no. 7; "Drzewiecki aux diverses critiques de son article 'Fausse route" April 1909, 154–55, vol. 17 no. 7; Sée, A., "La Querelle des hélicoptères un dernier mot sur l'article de S. Drzewiecki" May 1909, 203, vol. 17 no. 9; "Fausse route à M. Drzewiecki" 15 May 1909, 219, vol. 17 no. 10; Lecornu, L., "La Question des hélicoptères" 15 May 1909, 219–20, vol. 17 no. 10; Drzewiecki, Stefan, "La Question des hélicoptères. Réponse a M. Lecornu" 1 June 1909, 255, vol. 17 no. 11; Drzewiecki, Stefan, "La Querelle des héli-

coptères. Réponse a M. A. Sée" 1 June 1909, 255, vol. 17 no. 11; Drzewiecki, Stefan, "La Querelle des hélicoptères. Réponse a M. Lecornu" 15 July 1909, 315–16, vol. 17 no. 14.

[2.89] Donald R. Edgington and David D. Hatfield, *The Threshold of Flight* (Inglewood, California: Northrup Institute of Technology, 1968). Also: Fay, John, *The Helicopter-*History and How It Flies (London: David & Charles, 1976). 130.

[2.90] *Scientific American,* 13 March 1869, 169.

[2.91] Gabrielle de al Landelle, *Dans Les Airs-*aérostation-aviation etudes aérostatiques, parachutes, hélicoptères, cerf-volants, aéroplanes, orthopters (Paris: Louis Vivien, ca. 1876), Part VII, Hélicoptères, 175–200.

CHAPTER 3 SECOND PERIOD: EARLY TWENTIETH CENTURY

[3.1] *Aero and Hydro* (Chicago), 16 May 1914, 82.

[3.2] *Aero and Hydro* 12 September 1914, 298.

[3.3] New International Encyclopedia (New York: Dodd Mead, 1927) Supplement, Vol. XXIV.

3.4] "The British Helicopter Competition-Prizes of 50,000 Pounds Offered" *Flight* (London), 17 May 1923, 263–64, vol. 15 no. 2; "The Air Ministry Helicopter Competition" *Aeroplane* (London), 23 May 1923, 388, vol. 24 no. 21; "British Air Ministry's Helicopter Competition" *Aviation,* 28 May 1923; "The Air Ministry's Helicopter Prizes" RAS *Aeronautical Journal,* December 1923, 568, vol. 27 no. 156; Woodhouse, H., "Will the $250,000 Prize for Vertical Flying be Won?" *Scientific Age,* 23 August 1924, 101–104, vol. 7; Lee, C. E., "The British Air Ministry's Helicopter Competition" *Aero Digest,* July 1923, 24, vol. 3 no. 1. Also: The performance requirements were publicized in *The New York Times,* dateline London, for 8 May 1924, 15 May 1924, and 12 July 1924. The 15 May news item emphasized the importance of safe descent, power-off. Below the headline "To Check Helicopter Fall" was the following: "Among the most difficult problems to solve has been how to prevent such machines from falling, should the engine fail while in the air." The article mentioned two (anonymous) approaches, one can be identified as the Perry (1923) locked rotor concept. The other described the de-pitching approach and autorotation, "Several sets of whirling screws capable of being fixed in case of need, at such an angle to act like a parachute, reducing the speed of fall to ten miles per hour (16.1 km/h). Shock absorbing apparatus is provided to make the landing at this speed harmless." With the 8 May dateline the *Times* quotes the *London Daily Chronicle* ". . . . the conditions imply the production of a helicopter very much in advance of any experimental machine hitherto produced."

[3.5] Lamé (1934), 213. Also: *Aerial Age,* 30 May 1921, 280, vol. 13 no. 12; *Flight,* 28 April 1921, 299, vol. 13 no. 17; *Aviation,* 12 June 1922, 687, vol. 2 no. 24; *Aerial Age,* 30 May 1931, 280, *Popular Science,* March 1936; *Aircraft Engineering* (London), November 1936.

[3.6] "Le Premier circuit fermé d'un kilometre par Oehmichen" *L'Aérophile,* 1–5 May 1924, 161–62, vol. 32 no. 9–10; "L'Hélicoptère du premier hélicoptère" *L'Aéronautique,* June 1924, 137–38, vol. 6 no. 61; "First Helicopter to Fly a Circular Kilometer" *Aviation,* 18 August 1921, 889–89, vol. 17.

[3.7] "The Helicogyre" RAS *Aeronautical Journal,* July 1929, 573–614, vol. 33 no. 223; Lame (1934), 213–15; *Luftwissen,* May 1936, 125; "L'Hélicogyre Isacco" *L'Aérophile,* 1–5 March 1929, vol. 37 no. 5–6; "The Hélicogyre" *Flight,* 21 March 1929, 244; *Scientific American,* July 1929.

[3.8] Hermann Glauert, *The Elements of Aerofoil & Airscrew Theory* (Cambridge, England: University Press, 1948), 201.

[3.9] "Asboth Steilschrauber" (Asboth vertical-rising, screw craft) *Flugsport,* May 1936, 224–27, no. 11. Also: Lamé (1934), 216–18; *Flight,* 20 December 1934, 1358, vol. 36; *Les Ailes,* 17 November 1938, 4, vol. 18; *Scientific American,* December 1938 and December 1939, 348; *L'Air,* 20 January 1940, 10, vol. 22; *Flugsport,* 16 June 1943; *Aviation,* July 1946; *American Helicopter*, March 1947.

[3.10] Lamé (1934), 195–203; "Helicopter for Military Purposes" *Scientific American,* 26

February 1921, 173, vol. 124 no. 9; "Les Derniers essais de l'hélicoptère Pescara" *L'Aérophile,* 1–5 March 1922, 77–79, vol. 50 no. 5–6; *Aviation*, June 1921; *Aerial Age,* 18 April 1921, 134.

[3.11] A. R. S. Bramwell, *Helicopter Dynamics* (London: Edward Arnold, 1976), 46.

[3.12] R. P. Coleman and A. M. Feingold, "Theory of Self-Excited Mechanical Oscillations of Helicopter Rotors with Hinged Blades" *NACA* Report 1351, 1958. Also: Coleman, R. P. and A. M. Feingold, "Theory of Ground Vibrations of a Two-Blade Helicopter Rotor on Anisotropic Flexible Supports" *NACA* TN-1184, 1947. Both reports incorporated in Wagner, Robert A., *Vibrations Handbook for Helicopters* (Washington, D.C.: Department of Commerce, OTS, 1954), 73 pp. See also Appendix E, Volume 7.

[3.13] Jean Boulet, *History of the Helicopter As Told by its Pioneers 1907–1956* (Paris: Editions France-Empire, 1984), 52–54.

[3.14] Warren R. Young, *The Helicopters* (Alexandria, Virginia: Time-Life, 1982), 6–7.

[3.15] G. A. Crocco, "Inherent Stability of the Helicopter" *NACA* TM-324, 1923. Also: "Esperienze Analitiche Sulle Eliche Ascensionali" *Bollettino della Societa Italiana* (Rome), October 1904, 60–64; Catalanotto, Baldassare, "Il Contributo Italiana allo Sviluppo Dell'Elicottero" *Volabilita,* March 1991, 34, no. 10, mentions Crocco's 1906 ideas on autorotation and pitch change. These comments are from Giacomelli, R., in *L'Aerotecnia,* October 1929, 793–93, vol. XI no. 10.

[3.16] Lamé (1934), 31, 164–65; "Hélicoptère Cornu et fils à propulseur spécial" *L'Aérophile,* June 1906, 145–157, vol. 14 no. 6; "Successful Tests of Cornu Helicopter" *Scientific American,* 18 April 1909, 276, vol. 98; "A New Flying Machine: The Helicopter" *Illustrated London News* 2 May 1908, 654; Jane's 1910–1911; *Les Ailes* 24 August 1947, 4–5.

[3.17] Lamé (1934), 34; Luyties, O. G., "Advantage of the Helicopter Over the Aeroplane" *Aeronautics,* April 1908, 7–11, vol. 2 no. 4; "Experiments with a Helicopter" *Scientific American,* 11 July 1908, 26–27, vol. 99 no. 2; Luyties, O. G., "Helicopter and Aeroplane" *Scientific American* Supplement, 11 July 1908, 30–32, vol. 66; Jane's 1909, 295; Jane's 1910–1911.

[3.18] See Appendix E, *Helicopter Handbooks,* Volume 2, 90.

[3.19] Source information for the Paul narrative is courtesy of Tom Parramore, Raleigh, North Carolina, cultural historian for the state, in a letter 29 April 1996. The author is indebted to Mr. Parramore for the volunteered information on an otherwise unknown helicopter pioneer.

[3.10] "Paul Invented Queer Airship" *Raleigh News and Observer,* 18 December 1937.

[3.21] Granddaughter Lina Belar biography of Luther Paul. In typescript form, undated but ca. 1950. Courtesy, Tom Parramore.

[3.22] Letter from Paul, 23 March 1942 to National Inventor's Council, Washington, D.C. The sketch Figure 3.4 was included in the letter describing his "Bumble Bee".

[3.23] Angle (1940). Contains data on Gyro Rotary and Adams-Farwell rotaries.

[3.24] "Test of an American Helicopter" *Scientific American,* 27 November 1909, 403, vol. 101 no. 22; Berliner, E., "Elements of a Gyrocopter" *Aeronautics,* 1915, 51; *Scientific American,* 27 May 1921, 331, on the 1909 helicopter.

[3.25] "The Berliner Helicopter" *Aeronautics,* October 1908, 19, 47, vol. 3 no. 4.

[3.26] Jane's 1909, Berliner-Williams prototypes I and II. Type II 1908 (not illustrated) was similar except for blade construction. Blades were elliptical in plan form.

[3.27] "Williams Helicopter, *Aeronautics,* March 1908, 11, vol. 2, no. 3, and June, 1908, 35, vol. 2 no. 6; "Williams Helicopter" *Colliers Weekly,* 13 June 1908, 19, vol. 41; Jane's 1909, and 1910–1911.

[3.28] *Aeronautics,* May 1908, 15–16, vol. 2, no. 5; and February 1909, 58–61, vol. 4 no. 2.

[3.29] "The Kimball Helicopter" *American Aeronaut,* June 1908, 235–36, vol. 1 no. 6; "Kimball Helicopter" *Aeronautics,* September 1908, 18–19, vol. 3 no. 3; "The Kimball Helicopter" *Popular Mechanics,* December 1909, 802–803; Kimball. W. R., "A Wingless Flying Machine" *Air Travel,* February 1918, 262, 288, vol. 1 no. 8; Whitehouse (1965), 135; Young W. R. (1982), 38–39.

[3.30] Jane's 1909; "Metcalf Helicopter Multiplane" Jane's 1910–1911, 395.

[3.31] Jane's 1909, 294, and 1910–1911.

[3.32] Newspaper (anonymous) Wilmington, North Carolina, 21 August 1909.

[3.33] North Carolina, *Wilmington Morning Herald,* 17 December 1911.

[3.34] Jane's 1909, 291, and 1910–1911.

[3.35] Jane's 1909 and 1910–1911, 399.

[3.36] Jane's 1909.

[3.37] Jane's 1909, and 1910–1911.

[3.38] Jane's 1909, 269, and 1910–1911.

[3.39] "Davidson Gyropter" *Scientific American* Supplement, June 1909, 353; Jane's 1910–1911, 100; *Aviation,* 15 April 1919; Davidson, George L. O., "The Problem of Flight" *Engineering,* 14 August 1908, 206–207, vol. 86; *English Mechanics,* 2 July 1897, 460; Secrest, Clark, "It's a Bird, It's a Plane-It's George Davidson's Disintegrating Airship" *Colorado Heritage* (Denver) Autumn 1993, 36–41; AHS *Vertiflite,* September/October 1995, 48.

[3.40] Jane's 1909; Jane's 1910–1911, 397.

[3.41] Whitehouse (1965), 139.

[3.42] Jane's 1909; Jane's 1910–1911, 397; *Aeronautics,* July 1909, 29, vol. 5 no. 1; *Aeronautics,* February 1910, 50, vol. 8 no. 2.

[3.43] Mary Collett Farris, *The Short Happy Life of the Kansas Flying Machine* (Goodland, Kansas: High Plains Museum, 1982), booklet, 23 pp. illus.

[3.44] *Jetmore Republican* (Jetmore, Kansas) 23 May 1957; Young, W. R. (1982), 37.

[3.45] A. Rochon, "A Direct Lift Machine" *Aircraft,* May, 1911, 86–88, vol. 2 no. 1. Also: Liberatore, E. K. and R. Trainor, *"Rotorchute Handbook",* Prewitt Aircraft Company Report 28–93–3, 15 February, 1951.

[3.46] *American Heritage History of Flight* (New York: American Heritage/Simon & Schuster, 1962), 146; Young, W. R. (1982), 40.

3.47] *Flugsport,* 28 May 1941; *Flugsport,* 1943, 167–70, no. 12.

[3.48] Stella Randolph, *Lost Flights of Gustave Whitehead* (Washington, D.C.: Publication Places, 1937).

[3.49] Whitehead sources: Aircraft, May 1910, 119, advertisement; "The World Ignores Anniversary of Aviation Pioneer" *Bridgeport Post* (Connecticut) 18 August 1940; Whitehouse (1965), 137; Crouch (1981), includes an analysis of the Wright-Whitehead controversy; *Aviation History* (Leesburg, Virginia), March 1996.

[3.50] *Baltimore American,* Sunday Magazine Section, 16 September 1917.

[3.51] *Aircraft,* January 1913, 331, and other issues. The earlier ad from *Aircraft,* May 1910.

[3.52] *Aircraft,* April 1913, 43.

[3.53] Tom Parramore (Reference 3.19) supplied the following information on an unknown helicopter pioneer. He believes the activity took place in 1914, Carr being only 11 in 1904. In the Parramore letter (29 May 1996) he mentions his search of Raleigh newspapers but found no account of this work, nor is it covered in Jane's. The correspondent writes, "Booker was something of a con-man and he may possibly have fabricated the story". The Booker original source was a typescript possibly transcribed from a hand-written account.

[3.54] *Aeronautics,* December 1920; *Aerial Age,* 22 November 1920; "Helicopter Experiments" *Aeronautics,* 5 February 1920, 122, vol. 8 no. 329; "Les Hélicoptères modernes" *La Nature,* 10 July 1920, 21–30, no. 2414; Crocker, F. B. "The Hewitt-Crocker Helicopter" *Aeronautics,* 16–23 December 1920, 441–42, and 457–59, vol. 19 no. 374–75; *Aerial Age,* 22–29 November 1920, 295–97 and 323–25, vol. 12 no. 11–12.

[3.55] *New York Sun,* 23 November 1919.

[3.56] "Berliner Experiment" *Aerial Age,* 15 March 1920; *Washington Evening Star,* 8 March 1920; *Scientific American,* 27 May 1920, 331, vol. 122 no. 13; *Aviation,* 28 March 1921; *Aviation,* 20 February 1922; Boulet (1984), 35.

[3.57] *Air Beat Magazine,* Journal of the Airborne Law Enforcement Association (Orem, Utah) February/March 1983.

[3.58] *Aerial Age,* 26 January 1920; "The Beach Helicopter" *U.S. Air Service,* March 1920, 20, vol. 3 no. 2; Mancini, Luigi, *Grande Enciclopedia Aeronautica* (Milan: Edizioni "Aeronautica", 1936), 113.

[3.59] The information was obtained through correspondence with Exel. There is little contemporary reporting on his work; Mancini (1936).

[3.60] "The Leinweber Improved Helicopter" *Aerial Age,* 21 February 1921, 604, vol. 12 no. 24; "Neuere Schraubenflieger Projekte" *ZFM,* 31 December 1921, 360–61, vol. 12 No. 24; Lamé (1934), 184; Boulet (1984), 36; *Compressed Air,* (Inqersoll-Rand) July–August 1997, 8.

[3.61] "Hall Helicopter Airplane" *The Ace,* April–March 1920–1923 issue, April 1920; *Aerial Age,* 21 February 1921, 604.

[3.62] *Whirl Test,* Propeller Laboratory, McCook Field (Dayton, Ohio) January 1922.

[3.63] The Berliner lateral rotor machine was in its initial configuration a pure helicopter, but most the flights and publicity applied to the triplane arrangement. "Man-Carrying Helicopter Makes a Short Flight" *Popular Mechanics,* August 1922; "Berliner Helicopter" *Aerial Age,* August 1922, 395–96, vol. 15 no. 17; *Aviation,* 26 June 1922, 745, vol. 12 no. 26; "Helicopter That Flies-The Berliner Machine" *Scientific American,* September 1922, vol. 127; *Aviation,* 28 August 1922; "The Berliner Helicopter in Flight" *Aviation,* 18 September 1922, 356, vol. 13. no. 12; "Helicopter Ascends 7 Feet at Trials" *New York Times,* 17 June 1922, 2; "Hélicoptère Berliner" *L'Aéronautique,* August 1925, 291, vol. 7 no. 75; *L'Ala d'Italia,* August 1925, 259, vol. 4 no. 5; *Washington Herald,* 2 December 1925; *Luftwissen,* May 1936, 122; *Der Flieger,* November 1943; *Aviation,* July 1946, 57; Liberatore, E. K., *Convertible Aircraft* (Washington, D.C.: Department of Commerce, OTS, 1954), PB-111288, 79 pp. See also Appendix E, Volume 13.

[3.64] "Elicottero Berliner-Tipo 1924 Modificato" *L'Ala d'Italia,* June 1924, 147, vol. 3 no. 6.

[3.65] "Helicopter for Military Purposes" *Scientific American,* 26 February 1921, 173, vol. 124 no. 9; *Slipstream Monthly,* January 1923, vol. 4 no. 1; "Successful trials at McCook Field" *Aviation,* 22 January 1923, 97, vol. 14 no. 4; "Latest Helicopter Makes Flight" *Popular Mechanics,* March 1923, 331, vol. 39 no. 3; "The DeBothezat Helicopter" *Flight,* 1 March 1923, 125, vol. 15 no. 9; "Our Army's Helicopter" *Scientific American,* April 1923, 243, vol. 128 no. 4; "Les Hélicoptères" *L'Aéronautique,* May 1923, 183, vol. 5 no. 48; "New Trials of the DeBothezat Helicopter" *Aviation,* 21 May 1923, 262, vol. 14 no. 21; *Aero Digest,* July 1923, 23, vol. 3 no. 1; *Luftwissen,* May 1936, 123; "Flight on Rotating Wings" *Journal of the Franklin Institute,* September–October 1936, 255–88, 461–74, vol. 222 no. 3–4; *American Helicopter,* July 1948, vol. 11 no. 8; Wartenburg, Steve, "The First Helicopter-DeBothezat's Flying Octopus" AHS *Vertiflite,* March/April 1986; *Aviation History,* March 1996, 60–63.

[3.66] "Massapequa Developed Many Things" *The Southeaster* (Massapequa, New York), 2 July 1953, 6–7.

[3.67] "DeBothezat Puts Last Touch on Helicopter" *New York Herald Tribune,* 1 October 1939; "New Helicopter Makes Flight at 40 Foot Airport" *New York Herald Tribune,* 10 May 1940; *Mechanix Illustrated,* September 1943; "DeBothezat Coaxial Helicopter" *Aero Digest,* 15 January 1944; "The Late George DeBothezat" *American Helicopter,* December 1945, vol. 1 no. 1; *Aviation,* July 1946.

[3.68] Data mainly from a promotional brochure released by Chicago Helicopters in the 1920s. Also: Lamé (1934), 180–81; *Luftwissen,* May 1936; *Aviation,* July 1946, 57.

[3.69] The Pitcairn helicopter activity was so eclipsed by his work with autogiros that there is little published on the former. Illustrations and data mainly from conversations with his associate, Agnew Larsen in the late 1940s. Also: Hubler (1961), 53, notes "In 1920 Pitcairn told a friend he wanted 'a single-rotored helicopter' and that he did not care if it had a propeller in front or not". Presumably this remark was the explanation for his switch from helicopters to Cierva's autogiro. However Pitcairn did not abandon interest in helicopters until the Cierva agreement in 1928. Literature on autogiros is extensive. Of particular interest are the following. *The Autogiro: Its Characteristics and Accomplishments* Smithsonian Report 1930, 265–71; "Autogiros by Pitcairn, H. F." *Engineers and Engineering,* December 1930, 305–12, vol. 47; "Three Commercial Autogiros" *Aviation,* July 1931, 408–15, vol. 30 no. 7; "Full Scale Wind Tunnel Tests of a PCA-2 Autogiro Rotor" *NACA* TR-515, 1935; Gablehouse, Charles, *Helicopters and Autogiros* (New York: Lippincott, 1967). Also: Reference H.1.

[3.70] Piasecki, father of the tandem rotor machines flying today, formally began helicopter activity with PV Engineering Forum in 1943. Also: "Birth Notice (PV Engineering Forum)" *Air Facts,* 1 December 1943, 41–45, vol. 6 no. 12. That year the company flew America's second successful helicopter. As Piasecki Helicopter Corporation (1947) a series of tandem rotor helicopters were built. The largest for its time was the XH-16, described in AHS *Vertiflite* for May/June 1994. In 1955 Piasecki resigned from the company acquired by Boeing to reestablish his own research and development facility, Piasecki Aircraft Corporation. Through the years he has been responsible for development of 48 different vertical lift aircraft.

[3.71] David A. Brown, *The Bell Helicopter Textron Story,* (Arlington, Texas: Aerofax, 1995). A comprehensive account of Bell Helicopter activities.

[3.72] Wilford was an early advocate of large multi-passenger transport helicopters. He was active in rotary wing affairs in the Philadelphia area in the formative 1920–1950 era. Also: Liberatore, E. K., "E. Burke Wilford" *American Helicopter,* July 1949, 18–20.

[3.73] Appendix E, Volume 2. Also: *American Helicopter,* December 1946, 50; Hubler (1961), 63.

[3.74] Only information on Lux from British helicopter competition list.

[3.75] Information for this narrative is based on two photographs supplied the author by Ken West of Naples, Florida, in 1995, with appreciation. He in turn received them from an unnamed individual in the late 1940s who stated he had worked on the helicopter in the photos. The bulk of the narrative is derived from a study of the photos. There is little doubt it is a project of J. Newton Williams.

[3.76] "Plans Plane to Fly Forward, Backward, Up or Down by Newbauer" *Popular Science,* September 1927.

[3.77] *Science and Invention,* June 1924; Liberatore, E. K., *Convertible Aircraft* (Washington, D.C.: Department of Commerce, OTS, 1954), PB 111 288. See also: Appendix E, Volume 13.

[3.78] As for [3.74] and the cited patents.

[3.79] *Slipstream,* January 1923; Mancini (1936), 71; *Aviation History,* March 1996.

[3.80] Liberatore, Volume 13, *Convertible Aircraft,* 46.

[3.81] As for [3.74].

[3.82] As for [3.74] and patent review.

[3.83] Agnew Larsen along with Paul Stanley were the leading autogiro designers for Pitcairn. In the late 1930s the autogiro company went under the name Pitcairn-Larsen. In the 1940s when autogiro manufacturing ceased the parent company, Autogiro Company of America (ACA) survived with Stanley as head. ACA functioned to administer the numerous patents held by the organization. Larsen independently conducted rotor system developments. In 1948 he was head of Rotawings (North Wales, Pennsylvania), which became a unit of Glenn L. Martin Company. Also: Liberatore, E., K., *Rotary Wing Industry* (Washington, D.C.: Department of Commerce, OTS) PB 111 391, and Appendix E, Volume 14.

[3.84] In 1968 a design study by J. A. Moyer consultant to the state of Massachusetts, considered a steam turbine with condensing unit feasible for a propeller-driven airplane. The complete system (turbine, boiler, condenser) for a 149.2 kW (200 hp) engine was calculated to weigh 182 kilograms (400 pounds) or 1.22 kg/kW (2.0 lb/hp). Including a propeller reduction gear the unit weight becomes 1.6 kg/kW (2.63 lb/hp). The system would require a White flash boiler, which preheated the gasoline. The novel flash boiler was the invention (1899) of Rollin White and incorporated in the White (Sewing Machine Company) steam car, an organization active 1901–1909. The engine included a condenser (a simple radiator). This gave the car over four times the range of the Stanley Steamer, even so, it was not a fully condensing concept. Notes from *The Steam Automobile,* 1968 vol. 10 no. 3.

3.85 As for [3.74] and his patent.

[3.86] Crouch (1981), 125. Beach was a supporter of Whitehead and presumably provided a realistic evaluation.

[3.87] Data primarily from Appendix E, Volume 2, Myers' patents, and correspondence with him. Also: "Myers Helicopter Flights" *New York Herald Tribune,* 4 September 1926.

[3.88] *Aviation Yearbook,* (Greenwich, Connecticut: Fawcett), Flying Manual No. 7; "Pitts Helicopter" *Air and Airways,* February 1928.

[3.89] "Test Johnson Helicopter" *Aviation,* 16 November 1929, 995, vol. 27 no. 20; "Allison and Johnson Convertaplane" *Popular Science,* February 1930, 42. Note early use of word *convertaplane*. Random House College Dictionary (1992) gives *convertiplane* (sic) the earliest date as 1945.

[3.90] "The Curtiss Helicopter" *Scientific American,* February 1928, 161, vol. 138; *Popular Science,* September 1930; "Curtiss-Bleecker Helicopter" *Aero Digest,* July 1930, 110–12, vol. 17 no. 1; *Scientific American,* September 1930, 214–15, vol. 143; "The Curtiss-Bleecker Helicopter" *Aeroplane,* 24 September 1930, 723, vol. 36, no. 13; Lamé (1934),

218–20; Brenner, H. E., "Curtiss Bleecker Experiment" *American Helicopter,* January 1948 17, 26–27.

[3.91] Dorothy Cochrane, Von Hardesty, Russell Lee, *The Aviation Careers of Igor Sikorsky* (Seattle: University of Washington Press, 1989) 208 pp., three-view drawings, bibliography. A comprehensive account of Sikorsky's accomplishments in fixed and rotary wing aircraft. Illustration of 1930 tail rotor, 121. For a biography see Delear, Frank L., *Igor Sikorsky, His Three Careers in Aviation* (New York: Bantam, 1992), reprint of (New York: Dodd-Mead, 1969). On his early career, the following is a news item from *Aero and Hydro,* 27 June 1914, 555:

"St. Petersburg, Russia—Aviator Sykorski (sic), the famous Russian birdman and constructor of giant biplanes, made another new world's record today, when he flew for six hours, 33 minutes and 10 seconds in an aeroplane with six passengers."

[3.92] *Les Ailes,* 21 June 1947, 8–9; "Yur'ev Helicopter Model 1909" *Letectvi* (Czech) 3 February 1948; "B. N. Yur'ev" *Ogonek* (Moscow), April 1949, 23–24, no. 16; Liberatore, Eugene K., "Russia's Rapid Design Progress Based on Two Centuries of Experience" *Aviation Week,* 27 February 1956; Izakson (1964), 68–70; Mikheyev (1992) 152–162.

[3.93] Brown (1995). Also: "Two Bladed Rotor" *Aero Digest,* April 1946; Kelley, Bartram, "Contributions of Bell Helicopter Company" RAS *Aeronautical Journal,* March 1972; Schneider, John, "Out of the Past-Progress? Arthur Young-Inventor, Developer and Metaphysicist, the Developer of the Bell Teetering Rotor" AHS *Vertiflite,* March/April 1995, 36–39, vol. 41 no. 2; Boyne, Walter J. and Donald S. Lopez, *The Age of the Helicopter, Vertical Flight* (Washington, D.C.: Smithsonian, 1984) 73–83.

[3.94] Arthur M. Young, *The Bell Notes* (Mill Valley, California: Roberts Briggs Associates, 1979).

[3.95] "Radical Car Designed for All-Purpose Flying" *Popular Aviation,* March 1931. Also: "New Helicopter Developed" *American Aviation Daily,* 17 July 1943, 79, vol. 28 no. 14; *Aviation,* October 1944, and February 1945;

"The Landgraf Helicopter" *Western Flying,* August 1945, 48–49; Landgraf H-2 Jane's (1947), 246c.

[3.96] Appendix E, Volume 2, 123.

[3.97] Cordy information based on his patent. Illustration anonymous.

[3.98] Appendix E, Volume 2, 198.

[3.99] R. R. Hays, "Convertaplanes" *American Helicopter,* September, 1947, 12–13, 23, 24, vol. 8 no. 10.

[3.100] "Le Page Helicopter" *Journal of the Franklin Institute,* September 1936. Also: Wales, G. A., "Le Page Rotor Prop" *American Helicopter,* July 1947, 14, vol. 7 no. 8.

[3.101] *Science News Service,* August 1946. Illustration dated November 1941.

[3.102] "Focke Hubschrauber, FW-61" *Flugsport* 1937, 390, no. 14; *Flugspart,* August 1937, 436; Jane's (1937), 172c, *Les Ailes,* 8 June 1937, 4, vol. 17 no. 838; *Flugsport* 1938, 113, 138, 185, 226–27, 274, 299; "The Focke Helicopter" *NACA* TM-858, 14 pp; "Focke Helicopter" *Scientific American,* September 1938, 143–44, vol. 59 no. 3; "Development of the Focke Helicopter" ASME *Journal,* April 1939, 177–89, vol. 61 no. 4; "New Flying Methods Revealed by Invention by Focke" *Canadian Aviation,* January 1940, 38, vol. 13 no. 1; Zuerl, Walter, Seltsame Flugzeuge (Unconventional Aircraft) *Der Flieger,* December 1943, 362–65; "Helicopter Progress" *Flight,* 21 April 1938, 380–83, vol. 33 no. 1530; "The Focke Helicopter" RAS *Aeronautical Journal,* July 1938, 577–90, vol. 42 no. 331; Young, W. R., (1982), 71–74; Boulet (1984), 72–82; Apostolo, Giorgio, *The Illustrated Encyclopedia of Helicopters* (New York: Bonanza, 1984) 16–18.

[3.103] "Records de Hanna Reitsch sur l'hélicoptère FW-61" *Les Ailes,* 11 November 1937, 17, vol. 17; "Hanna Reitsch, célèbre virtuese de l'hélicoptère, a vol a l'intérieur de Grand Palais de Berlin" *L'Écho des Ailes* 24 February 1938, 92, vol 8; Boulet (1984), 73–75; Prins, Francois, "Foolhardly Patriot? Flugkapitan Hanna Reitsch" *Air Enthusiast* (Stamford, England), July–August 1996, 52–55, no. 64.

[3.104] Boulet (1984), 71–72, Carl Bode interview.

[3.105] *Luftwissen,* February 1938, vol. 15 no. 2. Also: "Le Focke Wulf est il vraiment un héli-coptère?" *Les Ailes,* 15 July 1937, 7–8, vol. 17 no. 839; "Helicoptere or Autogiro" *Vliegwereld* (Netherlands), 19 August 1937, 502, vol. 3 no. 29; Focke, H., "Les Six qualités de l'hélicoptère" *Les Ailes,* 28 April 1938. 7, vol. 19 no. 880.

CHAPTER 4
EPILOGUE

[4.1] Orville Wright, *How We Invented the Airplane* (New York: Dover, 1988); Kelley, Fred C., *The Wright Brothers* (New York: Dover, 1989); Jarrett, Philip, "Selling the First Aeroplane, Exploiting the Wright Flyer" *Air Enthusiast,* March/April 1996, no. 62.

[4.2] The doubt surrounding the helicopter in its early years was opposite the enthusiastic acceptance in Europe of the airplane at the end of its first decade of existence. A sampling of the critical look at the helicopter is in the articles below. Nothing like these views were applied to airplanes. In that case progress was slow but generally optimistic. The titles reveal the helicopter controversy, replete with question marks:

"Is Direct Lift Desirable or Possible?" R. Sharpe, *Aero,* February/March 1910.

"The Helicopter as a Possible Type of Flying Machine". *Aircraft Journal,* 31 May 1910.

"Is the Helicopter Possible?" C. I. Reynolds, *Flight,* 10 December 1910.

"Is the Helicopter Possible?" W. A. Weaver, *Flight,* 24 December 1910.

"What is the Use of the Helicopter?" N. M. H. Vernham, *Aero,* 28 December 1910.

"Is the Helicopter Possible?" C. J. Reynolds, *Flight* 7 January 1911.

"Do We Want the Helicopter?" D. Greig, *Aero,* 8 February 1911.

"Is Direct Lift Desirable or Possible?" R. Sharpe, *Aero,* February/March 1912.

"Is the Direct Lifter Desirable or Possible?" E. E. Green, *Aero,* May 1912.

"The Helicopter as a Possible Type of Flying Machine" *Aircraft Journal,* 31 May 1919.

"The Coming of the Helicopter" D. Shaw, *Aeronautics,* 2 December 1920.

"The Problem of the Helicopter" *Technical Review,* 4 January 1921.

"The Helicopter Craze" *Aeroplane,* 7 June 1922.

"Helicopter, Is It Worth a Prize?" L. Bairstow, *Nature,* 18 August 1923.

"The Helicopter and Such Things" *Aeroplane,* 21 October 1925.

"Helicopter Myth" W. L. Marsh, *English Review,* November 1925.

"What Use is the Helicopter?" D. L. Edwards, *Infantry Journal,* July 1941.

"You Will Fly a Helicopter" *Science and Mechanics,* Fall 1943.

"Let's Be Calm About the Helicopter" *Aviation,* November 1943.

"More Rotating Wings: America Experiences an Epidemic of Helicopter Designs" *Flight* 16 December 1942.

"Don't Believe All You See and Hear About Helicopters" G. Loening, *Air Transportation* December 1943.

"What's Wrong with the Helicopter?" C. B. F. Mcauley, *Air Tech,* March 1944.

"What You Can Believe About the Helicopter" H. F. Gregory, *Saturday Evening Post* 27 May 1944.

"No Helicopter for You Tomorrow" D. Francis, *Popular Science,* June 1944

"How About Helicopters?" C. Apponyi, *Skyways,* December 1944.

"Helicopters:Designs Flourish, but Public Has to Wait for a Practical Family Model" *Life* 26 February 1945.

"And the Cow Jumped Over the Hangar" A. F. Edwards, *Air Facts,* April 1945.

"The Helicopter, Promise and Contradictions" D. Francis, *Interavia,* September 1947.

"Is the Helicopter Ready?" J. Ray, *American Helicopter,* January 1948.

"Is it Worthwhile?" P. F. Simmons, *American Helicopter,* January 1948.

Chronologically the above shows a shift from skepticism of technical feasibility to tentative acceptance. The list conforms to the shift from the third to the fourth stages of response discussed in the Epilogue. In the case of the helicopter, and judging from a more extensive bibliography (not listed above) the fifth (general acceptance) stage occurred in the early 1950s.

[4.3] Igor Sikorsky, "Sixty Years of Flying" RAS *Aeronautical Journal,* November 1971.

[4.4] Despite the enthusiastic reception in Europe, America was cool to the flying machine in the period of 1908 to World War I.

Pull quotes from *Aero and Hydro,* 17 October 1914 editorial reveal the mood: "What is the matter with American Aeronautics?"; "Who is to blame?"; "Lack of teamwork"; "Devouring one another". The mood nominally suggests the helicopter experience cited in [4.2] above. However there was one big difference. In this period the airplane was a practical machine and the problem was an "internal" social-political one, rather than technical. Historically the helicopter did not experience this form of the problem. Once the helicopter was accepted in the early 1950s, technical progress advanced smoothly though competitively. Very likely the Army's commitment to this machine was a very stabilizing influence on its progress. Even the commercial operations end, which relies on a constant search for contract jobs, has never exhibited the wildcat approach revealed by the quotes from *Aero and Hydro.* It referred specifically to the aeronautic industry in general (manufacturers, clubs, pilots, factory employees, and others with a passive interest) "Ideals and cooperation are woefully lacking. . . .". In contrast French and German developments were pointed out as exemplary, even England caught up and ". . . . now has an aeronautical industry and organization unique in its record of efficiency and attainments, as well as its permanence". *The Aeroplane* 26 February 1914 (200) states: "It is not surprising to find in a country which puts so little attention to defense, that military aeronautics has been treated with consistent neglect." However the onset of World War I awakened America to the need for aeronautical research and development. This started with establishment of National Advisory Committee for Aeronautics (NACA), now NASA, in 1915.

[4.5] E. K. Liberatore, *Rotary Wing Industry* (Washington, D.C.: Department of Commerce, OTS, 1954) PB 111 391. See also: Appendix E, Volume 17.

[4.6] Alexander Klemin, "An Introduction to the Helicopter" *NACA* TM-340, 1925.

[4.7] David Diringer, *The Book before Printing* (New York: Dover, 1982), 67. Cites Krober's "stimulus" or "idea diffusion". Krober a cultural anthropologist from Hoboken, New Jersey, taught at University of California

(Berkeley). In *Configurations of Cultural Growth* (1945) he advanced the idea that geniuses and near-geniuses historically tend to appear in clusters rather than one at a time, irrespective of nationality.

APPENDIX A. OTHER PROJECTS

[A.1] *Scientific American,* 3 March 1849.
[A.2] Millbank (1943), 173; Mikheyev (1993), 59–60.
[A.3] Millbank (1943), 173, 1866 patent; Mikheyev (1993), 62–63.
[A.4] *Scientific American,* 22 July 1871, 52, vol. 39; Mikheyev (1993), 73.
[A.5] "W. D. G. Helicopter-Proposed Flying Machine" *Scientific American,* 5 December 1874, 357; *American Helicopter,* December 1945, 30; *Flight Before Wright.* Library of Congress Calendar, 1993 (Petaluma, California: Pomegranate Calendars and Books, 1992).
[A.6] Millbank (1943), 173–74; Chanute (1976), 106; Mikheyev (1993), 88.
[A.7] Chanute (1976), 65; Fay (1976), 130.
[A.8] Millbank (1943), 175.
[A.9] Chanute (1976), 65; Fay (1976), 130.
[A.10] *Fly Magazine,* November 1908.
[A.11] H. T. Keating, "Value of Inclined Propellers for Helicopters" *Scientific American,* 3 October 1908, 223, vol. 99.
[A.12] Jane's (1909), 291; Jane's (1910–1911). Featured eight, 12-blade shrouded screws, 0.61 meters (2.0 feet) in diameter, with 29.8 kW (40 hp) Curtiss engine. Weight 227 kilograms (500 pounds).
[A.13] Jane's (1909), 290; Jane's (1910–1911), 396.
[A.14] Jane's (1909).
[A.15] Jane's (1909) 291; Jane's (1910–1911), 393.
[A.16] Jane's (1909); Jane's (1910–1911).
[A.17] Jane's (1909), 294.
[A.18] Jane's (1910–1911).
[A.19] "The Irvine Aerocycloide" *Technical World,* August 1909, 682; Jane's (1910–1911), 392.
[A.20] Jane's (1910–1911), 394.
[A.21] Jane's (1910–1911), 395.
[A.22] Jane's (1910–1911), 387.
[A.23] Jane's (1910–1911), 386.
[A.24] Jane's (1910–1911), 387.
[A.25] Jane's (1910–1911), 390.
[A.26] Jane's (1910–1911), 391.
[A.27] Jane's (1910–1911), 396.
[A.28] Jane's (1910–1911), 394.
[A.29] Jane's (1910–1911), 286.
[A.30] "J. E. McWorter Autoplane of St. Louis, Missouri" *U.S. Air Services,* 13 August 1919.
[A.31] Mancini (1936), 556.
[A.32] Henry R. Velkoff, "An Evaluation of the Jet Rotor Helicopter" Journal of the American Helicopter Society, October 1958.
[A.33] Velkoff (1958); *Flugsport,* 1939, 117, 185; Zuerl, *Der Flieger* November 1943, 335–336.
[A.34] Hubler (1961), 64.
[A.35] Appendix E, Volume 2, 103. Around 1938 the Halligan brothers of Beardstown, Illinois produced a helicopter that featured a propeller-driven, two-blade rotor. The propellers were powered by tip-mounted engines.
[A.36] *Aero Digest,* December 1939.

APPENDIX B: COMPETITION ENTRANTS 1924

Those names without a reference are entries lacking source information other than that on a list from the British Air Ministry and transmitted to the author by R. N. Liptrot.
[B.1] See Newbauer (1924) narrative.
[B.2] See Perry (1923) narrative.
[B.3] *Aeronautics,* October 1911 and November 1911; Porter, James Robinson, *The Helicopter Flying Machine* (New York: Van Nostrand, 1912), 88 pp. Porter was a British entrant. In the November 1911 article he wrote it strange no lateral rotor configuration machine (his concept) was every built. (The narratives show the coaxial rotor was favored.) Since stability was so important he believed the lateral rotor should be developed. The Berliner (1922–25) showed more than rotor arrangement was necessary. Focke demonstrated flap-hinged blades and positive (two-position) pitch control were the missing elements. Porter like others in

his time failed to distinguish between design for stability and design for control. He presumed that regardless of the amount of (lateral) instability rotor control could overcome it.

[B.4] See Myers (1926) narrative.

[B.5] "L'Hélicoptère Hellesen-Khan HK-1" *L'Aéronautique,* October 1925, 382–83, vol. 7 no. 77; *Flugsport,* 1925, 439 no. 2; *Luftwissen,* May, 1936; *Der Flieger,* November 1943; *Aviation,* July 1946.

[B.6] See Berliner (1922–25) narrative.

[B.7] Appendix E, Volume 11, 127. Englishman F. Samide entered a paddle wheel rotorcraft in the competition. The paddles were partly shrouded and a tractor screw was used for propulsion. Samide failed to obtain financial support, and his design was not built.

[B.8] Von Baumhauer was one of the few entrants who had a reasonably practical machine for its time. The prototype was funded by the government but it was not completed in time for either competition. The helicopter featured a two-blade main rotor controlled by a swashplate, and a tail rotor driven by a separate engine. Initially a tractor propeller was installed but later removed. The final variant had a 15.3 meter (50 foot) diameter rotor, powered by a 149.2 kW (200 hp) Bentley rotary engine. An 59.7 kW (80 hp) engine drove the tail rotor. The first hover took place in June 1925. Weighing 908–1298 kilograms (2000–2860 pounds) the machine made hovering flights, but failed to rise more than a meter off the ground in drifting flight. Problems with vibration, mechanical failures, and financing, led to project abandonment, precipitated by a crash in August 1930. Pilots were successively, Captain Van Heyst, J. C. Grasse (Fokker pilot) and in 1928, Peter Six. The last recounts his experience in Boulet (1984) 47, 48. Also: Proceedings of the First International Congress for Applied Mechanics, 1924; Lame (1934), 211–12; *Luftwissen,* May 1936, 124; "Work of Dutch Pioneer" *Flight,* 14 October 1943, 16; *Der Flieger,* November 1943, 332.

[B.8] Michael Heatley, *The Illustrated History of Helicopters* (Greenwich, Connecticut: Brompton Books, 1985), 18–19.

[B.9] See Brown (1924) narrative.

[B.10] See Keefer (1924) narrative.

APPENDIX C: COMPETITION ENTRANTS 1925–1926

[C.1] See Curtiss-Bleeker (1930) narrative. Apparently Bleecker had a new design for the competition independently submitted.

[C.2] British patent the only information on American entrant Pusterla.

[C.3] Rudolph Chillingworth later emigrated to America. In the 1950s, in view of the helicopter fever of the time, the estate sought to exploit his patent (1,605,327). The design consisted of a rectangular framework with a lifting screw at each corner. Below each was a rotatable wing with a propeller mounted on each. In forward flight the wings were locked, the propellers serving as thrusters. The design was 26.1 meters (85.5 feet) long and 22.9 meters (75 feet) wide. Two 336 kW (450 hp) were to be used. Also: Appendix E, Volume 13, 26.

[C.4] See Pitcairn (1925) narrative and Agnew Larsen (1925–1926).

[C.5] See Anonymous (Williams) narrative.

[C.6] See Exel (1920–1923) narrative. Apparently the triaxial configuration was his entry, being the most developed.

[C.7] See Ford (1925–1926) narrative.

[C.8] Fernando Aldrovrandi of Turin, Italy, patented a coaxial rotor helicopter using slipstream vanes for control. It is possible a prototype was built, without success. Also: Appendix E, Volume 2, 2; Mancini (1936), 31.

[C.9] See Brown (1924) narrative.

[C.10] See Hellesen-Khan comments with Curtiss-Bleecker (1930) narrative.

[C.11] See Berliner (1922–1925) narrative. The monoplane configuration resembled the Johnson (1929), Figure 3.93. Thus the Berliner range of configuration experiments ended where Johnson began his.

[C.12] See Beach (1925) narrative. S. Y. Beach also was involved in fixed wing projects. One was a 37.3 kW (50 hp) biplane prototype with Whitehead in 1908. The other a monoplane built with Charles F. Willard. Also: Whitehouse (1965), 139, 140.

APPENDIX D: PATENTS

Copies of U.S. patents are available from:
U.S. Department of Commerce
Patent and Trademark Office
Washington, D.C. 20231

APPENDIX E: ROTARY WING HANDBOOKS AND HISTORY

[E.1] Also: Liberatore, E. K, "An Eclectic Bibliography of Rotorcraft", AHS *Vertiflite,* January/February 1988, 50–53, 132 items from 1768 to 1964).

APPENDIX G: SYSTÈME INTERNATIONALE UNITS

[G.1] "International Standard, ISO 1000", New York, *American National Standards Institute,* 1430 Broadway, New York, N.Y. 10018. Also: *SI Units in Engineering and Technology* (Elkins Park, Pennsylvania: Franklin Book Company).

[G.2] R. C. Pankhurst, "The Slug, an Erstwile Unit of Mass", RAS *Aeronautical Journal,* May 1970, 724.

[G.3] P. J. Wingham, "SI Units Applied to Aircraft Performance Calculations" RAS *Aeronautical Journal,* November 1972, 657–58.

[G.4] "SI Units" RAS *Aeronautical Journal,* February 1969. A one-page summary of SI Units, with conversion constants British to S. I. system. Also: RAS *Aeronautical Journal,* February 1968 for a more detailed account.

[G.5] Robert C. Weast, Editor in Chief, *CRC Handbook of Chemistry and Physics* (Boca Raton, Florida: CRC Press, 1985), 65 Edition, F-245 to F-248.

[G.6] *Jane's All the World's Aircraft* (Couldson, Surrey, England: Jane's) 1990–1991 and current editions. Power is listed in kilowatts, while fuel consumption is in micrograms per joule units, and temperature in celsius.

[G.7] Barnes W. McCormick, *Aerodynamics and Aeronautics and Flight Mechanics* (New York: Wiley, 1979), 621–623. The SI system (names, symbols, conversions) 624–28. Standard Atmosphere tables in both units.

[G.8] J. Seddon, *Basic Helicopter Aerodynamics* (Washington, D.C.: AIAA, 1990), xvi, xvii. Units and conversion table.

[G.9] Arnold M. Keuthe and Chuen-Yen Chow, *Foundations of Aerodynamics* (New York: Wiley, 1986), 4th edition, 1–2, SI units, 516, conversion tables, 518, Standard Atmosphere table.

[G.10] A. R. S. Bramwell, *Helicopter Dynamics* (London: Edward Arnold, 1976). Numerical calculations in SI units, figures use both systems.

[G.11] *The Chicago Manual of Style* (Chicago: University of Chicago Press, 1993), 14th edition, 478–81. Note 1, 479 on weight and mass distinction.

APPENDIX H: GLOSSARY

[H.1] Peter Brooks, *Cierva Autogiros* (Washington, D.C.: Smithsonian Institution Press, 1988), 384 pp. A comprehensive account of the autogiro including illustrations, 3-view drawings, chronology, registration numbers, early (non-Cierva) gyroplanes, and helicopters. Also: Brie, R. A. C., *The Autogiro and How to Fly It* (London: Pitman, 1933). 88 pp; Glauert, H., "A General Theory of the Autogiro" British *Aeronautical Research Committee* (ARC) R & M No. 1111, 1928. The first analytical treatment.

[H.2] Commercial helicopters must comply with Federal Air Regulations (FARs) in order to be sold commercially. The FARs are separated into two weight categories. FAR Part 27 "Airworthiness Standards: Normal Category Rotorcraft", for helicopters 6000 pounds (2724 kilograms) or less, and FAR Part 29 "Airworthiness Standards: Transport Category Rotorcraft" for the higher gross weights.

[H.3] *Engineering Design Handbook, Helicopter Engineering, Part One, Preliminary*

Design (Springfield, Virginia: NTIS), Headquarters U.S. Army Materiel Command AMC Pamphlet (706–201, 1966, 4.125–4.137. Fatigue life determination methodology.

[H.4] M. A. Miner, "Cumulative Damage in Fatigue" *Journal of Applied Mechanics,* 1945. The original presentation of the concept. The principles are incorporated in the FAA Federal Air Regulations for Helicopters.

[H.5] Bramwell (1976), 299–317. Also: Den Hartog, J. P., *Mechanical Vibrations* (New York: McGraw-Hill, 1940), 306–315 and (New York: Dover, 1985). Rotating blade natural frequency determination.

[H.6] Den Hartog (1940), 87–88.

[H.7] Franklin P. Durham, *Aircraft Jet Powerplants* (New York: Prentice-Hall, 1951), 47–75 on thermodynamic cycle analysis. Also: Zucrow, M. J., *The Principles of Jet Propulsion and Gas Turbines* (New York: Wiley, 1948), 257–309; Oates, Gordon C., *Aerothermodynamics of Gas Turbines and Rocket Propulsion* (New York: AIAA, 1984), 119–76, 219–59.

[H.8] Bartram Kelley, "Helicopter Evolution" *Journal of the American Helicopter Society,* January 1983, vol. 28 no. 1. Points out the notion that in thermodynamics, theory followed practice, the reverse of what one would expect.

[H.9] *L'Aéronaute,* November 1871.

[H.10] There are many government documents that cover the totality of systems engineering methodology, including the concepts of Life Cycle Costing (LCC), Configuration Management (CM), Work Breakdown Structure (WBS), and Functional Flow Diagrams (FFDs). The last are essential in creating requirements for a new, very complex and unique military system. The methodology is applicable to new helicopter procurement with many operating concepts (missions) to account for in defining requirements. The driving document on systems engineering is MIL-STD-499. Systems engineering is one element of the total military procurement process. For an outline of the overall process see: Przemieniecke, J. S., Editor, *Acquisition of Defense Systems* (Washington, D.C.: AIAA, 1993), 366 pp, including an appendix containing a glossary of abbreviations and acronyms, 357–66.

[H.11] There was a flurry of interest in cyclogiros in Europe and America in the 1930s. See: "J. E. McWorter Autoplane of St. Louis" *U.S. Air Services* 13 August 1919. A quarter scale model was evaluated at McCook Field in 1919; Kirsten, Frederick Kurt, "Cycloidal Propulsion Applied to Aircraft" ASME *Transactions* No. AER-50-12, 1928, 77-80, vol. 50; "Cycloplane C-1" *Aero Digest,* November 1931, 62, vol. 19 no. 5; Wheatley, John B., "Simplified Aerodynamic Analysis of the Cyclogiro Rotating System" *NACA* TN-467, 1933; "The Theory of the Strandgren Cyclogiro" *NACA* TM-727, 1933; "A Revolutionary German Aeroplane Now Under Construction" *Illustrated London News,* 20 January 1934, 94–95, vol. 184; "Paddle Wheel Plane to Fly Backwards" *Popular Mechanics,* April 1934; Strandgren, C. B., "The Strandgren Cyclogiro" *Mechanical Engineering,* September 1934, 535–37, vol. 56 no. 9; Wheatley, John B., "Wind Tunnel Tests of Cyclogiro Rotor" *NACA* TM-528, 1935; Laskowitz, I. B., *Designs for Helicopters* (Brooklyn, New York: Author, 1947) 22 pp; *American Helicopter,* March 1953 (Laskowitz); Foshag, William F. and Gabriel D. Boehler, "Cyclogiro Systems", Part B, *USAAVLabs* Report 69–13, March 1969, 80–169.

[H.12] Eugene K. Liberatore, *Special Types of Rotary Wing Aircraft* (Washington D.C.: Department of Commerce, OTS, 1954), PB 111 633, 51–105, an ornithopters. See also: Appendix E, Volume 11.

[H.13] Liberatore (1954), Volume 11, 55.

[H.14] Lafcadio Hearn, *A Japanese Miscellany* (Rutland, Vermont: Tuttle, 1954), 75–118.

[H.15] Gabriel D. Boehler and William C. Schneck, "On The Feasibility of a Very Heavy Lift Helicopter (VHLH) in Support of the Army's Force XXI Operating Concept" *American Helicopter Society,* 54th Annual Forum, June 4–6, 1996, 18 pp. A mission analysis of helicopters up to 227,000 kilograms (250 tons). Single and tandem rotor designs were considered, but no quadrotor configurations.

[H.16] *World Almanac and Book of Facts, 1996* (Mahwah, New Jersey: Funk and Wagnalls), 174. However the 1997 *Information Please Almanac,* 552, lists Focke as inventor of the "double rotor" helicopter (1936) and Sikorsky as the "single rotor" inventor (1939). This bland treatment does not reveal the importance of Focke's work.

[H.17] *Flettner FL-282* Luftwaffe Profile Series No. 6 (Atglen, Pennsylvania: Schiffer, 1996), 4. Also: *Aviation Week,* 29 November 1954. In his later years Flettner had a design office in Kew Gardens, New York, the author was chief engineer. Flettner recounted the anxious moments he had on the ground, and those the pilot in the air had in executing the first entry and recovery from autorotation. Theory does not always reassure practice. In its time the FL-282 was the best helicopter flying. First flown in 1941, over 20 were built and the type was used in service. After World War II the U.S. Air Force contracted Prewitt Aircraft Company to flight-evaluate a FL-282 they had acquired. The test pilot was J. D. (Dave) Driskill of Kellett Aircraft. His evaluation of the helicopter was similar. Also: Cobey, William E., "Evaluation and Tests of the Flettner FL-282 German Helicopter" *USAF, Prewitt* Technical Report F-TR-1193-ND, ATI 20283, September 1948, 146 pp.

[H.18] Alfred Gessow and Gary C. Myers, Jr, "Flight Tests of a Helicopter in Autorotation, Including Comparison with Theory" *NACA* TN-1267, April 1947.

[H.19] Young (1979), 86.

[H.20] Boulet (1984), 102; Brown, Textron (1995), 13.

[H.21] Cochrane, Hardesty, Lee (1989), 124.

[H.22] Norman Macmillan, "Rotaries Remembered" *Shell Aviation News,* 1964, No. 312.

[H.23] G. de Simone, R. S. Blauch, R. A. Fisher, "The Impact of Missions on the Preliminary Design of an ABC Rotor" *Journal of the American Helicopter Society,* July 1982, 32–43, vol. 27 no. 3.

[H.24] E. K. Liberatore, "ISR-Inherently Stable Rotor Systems" *Journal of the American Helicopter Society,* October 1960, 3–11.

[H.25] K. Hohenemser, "Dynamic Stability of a Helicopter with Hinged Rotor Blades" *NACA* TM-907, 1939. An early investigation of the stability parameters, followed by a later Hohenemser paper *AMC* T-2T Translation, August 1946; Cobey, W. E., *Stability and Control of Rotary Wing Aircraft,* (Washington, D.C.: Department of Commerce, OTS, 1954), PB 111 521, 1964, 64 pp. Includes an early

physical-analytical description of helicopter stability. Also: Bramwell (1976), 227–149.

[H.26] Arthur M. Young, "A New Parameter of Lifting Rotors", Second Annual Meeting, Franklin Institute, sponsored by *Institute of Aeronautical Sciences* (AIAA), 30 November-1 December 1939, 29–36. Young describes his model experiments and presents a qualitative description of the system principles. The analysis is in Kelley, Bartram, "Helicopter Stability and Young's Lifting Rotor" *Transactions, SAE Journal,* December 1945, 685–90, vol. 53 no. 12.

[H.27] John P. Reeder and James B. Whitten, "Some Effects of Varying the Damping in Pitch and Roll on the Flying Qualities of a Small Single Rotor Helicopter" *NACA* TN-2459, January 1952. Advantage was taken of this feature to investigate the stability range from a flybar lockout to an arrangement beyond application in a practical helicopter.

[H.28] Joseph Stuart III, "The Helicopter Control Rotor" *Aeronautical Engineering Review,* August 1948, IAS Preprint No. 110, 1948.

[H.29] E. K. Liberatore, "Design and Performance of Parks-Jaggers Remotely Piloted Helicopter" *Liberatore* Report 286 EM-4, July 1983. Includes a comparison of hovering stability characteristics for RPHs and the full scale Hiller UH-12.

[H.30] D. R. Jacoby, "Experimental and Theoretical Investigation of the Hiller Automatic Control-Final Report", *United Helicopters* Report 150.5, 4 April 1949, ATI 58 149.

[H.31] G. J. Sissingh, "Automatic Stabilization of Helicopters" *Journal of the Helicopter Association of Great Britain,* October 1948, vol. 2 no. 3; Sissingh, G. J., "Investigations on the Automatic Stabilization of the Helicopter (Hovering Flight) Part I" *RAE* Report No. Aero 2277, 1948. Shows the effect of stabilizing devices on the sample helicopter (Sikorsky R-4B). Without devices the amplitude theoretically doubles in 5 seconds. With an autopilot providing both proportional (attitude) and rate control, the helicopter is stable, with the amplitude halved in 3 seconds. The Young stabilizer bar system stabilized in 37 seconds, suggesting almost neutral stability. Apparently 5 seconds for the R-4B without devices was considered adequate for controllability. This is a relatively low value suggesting the R-4B was difficult to fly. Today subjective views are replaced by objective standards for handling qualities. See the following references.

[H.32] "Handling Requirements for Military Rotorcraft. Aeronautical Design Standard ADS-33C", August 1989. The associated specification is MIL-8501 updated; Harm, J. A., M. Metzger, R. H. Hall, "Handling Qualities Testing Using the Mission-Oriented Requirements of ADS-33C", *American Helicopter Society,* 48th Annual Forum, June 1992.

[H.33] The original unrevised diagram was a byproduct of a Navy Contract Definition program at Electric Boat Division, General Dynamics Corporation in which the author participated. Diagram also used in: Liberatore, E. K., "The Nuclear-Powered Ocean-Going Surface Effect Ship (SES)" *Jane's Surface Skimmers Annual,* 1970–1971 Edition.

[H.34] E. K. Liberatore, "Cold-Cycle Pressure-Jet Helicopters" AHS *Vertiflite,* Part 1, Ventures, November-December 1991, vol. 37 no. 6; Part 2, Design, January–February 1992, vol. 38 no. 1; Part 3, Costs and Developments, March–April 1992, vol. 38 no. 2.

ACRONYMS

The following acronyms have been used here. Note some of the source names are now out of use. For comprehensive list see:

Bill Gunston, *Jane's Aerospace Dictionary* (London): Jane's Information Group, 1988) 3d Edition, 605 pp.

Fernando B. Morinigo, *The Acronym Book* Washington, D.C.: AIAA, 1992) 2d Edition, 297 pp.

Slovar' Angliyskikh i Amerikanskikh Sokrascheniy

(Dictionary of English and American Abbreviations)

(Moscow, 1957) 767 pp. English and Russian translations of the acronyms.

AHS American Helicopter Society (Alexandria, Virginia)

AIAA American Institute of Aeronautics and Astronautics (Washington, D.C.) (Formerly IAS)

AMC Air Materiel Command, U.S. Army

ARC R&M Aeronautical Research Committee, Reports and Memoranda (London)

ASME American Society of Mechanical Engineers (New York)

ATI (CADO) Air Technical Index (Central Air Documents Office) (Dayton, Ohio) Current document agency is NTIS.

CRC Chemical Rubber Company Press (Naples, Florida)

FAA Federal Aviation Administration (Washington, D.C.)

FAR Federal Air Regulations (FAA)

HAGB Helicopter Association of Great Britain. Now integrated with RAeS.

HMSO Her Majesty's Stationery Office (Norwich, England)

NACA National Aeronautics and Space Administration (Washington, D.C.)

IAS Institute of Aeronautical Sciences. Now AIAA.

NTIS National Technical Information Service (Springfield, Virginia) Current, government central document service.

OTS Office of Technical Services, Department of Commerce (Washington, D.C.) See NTIS.

RAE Royal Aircraft Establishment (Farnborough, England)

RAF Royal Air Force (Britain)

RAeS (RAS) Royal Aeronautical Society (London, England)

RPH Remotely Piloted Helicopter

SAE Society of Automotive Engineers (Warrendale, Pennsylvania)

SES Surface Effect Ship

sf Science fiction. Preferred to *Sci-fi* by those in the literary field. The latter (Sci fi) is used by the literate in referring to "inferior" science fiction.

USAAVLabs U.S. Army Aviation Laboratories (Fort Eustis, Virginia)

ZFM Zeitschrift fur Flugtechnik und Motorluftschiffahrt (Munich, Germany) Journal of Flight Technology and Powered Airship Travel.

ILLUSTRATION CREDITS

Above and Beyond (1968) 3.12

Aerial Age (21 February 1921) 3.56

Aero Digest (July 1930) 3.99

Aeronautics (October 1908) 3.6, 3.7, 3.9

Aero News and Mechanics (June–July 1930) 2.1

Aerosphere (1939) 3.5

AHS Journal (October 1958) A.5, A.7

Air Beat (February–March 1983) 3.44

Aircraft (May 1910) 3.31, 3.37

Aircraft (January 1913) 3.36

Alexander and Mason, Views of 18th Century China (London: Studio, 1989) H.6

American Helicopter (December 1945) 2.30, A.1

American Heritage/AIAA (1962) 2.37, 3.29

Appendix E (Volume 1) 2.20, 2.28, 2.29

Appendix E (Volume 2) 3.93, 3.109, 3.113

Appendix E (Volume 11) 3.110

Appendix E (Volume 13) 3.57, 3.81, 3.94

Aviation Fundamentals (Englewood, Colorado: Jepperson, 1983) 2.11

Author's collection: 2.4, 2.5, 3.8, 3.26, 3.27, 3.28, 3.43, 3.45, 3.46, 3.47, 3.48, 3.50, 3.51, 3.52, 3.53, 3.54, 3.58, 3.60, 3.61, 3.62, 3.64, 3.65, 3.66, 3.69, 3.75, 3.76, 3.86, 3.87, 3.88, 3.89, 3.90, 3.95, 3.100, 3.112, 3.115

Author's preliminary design: 2.17

Author's sketches: 1.1, 1.14, 1.15, 1.16, 2.12, 2.13, 3.55, H.1, H.2, H.5, H.7, H.9

Baltimore American (16 September 1917) 3.32, 3.33

Bodelian Library, Oxford/Frazer (1966) 1.3
Figure 1.3 insets:
[Left] Medieval Life Illustrations (Dover, 1966)
[Middle] Larousse Encyclopedia of Ancient and Medieval History (Hamlyn, 1972)
[Right] Alberto Manguel, A History of Reading (Vintage, 1996)

Bouton, Etienne, 1.24

British Museum/Frazer (1966) 1.4, 1.5, 1.6, 1.8, 1.9, 1.10, 1.23

Brueghel/Children's Games (1560) 1.7

Chicago Helicopters brochure (ca. 1924) 3.73

Clute (1995) 2.39

Cochrane, Hardesty and Lee (1989) 3.100

Colorado Historical Society/Secrest (Denver, 1993) 3.20

Culin (1960) 1.13

Da Vinci, 1.21; Manuscript B, folio 83v, Bibliothèque de L'Institut de France (Paris). Most publishers of this famous helicopter drawing apparently are unaware that the owner expects credit as well as a fee for publication of 200 francs which the author paid.

Der Flieger (November 1943) 3.101, A.6

Der Flieger (December 1943) 3.116

Drees/AHS Vertiflite (1976) 1.2

Edgington and Hatfield (1968) 2.18, 2.40

Exel, J. G. (Clifton, New Jersey) 3.54

Flugsport (28 May 1941) 3.30

Fly (November 1908) 3.15

Focke-Wulf Company drawing 3.17

Gablehouse (1967) 3.59

Gibbs-Smith/RAS Aeronautical Journal (1974) 2.14

Harter (1986) 3.1

Heinken and Braun (1952) 3.70

High Plains Museum (Goodland, Kansas) 3.23, 3.24

IBM/da Vinci booklet (ca. 1950) 1.19

International Nickel Company advertisement (1963) 2.36

Izakson (1964) 3.16, 3.19, 3.102, 3.103, 3.104

Jane's (1909) 3.3, 3.21, 3.22, A.3

Jane's (1910–1911) 3.11

Kansas State Historical Society/Jetmore Republican (1957) 3.25

La Cucina Italiana (March 1978) H.4

L'Aéronaute catalog (1911) 1.18

Leslie's (1876) 2.27

Light Steam Power (September–October 1967) 2.2, 2.3

Mancini (1936) 3.61, A.4

Mechanix Illustrated (September 1943) 3.71

Mechanics Magazine (8 April 1843) 2.16

Mikheyev (1993) 1.22, 2.15, 2.21, 2.25, 2.26, 2.31, A.2

Musée d'Histoire de l'Éducation/Frazer 1.11

Musée du Mans, Le Mans, 1.22, 1.24

Nelson prospectus (ca. 1861) 2.23, 2.24

Tom Parramore (Raleigh, North Carolina) 3.4

Patent drawing: 1.17, 2.22, 2.32, 3.2, 3.10, 3.17, 3.18, 3.34, 3.35, 3.38, 3.39, 3.40, 3.41, 3.42, 3.49, 3.72, 3.74, 3.79, 3.80, 3.83, 3.84, 3.85, 3.92, 3.105, 3.107

Popular Science (September 1930) 3.96,
3.97, 3.98
Punch/Bradbury[?] (ca. 1950) 2.42
Science Digest (December 1985) 1.20
Science and Invention (1924) 3.82
Science and Mechanics (June 1936) 4.2
Science Museum/Gibbs-Smith (1967) H.3
Scientific American (9 May 1885) 2.33
Shell Aviation News No. 289 (1962) 2.6, 2.7,
2.8
Smith (1955) 2.10
Smithsonian Institution 2.41, 3.63

The Southeastern (Massapequa, New York, 2
July 1953) 3.67
Joshua Stopf, Picture History of Aviation
(Dover, 1996) 3.14
Unidentified: 2.38, 3.68, 3.91, 3.108, 3.111,
3.114, 4.1
U.S. Army H.8
Verne (1886) 2.34, 2.35
Ken L. West (Naples, Florida) 3.77,
3.78
Wise (1873) 2.19
W. R. Young (1982) 1.12, 3.13

INDEX